For Joan Dagle and Rich Weiner

D1202433

LACAN,
POLITICS,
AESTHETICS

SUNY Series, Psychoanalysis and Culture
Henry Sussman, Editor

LACAN,
POLITICS,
AESTHETICS

WILLY APOLLON AND
RICHARD FELDSTEIN,
EDITORS

STATE UNIVERSITY OF NEW YORK PRESS

Published by
State University of New York Press, Albany

© 1996 State University of New York

For information, address State University of New York
Press, State University Plaza, Albany, N.Y., 12246

Production by E. Moore
Marketing by Dana Yanulavich

Library of Congress Cataloging-in-Publication Data

Lacan, politics, aesthetics / Willy Apollon and Richard Feldstein,
    editors
        p.   cm.
    Includes bibliographical references and index.
    ISBN 0-7914-2371-9 (alk. paper). — ISBN 0-7914-2372-7 (pbk. :
alk. paper)
    1. Psychoanalysis and culture.   2. Psycholinguistics—Social
aspects.   3. Political psychology.   4. Aesthetics—Psychological
aspects.   5. Lacan, Jacques, 1901–   .   I. Apollon, Willy.
II. Feldstein, Richard.
BF175.4.C84L33   1995
150.19'5'092—dc20   94-10967
                                                                 CIP

10 9 8 7 6 5 4 3 2

CONTENTS

ACKNOWLEDGMENTS

We wish to thank Ericka McGowan for her work in preparing the index for this volume. We would also like to thank Maria Cimini and Chris DeGuilio for their aid in helping us to prepare the final manuscript of *Lacan, Politics, Aesthetics*. We would especially like to thank Rich Weiner, Dean of Arts and Sciences at Rhode Island College, and Joan Dagle, Chair of the Department of English when we compiled this anthology, for all their support. Without them, this volume would have been delayed for several years.

Richard Feldstein

Introduction I

By the end of the 1980s the first phase in the reception of Lacan's work by the English-speaking audience drew to a close. This stage presented numerous introductions to Lacan's writing that both defined basic concepts like the big Other, *petit objet a,* desire, and *jouissance,* and contextualized them in relation to each other. Because most of Lacan's seminars have not yet been translated for the Anglo-American audience and since his concepts do not easily lend themselves to intellectual comprehension, other texts will no doubt surface to redefine basic terminology and founding principles. Nonetheless, in the 1990s, we have entered into a second phase in the transmission of Lacan's work. In this stage, some writers continue to develop basic concepts that have proved confusing, while others concern themselves with the cultural connotations of Lacanian analysis. The recent exploration of multiculturalism has induced a second look at Lacan's work. Spearheaded by philosophical and literary activists like Slavoj Žižek and Juliet Flower MacCannell, this second wave of transmission applies Lacan's theories to cultural studies—to issues of race, gender, and class that help to delineate the boundaries of the new

psychopolitical movements that are a part of the cultural ethos of
our time.

   Lacan, Politics, Aesthetics is part of the second phase in the
dissemination of Lacan's thought through the cultural field. In this
volume psychoanalysts, cultural theorists, and literary critics
demonstrate the relevance of the unconscious economy to the
wider field of cultural studies. These writers have adopted a variety
of rhetorical positions when engaging cultural issues that deal with
representation, ideology, class, and gender. This volume was conceived to apply psychoanalytic cultural criticism to a broad range
of political and aesthetic issues related to the legal and ideological
superstructure of contemporary society. Our hope was to offer a di-
versified anthology to understand relevant Lacanian concepts as
well as to provide a conceptual network to challenge initiated
readers.

   The initial part of the volume is divided into three sections,
the first of which, "the politics of desire," contains essays by Slavoj
Žižek, Willy Apollon, and Richard Feldstein. In these essays the
writers examine the cultural dynamics of a range of political discourses legitimized by post-enlightenment bourgeois societies.
Žižek, in particular, is interested in the logic of the Communist
party as a carrier of the sublime body that becomes a fetish repudiating castration. According to Žižek, the political fetish presents a
lack in the Other where nothing is missing. This lack guarantees a
neutral knowledge or metalanguage of objective laws that enabled
Stalin and his cohorts to claim factual objectivity for themselves,
although their only claim to objective meaning was the performative nature of language. Apollon also questions the foundation of
politicized laws that legitimize authority while repressing any investigation of "the foundation of the Law as legitimate to authorize
political discourse." From this perspective, State authorities—including the police and military establishment—perpetuate a monopoly of violence in the practice of their political will as an end in
itself. By repressing an inspection of the political foundation and
jouissance related to it, the State regulates violence against those
who seek to uncover the cultural fissure that comprises the lack in
the Other and the monopoly of violence used to hide this lack. My
own article also examines the impulse to construct a symbolic organization that evades the lack in the Other, the fissure in its cultural
matrix, and the attempt to overwrite it within the framework of
fantasy. I claim that the phallic implementation of political power

is accomplished in part by the phallus's presumption of privilege in marking itself as the stripe of differential structure. The State attempts to appropriate for itself power associated with the intersection of the imaginary, symbolic, and real; at this disjuncture of registers, the State substitutes a repeated insistence of its mastery over the void. In its attempt at psycho-social colonization, powerful State interests use the trick of repetition to increase their status while trying to alleviate anxiety about their not having any basis for authority other than the manipulation of images and signs to repeat their claims and insist on their privileges.

In the second section, "jouissance, desire, and the law," Juliet Flower MacCannell and Judith Roof examine non-phallic *jouissance*, which escapes the parameters of masculine representation. MacCannell's essay is concerned with the distinctions between perversion and "a feminine ethics." In her analysis of perversion, MacCannell examines Adolf Eichmann, who helped to administer The Final Solution under Hitler. As MacCannell illustrates, Eichmann's crime—bureaucratic genocide—was murder by administrative edict. Instrument of a will-to-*jouissance* that was not his own, Eichmann wished to penetrate beyond the realm of law to the source from which the law originates. Obsessed with the bureaucratic officialese that conveyed Hitler's genocidal program, Eichmann was a sadistic pervert who executed the Furhrer's wishes, and, in the process, became an instrument of Hitler's will-to-*jouissance*. MacCannell carefully distinguishes perverse behavior from the feminine position in which women are aligned with the Other's *jouissance*. She notes that a feminine ethics "requires itself to find the path in the signifier and have it recognized in the social." While Eichmann wanted empty, formal signifiers, a feminine ethics demands full speech linking jouissance to the body of the signifier.

Judith Roof is also concerned with the interaction of desire, law, and *jouissance*. Roof claims that many legal reforms instituted to ensure gender equality have not produced the desired results because there exists confusion between statutory law and symbolic laws that "treat symptoms, not the underlying gender drama" or metaphors linked to the interpenetration of desire and law. Roof demonstrates how abortion laws treat the mother as a medium rather than as a subject. One can find a parallel between the analyses of Roof and MacCannell since both demonstrate how women are relegated to mere mediums of State authorities.

According to contemporary abortion laws, the State perpetuates the rights of the invisible father who stands for the paternal metaphor, the laws of kinship exchange, and, most insidiously, the rights of fetal ownership. Roof wonders how we can balance the interests of pregnant women while we dissolve patriarchal privileges protected by state and federal laws; she suggests that we jettison the pro-choice/pro-life dichotomy currently used to challenge androcentric reproductive laws and the kinship basis of property law.

In the section "the politics of mastery," Ellie Ragland contrasts the discourse of the master with that of the analyst. She shows that, from a Lacanian perspective, love is a sign of changing discourses, and the analytic discourse is, par excellence, that which typifies this ability to make such a shift. The analyst's discourse places desire in the position of the agent and evokes in the analysand a knowledge of his or her own desire. This is especially important if we consider love is a sign that we love in the Other what we lack in the Other. In contrast, the discourse of the master reduces life to a one-dimensional experience. To the master, knowledge is conjoined with truth to emphasize cognition, perception, and consciousness, in other words, the visible domain of logically provable experience. To establish this flat perspective, the master must repress unconscious ideation. As Ragland illustrates, the master is a purposely blind master—a cognitive specialist who scans experience within the limits of perceptual boundaries, and, in this way, makes the following equation: "I am; I am knowledge, I am the one who knows." The political effects of this discourse are obvious: since this is a discourse of conscious synthesis, it exists on a base of repressed affects excluded from the narrow purview of consciousness. To the master, having is knowing, and in a capitalist culture this equation runs the risk of making the possession of knowledge an endpoint in itself.

The second section of *Lacan, Politics, Aesthetics* presents a study of aesthetic representation, which invariably means a study of the dynamics of symbolization. In the Lacanian schema such a study indicates how the symbol is structured in relation to the imaginary and the real. According to Lacan's formulations, the real is that which escapes language and is experienced as affect, *jouissance,* and the death drive. Interacting structurally with the real is the representational ground of language, which includes signs (and their further division into signifiers and signifieds) used to forge a social link and form an attitude of adjustment toward what is irreducible to the field of representation. The essays in the second half of the book examine the itinerary of the signifier as it combines with the imaginary to prevent the subversion of the representational field and the cultural matrix placed in relation to it. As the writers in this section demonstrate, there is both an aesthetics and an ethics of representation. The various literary, filmic, graphic, and musical texts examined here introduce combinations of aesthetic representation framed in formal boundaries to produce a theatrical inscription of discourse, the social link that binds us to an ethics enacted in relation to human-all-too-human desire.

The section titled "literary representation" is comprised of four essays. In "Othello's Lost Handkerchief: Where Psychoanalysis Finds Itself," Elizabeth Bellamy invokes Jacques Derrida's critique of Lacan when examining the psychoanalytic ur-narrative of castration. This type of Derridean critique claims that psychoanalysis finds itself in an ur-narrative as it attempts to avoid anxiety related to the displacement of the unrepresentable thing itself. Through this form of self-presencing, psychoanalysis discovers itself where the thing is no longer a thing, precisely where a narrative trace foregrounds the stand-in logic which substitutes for the lost object of desire. Bellamy diverges from Derrida's wholesale condemnation of psychoanalysis, however, by suggesting that the process of overdetermination provides "the basis for a 'new' psycho-analysis that will not 'find itself' where it has (and has *not*) already been in the past." Bruce Fink's essay on *Hamlet* offers another slant on this issue. Fink argues that the work of psychoanalysis is not simply to read into aesthetic works psychological structures that have been previously identified but to seek new psychoanalytic insights as well. By taking this position, Fink proposes a counterlogic to Derrida's critique of psychoanalysis which also provides a rationale for Fink's own reading of *Hamlet*, one that disagrees with Lacan's analysis of the fifth act. In his famous essay on the play, Lacan claimed that before the Prince of Denmark died he discovered his own desire and distinguished it from that of the (m)Other. Lacan constructed his argument upon the assumption that once Hamlet was mortally wounded he could finally separate from the Other, stop procrastinating, and enact his will. Fink diverges from this reading by suggesting that "Hamlet's time never comes," that his "time is never now" because, when all is said and done, Horatio must speak for him and plead his case before the world.

The other two essays in the section on literary representation are also concerned with death. In her analysis of *The Unbearable Lightness of Being*, Maire Jaanus demonstrates that the protagonist Tomas recognizes his wife, Tereza, as a harbinger of death when they initially meet. For Tomas, death indicates desire associated with the infant's identification with the mother where there is the danger of absorption in the other. Tomas invokes this imaginary strategy while endlessly pursuing the *objet a,* the absent object that reappears after the symbolic cut as surplus *jouissance.* Jaanus states that, like all of Kundera's characters, Tomas lives fundamentally on the level of the drive, which has no specified object but instead circles endlessly around the absent object. This condition contributes to the death-of-love motif represented in the novel in the figure of the nocturnal butterfly that represents the unbearable lightness of being: unbearable because it refers to death, weight, and human suffering; light because it indicates flight, movement, and the metonymy of the dream image which provides us with the fundamental "truth" emanating from the unconscious.

Death also figures prominently as a motif in Elizabeth Bronfen's essay on Poe. In the final essay on literary representation, Bronfen testifies to the writer's "necrophic misogyny" revealed in the belief that the death of a beautiful woman is the most poetical of tropes. For Poe beauty is spiritually akin to an ecstatic elevation of the soul, and melancholia—the most legitimate poetic topic for Poe—finds its most pronounced form in death. According to this seasoned prejudice, the corpse of a beautiful woman provides the contour of an empty surface for projection, a mirror reflection for the masculine gaze. Here the readily visible dead body becomes an object of desirability in an "aesthetic event" captured by the shift of male fantasy from the proximity of unimaginable death to the more comfortable scene of viewing.

In the later sections of the book, which present essays on musical and graphic representation, there is a continuation of the investigation between the lost object, compensatory fantasy, and the transmission of lingual signs. Peter Widmer's point is tellingly simple: music aims for that beyond human mortality, but it must enter into the realm of knowledge for us to receive it. Traditionally associated with the invisible shadow realm of Hades, music reaches for the ecstatic dimension of human consciousness. But in order to capture the lost object of desire and summon us out of self-conscious, music must "pour into the folds of abstract language." The myth of music lies in the feat of overcoming the binary opposition of language, but any musical trance must eventually be broken because it cannot entirely shake off its linguistic dimension. Because of this inevitability, Widmer concludes, music cannot help us "attain its lost immediacy, a state eternal to the experience of time." In his essay on Dali, Hanjo Berressem emphasizes the lost object in relation to compensatory fantasy and the differing ways fantasy is read by Dali and Lacan. In Lacanian theory, the ego is the site of an imaginary alienating identification—the site of *méconnaissance.* According to Lacan, there is no pre-reflexive ego because reflection gives birth to the ego in the first place; the visual scene structures the ego, not vice versa, since the ego is a mirror-effect. While Lacan states that paranoiac hallucinatory systems represent a "symbolic expression with their own original syntax," Dali believes that being follows from the ability to hallucinate. Dali goes so far as to state, "I am because I hallucinate, I hallucinate cause I am." Dali considers himself a sane madman and sees in the paranoid image a variation of the normal hallucinatory system. For Salvador Dali the image becomes clearer at the point where it becomes more enigmatic. Seen from this perspective, it becomes apparent that Dali offers a shift in thinking: a transposition from interpretative paranoia within perception to paranoia as a signifier of perception itself.

As a counterpoint to the study of the imaginary, the section on filmic representation examines the psychotic fantasy of being delivered up to an all-powerful Other that requires—no, demands—human subjugation to its beastly demands. Danielle Bergeron shows how an alien species, the xenomorphs, invade the human terrain to create a sci-fi inversion where human beings are subordinated to another species. Once the alien creature comes on board the spaceship, humans live in terror of being reduced to objects of need for the xenomorph, mere bodily receptacles for its reproduction. In this way human beings become objects that fill in the lack in the xenomorph/Other. Bergeron stresses that the sci-fi inversion of species' dominance is equivalent to a psychotic fantasy because in psychosis the Other overwhelms the subject "by terrifying impressions, individual drives caused by the unpredictable wandering of the Thing." In her article on *Aliens,* Lucie Cantin states that the capture of the subject by the *jouissance* of the Other insists that the subject must comply with its demands. According to this logic, the human being becomes a thing of prey in the staging of trauma's structure. For humans to survive, the thing must be externalized to create a process of separation; to defeat the thing, humans must constitute an *objet a,* place the thing within limits, and identify its boundaries. But in *Aliens,* even after the humans are separated from the xenomorph, all who came into contact with the beast are permanently marked by their non-mediated relation to the real of the Other's *jouissance.*

The final section, "cross-genre representation," presents an analysis by Catherine Portuges that weaves together an intersecting fabric of literary and filmic perspectives. Portuges tells us that Duras, who is both a writer and a filmmaker, seeks in her films "the primary state of the text, as one tries to remember a distant internal event not lived out but heard told." For Duras the text presents an adjustment of distance between memory and narration—an attempt to find the correct distance to experience the object of narration without fear or trepidation. As Portuges shows, if we come too close there is suffocation, if we get too far away separation anxiety ensues. Perhaps that is why Duras often adds two layers to her depiction of experience, literary and filmic: surrender to the cinematic transference involves a risk of entrapment and the compensatory desire to remain within the tug of the narrative, while Duras's cinema insists on narration as its modus operandi even as it deconstructs the audience's narrative impulse. In films like *Aurélia Steiner,* Duras introduces the narrative voice as an off-screen track of pure narration superimposed over the visual sequence, in this case, a boat on the Seine. Through this technique, the filmmaker conflates herself with the narrator of the written text. Duras speaks through Aurélia in order to create a textual locus so everything can be read, including "the empty place" in the Other.

It is this lack in the Other that so many writers in *Lacan, Politics, Aesthetics* address from varying perspectives. How this lack is denied or filled—through aesthetic technique or political manipulation—proves to be a prominent point of focus in this collection. In fact, it becomes a manifestation of form itself, of the structural attempt to negotiate lack and the surplus *jouissance* that issues from it.

Willy Apollon

Introduction II

Psychoanalysis is possible only if language is considered to be the foundation of the human. The field of representation in its entirety then becomes the realm in which the human is reduced to what can be represented, abandoning what, in keeping with Lacan, must be taken as the real—that which cannot be reduced to representation. A decisive stake in language thus becomes its foundation, what guarantees the representation of representing, or, in other words, what represents a new, adequate form. The ancients saw the roots of morality and law in that hypothesis of truth where assumed presence bore witness to the preciseness of representation. Until Marx, Freud, and Nietzsche, who initiated the philosophies of suspicion, that illusion of truth dominated our thought processes.

The injury that psychoanalysis inflicts upon the representation of the human is the subversion of truth as central to knowledge, experienced as an effect of what the structure of language excludes from representation. The real, excluded from language but returning in representation as an erosion of the interior, is what Freud designates in the human as the death drive and what Lacan sees as the paradigm of *jouissance*. What psychoanalysis after Lacan designates by *jouissance* is that part of satisfaction lost for the living speaking beings, not because it is prohibited, but because the loss is logically implied in the structure of inadequacy of the language to the real.

The inadequacy of the object of demand to the object of need leaves stranded an undecidable portion of need-satisfaction, which returns indefinitely in every quest of the drive and whirlwind of fantasy. That portion of impossible jouissance over and above prohibited satisfaction is what Lacan refers to as *objet petit a*, the cause of the subject's desire and the final identification with its truth in fantasy. The reintroduction of the subject into every consideration of things human is the constant wound, termed the plague by Freud, that psychoanalysis inflicts upon every science of humanity.

Any such problematic in the relationship of humanity to truth subverts the entire field of representation. What subsequently emerges is no longer the relationship of representational truth to the real insofar as the real is what is focused on by representation. The real is now the jouissance left stranded owing to language, and representation is the representation of the real. Representation thus becomes the special mode whereby an impossible *jouissance* is the object of an irreducible quest, "in spite of" and/or "over and beyond" what organizes itself as a prohibited modality of *jouissance* in this field of representation. A prohibition such as incest or parricide is what founds the social link as a loss and debt to pay to derive satisfaction from the social link. The psychoanalytic discourse reduces the field of representation to this articulation of the prohibited and impossible as a cultural and historical delimitation of the possible for a given social group. A knowledge about *jouissance,* whose reckoning is a logical function of the prohibition founding the social link, is therefore introduced by the psychoanalytic discourse into the real of the human.

Taken from the standpoint of the psychoanalyst who assumes this knowledge of what is creating the cause in the social link, we maintain that the subversion of the representational field is not without consequence to political and aesthetic thought. Our claim emphasizes and founds the extension of psychoanalysis into the various disciplines in which reintroducing a subjective problematics into scientific consideration is essential if the human is not to be reduced simply to something that can be managed, a set of realities constituted by science. The extremes in the field of social representation—politics and aesthetics—may consequently be moved closer to one another.

politics as a structure of repression in the field of representation

Politics makes a promise it cannot keep. Would that have something to do with the fact that the field of representation from which politics draws its credibility cannot deal with the realities it espouses without deforming and losing some part of them? Both the loss and deformation sustain the dimension of deceit embodied in politics, and what the media imagines and constantly searches for, without ever realizing it, fuels their desire to know about the jouissance of politics. Doubtless then, the representation of politics must strictly be considered an aesthetic, where the inescapable stakes of the loss are asserted in the criticism of the unkept promise and in the questioning of jouissance attributed to politics. Would that be the indirect pathway through which politics, confronted with the impossible, finds itself in ethics? These questions warrant examination.

The promise of politics is to strike a balance between personal happiness and the common good. The current tendency throughout the world is toward a liberalization of policies; generalized liberalism whose object par excellence in fantasy if not in the fetish of the political discourse is private ownership. The balance exacted between personal happiness and the common good in the political promise is thus a balance that turns principally on private ownership as such. In a sense it could be said that the premise of the promise is that private ownership would cover over the locatable contradiction between personal happiness and the common good. Private ownership is lifted to the status of a desirable object as a solution to a contradiction in current political discourse to the extent that a discourse can survive and maintain itself before the voters in a democratic perspective only as a promise of enhanced well-being.

But what is this contradiction at play in the political discourse? In its liberal electoralist version, the political discourse highlights the unbridgeable gap, from the subject's point of view, between so-called personal happiness and the common good. It does so by stressing the difference rather than the contradiction. The liberal discourse would have us believe that there is a gap capable of being improved upon, not an insurmountable contradiction. Subtle and highly skillful economic maneuvering in such areas as taxes, job creation, support for various sectors in the national and regional economies and in public services would enable the gap to be managed and national riches to be better distributed.

Turning to the psychoanalytic problematics where *jouissance* is at stake as the cause, we are confronted with an unbridgeable gap? The rules governing economics as a scientific discipline and as a technology have not been tailored to respond to satisfying personal needs, and even less so to meeting the quest for impossible *jouissance* for those persons. But the fact does remain that when those subjects speak of economics, they do so by involving their own specific quest. Even the economic reality is predicated on fantasy, and thus the irrational dimension is paradoxically taken on by any economic consideration from the standpoint of the potential voter for whom the politician's message is directed.

The point of view of the "common good" is necessarily a statistical and scientific one, where consideration of the subject is unwanted and even heretical. The "common good" is the precise opposite of personal interest because the subjective dimension obliterates any possible objectivity in such an interest. Likewise, one must accept the obvious—that the very notion of private ownership is far from being subjectively insinuated in the political discourse. There is nothing subjective about private ownership; it must be objectifiable to be scientific. It is linked to economic and legal imperatives determining its exact scope in society independent of the ideas that each citizen may have of it and unrelated to any comparison with the object at stake in the *jouissance* for any given subject.

This "common good" in its economic sense and personal dimension of "private ownership" fails to respond to the fundamental question of the relationship of the subject to *jouissance* and to the impossible dimension where the relationship of the object of ownership substitutes for objects of need. This failure is of course structural and accounts for the impossible that the political discourse consists in repressing. The question thus arises as to whether this operation of repression is part and parcel of *jouissance* where the passion of politics is founded as one of its conditions. But the repression itself is only partial and thus hides a more radical repression in liberalism, thanks to the historic failure of the socialist discourse. The liberal promise in fact erases the internal division in the notion of a common good, which is the contradiction that the notion is designed to expunge.

Private ownership as an objective concept carries with it a dichotomy that is removed between the individual in the social linkage and the subject in relation to *jouissance*. When only the individual is considered, the political promise erases the subject, and that exclusion becomes a necessary and sufficient condition to allow for the hope of a reduction in the insistence of *jouissance* whose demands are scattered throughout the filaments, ambiguities and objects of the social link. Lulling the subject to sleep and ensuring that s/he does not wake up thus becomes the driving force behind the discourse of a political promise, whether liberal or socialist.

The revolutionary discourse is one that seeks to waken the subject, and for that reason is dangerous and heretical. The only efficient counter-logic is to confront the subject prematurely with the violent return of the drives and to accuse the subject of stirring up this violence, which constitutes the return of the repressed. The nationalism of the former Eastern-bloc countries, the would-be religious fanaticism in the Middle East, and the political movements sustained by a supposedly new democratic problematics in Latin America—each signify in different manners and in varying contexts an unforeseen awakening that is accompanied by an unavoidable violence. It would be surprising to see international diplomacy, built on the exclusions of its promises of "well-being" and worldwide peace, be able to put down these forces that are now awakening abandoned subjectivities.

The erasing of subjectivies in the social link confirmed on the personal level by notions like "private ownership," personal and collective "well-being," and "social peace" may also be found at the collective level. The social relations of inequality are done away within the *jouissance* of rights, social injustice, poverty, and inequality in access to social and public services and in the economic strategies commonly referred to as equal opportunities. The blotting out of social relationships of inequality by resorting to equalizing economic schemes is embodied in the concept of "well-being," where any apportioning for those included and excluded by the structure is done away with, so that the apportioning becomes scientifically and technically possible.

Thus, in the field of representation, the political discourse maintains a promise that cannot be kept. Today's political discourse dominates the entire field of representation and operates like a vacuum or vortex. It is a discourse that requires its visibility, and now it has the greatest array of production means to ensure that visibility. One could logically posit the following hypothesis as the most profitable and economical for an analysis of the field of representation: the visibility required by a discourse in the field of representation is directly proportional to the invisibility of what the discourse is intended to exclude from that field; showing more in order to hide better is the principle of what the discourse of a political promise requires of visibility in the field of representation. Both this principle and the visibility it requires are extraneous to the individual politician's intentions and wishes. A politician most certainly may be driven by the best of all possible intentions. What is involved, however, is the ordering of the promise as a political discourse in the structure of the field of representation as such.

aesthetics against ethics

The media discourse takes after the visibility required in the field of representation, but it duplicates it with a criticism that, far from attacking and diminishing the visibility, promotes it. The visibility feeds the mass media discourse and, in so doing, blinds the media to the element of impossibility around which the political discourse of promise revolves. Media criticism always remains oblivious to the greatest weakness in the political discourse, which leaves unscathed the failure where the discourse is constantly unraveling and reweaving itself. The media discourse succeeds in unceasingly questioning the politician's *jouissance*, leaving for the individual what at the outset s/he is destined not to grasp on the level of structure. The politician's relationship to the political discourse is the particular relationship of an individual to the impossible in the social link. This impossible is embodied in the structure of the political discourse as a promise; it is not the subject's breaking point where *jouissance* has been made impossible by language. This distinction illustrates the extent of error in the media discourse. After leaving aside what constituted the structural failure of politics as a promise, it becomes concerned solely with the *jouissance* of the politician as the object of criticism.

Politics addresses the ethical questions posed by the media discourse arising from the errors found in their objects of criticism by resorting to a strategy of aesthetics. And this tactic is unavoidable because it is the only logical strategy within the structured field of representation. An aesthetics of representation, primarily in the ritualization of the staged political ploy, presents what the media sees as an exercise of democracy in its right to question and to criticize. The target is not the failing, which renders the politician's promise worthless, but the verbal performance of the politician, i.e., his or her relationship to the lack that nourishes the lust for power.

If it is true that the field of representation is dominated by the blinding of visibility in politics, then what does the media's strategy of ethical questioning bear on? The structural blindfold induced into the field of representation is based on the impossible at stake in the political promise. As repression of the impossible, the blinding is maintained outside the field of visibility by the created theatricalization, ritualization, and projection of events by the media to the entire nation. The media's ethical question therefore may never have any credible bearing on an object kept out of its reach by the very function that politics assigns to the media discourse of promoting the theatricalization of power on the national level.

What then does the ethical questioning focus on? Beyond what is presented as moral, above a system of implicit and explicit prohibition where the limits of acceptability in social relationships are conditioned, an ethics questions what appears as impossible. Morality attempts to confine the social link within the limits defined by prohibitions in their personal and legal implications. But over and above the social link, an ethics questions the impossibilities underlying the quest in human desire, i.e., what the human being cannot reject without giving up his or her status as human. The subject's demand in relation to the impossible is truly the site where historically s/he disputes and modifies the limits of orality but without abandoning the prohibited as a condition of the social link. Thus, in the field of representation, ethical questioning should address the conditions of impossibility underlying the political promise. Visibility staged as a political space makes this flaw in the political discourse the blind spot in the field of representation hidden by the theatricalization of power and the ritualization of the democratic process of political questioning.

The field of representation, reduced by the staging of political discourse, becomes a theater where interest in the behind-the-scenes and on-the-scene lifestyles and performances of its actors has been replaced by the anxiety the text was intended to sustain in the relationship of the spectator to the impossible. The structural shifting of criticism, from the impossibility at stake in the political promise to the *jouissance* sustaining the politician's quest for such an impossibility, determines the particulars governing the ethical questioning of the politician rather than the questioning of political discourse. In North America, the process takes place as if the political discourse were capable of standing on its own, not having to be questioned in its prerequisites and conditions of possibility.

The political discourse seems to determine the structure of the field of representation as a received discourse establishing the relative position of all others. To question the possible conditions of the political discourse is to tackle the entire field of representation as it itself is received. This would imply modifying the conditions for devising dominant currents such as the media's encapsulated mentality, the dominance of the feminist critique of human sciences, the dominance of biological and legal problematics in the realm of scientific justification so exaggerated in prevailing currents, and so on. The specific blinding of the structural contradiction between economics and social policies, which renders the promise of political discourse unfulfillable, corresponds to an equally specific repression of subjectivity in its insistence on desire and demand.

The repression of the subject, sustained in dominant currents by scientism and juridism, reduces the question of ethics to one of private morality projected onto the scene of representation as public visibility. The argument sustaining the questioning of moral visibility lies in a principle devised to fit these circumstances: the public has a right to know. Any media questioning of a politician is thus centered on private and public morality as the right of the public to know. But what it has a right to really know, the structural failure of the discourse of promises, the public will never know. The public will be either entertained or bored for want of being able to be informed about the structural limits of politics in human affairs. The entire ethical questioning supports and shores up the theatricalization of power and the ritualization of the democratic process as an aesthetics of political representation.

This "showing to hide" can achieve its objectivity only if it provides an aesthetic dimension to the visibility required for the political discourse, where the subject's lack can be substituted for the structural failing. What is at stake in the aesthetics of politics is a specific prohibition—the prohibition of thinking! The psychoanalytic discourse, introducing the knowledge of analysis into the political field, constitutes the particular real of a *jouissance*—that promised by politics but that turns out to fail in the accompanying discourse. Applying psychoanalysis to the political discourse can only bring out the dominant function of the discourse in the field of representation, while at the same time it entraps *jouissance* motivating the impossibility inherent in that discourse.

The extension of psychoanalysis by its application to realms of discourse other than those related to the subject in transference can obviously not be affected without giving rise to specific epistemological difficulty. But those extension-related problems can be discussed and solved only in that very context. Applied to literature, theater, and film, psychoanalysis operates differently than when applied to painting, sculpture, or even music. Put another way, those fields of psychoanalytic extension impose on knowledge and on the theory of psychoanalysis the resistance of a real that is particular to each case—the real of *jouissance* itself at work in each domain where the subject of the word and desire finds that singular matter of identification to his or her own truth. The articles published in this volume are intended as a modest contribution to this emerging undertaking that extends the work of psychoanalytic knowledge outside the social kind of transference structured by the response that the analyst's desire prompts from the drive.

the politics of desire

Slavoj Žižek

THE FETISH OF THE PARTY*

The Totalitarian Body

At the beginning of the "Pledge of the Bolshevik Party to its Chief Lenin," Stalin says: "We are, us communists, people of a different making. We are cut in a different fabric" (*History* . . . 1971, p. 297). Here we immediately recognize the Lacanian name of this "different fabric:" the object small *a*. The weight of Stalin's sentence comes from the basic fetishist functioning of the Stalinist Party; it comes from the basis that the Party functions as the miracle of an immediate incarnation of an objective and neutral Knowledge that serves as a reference point to legitimate the activity of the Party (the so-called "knowledge of objective laws"). Marx determines money in its relation to other merchandises as a paradoxical element that immediately incarnates, in its very singularity, the generality of "all," that is to say, as a "singular reality, that includes in itself all the really existing species of the same thing":

3

It is as if, next to and other than lions, tigers, hares, and all the other real animals that constitute in a group different races, species, sub-species, families, etc, of the animal kingdom, existed, furthermore, *the animal*, the individual incarnation of the animal kingdom. (Dognin, 1977, p. 73)

This is the logic of the Party: it is as if, next to and other than classes, social strata, social groups and subgroups, and their economic, political, and ideological organizations, that constitute in a group the different parts of the sociohistorical universe ruled by the objectives of social development, existed, furthermore, the Party—the immediate and individual incarnation of these objective laws, the short circuit, the paradoxical crossing point between the subjective will and objective laws. Therefore, the "different fabric" of the communists is the "objective reason of history" incarnated. Since the fabric in which they are cut is, after all, their body, this body undergoes a true transsubstantiation; it becomes the carrier of *another* body, the *sublime* body. It is interesting to read the letters of Lenin to Maxim Gorki on the basis of the logic of the Communists' sublime body, especially those letters of 1913, related to the debate on the "Construction of God/bogobraditel'stvo/" of which Gorki was an advocate (Lenin, 1964). The first obvious thing is an apparently not-so-important trait, lacking theoretical weight. Lenin is literally obsessed by Gorki's health. Here are the ending of a few letters:

- "Please write to me about your health./ Yours, *Lenin.*"
- "Are you in good health?/ Yours, *Lenin.*"
- "Enough of this joking. *Stay well.* Send me word. *Rest more./* Yours, *Lenin.*"

When, in the fall of 1913, Lenin hears of Gorki's pulmonary illness, he writes to him immediately:

That a Bolshevist, old it is true, treats you by a *new* method, I must confess that it worries me terribly! God save us from doctor friends in general, and from Bolshevist doctors in particular! . . . I assure you that one must be treated *only* by the best specialists (unless for benign cases). It is horrible to experiment with the invention of a Bolshevik doctor on oneself! Unless under the supervision of professors from Naples (at this time, Gorki lived in Capri). If these professors are really knowledgeable. . . . I would even tell you that if you are leaving this winter, consult *without fail* the best doctors *in Switzerland* and *in Vienna*—You would be unforgivable if you fail to do it!

Let us leave aside the associations that a retroactive reading of these sentences of Lenin triggers (twenty years later, all of Russia experimented with the new methods of a certain Bolshevist). Rather, let us set the question of the *field of meaning* of Lenin's worry for Gorki's health. At first sight, the question is clear and quite innocent: Gorki was a valuable ally, thus worthy of care. But the following letter sheds a different light on the affair. Lenin is alarmed by Gorki's positive attitudes toward the "Construction of God" that should be, according to Gorki, only "postponed" and put aside for the moment but not at all rejected. Such attitudes are for Lenin incomprehensible, an extremely un-pleasant surprise. Here are the beginning and the end of this letter:

Dear Alexis Maximovitch, /But what are you doing? Really, this is simply terrible!// Why are you doing this? It is terribly unfortunate./ Yours, *V.I.*

And here is the postscript:

Take care of yourself more seriously, really, so that you can travel in the winter *without catching a cold* (in the winter it is dangerous).

The true stakes are even more clearly observable at the end of the following letter, sent together with the preceding letter:

I enclose my letter from yesterday: do not hold it against me if I got carried away. Perhaps *I did not* understand you cor-rectly? Perhaps you were *joking* in writing "for the moment?" Concerning the "construction of God," perhaps you were not serious?/ For heavens sake, take care of yourself a little better./ Yours, Lenin.

Here, it is stated in an explicit and formal manner that, in the last resort at least, Lenin takes Gorki's fluctuations and ideological confusion for an effect of his physical exhaustion and illness. Thus he does not take Gorki's arguments seriously. Finally, his response consists in saying: "Rest, take care of yourself a little better. . . ." The foundation of Lenin's procedure is not a vulgar materialism nor an immediate reduction of ideas to body movements. Quite the contrary, his presupposition and implication are precisely that a Communist is a man of a "different fabric." When the Communist speaks and acts as a Communist, it is the objective necessity of history itself that speaks and acts through him. In other words, the spirit of a true Communist cannot deviate, since this spirit is immediately the self-awareness of the historical necessity. Consequently, the only thing that can disturb or introduce disorder and deviation, is his body, this fragile materiality serving to support another body, the sublime body, "cut in a different fabric."

Phallus and Fetish

Can we also maintain the proposition of the fetishist character of the Party in the analytic use of this term? The fetish is, as we well know, the *ersatz* of the maternal phallus: it is a question of repudiation of castration. Thus, we should approach fetishism from the phallic signifier.

One side of the "Meaning of the Phallus" was already developed by Saint Augustine. The phallic organ incarnates the revolt of the human body against mastery by man. The phallic organ is the divine punishment for the arrogance of man who wanted to be God's equal and become the master of the world. The phallus is the organ whose pulsation and erection mostly escape man, his will, and his power. All the parts of the human body are in principle at the disposal of man's will. Their unavailability is always "de facto," with the exception of the phallus, whose pulsation is unavailable "in principle." However, we must relate this aspect to another, indicated by this witticism: "Which is the lightest object in the world? The phallus, since it is the only thing that can be raised by the very thought of it."

That is the "Meaning of the Phallus:" the short-circuit where the "inside" and the "outside" intersect, the point where the pure exteriority of the body unavailable to the subjective will passes immediately into the interiority of the "pure thought." We could almost recall the Hegelian critique of the Kantian "chose en soi" where this transcendental "chose en soi," inaccessible to human thought, is revealed being only the interiority of pure thought with the abstraction of each objective content. Such is precisely the "contradiction" that could be described as the "phallic experience:" I can nothing (the Augustinian moment) although everything depends on me (the moment of the above mentioned witticism). The "Meaning of the Phallus" is the very pulsation between the EVERYTHING and the NOTHING. Potentially, it is "all meanings" or the very universality of meaning (in other words: "in the last instance, we only talk about this"), and for this reason the "Meaning of the Phallus" is effectively without any determined meaning; it is the signifier-without-signified. Naturally, this is one of the commonplaces of the Lacanian theory. As soon as we try to grasp "all" the signifiers of a structure, as soon as we try to "fill" its universality by its particular components, we must add a paradoxical signifier that does not have a particular-determined signified but that incarnates in a way "all meanings" or the very universality of this structure while at the same time, being "the signifier without signified." A passage from *Class Struggle in France* by Marx is of special interest to us here since it develops the logic of the phallic element precisely relative to the political party. It is a question of the role of the "party of order" during the revolutionary events in the middle of the nineteenth century:

> The secret of its existence, *the coalition in a party of the Orleanists and Legitimists . . . the anonymous kingdom of the republic* was the only one under which the two fractions could maintain with equal power their common class interest without renouncing to their reciprocal rivalry. . . . If each of their fractions considered separately was royalist, the product of their chemical combination must necessarily be *republican.* (Marx, 1973, p. 58–59)

According to this logic, the republican is a species inside the genus of royalism. Within (the species of) this genus, the republican stands for the genus itself. This paradoxical element, the specific point where the universal *genus falls on itself* among its particular species, is this very phallic element. Its paradoxical place, the crossing point between the "outside" and the "inside," is crucial for grasping fetishism: it is precisely this place that is lost. In other words, the *castrative* dimension of the phallic element is repudiated with the fetish, the "nothing" that necessarily accompanies its "all," the radical heterogeneity of this element relative to the universality that it is meant to incarnate (the fact that the phallic signifier can bring the potential *universality* of meaning only as a signifier-*without*-signified, that we can be royalist *in general* only in the form of *republicans*). The fetish is the S1 that, by its position of exception, immediately incarnates its Universality, the Particular that is immediately "merged" with its Universal.

This is the logic of the Stalinist Party that appears as the immediate incarnation of the Universality of the Masses or the Working Class. The Stalinist Party would be, to speak in Marx's terms, something like royalism in general in the very form of royalism, which is also the fetishist illusion. In fetishism, the phallic element, the *intersection* of the two species ("Orleanists" and "Legitimists") is immediately set as *All*, "the general line," and the two species whose intersection it is, become two "deviations" (that of the "right" and that of the "left") of the "general line.

In the "short-circuit" between the Universal (the Masses, the Class) and the Particular (the Party), the relation between the Party and the Masses is not dialectized, such that if there is a conflict between the Party and the rest of the working class (as today in Poland), this does not mean that the Party is "alienated" from the

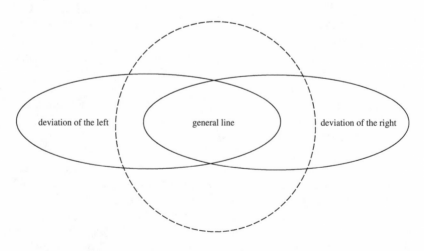

FIGURE 1.1

working class but that, on the contrary, elements of the working class itself have become "strange" to their own Universality ("the true interests of the working class") incarnated in the party. It is because of this fetishist character of the Party that there is, for the Stalinist, no contradiction between the demand that the Party should be open to the Masses and merged with the Masses, and the Party in the position of Exception, the authoritarian Party, concentrating power in itself. Let us, for example, take up this passage from *Questions of Leninism:*

> Speaking of the difficulties of stocking wheat, the communists generally put the responsibility on the peasants, pretending that the latter are guilty of everything. But this is completely wrong and absolutely unjust. The peasants have nothing to do with it. If it is a question of responsibility and guilt, the responsibility falls entirely on the communists, and the guilty ones in all of this are us and only us, the communists.
>
> There is no power as strong, and never has been, with as great an authority as ours, as the power of the Soviets. There is no party as powerful, and never has been, with as great an authority as ours, as the Communist Party. Nobody is or can prevent us from leading the Kolkhoz as their interests require, the interests of the State. (Stalin, 1977, p. 659–60)

Here, the authoritarian character of the Party is directly accentuated. Stalin insists explicitly that all power, without any division, is in the hand of the Party and that people, the "ordinary" people, "have nothing to do with it," that they are neither responsible nor guilty. However, this exclusive and authoritarian power is set *immediately* as a truly democratic power, as an effective power of the people. From there a certain "naivety" of the "dissident" critiques follows. The Stalinist discursive field is organized in such a way that the critique misses its aim; *one can guess in advance* what the critique bothers to demonstrate (the authoritarian character of power, etc.) in giving to this fact another scope, in taking it precisely for the proof of the effective power of the people. In short, to speak in the usual way: the critique tries to attack the Stalinist at the level of facts within a presupposed common code that plays on the contradiction between effectiveness and ideological legitimation ("in principle, the USSR is supposed to be a democratic society, but effectively . . ."), while displacing in advance the conflict at the level of the code itself.

Here is the "impossible" position of the fetish: a singular that immediately "incarnates" the general, without signifying this with "castration." It is an element that occupies the position of metalanguage while being part of the "very-thing" itself; it is at the same time an "objective" gaze and an "involved party." In *Bananas*, Woody Allen's political comedy, there is a scene that perfectly illustrates this point. The protagonist, who is in a non-identified dictatorship in Central America, is invited to dinner by the ruling general, an invitation that is delivered to him in his hotel room. As soon as the messenger is gone, the protagonist throws himself on the bed in joy, turns his eyes toward celestial heights as the sound of harp is heard. As spectators, we perceive this sound, of course, as a musical accompaniment and not as a real (quasi-) music present in the event itself. Suddenly, however, the protagonist sobers up, rises, opens the armoire and discovers a "typical" Latin American who plays the harp. The paradox of this scene is this passage from outside to inside: what we had perceived as "external" musical accompaniment is affirmed as "internal" to the (quasi) "reality" of the scene. The comical effect comes from the position of the impossible knowledge of the protagonist. He behaves as if he is in a position from where he could hear at the same time what is in the realm of cinematographic (quasi-) "reality" *and* its "external" musical accompaniment.

It is not surprising that we find this same "short-circuit" clue of the position of the fetish in the "totalitarian" discourse, and precisely where it is necessary to affirm at the same time the ideological "neutrality" and the "professional" character of the regions of "culture" (art, science), *and* their submission to the ruling "doctrine" and to the "people." Let us take up this passage of the famous letter of Joseph Goebbels to Wilhelm Furtwangler of 11 April 1933:

> It is not sufficient that art be excellent, it should also present itself as the expression of the people. In other words, only an art that takes inspiration from the people can at the end be considered as excellent and mean something for the people it addresses.

Here is the pure form of the logic that is in question: it is *not only* excellent *but also* an expression of the people, since *to tell the truth,* it can be excellent only in being an expression of the people. In replacing art by science, we obtain one of the topics of the Stalinist ideology: "scientificness alone does not suffice, we also need a just ideological orientation, a dialectic-materialistic vision of the world, since it is only through a just ideological orientation that we can achieve true scientific results."

The Stalinist Discourse

The fetishist functioning of the Party guarantees the position of a neutral knowledge, *"décapitonné,"* that of the agent of the Stalinist discourse. The Stalinist discourse is presented as a pure metalanguage, as the knowledge of "objective laws," applied "on" the "pure" object, S2, descriptive [constatif] discourse, objective knowledge. The very engagement of theory on the side of the proletariat, its "hold over the party," is not "internal"—Marxism does not speak *of* the position of the proletariat; it "is oriented to" the proletariat from an external, neutral, "objective" position:

> In 1889–90, the proletariat of Russia was a minute minority relative to the masses of individual peasants who formed the great majority of the population. But the proletariat was developing insofar as class, while the peasantry insofar as class was disintegrating. Since it was precisely the proletariat that was developing as a class, Marxists founded their actions on them. In this they were not mistaken, since we know that the proletariat, that was only a force of little importance, later became a first rate historical and political force. (*History,* 1871, p.121–122)

At the time of their struggle against the Populists, from where could Marxists speak to be mistaken in their choice of the proletariat? They could of course speak from an external place where the historic process extends as a field of objective forces, where one must "be careful of not being mistaken," and "be guided by just forces," those that will win. In short, one must "bet on the right horse." From this external position, we can approach the famous "theory of reflection:" one must ask the question of who occupies the "neutral-objective" position from where this "objective reality," reflected yet external to reflection can be judged, whence the reflection can be "compared" to the "objective reality" and judged if the reflection corresponds to it or not.

We have already touched the "secret" of the functioning of this "objective knowledge": this very point of "pure objectivity" to which the Stalinist discourse is related and by which it is legitimized (the "objective meaning" of facts) is already constituted by the performative. It is even the point of the pure performative, the tautology of pure self-reference. It is precisely there, at the point where, "in words," the discourse refers to a pure reality outside language, that "in (its own) act," it refers only to itself. Here, we could almost recall the Hegelian critique of the Kantian *"chose en soi"* where this transcending entity, independent of subjectivity, is revealed to be only the interiority of pure thought, abstraction made of each objective content. In classical terminology, the propositions of validity (just-unjust) take the form of propositions of being. When the Stalinist pronounces a judgment, he pretends to describe and "observe" the "objective" state. In short, in the Stalinist discourse the performative functions as the *repressed truth* of the descriptive [constatif], as it is pushed "under the bar." Consequently, we could write the relation between S1 and S2 in the following manner: S2/S1. This means that the Stalinist discourse presents a neutral-objective knowledge as its agent, while the repressed truth of this knowledge remains S1, the performative of the master. This is the paradox where the Stalinist discourse finds the victim of the political process. If I insist on the descriptive [constatif] falsehood of the judgment of the party ("you are a traitor!"), *in reality* I act against the party and "effectively" break its unity. The only way to affirm my adherence to the party "by my acts," at the performative level, is, of course, to confess. What? Precisely my exclusion, the fact that I am a "traitor."

Then, what takes the place of the *other?* At first the answer appears rather easy. The other of the "objective knowledge" is obviously only a subjective knowledge, a knowledge that is only a seeming of knowledge like "metaphysics" and "idealism," relative to which the Stalinist "objective knowledge" ("different from metaphysics that . . .") is defined. The paradoxical nature of this opposing pole appears as soon as we look more closely at the Stalinist divisive procedure. We can read the four famous "Fundamental Traits of the Marxist Dialectic Method" in opposition to the traits of metaphysics as a process of differentiation, of disjunction, proceeding by a choice in four stages:

1. *either* we look at nature as an accidental accumulation of objects *or* we look at it as a unified, coherent all;
2. *either* we look at the unified All as a state of rest and immobility *or* we look at it as a process of development;
3. *either* we look at the process of development as a circular movement *or* we look at it as a development from the inferior to the superior;
4. *either* we look at the development from the inferior to the superior as a harmonious evolution *or* we look at it as a struggle of the opposites.

At first sight, we are dealing with a classical case of exhaustive disjunction: at each level, the genus is divided in two species. However, if we look at things more closely, we will immediately perceive the paradoxical character of this division. There is basically an implicit affirmation that all the variants of metaphysics are "by their essence," "objectively," "the same thing." We can verify this by reading the scheme "backward." The harmonic development, "by its essence," "objectively," is in no way a development from the inferior to the superior, but a pure and simple circular movement. The circular movement, "by its essence," is not at all a movement but a conservation of the state of immobility. This means that there is at the end *only one choice:* that between Dialectics and Metaphysics. In other words, the diagonal that separates dialectics from metaphysics is to be read as a vertical line. If we choose the harmonious evolution, we lose not only the struggle of the opposites but also the very common genus, the development from the inferior to the superior, since, "objectively," we fall in the circular movement.

This vertical reading of the diagonal unifies the "enemy." We can evade the fact that it is a question of a gradual differentiation. First it was Bukharin who, together with Stalin, got rid of Trotsky. The conflict with Bukharin emerged only later, in the same manner that it was first the circular movement that, in connection with the evolutive movement, was opposed to immobility and became its opposite only after the "expulsion" of immobility. With all these oppositions, we construct *only one* "Bukharin-Trotskiist plot." The "short-circuit" of such a "unification," is, of course, a particular perversion of the "primacy of synchrony over diachrony." We project backward the present distinction, the opposition that determines the present "concrete situation." Thus, the implicit presupposition of official historians of East Germany is that it was West Germany that began the Second World War.

What is thus the "secret" of this process of division? The *History of the Communist Party (b)* characterizes the "monsters of the Bukharinist and Trotskiist gang" as "scraps of the human kind." This distinction is to be taken literally and must be applied to the very process of differentiation. In this process each genus has only one true and *proper* species; the other species is only a *scrap* of the genus, the nongenus under the appearance of a species of the genus. The development from the inferior to the superior has only one species, the struggle of the opposites; the harmonious evolution is only the scrap of this genus.

From there, unexpectedly we fall into the scheme of the division encountered in the process of the Hegelian dialectics: each genus has only one species, the other species is the paradoxical negative of the genus itself. Just as in the case of the "limit case" of the logic of the signifier, the All is divided into its Part and a remainder that is not nothing but a paradoxical, impossible, contradictory entity. Metaphysics pretends at the same time that (1) nature is an accidental accumulation and not an All and (2) nature as All is a state of immobility and not a movement. Unlike the Hegelian division, however, instead of *including* through its specification/determination, the genus *excludes* its own absence and "negativity." The development from the inferior to the superior as a concretization of the process of development "in general" is not a "synthesis" of initial abstract universality and its negation (of the "circular movement") but precisely the exclusion of the "circular movement" from the "process of development" in general. Through its specification, the genus is purified of its scraps. Far from "particularizing" it, the division "consolidates" the All as All. If from the All of the genus we subtract its scrap, we subtract nothing and the All remains All. The "development from the inferior to the superior" is no less "all" than the process of development "in general." From there we can grasp the logic of this apparently absurd formulation: "In its immense majority the party wholeheartedly rejected the platform of the bloc." The "immense majority" is equivalent to "wholeheartedly," the rest (the "minority") does not count. In other words, we are dealing with a fusion between the Universal and the Particular, between the genus and the species. This is, in reality, why one does not choose between Nothing and the *Party*. Each Particular is immediately fusioned with the Universal and we are thrown in this way toward the "ou bien ou bien absolu," between the Nothing and the *All*. Thus, the Stalinist disjunction is precisely the contrary of the habitual disjunction in two particulars where we can never "catch up with the turtle," (to be understood on the account of the movement of ennunciation itself), to divide in a part and a remainder that would not be nothing, that would come in the place of the ennunciation itself (this division functions as an inaccessible asymptotic point). In the Stalinist disjunction, the problem is rather to get out of "ou bien ou bien absolu:" the inaccessible is a division in particulars, a division where one of the terms would not evaporate in a "nothing" of pure seeming.

"Metaphysics" consequently functions as a paradoxical object that "is not nothing," an "irrational" surplus, a purely contradictory element, nonsymbolizable, that is the "other of oneself," a lack where "nothing is missing," precisely the *object-cause of desire* or the pure seeming that is always added to S2 and forces us in this manner to continue with the differentiation. Or, in terms of the order of classification and articulation of genuses and species, "metaphysics" functions as a "surplus" that disturbs the symmetrical articulation and as a paradoxical species that "does not want to be limited to being only a species" or the "unilaterally accentuated partial object" ("absolutization of a determined moment," as Lenin used to write). Thus, we can write the relation between the agent of the Stalinist discourse, the "objective knowledge," and its other in the following way: $S2 \rightarrow a$, the arrow indicating the repetitive differentiation by which knowledge tries to penetrate its "positive" object and grasp it in demarcating it from the "surplus" of the "metaphysical" seeming-object that always prevents the accomplishment of the "objective knowledge of reality." In other words, the object of the Stalinist discourse in the sense of "positive object" is of course the so-called "objective reality." It is, nevertheless, far from occupying the place of the object-cause of desire. The *plus-de-jouir* that "pushes forward" its process of differentiation is to be sought rather in the pure seeming of "metaphysics."

The Stalinist political process functions precisely as a hallucinatory "mise-en-scene" of this desire, which the Stalinist renounces and with which he refuses to be identified. The condemned (the "victim") is the one who acknowledges desire (his own desire and thereby, in accord with the hysteric's formula of desire, the desire of the Stalinist other). This function of "victim" in the Stalinist discourse is not at all comparable to the same function in the fascist discourse. For the fascist, the Jew is sacrificed as the *object* of desire. The logic of this sacrifice is: *I love you but since unexplainably I love in you something more than you, the object a, I mutilate you.* The Stalinist "traitor" is not at all in the position of the *object* of desire. The Stalinist is not at all in love with it. Rather, he is $, the desiring divided *subject*. This division indicates the very confession that is purely unthinkable in fascism.

In fascism, the "universal" medium is missing, the medium that the accuser and the guilty would have in common and by which we could "convince" the guilty of his or her fault. One of the fundamental mechanisms of the Stalinist trials consisted in displacing the split between the neutral place of the "objective knowledge" and the hold of the particularity of the "scraps" over the victim. The victim is guilty and at the same time capable of reaching the "universal-objective" point of view, from which s/he can recognize his or her fault. This fundamental mechanism of "self-criticism" is unthinkable in fascism. In its pure form, we can find it in the self-accusations of Slansky and Rajk during the well known trials. To the question of how did he become a traitor, Slansky responds very clearly, in the style of a positivist observation or of a pure metalanguage, that it was because of his bourgeois milieu and education that he could never be part of the working class. This is the moment where the Stalinist discourse is the heir of the Lumières. They share the same presupposition of a universal and uniform reason that even the most abject Trotskiist scrap has the capacity of "comprehending" and from there confessing.

The Real of the "Class Struggle"

At this point, we can link all the moments we developed. The Stalinist discourse is presented as a neutral "objective knowledge," S2, whose other is a pure seeming of a "subjective" (metaphysical) knowledge. The reality of this neutral knowledge is the performative gesture of the master, S1, who addresses S, the hystericized-split subject of desire. This result is disenchanting as this is something known for a long time: the formulae of the discourse of the University. The Stalinist discourse is perhaps the purest form of the discourse of the University in the position of the master (a possibility already envisioned by A. Grosrichard).

We can add a series of additional distinctions between fascism and Stalinism by examining, for example, *The* book of Fascism and *The* book of Stalinism. On the one hand, in *My Combat*, the immediate speech of the Master presents his vision "in person" with a quasi-"existential" passion; on the other, the *History of the Communist Party, Abridged Course (b)* is an anonymous "objective" summary whose "academic" character is already revealed by its subtitle. The latter book is not the immediate word of the Master but a commentary. On the other hand, the fascist discourse's medium *par excellence* is the living *speech* that hypnotizes by its very performative strength, without taking into account its signified content. To cite Hitler himself: "All great events that have shaken the world have been provoked by speech and not writing." In addition, the Stalinist discourse's medium *par excellence* is really the *writing*. The Stalinist is almost obliged to *read* his very discourses in a monotonous voice clearly attesting that we are dealing with the reproduction of a prior writing.

In the Lacanian theorization, the real has two principal sides. One is the real as a remainder impossible to symbolize, a scrap, a refuse of the symbolic, a hole in the Other, (it is really a question of the real side of the object *a*, the voice, the gaze) and the other is the real as writing, construct, number, and matheme.

These two sides precisely correspond to the opposition fascism/Stalinism. The hypnotic power of the fascist discourse is supported by the "gaze" and especially by the "voice" of the Chief. The support of the Stalinist discourse is in turn the writing. Which writing? We must consider the decisive difference between the "classical" texts and their "commentaries" and "applications." The impossible-real is the institution of the "classics of Marxism-Leninism" as the sacred-incensed Text, approachable only through the proper-just commentary that gives it its "meaning," and vice versa. It is precisely the reference to the nonsense of the "classical text" (the famous "citation") that "gives sense" to the commentary-application (to take up again the distinction between "sense" and "meaning": sense = meaning + nonsense).

We could prolong this *ad infinitum* but let us rather remain at a general level. In linking what we just said to the fact that the capitalist discourse is that of the Hysteric, we can read the scheme of the four discourses as providing a schema for three types of current political discourses: the capitalist discourse of the Hysteric, the attempt of its suppression by a return to the discourse of the

Master in fascism, and the discourse of the University of the post-revolutionary society, that is to say, the Stalinist discourse.

As far as the idea that the capitalist discourse is the discourse of the Hysteric, we should add the proposition I have suggested elsewhere: it was Marx who discovered the symptom. What does hysterical-capitalism "produce" as its symptom? The proletariat, of course, as its "own gravedigger," the "irrational" element of the given totality, the "class whose very existence is the negation of the rationality of the existing order," S2, the place of a knowledge (the "class awareness") that later (after the revolution) will take the place of the agent. Lacan precisely links this to the Marxian discovery of the symptom: the existence of the proletariat as pure subjectivity, freed of the particular links (of states, corporations, etc.) of the Middle Ages. We also recall the connection established by Lacan between *plus-de-jouir* and the Marxian surplus value. Capitalism, really the common ground of historical materialism, is different from preceding formations in that an internal condition of its reproduction is to surpass itself constantly, revolutionize the given state, and develop the productive forces. The reason should be sought in surplus value as a "driving goal" that pushes the mechanism of social reproduction. In short, in the place of the "truth" of the capitalist discourse we find the *plus-de-jouir.*

And the fourth moment, the analytic discourse? Is it really the destiny of the political field to wander between the three positions of the Master, who constitutes the new social contract (the "new harmony") of the Academic, who elaborates it in a system, and of the Hysteric, who produces its symptom? Should the void in the place of the fourth discourse be read as a mark of the very fact that we are at the political level? We are tempted to suggest some indications that go a different way.

Marx writes in a letter that *The Capital* must conclude with class struggle as the "dissolution of all this shit." It is of course precisely this dissolution that "does not stop from not being written," and that is lacking in the very text. The third book of *The Capital* is interrupted, as we know, at the beginning of the chapter on classes. In this manner, we could say that class struggle functions in a strict sense as the "object" of *The Capital,* that which precisely cannot become the "positive object of research" and that which necessarily *falls* outside and thus makes of the totality of the three books of *The Capital* a "not-all" totality. This "object" never arrives "at the end," as some "subjective expression of objective economic processes." Rather, it is an agent always at work at the very heart of the "positive content" of *The Capital*. All the categories of *The Capital* are already "colored" by class struggle, all "objective" determinations (labor value, the degree of surplus value, etc.) are already achieved "by struggling."

If we say that an aspect of class struggle is of the real, we are only reiterating the Lacanian formula of the impossibility of the sexual relation. "There is no class relation"; classes are not "classes" in the usual or logical-classificatory sense; there is no universal medium. The "struggle" (the relation that is precisely a nonrelation) between classes has a constitutive role for the very same classes. In other words, class struggle functions as this "real" because of which the socioideological discourse is never "all." Consequently, class struggle is not some "objective fact" but rather the name (one of the names) of the impossibility for a discourse to be "objective," to be at an objective distance and to tell "the truth on truth," the name of the fact that each word *on* class struggle falls *into* class struggle.

From this logic it follows that the Stalinist discourse dissimulates the essential dimension of class struggle. The "objective knowledge" is presented as a neutral discourse on society, stated from an excluded place, a place that is not in itself split or marked by the separating line of class struggle. That is why one could say that for the Stalinist discourse "all is politics," or "politics is all," which is different from the Maoist discourse where, for example, politics is inscribed on the "feminine" as "not-all." However, it is here that we must be most careful of the paradoxes of not-all. Precisely because "all is politics," the Stalinist discourse always needs *exceptions*, "neutral" foundations in which politics is invested from outside such as the innocence of technology, language as the neutral-universal tool at the disposition of all classes, and so forth. These traits are not at all indices of some "de-Stalinization" process but precisely the internal condition of Stalinist "totalitarianism."

Stalinism Versus Fascism

Class struggle today seems, of course, like something outmoded. However, the reasoning by which we reach this conclusion is very much homologous to that which leads us to affirm (in the era of the so-called "permissive sexual morals") the obsolescence of the object of psychoanalysis (the repression of sexual desire). During the "heroic" epoch of psychoanalysis, it was believed that the "unleashing of sexual taboos" would bring or at least contribute to a life without anxiety, without repression, a life full of free enjoyment. The experience of this so-called "sexual liberation" helps us rather to recognize the dimension proper to the constitutive law of desire, of a "crazy" law that inflicts *jouissance*. Likewise, at the "heroic" epoch of the labor movement, it was believed that with the abolition of private ownership, classes and their struggles would be abolished and that we would arrive at a new solidarity. The experience of so-called "Stalinism" helped us rather to recognize, in "real socialism, the realization of the very concept of class struggle in its "distilled" form, no longer clouded by the difference between the "civil society" and the State.

Here again "real socialism" differs radically from fascism. Let us start with the latter: how can we link class struggle (insofar as the core of an "impossible" difference) to the fact that, in the fascist discourse, *a* is really the Jew? The answer is that the Jew functions as a *fetish* that masks class struggle and comes in its place. Fascism struggles against capitalism and liberalism, which are supposed to destroy and corrupt the harmony of the society as "all organic" where particular "states" have the function of "members," that is to say, where "each and everyone has his natural and determined place" (the "head" and the "hands"). Fascism thus tries to restore a harmonious *relation* between the classes in the framework of an organic all, and the Jew incarnates the moment that introduces a discord "from outside." The Jew is the surplus that "disturbs" the harmonious cooperation of the "head" and the "hands," of "capital" and "labor." The "Jew" suits this in multiple ways by his historical "connotations." He is there as a "condensation" of the "negative" traits of the two poles of the social scale. On the one hand, he incarnates the "exorbitant," nonharmonious behavior of the ruling class (the financier who "drains" his workers), and on the other, the "dirt" of the lower classes. Moreover, the Jew appears as the personification of the mercantile capital that is (according to the spontaneous ideological representation) the true place of exploitation and thereby reinforces the ideological fiction of capitalists and "honest" workers, of the "productive" classes exploited by the "Jewish" merchant. In brief, the "Jew," in playing the role of the "disturbing" element and introducing "from outside" the "surplus" of class struggle, is really the "positive" repudiation of class struggle and of "there is no class relation." It is for this reason that fascism, as distinct from socialism, is not a *sui generis* discourse, a global social contract, determining the whole social edifice. We could say that fascism, with its ideology of corporativism, of returning to the prebourgeois Master, causes in some way interference on the capitalist discourse without changing its fundamental nature, with the proof being precisely the figure of the Jew as enemy.

To grasp it, we should start from the decisive cut in the relation of domination that occurs with the passage from the prebourgeois society to the bourgeois society. In the prebourgeois order, the "civil society" is not liberated yet from the "organic" links, that is to say, we are dealing with "the immediate relations of domination and servitude" (Marx). The relation of the master to his subject is that of an "interpersonal" link, of a direct subjection, paternal concern on the part of the master and veneration on the part of the subject. With the advent of bourgeois society, this rich network of "affective" and "organic" relations between the master and his subjects is tattered. The subject frees himself from tutelage and stands as an autonomous and rational subject. Now, Marx's fundamental lesson is that the subject remains nevertheless subjected to a certain master, that the link to the master is only displaced. The fetishism of the "personal" Master is replaced by the fetishism of the merchandise. The will of the person of the Master is replaced by the anonymous power of the market or this famous "invisible hand" (A. Smith) that decides the destiny of individuals behind their back.

It is in this framework that we must place the fundamental stake of fascism. While preserving the fundamental relation of capitalism (that between "capital" and "labor"), fascism wants to abolish its "organic," anonymous, and savage character. That is to say, to make of it an "organic" relation of patriarchal domination between the "hand" and the "head," between the Chief and his "escort," and replace the anonymous "invisible hand" by the Will of the Master. Now, insofar as we stay in the fundamental framework of capitalism, this operation does not work. There is always a surplus of the "invisible hand" that contradicts the design of the Master. The only way of recognizing this surplus is (for the fascist whose "epistemic" field is that of the Master) to again "personalize" the "invisible hand" and imagine another Master, a hidden master who in reality pulls all the strings and whose clandestine activity is the true secret behind this anonymous "invisible hand" of the market, i.e., the Jew.

As to "socialism," it should be conceived as a paradox of the *class society with only one class*. This is the solution to the question of whether "real socialism" is a class society or not. The so-called "ruling bureaucracy" is not just the "new class"; it comes in the place of or stands for the ruling class. This must be taken literally and not in an evolutionist-teleological perspective (in a way that the "new class" already has some traits of the ruling class and the future will show that it will be consolidated as a ruling class). This "in the place of" is not at all to be seen as a mark of an unfinished, half-way character. In "real socialism" the ruling bureaucracy is found in the place of the ruling class, which *does not exist*, holding its place empty. In other words, "real socialism" would be this paradoxical point where class difference really becomes differential. It is no longer a question of difference between the two "positive" entities but rather a difference between the "absent" class and the "present" class, between the lacking class (ruling) and the existing class (working). This lacking class can really be the working class itself insofar as it is opposed to actual "empirical" workers. In this manner, class difference coincides with the difference between the Universal (the working class) and the Particular (the empirical working class), with the ruling bureaucracy incarnating its own Universality facing the "empirical" working class. It is this split between The Class as Universal and its own particular-empirical existence that clarifies an apparent contradiction of the Stalinist text. *History* ends with a long quotation of Stalin against the "varnish of bureaucratism" that reveals for us the "secret of the invincibility of the Bolshevik direction:"

> I think that the Bolsheviks remind us of Antaeus, the hero of the Greek mythology. Just as Antaeus, they are strong because they are attached to their mother, to the masses that gave them birth, fed them, and educated them. And as long as they stay attached to their mother and to the people, they have all the chances of remaining invincible. (*History*, 1971, p.402)

The same allusion to Antaeus is found at the beginning of Marx's *18th Brumaire* as a metaphor of the class enemy in the face of proletarian revolutions that "knock their adversary to the ground only for the adversary to regain his strength so he can reemerge in front of them even bigger." We must read these lines in relation to the beginning of this famous "Pledge of the Bolshevik Party to its Chief Lenin who will live through centuries:" "We are, us Communists, people of a different making. We are cut in a different fabric." At first sight, these two passages seem to be contradictory: on the one hand, it is a question of fusion of Bolsheviks with "masses" as the source of their strength; on the other, they are "people of a different making." We can resolve this paradox (how does the privileged *link* with the masses *separate* them from other people, precisely from the masses?) if we take into account the above mentioned difference between the Class (the "working masses") as All and "masses" insofar as "not-all," i.e., an "empirical" collection. The Bolsheviks (the Party) are the only "empirical" representatives, the only "incarnation" of the "true" masses, of the Class as All. (1)

From there it is not difficult to determine the place of the "Party" in the economy of the Stalinist discourse. This "striking force of the working class," composed of "people of a different making" and at the same time intimately attached to their mother or the masses, really takes the place of the "maternal phallus," the fetish that rejects the real of class difference, of the "struggle," of the nonrelation between All of the class and its own not-all. While, in the fascist discourse, the role of the fetish is played by the Jew, or the enemy, the Stalinist fetish is the Party itself.

Although already in Lenin, we find this logic of the Party, the incarnation of the historic objectivity, the continuity between Leninism and Stalinism should not lead us to an immediate identification of their discursive positions. On the contrary, it is precisely on the basis of this continuity that we can highlight their difference, the decisive "step forward" relative to Leninism accomplished by Stalin. In Lenin, we already find the fundamental position of a neutral-objective knowledge and the "objectivation" of our "subjective intentions" that follows: "the important thing, is the objective meaning of your acts, regardless of your subjective intentions, sincere as they may be." The "objective meaning" is determined, of course, by the Leninist himself from his position of neutral-objective knowledge. Now, Stalin takes a step forward and again subjectifies this "objective meaning," projecting it on the subject himself as his secret desire: what your act objectively means, is what you in fact wanted.

We can also deduce the different status of the political adversary: for Lenin, the adversary (of course, always the "internal enemy," the Menshevik, the "social revolutions of the left," the "opportunist," etc.) is, according to the rule, determined as the *hysteric* who has lost contact with reality, who, unable to be his own master, reacts emotionally when reasoning is required, who does not know what he is talking about, and who is all talk and no action. The elementary figures are Martov, Kamenev, and Zinoviev at the time of October, and Olga Spiridonovna (arrested after the missed coup attempt of the social revolutionaries of the left in the summer of 1918 when, at the Bolshoi Theater where the Constituent Assembly took place, she played the role of the hystericized speaker and was later interned in a psychiatric hospital). The hidden truth of the Leninist is, of course, the fact that he, by his position as holder of the neutral-objective knowledge and a universal and uniform reason, *produces the hysteric.* This position of the "objective knowledge" implies that there is basically no dialogue, as it is impossible to have a discussion with someone who has the access to reality itself, with the one who incarnates historical objectivity. Any different position is, in advance, defined as a seeming, as a nothing, and the dialogue is replaced by pedagogy, by the patient work of persuasion (the elegy of Lenin's great art of persuasion is, it is well known, a common place of the Stalinist hagiography). In this climate of total blockage, the only possibility open to the one who thinks otherwise is the hysterical cry that announces a knowledge that escapes this universality. Now, with Stalin, we are done with the hysterical game: the Stalinist adversary, the "traitor," is not at all the one who "does not know what he is talking about" or "what he is doing," but on the contrary, it is precisely the one who, to use a Stalinist turn of phrase *par excellence,* "knows very well what he is doing." With the menace implied by this syntagm, a conspirator is the one who plots consciously, with intention. In other words, while Leninism remains a "normal" academic discourse (knowledge in the position of the agent produces as its result the barred-hystericized subject), Stalinism takes a step into "madness," the academic knowledge becomes that of the paranoid and the adversary becomes the intentioned and literally "divided" conspirator, the rubbish, the pure scrap, who has nevertheless access to neutral-objective knowledge whence he can recognize the importance of his act and *confess.*

The Totalitarian Phantasm,
The Totalitarianism of the Phantasm

What is essential here is not to reduce this "psychotization" to a simple "excess" but to grasp it as an immanent possibility that brings out the truth of the fundamental position itself. This is already Marx's truth. This allows a new approach to the passage from "utopian" socialism to the so-called "scientific" socialism. Although Marx discovered the symptom and developed the logic of the social symptom (the moment when the fundamental blockage of the given social order emerges and when it seems to call on its own "revolutionary" practical-dialectical dissolution), he underestimated the importance of the *phantasm* in the historical process, and the importance of inertia that does not dissolve due to its dialectization and whose exemplary intrusion would be what is called the "negative behavior of the masses," who appear to be "acting against their true interest" and let themselves get entangled in diverse forms of the "conservative revolution." The enigmatic character of such a phenomenon is to be sought in the simple *jouissance* that they imply through their actions: social theory tries to get rid of what is worrisome in this *jouissance* by designating it as the "delirium of the masses," its "mindlessness," its "regression," its "lack of conscience."

Where is the phantasm here? The phantasmatic scene aims at the realization of the sexual relation, blinding us with its fascinating presence, to the impossibility of the sexual relation. Similarly with the "social" phantasm, the phantasmatic construct supports an ideological field. We are always dealing with the phantasm of a *class relation*, with the utopia of a harmonious, organic, and complementary relation between diverse parts of the social totality. The elementary image of the "social" phantasm is that of a *social body*, with which one eludes the impossible, the "antagonism" around which the social field is structured. The anti-"liberal" ideologies of the right that serve as a foundation for the so-called "regressive behavior of the masses" are precisely distinguished by recourse to this organicist metaphoric. Their *leitmotif* is that of society as a body, an organic totality of members corrupted later by the intrusion of a liberalist atomism.

We already find this phantasmatic dimension in so-called "utopian" socialism. Lacan determines the illusion specific to

Sade's perverse phantasm as "utopia of desire" (Lacan 1966, p.775). In the sadist scene, the split between desire and *jouissance* is suppressed (an impossible operation insofar as desire is supported by the interdiction of *jouissance*, that is to say, insofar as desire is the structural other side of *jouissance*), and at the same time the gap that separates *jouissance* from pleasure is removed. By way of pain, or the "negative" of pleasure, an attempt is made at reaching *jouissance* in the very field of pleasure. The word "utopia" should also be taken in the political sense: the famous sadist "One more effort . . ." (in *Philosophy in the Boudoir*) should be placed along the same line as "utopian socialism," as one of its most radical variants since "utopian socialism" always implies a "utopia of desire." In the utopian project from Campanella to Fourier, we are always dealing with a regulated and finally dominated phantasm of enjoyment.

With the passage to "scientific socialism," Marx has foreclosed this phantasmatic dimension. We must give to the term "foreclosure" all the weight it has in Lacanian theory: that is to say, not only the repression but also the exclusion and the rejection of a moment outside the symbolic field. And whatever is foreclosed in the symbolic, we well know that it returns in the real, in our case, in the *real socialism*. Utopian, scientific, and real, socialism thus form a sort of triad. The utopian dimension, excluded by its "scientification," returns in the real, or in the "Utopia in Power," to borrow the well-justified title of a book on the Soviet Union. "Real socialism" is the price paid in the flesh for the misrecognition of the phantasmatic dimension in scientific socialism.

To speak of the "social phantasm" seems nevertheless to imply a fundamental theoretical error insofar as a phantasm is basically *nonuniversalizable*. The social phantasm is particular, "pathological" in the Kantian sense, "personal" (the very foundation of the unity of the "person" insofar as it is distinguished from the subject and the signifier), the unique way that each of us tries to come to terms with the Thing, the impossible *Jouissance*. That is to say, the manner in which, with the help of an imaginary construct, we try to dissolve the primordial impasse in which *parlêtre* is situated, the impasse of the inconsistent Other, of the hole at the heart of the Other. The field of the Law, of rights and duties, on the contrary, is not only universalizable but universal in its very nature. It is the field of universal equality, of equalization effected by exchange in equivalent principal. According to this perspective, we could designate the object *a*, the *plus-de-jouir* as a surplus, and that is why the formula of the phantasm insofar as it is nonuniversalizable is written S<>a, that is to say, the confrontation of the subject with this "impossible," nonexchangeable remainder. There you have the link between *plus-de-jouir* and surplus value as a surplus that contradicts the equal exchange between capitalism and the proletariat, a surplus that the capitalist appropriates in the framework of the equal exchange of capital for the labor force.

Now, there was no need to wait for Marx to experience the cul-de-sac of the equal exchange. In its effort to enlarge the bourgeois form of the egalitarian and universal law, does not Sade's heroism rely precisely on the universal exchange, on the rights and duties of man in the domain of *jouissance*? Its starting point is that the Revolution stopped midway, since in the domain of *jouissance* it continued to be a prisoner of patriarchal and theological prejudices, that is to say, the Revolution did not get to the end of its project of bourgeois emancipation. Now, as Lacan demonstrates in "Kant with Sade," the formulation of a universal norm, of a "categorical imperative" that would legislate the enjoyment necessarily fails and ends in an impasse. Thus, we cannot, according to the model of formal bourgeois rights, legislate the right to *jouissance* in the mode of "To each his phantasm!" or "Each has a right to his particular mode of enjoyment!" Sade's hypothetical universal law is reinstated by Lacan as a "I have the right to enjoy your body, someone may say to me, and this right I shall exercise without any limit stopping me in the caprice of (whatever) exactions I have the fancy to gratify" (Lacan, 1966, p.768–69). Its impasse is glaring, the symmetry is false: to occupy in a consistent manner the position of the torturer is revealed impossible since each is in the final analysis a victim.

How can we, then, repudiate the reproach that speaking of a "social phantasm" is equivalent to an *in adjecto* contradiction? Far from being simply epistemological, far from indicating an error in the theoretical approach, this impasse *defines the thing itself*. The fundamental trait of the "totalitarian" social link, is it not precisely the loss of distance between the phantasm that gives the indicators of the enjoyment of the subject and the formal-universal Law that rules the social exchange? The phantasm is "socialized" in an immediate manner as the social Law coincides with the injunction "Enjoy!" It starts to function as a superego imperative. In other words, in totalitarianism, it is really the fantasy (phantasm) that is in power and this is what distinguishes the *stricto sensu* totalitarianism (Germany in 1938–45, the Soviet Union in 1934–51, Italy in 1943–45) from the patriarchal-authoritarian regimes of law-and-order (Salazar, Franco, Bolfuss, Mussolini until 1943) or from the real "normalized" socialism. Such a "pure" totalitarianism is necessarily self-destructive; it cannot be stabilized; it cannot arrive at a minimum of homeostasis that would allow it to reproduce in a circuit of equilibrium. It is constantly shaken by convulsions. An imminent logic pushes it to violence directed at the external (Naziism) or internal (the Stalinist purges) "enemy." The theme of the post-Stalinist "normalization" in the USSR was for good reason that of the "return to the socialist *legality*." The only way out of the vicious circle of the purges was perceived to be the reaffirmation of a Law supposed to introduce a minimal distance toward a phantasm, of a symbolic-formal system of rules that would not be immediately impregnated with *jouissance*.

This is why we can determine totalitarianism also as the social order where, although there is no law (no positive legality with universal validity, established in an explicit form), all that we do can at any moment pass for an illegal and forbidden thing. The positive legislation does not exist (or if it does, it has a totally arbitrary and nonobligatory character), but despite this we can at any moment find ourselves in the position of the infractor of an unknown and nonexistent Law. If the paradox of the Interdiction that founds the social order consists in forbidding something already impossible, totalitarianism reverses this paradox in putting us in the no less paradoxical position of the infractor who transgresses a nonexistent law. In the law-less state, although the law does not exist, we can nevertheless transgress against it, which is the supreme proof that, as Lacan emphasizes in *Seminar II*, the famous proposition of Dostoevski should be turned around: if God (the positive legality) does not exist, everything is forbidden (Lacan, 1978, p.156).

From there the difference between the fascist chief and the Stalinist chief is also explained. Let us start from the duality of power developed by A. Grosrichard: despot/vizier corresponds approximately to the Hegelian duality monarch/ministerial power. This means that despotism is not at all the phantasm of the "totalitarian" power, which is defined precisely by a "short-circuit" in the relation despot/vizier. If the fascist master wants to rule in his own name, if he does not want to part with the "effective" power but wants to be "his own vizier" (at least in the domain of war as the only domain worthy of the master), he discovers that the impossibility of the operation of integrating the "effective" knowledge, S2, provokes the phantasmatic transposition of this knowledge in the "Jews," who "hold effectively all the lines." The Stalinist chief is by contrast the paradox of the *vizier without the despot-master*. He acts in the name of the working class itself and constitutes it as a master opposed to the "empirical" class (cf. Grosrichard, 1979).

Note

*Translated and edited by Aïda Der Hovanessian.

References

Dognin, P.D., *Les "Sentiers Escarpes" de Karl Marx, Tome I: Textes*, Paris, 1977.

Grosrichard, Alain, *La Structure du Serail*, Paris, 1979.

Histoire . . . , *Histoire du Parti Communiste/Bolchevik/de l'U.R.S.S.*, Paris, 1971.

Lacan, Jacques, *Écrits*, Paris 1966.

———. *Le Seminaire, Livre II*, Paris, 1978.

Lenine, V.I., *Oeuvres, Tome 36*, Paris, 1964.

Marx, Karl, "*Die Klassenkampfe in Frankreich 1848 bis 1850*," in *MEW 7*, Berlin (Democratic Republic), 1973.

Staline, Iosif, *Les Questions de Leninisme*, Pekin, 1977.

Willy Apollon

A LASTING HERESY,
THE FAILURE OF POLITICAL DESIRE

The heretic is said to be someone who is an unbeliever. S/he does not follow the way granted for the majority. S/he contests orthodoxy. To some extent s/he represents a weakness or a default in the development of society as far as such a development is subordinated to the mastery of political power. The heretic is then an opponent. S/he challenges the dogma that establishes a legitimacy for political power. In effect, political power is acknowledged as the authority that guarantees the society against a violent contradiction where its existence may be challenged. The power of that authority is legitimated through the political discourse that sustains the theory of the Law defining the monopoly and the right of violence.

From my point of view, because I am an analyst and, secondarily, because I am Lacanian, I think that the analyst acts as a heretic in the field of politics. In doing so, s/he is on the side of the psychotic, taking for granted the hysterical contest of the signifier and authority as a nonfounded use of violence. We are aware that such an assertion introduces a link between politics and religion and that link is based upon a psychoanalytic approach. What is so common between religion and politics in the field of psychoanalysis? Freud suggested that religion was a solution for neurosis. The experience of the psychoanalytic treatment of psychosis leads us to think that it may be the same for it. Nevertheless, that experience will be the background of my theoretical position.

The heretic is said to be one because s/he scrutinizes the failures in the system, and s/he questions those points that should remain untouched, beyond any investigation. Those points are answers of the big Other. Their function is to found and to maintain the legitimacy of the discourse of political power. In any society the question of legitimizing the discourse of political power is the most important one. The unity and the survival of society appear to be subordinated to the way religion or the political or scientist ideologies in Western culture answer the question of the foundation of the Law and the legitimacy of authority. Such answers have the consistency of dogma and must be obeyed as such. The personal assent to that dogma is a guarantee, not only for the subject in his or her identification as a citizen but also for society in the great affair of an allegiance of the subject to that society.

the signifier and the repression of an investigation

To some extent such a function of religious discourse and political ideology is relayed in our societies by the theory of the Law and human rights. Laws and rights establish the legitimacy of political power and the authority of discourse, the same way that dogma has been established by religion. Where we referred yesterday to the will of God, today we invoke the authority of the Law. The structure of the reference we conjure up is the same. We assume that the law is nobody's will but everyone's assent or consent. And God is nobody. We can change laws and modify Rights, as we did with God's injunctions. Such reference is eventually one to the empire of the signifier. The question of the foundation of the Law as the legitimacy of its authority is a repressed question in the political discourse. In the same way, religion cannot sustain the interrogation of the nonexistence of God. That repression of the question of the foundation is necessary to the practice of political power. In our industrial and postindustrial societies, political power appeals to the sovereign use of violence, through the concern of the Law that establishes that sovereignty. The right of the State in using legal violence is made difficult to challenge in our societies.

We may assume that the theory of human rights alleviates, in some way, the monopoly of the State in the use of violence. Such a monopoly, however, stands as a guarantee to those rights. The investigation of the foundation of the Law is repressed in the theory of human rights as it is in the theory of political discourse. The appeal to the natural Law as a foundation to legitimate the political power, as a use of violence, is not an answer to the question we are discussing. The natural law is always a specific and cultural solution to the request of legitimacy. That which is called natural in a given society is but a cultural arrangement of the question of the metaphor, or the way such a culture shoulders the relationship between the words in the language and the things those words cut up in the so-called universe. Ultimately, the reference to the natural law is in any case a reference to the power of the signifier.

That which is considered natural is what a given culture determines as such. The natural Law as a foundation of political power is the way that the monopoly of violence is dispersed through political discourse in the entrapment of the subject's desire. In the consideration of the question of the foundation, the idea of natural Law remains untouched; such an idea in theory is an obscure and enigmatic point that cannot be enlightening and upon which any contest is repressed. The inquiry into such an excavation point digs up the lack of foundation, which motivates the weakness of the Law. And it sustains sufficient grounds for a monopoly of political violence in the repression of the contest of the subject.

Therefore, the repression of the investigation on the foundation of the law as legitimate to authorize political discourse and the monopoly of violence in the practice of political power and its ends are inseparable. The question of the legitimacy of political authority stands for an ethical taboo, as far as the foundation of the Law must be enclosed in myths and rituals that sustain the concept and practice of reason or science. There is no way out for such a dilemma. The subject as a potential breach in the political attempt to answer the lack of foundation of the Law is to be kept away from any attempt to investigate the foundation of the Law or the legitimacy of the political authority. That repression of the subject may be savage or subtle. It depends upon historical and social circumstances.

the political enterprise

We will favor the hypothesis that the political venture has a hidden purpose linked to the repression of any investigation of the foundation. It is the reason why I suggest that the analyst in politics acts as a heretic does in the field of religion. The analyst cannot help but know the action of *jouissance* in any hidden undertaking or repressed affair. The knowledge of what the analysand has access to in the working of the unconscious representations of desire can not take for granted the political discourse in its attempt to justify the "natural" violence of power. It is why we always have to keep in mind the position of the analyst as an outsider regarding what is at stake in the political affair.

The political discourse that regulates and legitimates the use of violence in a given society has a lot to do with the beliefs that sustain the myths and rituals of society. Political discourse does not fundamentally change when it is supported by our scientific knowledge or even the technological structure of the free market. It is still dealing with the same secret enterprise, manipulating the same crude violence against the return of the subject to the investigation of its foundation. No matter the time or the society, the discourse that legitimates the monopoly of violence is always dealing with the basic truths that confront the subject to its difference, its identity, its *jouissance,* and its death. By the way, that affair of Law as political discourse deals with the absence of foundation of any authority as an injury bleeding or seeping out the side of society. To hide that rupture and to maintain an impassable distance to that point of greatest weakness in the social organization, such is the concern of any attempt of legitimacy.

The political discourse does not only hide the lack of foundation of power, neither does it only maintain a distance from questioning such want for it is mainly involved in a process of supplying and fulfilling such a lack. Any society has to face that singular default in the representation of authority. As far as authority is a guarantee that using words and granting the law in negotiating satisfaction in society is better for anyone than fighting for the same goal, the representation of authority is a major social challenge. The absence of any representation of authority in a group as in a society is an open way to initiate violence as the fireback of the death drive. The absence of common rules offers the monopoly of violence to the stronger, and it is an image of what psychosis would be as a formless model for society. In *Totem and Taboo* Freud highlights the father of the primal horde as a paradigm to think that human enigma.

What is singular to any society or human gathering is the way that it masterminds the absence of a foundation in its erection of the representation of authority. Freud pointed out this challenge with the question of the father, as well in his elaborations of the Oedipus complex as in his formulations in *Totem and Taboo, Moses and Monotheism,* and *Civilization and Its Discontents.* With the concept of the lack in the Other, Lacan opened a new perspective for the investigation of that fundamental default in the organization of speaking beings. Insofar as the lack in the Other is interpreted not in terms of castration of the mother, but as a default in language and in the human incapacity to represent the real or the lack in the signifier as Lacan termed it, we discover a reference to a structural absence of foundation, what I refer to with the concept of *Infondé* or the unfounded. It is on the ground of such a lack that any society has to build the representation of its authority, as a solution to the void and the emptiness men and women face, when they confront an absence in the signifier. The anxiety and despair confronted in that discovery, which is always fortunate for the subject, must be removed by repression on the one hand and the structure of authority on the other. The way a society answers that dilemma determines the mounting of a specific enigma that will characterize it.

The discourse founding political power and its monopoly in the use of violence in a given society cannot be investigated without a specific outlook on such an enigma as its mysterious root. Therefore, the political enterprise as a guarantee or as a management device cannot be separated from the exercise of power against the subject, no matter the subtlety of such a use of violence for it must guarantee the permanency of the authority's representation and its efficiency. Insofar as the State formulates the machinery of the political enterprise, it is an apparatus of terror. That basic aspect of State terrorism is hidden by the discourse and the procedures in political affairs, but any attempt to jeopardize or even to challenge the structure of the state or its monopoly of violence brings out instantly the first steps of State-sponsored terrorism. We have in our time a lot of examples of such a reversion to this fascist alarm around the world.

The political enterprise usually seeks closure to break the

want and to maintain under the law the monopoly of violence that lack provides for. It cannot get rid of the "right" that the authorities insist on using for coercion, repression, and violence in order to obtain obedience and compliance from its subjects. In spite of what may seem to be the strength of such an assertion, we have to think of the State as structurally terrorist. The political signifier supposes such an extremity as a hypothetical or actual limit where the apparatus of the political enterprise may be forced. The conjunction of an inscrutable terror with the mysterious origin of the law determines the threat carried out by the authority figures. Cultural myths and rituals that hide the emptiness implied in the default of any foundation of law, prompt and attach any meaning of life to the uprising of such figures. Thereafter authority becomes Other, with a big O; it is assumed as such. Political discourse is carried on through a misunderstood connection with the enigma and power of authority. The political purpose to solve the enigma of the foundation of meaning through the legitimacy of the monopoly of violence goes on without any possible investigation of that goal.

the heresy, the structure of an unavoidable rise

The heresy has been to contest the authority as Other, by investigating the foundation of political discourse as a legitimate monopoly. Psychoanalysis recognizes the action of the signifier in the enterprise of political discourse. The object is to unify the opposite forces in civil society around a public goal of consent that might stand in for a fulfillment of the emptiness opened by the lack of foundation in the political affair in which the society lives. The lack in the signifier is sustained and erased by the enigma of the magnetism and influence of authority; that enigma is the "black continent" of politics. It opens and structures the place of the hypnotic power of the leader. From then on the inquiry of that enigma opens to the heresy and the return of a specific violence in which we acknowledge the working through of the death drive. Psychoanalysis gives us some indirect information in how to proceed in investigating that enigma.

That questioning is a preliminary one for the philosopher, as far as s/he stays on the inquest, refusing to receive any answer; it also has a reference in the adolescent, in the construction of femininity and psychotic discourse. In those three cases the interrogation refers to the figure of the father as the signifier of authoritative law, which introduces a loss of *jouissance* in the speaking being. They support three questions that have come with the heresy in the genesis of civil society when fighting the supremacy of the state in liberal democracies. Those questions form a ground in the fight against the political answer to the lack in the Other. The first, the one an adolescent could support, is the investigation of the foundation toward lack. It opens to the creativity of the subject an excavation that digs its way through aesthetics. In the second, concerning feminine heresy, the signifier is objected to as a limit and a frame to the void against the rebel, a leftover of *jouissance*. Within the third, the ethical choice of the psychotic takes for granted the *jouissance* against the signifier as a ground for a political counter-enterprise (if I may use that neologism).

We assume that modernity and our industrial civilization have been the groundwork of a tremendous transmutation in civil society and in its struggle against the state. Modernity begins with the investigation of the foundation where lay the legitimacy of the power in authority. It stands for the adolescence of Western civil society entering a movement of contestation against the supremacy of the state. It causes the passage from the power of the one—God, the King, or anyone else who is invested with such authority—to the power of the people by the means of their representatives. Such a transformation in the exercise of the monopoly leads to crucial changes in the political discourse. The answer to such a lack in the foundation of authority can no more be concealed in the sovereignty and the power of one, or in the servility and submission of all. It is therefore the concern of political discourse and the role of political parties to offer different versions of the unique answer to the lack that the political discourse dictates.

The second step in the transmutation of civil society in Western civilization is the rise of capitalism within the industrial market. This marks a time when the main concerns are with an independent civil society, individual autonomy, a free-market economy, and profit and loss with regard to the investigation of the political authority of the state; this becoming of Western civil society may be interrogated through the model of the relationship of the hysteric with the signifier of the Father. The hysteric is in opposition to the signifier of the Father. S/he considers the signifier as insufficient to border and limit the return of *jouissance* that she thinks jeopardizes her subjective identity or presents a danger to be submerged. S/he does not trust the logic of the signifier, which is grounded in the chain that the signifier of the Father guarantees. S/he looks for a master who will be stronger than the Father; she searches for a true limit in the signifier to sustain the framing of the returning *jouissance* and its transformation into sexuality and something else that aesthetic creations will provide.

In a similar vein, the civil societies of Western civilization do not entrust political discourse and the machinery of the state with its private concern with profit and loss as an expression of freedom. At the same time, the independence and autonomy of the civil society are used against the authority and power of the state. At the same time, the attitude regarding the authority and power of the state is one of suspicion toward the populace. According to political discourse, the state is supposed to provide a principle of unity; it has to bring the various antagonistic forces fighting in society into the camp of a common and public good. The object of suspicion, the state is unable to achieve its promise, that goal regarding the interests of the struggle that structures civil society. The antagonism between the forces in civil society, which is a permanent challenge to any public concern, is a source and power of creativity and innovation. The leading groups and factions in civil society—the business men and women, high tech managers, international financial technocrats and managers, think of the apparatus of the state as a hindrance and stopgap to their aspirations.

The key contradiction between violence and creativity that works through the structure of civil society is in the structural conflict that opposes the various economic forces to the many evolving social and cultural trends. The development of the Law in the Province of Quebec, Canada, has in the last decades been directed toward enforcing the ways and means of economic power. Its political discourse was oriented to the solutions of the liberal democracies with their goal of instituting a welfare state. In the last ten years, on the contrary, the strengthening of social trends through the ascending power of the media has ruptured the supremacy of economic irrationality. In Quebec the providential state has been obliged to intervene to neutralize or counterbalance the effects of economic irrationality. In spite of that, the strategy of current social trends in our civil society, as one of contestation with political authority, is to make use of the Law against the political authority that founds that Law, not only in the fight against the strategy of economic forces but in order to enforce the meditation of the State in providing for social needs.

Therefore, civil society is divided into two antagonistic forces that overdetermine the structure of political discourse. The economic forces in civil society are decisive in becoming those that befit a liberal democracy. They also have a stake in the despotic dictatorships or militarist regimes where the economic organizations are submitted to the goal of an oligarchal or hegemonic social class, to little groups or even family structures. So the social trends and forces in civil society are always suspicious when regarding the connections that relate the state to economic forces, no matter what such connections exist. The political discourse is seen as a repression and a substitute to the analysis and investigation of complicity between the economic forces and the monopoly of violence in the State. From another point of view, economic forces and social trends are divided into several conflicting groups of interests between which any consensus seems welcome.

In spite of the personification of State authority, which looks like a necessity in some conjectural situation in certain liberal democracies, the representation of State authority as a guarantee against the irrationalities arising from the conflictual structure of civil society is the main problem of political discourse. Fascism, dictatorship, military regimes, religious and political system—they all present different issues of that unresolved and mysterious contradiction between the lethal irrationalities that are an outgrowth of the conflictual structure of economic forces and the contention of social needs bounded to cultural and historical exigencies. The leader, a De Gaulle, Reagan, Khomeny or Mao, is never a perfect representation of a unified nation that enables the civil society to master the mysterious contradiction that permanently endangers its consistency. Like the State, they are insufficient signifiers to fulfill the lack that causes political affairs. They cannot provide for the fault that a splintered society tries to complement.

Thus, in spite of certain state monopolies and their authority in sustaining political desire to produce the object of "common love," which tends toward lack, a permanent heresy breaks up the political enterprise from inside civil society. Since the great contest of personal authority in the French and the American revolutions and the questioning of the foundation with the October revolution, the Western political quest has been to establish a new mythical legitimacy for the monopoly of violence in the place where the lack and the default of the signifier jeopardize any attempt to gather the social into a common term with a common goal. The lack—the default in language—deepens in the speaking being, maintaining the work of desire in the political discourse out of the range of what is going on in the main stream of civil society.

Political desire strives to house all of the antagonistic economic and social forces under a common myth, regardless of the cost for achieving that end. What is on the go in civil society operates to divide and to partition any gathering. There are many partial organizations with specific and contradictory goals working at the same time in various directions. Their strategy, if they have any, is not a logic of long-term procedures. They maneuver by trying this or that and evaluate the results, seeking only a calculus of a frame for the *jouissance* in the social link. That maneuver I have called the strategy of the expedient shot, based upon a practice of the letter in hysterical and psychotic cases, does not take for granted the logic of the signifier. The framework of that practice is what I pointed out as the letter constituting the body in opposition to the organism.

I relate the letter to the erogenous zones of Freud as a source for the drive, because of its function in writing the excluded *jouissance* on the body, and the Letter of Lacan in "Lituraterre" for its function as littoral and limit in the calculus of the real. The litter, leftover of the trauma as a parcel of the body, is the groundwork of any practice where writing is a calculus of the real. This much (the process of the writing as a calculus of the real) is opposite to the notion of speech as a chaining of the signifier; it distinguishes the strategy of the expedient shot with both a hysterical and psychotic flavor. It is a heretic praise with regard to the logic of the signifier that prevails in the symbolic order as the frame of political desire. The real *jouissance* escapes the power of the signifier, and its partitioning and molding of the heretic strategy aims precisely at what the logic of the signifier is repressing. The political discourse that is concerned with the chaining of the signifier organizes the substitution of a fireback of *jouissance* against the social order with the representation of political desire. As a result, the strategy of the calculus of *jouissance* through the lack in the signifier or in political discourse sustains the changes and alteration in the social linkage in what civil society continues its struggle against, the state enterprise. The strategies of try and shot of civil society in its quest for new forms and frameworks for a fireback of *jouissance* always jeopardize political desire, summoning it to answer for the lack of a foundation of state monopoly, destabilizing it through economical, technological, scientific, or managerial standards of unification of social conflicts.

Therefore, that structure of heresy is always at stake in the confrontation of civil society with the enterprise of the State. That encounter is the insoluble contradiction of two logics: the one, State, based upon the chaining of the signifier as a representation of desire repressing lack, and the other, the various, opposite groups or organizations in civil society that seek a strategy of shot for the framing of a return back to a demonstration of *jouissance.*

the undefined structural limit before the horror

The question involved in the contradiction that opposes the fireback of the real in civil society to the illusory but significant order promoted by political desire is the limit beyond which the system has to face horror. From subtlety to brutishness, State terrorism is a final barrier against such causality. The horror is that civil society vanishes under the violence of the state; if not, the result is translated as the overwhelming of the State order and the substitution of a new social strata of influence. That limit is the ultimate meaning of the monopoly as a foundation to political authority. Its occurrence initiates the end of the political enterprise and the state of war between the state and the civil society.

The clinic that deals with psychosis suggests a conceptual frame to formulate the intricacy of that limit of terror. I shall refer to the two faces of terrorism. The first one, State terrorism, wants to maintain a universal frame of meaning as a protection against the overthrow of authority. It creates a state of war in the nation, where the enemy is an internal one. Under the pressure of the events in civil society and in a specific historical situation of political conflicts, the state moves out of the political enterprise, back to a state of terror. The second type involves one or several little groups in civil society that aim to overwhelm the established order for the promotion of a new universal frame of meaning where the state is supposed to be congruent with the new order. This much, terrorism as a hardening of political desire, always presents a monopoly of violence seeking a foundation of legitimacy. It is always involved in determining the edge where violence founds the legitimacy of authority in the political discourse, in other words, in the signifier that the Master's discourse is provided with.

The clinic for the study of psychosis suggests to us a conceptual frame to formulate that collusion between the signifier and the violence that political terrorism makes so obvious. The relation of the psychotic with the signifier is a singular one. The psychotic is invaded by the signifier, captured in its power and his or her whole life seems to be a result of the violence of the signifier. The reality s/he has to deal with as a subject is completely submerged by the autonomy of the signifier whose logic and action looks like it had nothing to do with the social link the psychotic is involved in and, furthermore, appears to hazard such a social link.

Hence the psychotic relates to the signifier as to the absolute power of an Other who is possessing him or her within an undefined pleasure. What is unbearable for the psychotic subject under that possession is the arbitrariness of the signifier's power from the Other that oppresses the individual. As a matter of fact, s/he is aware of the absence of foundation whose investigation annihilates the legitimacy of the master's authority. S/he does not underestimate the intricacy between such a failure in the signifier and the ferocity of the Other. The whole enterprise of the political desire that sustains the master's discourse is irrelevant from her or his standpoint. S/he cannot believe the common myth with its background of violence, nor can s/he trust the signifier of the father as a warrant of good faith in the use of that violence.

Since Jacques Lacan's work has been published, psychoanalysis can refer the position of the psychotic with regard to the signifier to a foreclosure of the Name of the Father—the signifier that installs the father as the guarantee of the "good faith" of the Law or the harmlessness of the signifier. The clinician becomes aware of the opposite side of the foreclosure in the transference where s/he encounters the psychotic belief, what I have called the unfounded framework of the signifier of the whole symbolic order. That may be the understanding, in the field of psychosis, of the concept of the signifier of the barred Other that Lacan put forward to underline the question of the want in the Other. It is also from that wounding discovery that the psychotic distrusts the father or the authority of the social law as a groundwork for the practice of language and the production of meaning. It is also from such a stance that s/he will try through delusions to build a new foundation for language to neutralize the default in the symbolic order and the insufficiency of the signifier. So the psychotic develops his or her delusion as a political discourse drawing into an outline a reformation or a renewal of the world.

The psychotic position with regard to the politics of the signifier suggests the function of belief where the key signifier is missing to endow the delusional reconstruction of its legitimacy. It hints at the formation of the relationship of legitimacy and the belief in a political enterprise of reformation for societies based on a common goal. The analyst cannot help taking into account the structural proximity between the delusional reconstruction of the symbolic world on the ground of psychotic belief and the ideological and political enterprise of unifying those differences that split the patchwork of civil society on the ground of a dreamlike common good.

Psychosis represents in some way the structure of a limit to any enterprise for managing or reforming society on the ground of a belief in a common good. For both the State and civil society it refers their conflictual coexistence and affront to the wakening of violence that the failure and want in the signifier implicate. Such a limit is the result of the antagonistic encounter of two strategies, even if it is difficult to speak of a strategy in the specific case of civil society. The multitude of groups with various and conflicting interests that parcel civil society is an obstacle to any global, common, long-term strategy. So the strategy of civil society is a short-term one based upon a maneuvering of expedient shots leading to a limited but adequate profit for a specific group or a parcel of society in a given time. I have noted such a strategy as based upon the letter, as far as the writing is to be considered as a calculus of a border or a limit to the real or the computation of a frame for the fireback of *jouissance.* We acknowledge in fantasy the structure and tactics of such a practice of the letter reckoning a *jouissance* against the authority of the signifier.

Femininity and the hysterical subjective position have carried that strategy of the letter to a degree of efficiency that psychosis hardly reaches in its attempt to represent most of the time the limit of such a maneuvering. The procedure and tactics of that maneuver always bring the opposite side to the edge of what is bearable for him or her, guessing the limit over which it is again possible to go too far, that is, out of the range of the logic of the signifier.

Confronted with such an approach of multilevel and multilateral attacks, the State restlessly stays on the battlefield of political discourse within the logic of the signifier, sustained by its intrinsic violence. There is a structural limit to that encounter of those two antagonistic logics. There is a time where both the State and the civil society are forced into the necessity of giving a new form to their mutual acknowledgment in order to escape the horror of a terrorist violence. All over the world we notice that sort of conjunction, in the Eastern and Communist countries, in Asia, in South Africa, in the Middle East, in Central and South America. The structure of such a limit is the open political goal that the strategy of expedient shots in civil society is looking for to reach a conjunction of global reformation. At the same time that limit is what is unbearable for the structure and the logic of the State, which has condemned such a strategy as treason.

Obviously the solution to such a tragedy is a question of aesthetics contingent upon the singular genius and creativity of civil society in each concerned person. Eventually the State and the specific form of the political order provides the factual limit that supplies the action and opposition of civil society in the same way as the fireback of *jouissance* is not conceivable without the action of repression by the signifier. The structure of the relationship of the contest and creativity of civil society to the necessary but insufficient action of the political order that the State maintains overdetermine the limit that the lasting heresy encounters in jeopardizing political desire. And that relationship presents the boromean knot that Lacan indicates as a model to evaluate the structure of human affairs.

Richard Feldstein

Subject of the Gaze for Another Gaze

knoting the imaginary, symbolic, and real

Much of the work of feminist film criticism in the last decade has been to identify the look produced for patriarchal viewers as an introjected gaze that lingers over the bodies of women as it effaces them. Feminist film critics tell us that this look, which circumscribes us as beings to be seen in a specular world, has been used in cinema to filter commercialized phallic images through the camera's eye as a form of visual presencing. This filmic maneuver reestablishes the look which, projected through the lens, demarcates a series of visual boundaries and delimited viewpoints that indicate the sexist and racist inclination of the sanctioned production of perspectives.

Feminist film critics have identified these perspectives with patriarchal lines of sight that reveal "castrated" lines of desire. For many critics vision is not attributable to a biological or an ahistorical essence; vision is socially constructed, built upon dialectical determinants that in a New York glance tell us who has the right to look and who has become an object-to-be-seen. Who has the right to look has implications for the way women are viewed in the desire-infused glare of the gaze. The gaze invariably negates women to viewed objects of desire who are assigned positions of fantasy by a masculinist society but who, nevertheless, remain marginalized as a point of address that is unrepresentable within a patriarchal focus of attention.

The gaze that helps to structure the visual field is a psycho-cultural hybrid introjected as the very lining of perspective. Subjection to it induces a fantasized identification with the symbolic Other, which produces social perspectives linked to our predisposition to be looked at. In this way we identify with cultural perspectives that look as we introject versions of being seen and become subjects of the signifier.

As barred subjects of the Other, we are to double business bound: we are identified with a seemingly endless perspectival horizon (whose border expands into the unconscious); and we are localized by the parameters of perceptual consciousness that are structured by signifiers. But in both instances we are subjected to the introjected gaze and the cultural logic it represents. In the gaze there is a predisposition to be seen that is expansive because it reaches beyond the geometric to one's horizon of observability, then fades into the unobservable, a glitch on the visual screen projected reflexively at us. Being subjects of the gaze, we are pictured as objects of a self-reflexive given-to-be-seen. We are given coordinates within the parameters of the picture. We are produced as looking and looked at, constructed from successive instances of being seen by others that go beyond the particular instance or any succession of them, taking on the expansive characteristics of structure itself. It is a structure of seeing/being seen or imaging-as-consciousness that reduces us to "beings who are looked at, in the spectacle of the world" (Lacan, *Four*, 75).

Something more than the dictates of space and time influence this imaging process of the subject within the patriarchal structure. Within this structure words materialize the lexical arms of the dead fathers from beyond the grave in an archival resurrection of phallic discourse that institutes the law at the cut of desire. Incognito, veiled, *already castrated*, the phallic presumption is projected onto us regardless of gender. *Ironically, the phallus veils the true site of penis envy—within men themselves—who, already castrated, imaginarily backtrack, wishing for what they never had.* This syndrome creates a male anxiety that is metonymically projected onto systemicity itself, there structured as a fearful, already castrated desirousness that seeks *jouissance* beyond the phallus. In this way, women are subjugated as objects of a male spectatorial desire, which foregrounds white heterosexual male fantasies as a prominent point of address.

For centuries women have withstood the search and seizure of the visual once-over while they were simultaneously held accountable by male voyeurs for the scopic stimulation which reactivates castration anxiety that undermines the fantasy of oneness. This fantasy finds its limit in the disjunctive sexual relation that resists inscription within a comprehensive, fundamental, universalizing fantasy because the sexual relation only takes place between men and women through a secondary process—at one step removed—wedged by the Other. Still somewhere in the imaginary visual gestalt, a mythic nexus between figure and ground is guaranteed, certifying the signifying Other's knowledge as sufficient. Such knowledge, however, is grounded only by the phallic signifier that marks structure with no signified, and thus no conceptual basis other than the signifier itself. Thus, structure is marked "in relation to meaning, [which] symbolizes its failing" (Lacan, "Love," 151).

The phallic revolution was accomplished in part by the phallus's presumption of privilege in marking itself as the stripe of differential structure. This remains true today in our semiotic age of televisual simulation. The postmodern endlessly plays with this structural logic where logos is graphed onto desire in an inversion that leaves the subject subjected. At the phallic cut we submit to the mark of language, which produces the signified in a signifiable becoming as effect of the signifier (Lacan, "Phallus," 80). Subsequently at the phallic cut there is a psychocultural fissure where the insertion of the bar between the signifier and signified beckons us back to it, summoning us to the site of trauma. Summoned by the Other, we invert perspective and, represented by a signifier for another signifier, become effects of language. For once the phallus is raised to the function of a signifier, we are reduced to signifiers "determined by it," to the synchronic network that produces diachronic effects (Lacan, *Four*, 67).

At the phallic cut the imaginary converges with the symbolic, activating mirror-phase experiences and reactivating affects associated with the first transpositional twist at the site of the mirror where we initially switched subject positions—became seer and seen—in a specular drama that shaped both imaginary and symbolic identifications through repeated misencounters with the real. In this imaginary gestalt we are confronted with an overlay of identifications: we can identify with the figure (an image of our displacement into the object) or with the ground (the place from which we observe ourselves as well as the sphere of signifiable influences associated with that site). This identificatory overlay consists of innumerable figures pictured against varied backgrounds understood as both physical surroundings and signifying chains that enable us to arrange visibility within a perceptible gestalt. In *The Sublime Object of Ideology*, Slavoj Žižek explains that any either-or perspective "overlook[s] the fact that imaginary identification is always on behalf of a certain gaze in the Other" for whom we project our intentionality (106). This imagined gaze of the Other is thus subject to symbolic influences that help constitute the repression of need by demand and its sublation into desire.

Because of its association with the real, the gaze elludes the semiotic confines of construction. The look introjected as the gaze is an aspect of the *objet a*, the "privileged object, which has emerged from some primal separation" and which radiates beyond signification and the geometric field of vision (Lacan, *Four*, 83). Facet of the intersubjective split in the scopic dimension, the *objet a*-as-the-gaze can be understood as a letter in the writing of the real, which cannot be represented symbolically. For the symbolic grid upon which masculinity assumes its privilege is always insufficient to constrain the surging impetus of the drive. Though not a facet of the symbolic, the *objet a* is nevertheless a letter in the real because it appears as a result of the Other written on body parts exposed to the environment (the mouth, eyes, ears, etc.). These parts become effectively split-off and objectified bodily aspects colonized by the laws of the signifying Other.

The gaze is an aspect of the *objet a* in the scopic register. As such it manifests as a cut when the body screws up in "the grimace of the real" whose proximity we assiduously avoid yet upon whose hook fantasy is hung to deny the trauma associated with the cut (Lacan, *Television*, 6). For in the scopic register the gaze provides the _____ which is avoided through the construction of fantasies of wholeness. Because we are traumatized by repeated misencounters with the real, which remains unsymbolizable to a geometrical perspectival mapping, those who wield power enfranchise themselves by filling the void with transcendental signifieds. These sig-

nifieds perpetuate the fantasy of Knowledge believed capable of removing uncertainty in relation to the Other and the split in subjectivity associated with it. So a paradox is created: because the gaze
is more than the eye, it defies the logic of the signifier even as it is
structured by it.

Those in power learned long ago that the expansive quality
that exceeds the representable is desirable to us, that we will
follow the trajectory of the gaze where its horizon expands into
evanescent departure, even though we vanish at the bar which is
covered over by fantasy in a phantasmatic dusting that fortifies the
reassuring illusion of presence reinforced in the fantasy of "seeing
oneself see oneself" (Lacan, *Four*, 83). Patriarchal filmmakers and
the advertising moguls who stoke the capitalist engine—aware of
the gaze's sublime quality and the desirability of transcendence for
us—conflate themselves with its transcendental overreach and
equate it with their scriptorial power by turning the gaze into a
local universal. The gaze, sometimes confused with the look of
God, is structured by signifiers that localize their interests and, in
defining the line of sight, distinguish the interpretable from the repressed.

The incalculability and expandability and extensiveness of
the gaze's horizon parallels the transcendent quality of identification appropriated by secular and religious leaders who manipulate
the affects we experience in the identificatory process. Imaginary
identification with the desire of another invokes going beyond the
self, a process of trading places that becomes more pronounced in
symbolic identification, where we identify with the place from
which we imagine ourselves with society's eyes. If imaginary identification enables us to shift intersubjective positions in the realm
of fantasy, symbolic identification melds us with the social body:
the extensive interlinking lexical grid of metonymic signifier
sliding into signifier—the vast cultural body marked by phallic
privilege.

Internalized experiences of sliding in metonymic sequence or
experiencing oneself in the Other reinforce fantasies originating in
the mirror stage. In the internalized mirror, the repeated reflection
produced in the illusion of "seeing oneself see oneself" grounds our
fantasy of repetition and enables the creation of an illusion: in it
we become our own progenitors who retrospectively conceive ourselves as beings of logos bound by cohesive memory systems that
help the ego map itself within geometrical parameters. To do so

the ego doubles itself. In the doubled construction of "seeing one-self see oneself," the initial one, though not mentioned, is implic-itly claimed as the ego's privileged sight of looking: it is "[one] seeing oneself see oneself." The first inscription of *oneself* as the objectified other receives passing mention; that is, the identifica-tion of self-as-other is reduced in significance to one strophe while the ego reserves for itself two strophes: the ego sees the objectified other seeing the ego—which appears in the second inscription of *oneself* as the ultimate object of its internalized picture. This double mention as the site of sight and the object seen gives the ego a prominence upon which are built its illusions.

The State uses the same trick of repetition to increase its status while attempting to alleviate anxiety about its not having any basis for authority other than the manipulation of images and signs to repeat and/or to double the insistence of its privilege. Irigaray says as much when she insists that the heterosexual system of shared images constitutes a doubled reference that is al-ways between two men so that woman is passed "from one man to another, from one group of men to another" in a "hom(m)o-sexual" monopoly of representation (171). This is especially true of the vi-sual commodity because the law valorizes the desires of men who visually use, then exchange women in a self-same hom(m)o-social logic of looking that contextualizes gender-marked cultural con-ventions in light of predominant social fantasies.

The cultural exchange that Irigaray identifies here mirrors the egocentric pattern previously discussed where the same-old-self uses women to simulate the real and with it the circuit of "seeing oneself see oneself." Reticulating an intersubjective circuit to as-sure patronymic privilege, the patriarchal powerbrokers mask their investment in the Other-which-seems-whole-unto-Itself. Because patriarchal image makers know that when people see themselves it is through the eyes of the Other that they habitually look, such policy crafters prop up the psychocohesion of the phallic system by scripting cultural identities in their own images through the repe-tition of myths and rituals that bestow upon the technostructure its authority. This attempt to create cohesive identities, however, ignores the precarious position of the phallus—the fact that it is lacking in the real. This attempt at psychocohesion pretends that, if the symbolic is successfully colonized, the real will somehow be encompassed. It denies that the impenetrability and incomprehen-sibility of the real negates the symbolic attempt to link the subject relationally to the cultural interchange, a project whose basis for empowerment rests on the repetition produced in the symbolic exchange of signifiers and the *méconnaissance* produced by the individual or State in its propensity to map the geometric surety of constructed parameters.

The State accomplishes this psychosocial colonization through the institution of a *point de capiton,* which inserts a master signifier at the point of inversion where the cultural takes primacy over the natural. Through the *point de capiton* the State claims the indeterminate as its own; it delineates it as a point of origin in the process of [the State] seeing itself see itself. This usurpation allows the State-changeling to inscribe its privilege at the established point of anxiety where there is no foundation other than imaginary and symbolic justification on the faultline of illusion. Within such objectivist illusions, representative authority reserves its privilege, situated as the empire of signs that conscripts perceptual consciousness in an alliance to deny the lack in the Other. Such tactics encourage us to blink away the signifying system's "absence of foundation" (See Apollon's essay in this volume). By mimicking the ego's trick and allowing consciousness to double itself into an ideal, patriarchal powerbrokers habitually construct trumped up, inflated images of themselves for consumption.

Problems occur, however, when such constructions use women to s(t)imulate an encounter with a real whose extension beyond symbolic limits likens it to the imaginary and the identificatory processes associated with it. Because each encounter with the real presents an irreducible impediment to the sweep of symbolization, transcendental fantasies appear to brokered advantage in the patriarchal mapping of visual experience. In each register— imaginary, symbolic, and real—there is an expandable quality knotted to the social symptom at the juncture where a *point de capiton* is appropriated by patriarchal interests to effect the "'miraculous' turn, in this quid pro quo by means of which what was just prior the very source of disarray, becomes the proof and the testimony of a triumph" (Žižek, "Semiotics," 92). To aid in this deception, the *point de capiton* becomes a pretense to perfection that dismisses lack as a "source of disarray." When a *point de capiton* recasts numerous free-floating signfiers into a unfied field of meaning that reads each term in relation to this deterministic signifier, the disarray is recast into coherence. Lack is converted into the "proof and testimony of a triumph" that gives a phantasmatic guarantee to self-presencing certainty as a means to chart directed paths through the uncodifiable real.

In the imaginary, this type of reversal occurs when we go beyond a one-to-one identification; then we believe ourselves identical to the "place" of signification from which we look. In the symbolic, most people become subjugated through a logic that leaves them subjects represented by a signifier for another signifier. In the real, a simulation occurs in which the logic of the signifier is transposed onto the real in an attempt to negotiate it. In this transposition (in so far as the fantasy of oneness assures us that closure is possible in the symbolic network), the real becomes imbued by the symbolic with its characteristics and the subject believes herself or himself to be represented by the gaze for another gaze. This representation of a gaze for another gaze is only thinkable as a symbolic logic; it has nothing to do with the gaze as an aspect of the *objet a* in the real. Yet this real impossibility is given credence by those who use the power of the gaze as a signfier to substantiate their own positions.

As long as the State projects its desire into the scopic dimension that demarcates gender, race, and class privileges, the authorization of the social will be accompanied by fantasies of transcendental signifieds that substitute the cohesion of the cultural body for the indivisibility of God. Through such tactics the state takes onto itself the power to govern its citizens, who are reduced through this process of objectification as they project themselves for the crafted, staged look that ironically imposes the incomprehensibility of the real upon them in a dialectical charade. Confronted with the geometric, we fit ourselves to its coordinates, turn ourselves into pictures for an externalized look introjected as the gaze. Geometrically pictured as such, we stage ourselves where the gaze becomes a conduit for light's reflection in the eye. In its glint, as the light flickers, we become subjects of the symbolic—beings who are looked at and act for the Other-as-audience and imaginary ground of desire. In the scopic dimension, there is an implicit summons to capitulate, to lay down our gaze in visual surrender. Little wonder the State, aided by the mesmerizing power of the advertising industry, constructs the look for visual enslavement. As recipients of media dissemination, we receive a selection of stylized pictures in a lure of presented possibilities validated by the socialization process for our consumption.

Since, in the imaginary, the real can be annexed by the symbolic, on some level, the gaze is pitched for the gaze of another, and this has political consequences. Because the State's transcendental signifieds are erected in homage to its own cultural prerogative, we are strapped with a political agenda to which these signifieds testify. Subject to such ideological grooming, the gaze becomes a *trompe d'oeil* or surface appearance whose only reassurance lies in the double strophe of seeing itself see itself. Thus, according to the signifier's logic and inasmuch as it holds sway, we are subjects of a gaze seemingly staged for another gaze, but really established, in instances of scopic exchange, as a repetition, insistence, or doubled enactment of the imaginary and the symbolic in the foregrounding of these positions as prominent. Here the imaginary-symbolic hybrid is like the Dutch boy at the dike who believes there are options to sopping up the (w)hole in the real, which knows nothing of his designs, nor the State's privilege, nor women's place in the construction of simulated fantasy structures.

In androcentric State fantasies, women are positioned as objects of State-controlled scenarios established for audiences whose gender and race are taken for granted, as if these variables were prompts in a rigid computer logic. Women have been objectified by the look while staged for the fantasy of the Other—on behalf of its desire and imagined *jouissance.* Linking themselves to the identificatory process itself, patriarchal chameleons have used camouflage and travesty to intimidate others and overvalue themselves. They lure the eye and feed on the inflation experienced through the s(t)imulation of the real over the bodies of women who have been positioned in proximity to the real. In compensation for this s(t)imulation, we are presented pictures and proffered patriarchal narratives that assure us that our subjectivity retains its certainty and, more importantly, that geometric coordinates exist so that we can readily chart a frame of reference. Captured in pictures set in narrative progressions sold for scopic exchange and profit, women are positioned by patriarchs in the overdeveloped glare of their manufactured iconography. In this way a jealous, castrated phallic insistence uses women to kick start faltering fantasy, to *reve* up the real, to transfer the white, male metaphor through metonymic channels to various nexus points of intersecting experiences, where, in the crossing of registers, lies the experience of transcendence.

Baudrillard's theory of simulation

We have seen that insofar as the imaginary fantasy of unity gives assurance to the subject, tears in the symbolic envelope are restitched in fantasy to defer the signifier's metonymical displacement to the far reaches of dispersion. In other words, insofar as symbolic closure is believed possible, the imaginary and symbolic combine to form a hybrid that simulates the real so convincingly it seems authentic enough to attribute nongeometrical qualities to its referents. This hybrid is transposed to the real as a way to defer our encounter with it by overreading nonsensical gaps in symbolic transmission around which signifiers cluster to structure lexical privilege.

For a different angle on this combinatory hybrid, we turn to Jean Baudrillard's theory of simulation, which offers a means "to feign to have what one hasn't," like a psychosomatic illness that retroactively creates real symptoms so that one is left questioning whether a person is sick or not. Baudrillard claims that in the present historical period where simulation predominates, one can no longer tell where the effects of the real begin and where those produced by signs leave off. According to this kind of postmodernism, simulatory imagoes become self-progenitors of a hyperreal that murders the real rather than acts as a dialectical mediator of visible and intelligible referents. This postmodern failure of reference gives rise to the "precession of simulacra," which radiate as points of fascination, referring more to their own splendor than to a linear exchange of meaning (Baudrillard, *Simulations,* 2). These "simulacra radiant with their own fascination" are part of a model in "orbital circulation" that Baudrillard associates with the-media-as-first-cause and its audience as effects of a magnetic field of events (*Simulations,* 9). In this way Baudrillard's theoretical trajectory darts beyond the dialectical polarity and its antinomy—the implosion of the poles—to the realm of simulation. Through this theoretical attainment we become our own progenitors in a system of self-referential simulation introjected as a media experience in which the "nuclear and genetic" replaces the "specular or discursive" beyond the mirror, the gaze, the symptom, and a theory of history—either personal or cultural in origin.

For Baudrillard, the postmodern image no longer reflects reality, masks its absence, nor plays at being an appearance. His rendition of the postmodern image "bears no relation to reality" and is therefore sublated from the order of appearance to that of simulation (11). Moreover, "the hyperrealism of simulation is expressed everywhere by the real's striking resemblance to itself" as a contrived real functioning as an operation among operational models (*Simulations*, 45). This combinatory logic exists in a "hyperspace without atmosphere" from which the hyperreal is born unto itself, an operational double that deters every real process through its satellization in an "orbital recurrence of models" (*Simulations*, 4).

In his theory, after the murder of the real comes the resurrection in hyperspace. After the murder comes the theft or transfer of power from the real to the Other originally conceived as unbarred and now conflated by Baudrillard with the real-as-Other. This confusion becomes apparent every time he uses terms for the real like "the work-real, the production-real" that was fostered by capital into "the reality principle," and that, in turn, was liquidated by capital in its "extermination of every use value, of every real equivalence, of production and wealth. . . ." (*Simulations*, 43). Baudrillard mistakes the real-as-register with the Other-as-site-of-reality in a culturally introjected nexus of desire and law. This is further confounded by another type of confusion, that of the simulatory gesture which poses a transcendental logic with ahistorical suppositions.

For self-progenitive simulation denies the historicity of the image. This historical archeology is described by Baudrillard as a genealogical progression that passed through the following stages: (1) image as "the reflection of a basic reality," (2) image as that which "masks and perverts a basic reality," (3) image as that which "masks the *absence* of a basic reality," and (4) image as that which "bears no relation to any reality whatever: it is its own pure simulacrum" (*Simulations*, 11). But Baudrillard assumes that these sequences have completed their course when they are circuits in process that haunt the unconscious of postmodern simulation with historical and political discourses that subject it to alternate structures. These paradigms from previous ages appear symptomatically as the unconscious provides traces of past cultural introjections that reappear to alter the structural gestalt and reframe figure and ground according to past logics that historize the Other. Remnants of these past structures appear, are repressed, and reappear to articulate other logics with different historical grounds that relate to the dissociated and unintegrated aspects of the Other in us.

s(t)imulation of the real over the bodies of women

This detour through Baudrillard's hyperreal can help us to reread his theory of simulation as a variant of another strategy related to the attempt to add the t to s(t)imulation as the trace of a stimulus. Because the real has been displaced and its power appropriated by an imaginary-symbolic hybrid, for those empowered who would benefit from this appropriation, the stimulus becomes a secondary means of reviving the real. When reviving the real, there is an evocation of a particular, not a universal, stimulus whose force is tapped for symbolic purposes. The stimulus is evoked over the bodies of women as a means of resuscitating what would be killed—*feelings* experienced without the imaginary or symbolic to screen off the traumatic real. It is this quality that is appropriated each time patriarchal interests repeat their ritual of narcissistic self-replenishment. To resuscitate the real, those empowered must summon the impetus of the drives, especially their nontemporal trajectory validated in fantasy as transcendent. Driven to revitalize what is lost in their appropriation of the real, enfranchised patriarchs add the *t* to simulation. They add the evocative aspect of titillation when evoking the real in relation to the female body as seen through male fantasy.

In the imaginary-symbolic appropriation of the real as significatory Other, an identification with the phallus is induced as a result of the constitution of male desire at the moment of simulation. This identification positions women-as-other in an adequation of gender difference with the lost borders of knowledge. The two are repeatedly equated as women are positioned by patriarchy on the other side of discourse, as a s(t)imulus in its evocation of the real.

Contemporary feminist critics have denounced the timeworn tactic of placing women at the limit of what is theorizable, where knowledge doubles upon itself to prevent an unmediated experience of *jouissance.* For centuries women have preferred being not-all to the phallic domain. Then as now, few women relish being labeled phallic, castrated, or envious of the phallus. This is very different, however, from making the equation, in a calculated sweep of generalization, that being not all for the phallus is the same as being representative of not-allness, that is, of the gaps and inconsistencies in the Other. This is the appropriatory two-step that comes as an effect of s(t)imulation: first, women are displaced to the far reaches of signification; then they are asked to embody that position as a mark for the Other.

As a means of accomplishing this agenda, women have been historically placed on the cross of the real as fortification to bar unbarred signification. In this appropriation, women have been thrown to the far reaches of the symbolic and their position fetishized in two ways: because male fantasy elevates women to the status of sexual icons, they function in the process of s(t)imulation as a screen to block the real and as a lighting rod to revive male desire for which women have become conduits. This is done because patriarchs subject to symbolic castration like to pretend that this is not the case. One means they use to escape symbolic castration is to institutionalize the s(t)imulatory gesture. They are thus driven to s(t)imulate *jouissance*, but not directly. Rather they use women as screens that solicit a particular, not a universal, dose of *jouissance* targeted for the adolescent desire of male fantasy that has for centuries refused to grow up.

For Baudrillard the present historical age supersedes the paradigm of the map which represents the real territory. For him the map precedes the territory, whose vestiges persist as traces of a hyperreal technological circulation in hyperspace. Hyperspace, by definition, is not a spatial actuality because it defies the geometrical attempt to place spatial-temporal boundaries upon the transmission process. I have used simulation here to refer to an imaginary-symbolic hybrid that masquerades through immeasurable permutations as the real. In the simulatory dimension of s(t)imulation, the writing of the real leaves an imprint (as if on a magic writing pad) that reinscribes the signifier's trace as the real is appropriated in the name of an unmitigated phallologocentrism. These interests are represented by individuals, groups, the State and its ideological apparatus. The defining feature here is the attempt to manipulate a preferred logic of signification for the brokered advantage of those who would share in the treasury of the signifier's production. Such s(t)imulation, then, is born retroactively from repeated misencounters with a real that is overwritten by fantasies given value by transcendental signifieds. Hybrid imaginary signifieds are created, mapped, appropriated in a process that retains symptomatic amnesia with regard to the coding of patriarchal structures. These signifieds have been established in relation to an unsymbolizable lack that must be refused through the creation of virtual images of the real to compensate for and to defend against its direct apprehension.

conflation of the imaginary and symbolic phallus

The site of s(t)imulation is the place of the Other's inconsistency that has been colonized at structural points of weakness. Points that indicate structural weakness in the Other induce a hypnotic blindness and symptomatic stupidity where signification breaks down in its misencounters with the real. Coming and going, S1 ("the master signifier," which stands for the subject in the unconscious) traverses a gap that the subject would deny in its transmission with S2 (the battery of other signfiers that pair with S1 in the production of signification). As we approach the real, gaps appear in the topological mapping of "a geometry without measurement where there is no question of distances, where only the schematic network of the signifier supports objects" (Miller, "Elements," 30). In this encounter, however, weaknesses in the structure leave the symbolic more and more dependent on the imaginary to graph *incomprehensibility* submitted to symbolization. Produced through the real's interchange with the symbolic, the *objet a* is the refuse of the real sifted through the grid of the symbolic—a product of the Other in us, an Ur-object inscribed on the body. Although the *objet a* has no recognizable narrative or temporal dimension, it returns in time, and we narrativize its lost quality, label its temporality atemporal—even immortal—although it exhibits no such qualities. Instead, lost *jouissance* settles as *objet a*, which, once filled, now evacuated, becomes an impediment that interferes with the symbolic process.

Signifying chains falter as they approach the real. Signs fall apart, centers of signification cannot hold, and simulation is loosed upon the world by a passionate, untutored *jouissance* that settles stupidly, statically, interrupting the transmission of signifiers. The settling of *jouissance* represents an unsymbolized nonsense sacrificed at the altar of signification to the phallus, the signifier of pure difference that isn't so pure. The "master signifier" produces signification that occupies the place where reference is lacking, and this lack haunts or shadows the phallus in the presentation of its fantasmatical counterpart, the imaginary phallus which conflates the phallus as function with the penis as organ. Because the registers—real, imaginary, and symbolic—are knotted symptomatically to each other, the phallus is always a little tainted since its effects escape the cut to constitute fantasmatic slivers of signification.

Such combinatory formulations like the imaginary-symbolic

hybrid lead us to questions of agency and the authorization of privilege. That is why I introduce the term *the* patriarchy (without a bar) to situate it in the West as a fast-food position produced by quick capital in the wholesale s(t)imulation of the real. Barred subjects of the Other (individuals, groups, nations, groups of nations) are induced to project their positions with that of the signifying chain. Through the institutionalization of structural parameters, subjects are encouraged to project themselves onto the big Other, imaginarily graphing the symbolic even as the imaginary phallus is projected onto the phallic function. The projection of the imaginary phallus onto its symbolic counterpart filters the operation through a metaphorical regulation of iconic and lexical information. This process enables a patrimonial appropriation of topological neutrality for narcissistic purposes. To the extent that people accept the truth of the signifier's topological neutrality, knowledge gains consequence, the barred Other appears less barred, and the magnet of transferential love-of-knowledge and love-for-the-knowledgeable is used to establish a transference between s(t)imulated patriarchy-as-Other (the big brother of the unconscious) and the fast-food subject of capital.

On the other hand, to the extent that people accept the half-truth of the signifier's topological neutrality, they recognize that, although the symbolic is a distinct register, it is repeatedly overwritten by the imaginary that blends into its blind spots. Only then can the unconscious be taken as a gap that reveals itself at the faultline of significatory illusion. There the Gods (originally of the real) were transposed into the realm of knowledge at the behest of the big Other—unbarred, inflated as the idea-become-ideal in a genealogy of appropriation. For in the imaginary the barred Other must have been conceived initially without its bar in resistance to the subject's construction under the signifier. This transposition of the unconscious gods from the real-as-register (defined structurally in topological difference from the imaginary and symbolic registers) allows for a mortification of the real and its conversion into God as knowledge, the love of knowledge, and love for those who mediate knowledge to place themselves between desire and the known.

As the real is displaced into a symbolic-imaginary reduction, it allows for the construction of the subject of certainty, the subject of knowledge and, through the appropriation of the phallus, of the omnipresent patriarchal subject of the four corners of the earth.

In the West, with each new technological breakthrough, the inflation of the high-tech, fast-food subject of desire continues.
Continues only insofar as the fantasy attached to the wedding of
logos to desire finds its point of imaginary coherence in backroom
conversations, or, if there is no actual room, in the backroom discourse of appropriation used to demarcate privilege. Here, men and
women, doctors and lawyers, business executives and advertising
moguls, academicians, politicians, and others empowered by our
culture draft attempts to deceive others, to manipulate rhetoric for
their own purposes, to play upon the public's inability to distinguish the enunciated subject of consciousness from the enunciation of unconscious desire.

The smuggling of the Gods from the real to the Other has
been accomplished to confirm the equation of God-as-Knowledge.
State apparati, set up to mediate the message long before God was
declared dead, have equated themselves with knowledge's privilege, constructing it as a local universal to empower themselves.
Governments that ask their citizens to rally round the flag project
simulations that reconfigure the real as nationalist identity is inserted in the gaps of inconsistency in the signifying Other. Their
success is in some way measured by our inclination to make ex-
emptions for structural neutrality, symbolic dominance, and the
belief in knowledgeable foundations. Their success is also measured by our internalization of the dead fathers' words, codes, and
values. Such internalization enables enfranchised patriarchs to
conflate their privilege with the overreach of the real in order to
promote an identification with their power at the point of failure.
Governments count on us to identify with the symbolic mandate
that produces the subject of language coded by a sequence of dominant perspectives. Bound to language means bound to a trace used
to alter the subject's position through its identification with a signifier in the Other and one's fantasies related to it.

In the inconsistencies in the Other the State projects its
hyped-up "infinite" privilege that is propped up by the imaginary
fantasy of the State seeing itself seeing itself. In the imaginary register, within a self-same instant, the gaze is avoided and nationalism reaffirmed, the expansive transcendent quality of national-
istic interests tied to the transformational experience of imaginary
and symbolic identification. In the symbolic, the State reduplicates
its privilege through the institution of a retroactive process of signification used to cover over gaps in the Other with the smooth-

running fantasy of significatory interchange. And in the real, the hutzspah of s(t)imulation allows for the imaginary fantasy of one gaze being posited for another gaze, as if they were two signifiers. In this hybrid of the symbolic and the real, the hyperreal gaze that mimics the attributes of the signifier simulates a real exchange. But we are left with dialectical juncture, yet no interchange, no relationship—just simulatory give and take.

Works Cited

Baudrillard, Jean. *Simulations*. Translated by Paul Foss, Paul Patton, and Philip Beitchman. New York: Semiotext(e), 1983.

Irigaray, Luce. *This Sex Which Is Not One*. Translated by Catherine Porter. Ithaca: Cornell University Press, 1985.

Lacan, Jacques. *The Four Fundamental Concepts of Psycho-Analysis*. Translated by Alan Sheridan. New York: Norton, 1977.

———. "A Love Letter," in *Feminine Sexuality*. Edited by Juliet Mitchell and Jacqueline Rose. Translated by Jacqueline Rose. New York: Norton, 1982.

———. "The Meaning of the Phallus," in *Feminine Sexuality*. Edited by Juliet Mitchell and Jacqueline Rose. Translated by Jacqueline Rose. New York: Norton, 1982.

———. *Television*. Translated by Denis Hollier, Rosalind Krauss, and Annette Michelson. New York: Norton, 1990.

Miller, Jacques-Alain. "Element of epistemology," in *Analysis* 1 (1989): 27–42.

Žižek, Slavoj. *The Sublime Object of Ideology*. London: Verso, 1989.

———. "The Limits of the Semiotic Approach to Psychoanalysis," in *Psychoanalysis and . . .* Edited by Richard Feldstein and Henry Sussman. New York: Routledge, 1990.

jouissance, desire, and the law

*Juliet Flower MacCannell**

FACING FASCISM:
A FEMININE POLITICS OF JOUISSANCE

By combining the work of Lacan with the earlier insights of Lacan's contemporary, Hannah Arendt (1963/4), I seek to position a current problematic for feminist thinking in relation to ethics.[1] My critical question regards the special relation Woman has, via femininity, to *jouissance*—meaning to her own *body,* to *voice* and to the *Death Drive.* This special relation has bearing for any politics involving the feminine. But beyond this, it has bearing on the politics of postmodernity, an era opening with much promise, but a promise not yet "fulfilled" and possibly already forfeited due to its prehistory of sheer catastrophe.

In writing this I hope to steer around the prevailing impasse in defining where ethical thinking about woman must go "after the patriarchy," in a postmodern world that is moving away from Oedipal ethics.[2] We are no longer, in democracy, supposed to be governed by the patriarchal family; the classic patriarchal containments for "woman" are in remission, if not yet in default. But we are very far from having fulfilled the promise of the political liberation from the family made by our political innovations; the Mother and Father—as well as the Brother—have remained the "future of an illusion" that was supposed to be overcome in the democratic revolutions after the Enlightenment. The peculiar position of woman, on the edge between two possible ethical worlds, models a larger ethical predicament.

In Drive

An ethical relation to one's desire is the aim of "balance" for the subject: "Civilization" must stand or fall on how its ethics manage to temporize with "a hitch, an impediment that gives rise to ever new symbolizations" (Žižek 1991:100).[3] The first "hitches" Freud discovered concern the real (animal instincts, death, and so on). The original compromises civilization makes with animal "instincts" are the "Drives," those pulsations of absolute lack and absolute excess over nature and animal *jouissances:* Drive is not identical with these latter terms (nature/animal/*jouissance*), for it is, according to Freud, their first "violation." Natural and animal life is cyclical; what breaks this cycle and institutes a protosymbolic order is "drive." (Freud's alternative term is "principle": death drive and pleasure principle.) Drive sutures the breach it creates in the circle of life, but always in excess of it. Drives are the *sine qua non,* therefore, the absolute precondition of the Symbolic Order. Yet Drives are only perceived as such after they have instituted the symbolic, which covers over its own breaching of the Natural (as a cyclic whole): for Freud, the Natural-as-whole only appears through the "break" made by Drive, which is, Lacan reminds us, *modeled* on the instinct, not coterminous with it.

The Symbolic requires the regulation of lack/excess, but this "regulation" as the pulsation excess-lack already exists in principle—in The Drives themselves. Drives are directly linked to the original violation of nature and are themselves residues of a traumatic experience, a radical break with real enjoyment,[4] which, were it ever fully experienced, would require the "fainting of the subject." Satisfactions must be symbolically organized for the subject under laws (partial cuttings that produce both the retroactive "memory" of real enjoyments and the struggle against going beyond—and *back* to them—the Drives). Real enjoyments must be forgotten as "the price" of achieving civilization.[5]

Drive challenges what civilization sees as its only resource—the word, or the Law. But what civilization maintains as principles, Drives as unremembered or unmarked struggles that are more than just a labor or working-through—are civilization's first resource. Drive careens between a will-to-*jouissance* and its surmounting: outside the Word or Law of the Father, drive stands as the "violence" at the origin of the Law—however little we might wish to recall it.[6] At times Drive nevertheless must reclaim its status as a primary mode of limiting *jouissance*. This is the case in Lacan's (based on Freud's) theory. It is also the case in contemporary life where so-called "Symbolic" or Paternal laws are fading from the picture.[7] In their place, the fantasy objects that organize or structure the Drive emerge.[8]

What is new in Lacan's reading of Law and the Drives is his perception that the symbolic tactics civilization employs to open and close its self-inflicted wounds (the wounds that make us human) are no longer compelling fictions. More "balanced" modes of symbolic temporizing have taken a back seat. A direct, "imbalanced" relation to "Drive" displaces them. Under Holocaust, nuclear and global catastrophic threats, the will-to-*jouissance* insists with immediate virulence—at issue is, of course, the Death Drive.[9] Law, "the Symbolic order," are being experienced less and less by the modern subject as tempering its violent constitution of and by the Drive. The aporetic structure of the object of Drive (it confronts both pain and pleasure, both life and death) is a "traumatic, meaningless" experience of something that "cannot be integrated into [the] symbolic universe" (Žižek, 1991:274). Symbolic resolution (acceptance of castration and the signifier of the phallus, of lack in the big O Other) must be, literally, unimaginable to be effective. Yet fantasy grounds our contemporary culture; it inverts the logical (symbolic) structuring of necessary lack in us as the Other's *bliss*, or *fulfillment*.[10] Our fantasy will-to-*jouissance* seems limitless in a contemporary culture that promises, now more than ever, *jouissance* or fulfillment to its members. Fantasy's real limitations on the subject's relation to enjoyment are specifiable and have been found ethically instructive, as in the work of Jacques-Alain Miller.[11]

Certain subjects—fascists and "women"—hold a dubious "privilege" under such conditions. The fascist is on the way to a *jouissance* not restricted by the word, by the ethical framing of excess and lack. The fascist's will-to-*jouissance* must not, that is, be mistaken for Drive as such. "Women" as subjects, are, on the contrary, to be recognized as potentially exemplary with respect to "the other *jouissance*," the unlimited, or nonphallic one. Femininity provides at least two models for responding to the exigencies of unlimited *jouissance*:[12] sacrificing to it, as the fascist does, but, more crucial for the ethical question here, fending it off without complete submission to the phallic contract.

If women as a class do not accept fully symbolic-paternal limitation of the phallic word, they nonetheless face "the worst": the absence of a sheltering paternal metaphor. The father or the worst, said Lacan, *le père ou le pire*, and it is women who, without telling us in so many words, know the insistence of excess, the remainder of insistent *jouissance* created by the demand for love. The feminine subject position is forged by a speech that fails it; it cannot afford to "give way on its Drive."[13]

In his *Seminar VII*, "drive" became for Lacan, an "ethical attitude" (Žižek, 1991: 272). Drive, more than Oedipalized desire, is a pulsion and compulsion that places us unremittingly under the pressure of the conflictual, ex-centric "core" of our human being. Lacan had suggested early, in *Seminar I*,[14] that what constituted Freud's "Copernican" revolution was his insight into the traditional ruses (myths, laws, religions) that regulate and manage the contradictions inherent in human civilized life. For Freud, all symbolic systems of accommodation were equally ex-centric to and yet "intimate" with the human psyche. All are products of a *cause* (a will-to-*jouissance*), lost in advance, of which they are also the source. With that discovery, *the cause*, not the Law that rationalizes and covers it up, takes analytic precedence. As Lacan puts it, the suicide crushed on the sidewalk has obeyed the "rational" *laws of physics*, but his presence as dead body in the street is due to a *cause* fallen from the chain of reason. ("The Freudian Unconscious and ours"; 1978/73b). *Cause* faces starkly the essence of Drive (the violent impossibility of existing between excess and lack—the famous ambiguity of *plus-de-jouir*); it is also therefore a *cause* whose impossibility can and may be resolved by a will-to-*jouissance*, the ending or fulfillment of the death drive.

Drive therefore assumes a crucial role in the ethical picture. It affects the whole sense we have of our "Rights" realized through our collective emergence from the master/slave relation (the literal ownership of one's person by another) in the post–Cartesian Enlightenment.[15] "Right" has closer affinities with nonnegotiable "demand"—the "right to *jouissance*" working through Drive and its link to the superego—than does compliance with exigencies of a "paternal" monarch, an Oedipal figure, working through desire.[16]

Right and the Will-to-Jouissance

That a ferocious will-to-*jouissance*, expressed through fantasy, inhabits "right" is not to be doubted. If a preeminent, classic social-symbolic, political model—one that figured the differential of excess and lack—was the master/servant or master/slave relation before the revolutions of the eighteenth century, democracy reconfigured this differential by directly expressing it, as in this text (which inspired Hegel), Diderot's *Neveu de Rameau:*

> Je trouve qu'il n'est pas du bon ordre de n'avoir pas toujours de quoi manger. Que diable d'économie, des hommes qui regorgent de tout, tandis que d'autres qui ont un estomac importun comme eux, et pas de quoi mettre sous la dent. (`Le neveu,' p. 177–8).[17]

Under the recent policies of conservative economics, excess and lack have appeared before us more starkly than ever—as the Los Angeles riots recently demonstrated.[18] While fascism for our time has exhibited an unmistakeable will-to-*jouissance*, just as early capitalism understood this possibility in the dream of unlimited profit, the more critical figure for my argument here is Sade. Ex-aristocrat, he provided Lacan, not to mention Horkheimer and Adorno, as well as Arendt, with fantasy figures for the unlimited "will-to-*jouissance*."[19] One should not too casually connect fascism and sadism. Lacan argued all social linkages formally via Discourses. If we do not operate through the Discourses we risk equations that are overly simplistic, and we will miss the difference between "the feminine"—as what is without discourse—and the "sadistic," which is my concern here.

Sadism is a response, in Lacan's work, to the *jouissance* of the Other as *voice*, rather than to the Other as *speech*. Speech is here defined classically, as the signifier, the symbolic pact, the social contract that divides us from each other as mutual aggressors: "Speech is always a pact, an agreement, people get on with one another, they agree—this is yours, this is mine, this is this, that is

that," writes Lacan. The signifier determines the unconscious relation of the subject to enjoyment (*jouissance*). *Voice* is already *object a;* the embodiment or bearer of a "principle behind the law." It
took shape in Lacan's discourse as one of the four fundamental *objects a* (gaze, voice, breast, feces)[20] around which the fantasy that
structures drive circulates.

Lacan argued that the *perverted* position with respect to the
voice as *object a* is taken up by Sade (and I will argue below, it provides a certain instructive model for analyzing Adolf Eichmann,
who administered the Final Solution under Hitler). The perverse
position, which disavows castration, differs, however, from the
feminine solution. The pervert *identifies himself with the object a*
in its role as *agent* of the *Jouissance de l'Autre.*[21] Femininity's position vis à vis the Other *jouissance* does not follow this model, insofar as it works the distance between object and other. Its
"Ethics" reinvolve the Other *jouissance* as speechless, as "let-
tered," with speech as its horizon of impossibility. Lucie Cantin
calls this femininity's ethic—an "Ethic of the Impossible,"
(1993:17) For femininity, the link with the Other is necessarily the
"path of the signifier," since it accepts the division by sexuality
that the signifier alone—language—incurs. But at the same time,
given that the Other is, for femininity, structurally absent, femininity is left to face, without assurance of the support of the Law,
the "other" Other, the nonbarred Other of unlimited *jouissance.*
This Other "writes" on the body of woman with the broken logic
of "the letter."

To have a woman philosopher, Arendt, treat the ethical problematic of Nazism, and a male analyst, Lacan, initiate inquiry on
femininity and *jouissance* provides the researcher with an unbe-
lievably lucky moment. Though neither Arendt nor Lacan were
connected to each other (as far as I know), Arendt's connections to
the thinkers of the Frankfurt School as well as Lacan's interest in
German philosophy (especially Arendt's teacher and purported
lover, Martin Heidegger) enriches their potential enlistment as
coworkers in the study of the ethics of drive and resistance to the
will-to-*jouissance.*

Woman retains a special—and I believe exemplary—relation
to "limitless *jouissance*" (hers by virtue of her "femininity": non-
castration, nonsubmission to the signifier; Brousse, 1992; Salecl,
1993). Woman is—from the phallic signifier's viewpoint, "fulfillment," the final term, the signified of all signifiers, or the one "ex-

ception" to the universal rule of castration that proves that rule (the one who fully enjoys). But, from her own viewpoint, she cannot absolutely equate her existence with this final signified, which is nothing other than the final *jouissance*—death, the absolute *enjoyment*. She finds a different way to respond to and resist the Other *jouissance*. It is a way that works in tandem with, and in contradiction to, the (phallic) signifier. She will not, like the pervert, disavow the work of the word, the Law, but she will not accept it entirely either.[22]

The Ethical Problem:
Genocide and the Will-to-Jouissance

Let me state my own hypothesis bluntly: that the origin of the possibility of the "new crime" of *bureaucratic genocide* arises *only* with the opening of modern democracy (the attribution of will to the people); that it is its chief and most constant danger; and that the reasons why it threatens democratic civilization continually is that there is no written commandment, no written law against genocide. A law against genocide would prohibit the annihilation of one people by another as the moral equivalent of murder for the individual. The "people," not the individual, would be the subject of such a law. Under such a hypothetical law, many "issues" would be subjoined. For example, capital punishment, abortion and state-run sterilization programs, destruction of viable lands, euthanasia, suicide doctors, and so forth, would all be argued as matters transcending individual rights and choices and subject to other kinds of questions: the racial makeup of death row inmates,[23] the statistical distribution of availability of prenatal care, sterilization, of abortion by race, and so on.

There is a technical and crucial reason *why* genocide has not been (and possibly cannot be) legislated against in our modern democratic states.[24] Here we must go back to the transformation of the notion of law in the postrevolutionary age (or at birth of modern democracy) and what it does or does not do after this moment. We must go back, as well, to Kant, and to the notion of *will*, or *good will* as the principle of *Law*, rather than the traditional prohibition ("Law as the repression of a desire") that vexes us.

In Kant, the Law becomes a formal, empty universality by evacuation of all content. But it does not remain inert in its formal emptiness; instead, the emptiness of its form permits a certain kind of universality to be expressed as universal "Ought" or pure positive command to duty:[25] "You must!" rather than an inhibition against an action "You must not!"[26] Kant's spirit demands, in the form of duty, "that a man do more than obey the law": he must "go beyond the mere call of obedience and identify his own will with the principle behind the law—the source from which the law sprang. In Kant's philosophy that source was practical reason. . . ." (Arendt, 1963/4: 136).

But Lacan read Kant a bit differently. If you look closely enough at the "purity" of Kant's form, you will find an object—no longer the pathological object Kant has ejected from its contents, but the "object" that is present as cause in and of all Drive, the *object a* of pure excess or pure lack (the hallucinatory or fantasmatic, surplus enjoyment of *plus-de-jouir*). In other words, by stripping Law of its mythic-rhetorical veils, Kant put us right on the edge, in Drive. (Žižek, 1991: 231). By evacuating "content" from the Law, while avoiding recognition of the emergence of the new, "nonpathological" object, Kant founded ethics on a nonpathological basis—and unwittingly empowered the Thing (*das Ding*).

Kant's refusal of a pathetic foundation for the law opened many positive possibilities, but it also opened the way to multiple potential horrors. Like Adolf Eichmann, for example. Indeed, as the documentation and testimony piled up in his trial in Jerusalem, it became quite clear to Hannah Arendt, who reported on it, that Eichmann's Jews were killed not out of blood lust nor any of the traditional passions. He did not participate in the *Endlosung* "in the name of" some more-than-human principle, some "God." Eichmann was, as Arendt showed, a murderer only "by administration." He "felt" and desired very little if anything at all (at most he wanted to rise and succeed in the government's hierarchy). He always acted in accordance with the rules, but more than that, and more than simply following orders, he felt compelled to "go beyond" the written law, the norms of constraint, beyond the limit. He was the instrument of a will-to-*jouissance* not necessarily his own.

Kant's moral philosophy, Arendt reminds us, is closely bound to man's faculty of judgment, which rules out blind obedience and condemns the instrumentalization of the other (although his views on marriage as the even exchange of sexual parts could give us, as it has others, pause). Yet, Arendt and Lacan, two thinkers from quite different fields, found themselves disturbed at precisely the same moment by the excess or perversion to which Kant's moral philosophy seemed to lend itself.[27] Lacan published "Kant avec Sade" in 1963, and Hannah Arendt published the series she had written for the *New Yorker* on *Eichmann in Jerusalem* that same year. Lacan found the implications of Kant's maxims—the voice within—scandalously close to Sade's. Arendt, looking at a different kind of perversion, found Adolf Eichmann's self-proclaimed inner sense of his own "duty" a "version of Kant 'for the household use of the little man.' "

In Arendt's account, and by his own, Eichmann was motivated by only one thing: his sense of duty (1963/4: 134).

> He did his *duty*, as he told the police and the court over and over again; he not only obeyed *orders*, he also obeyed the *law*.

Dimly struggling, nonetheless, to make clear that he was not just a "soldier carrying out orders that were clearly criminal in nature and intent," (135) Eichmann "suddenly declared with great emphasis that he had lived his whole life according to Kant's moral precepts, and especially according to a Kantian definition of duty." (135–6)

Arendt objected, on massively philosophical grounds, to Eichmann's self-declared Kantianism—it is patently absurd on its face:

> In this household use, all that is left of Kant's spirit is the demand that a man do more than obey the law, that he go beyond the mere call of obedience and *identify his own will with the principle behind the law—the source from which the law sprang.* In Kant's philosophy that source was practical reason; in Eichmann's household use of him, it was the will of the Führer. (136; ital. mine)[28]

Yet, although he had clearly distorted it, Eichmann actually specifically singled out *The Critique of Practical Reason* as his personal moral guide and spontaneously spouted an "approximately correct definition of the categorical imperative" (136) to the astonishment of Judge Raveh and the audience at his trial in Jerusalem:

'I meant by my remark about Kant that the principle of my will must always be such that it can become the principle of general laws' (which is not the case with theft or murder, for instance, because the thief or the murderer cannot conceivably wish to live under a legal system that would give others the right to rob or murder him).

Eichmann added that he had

read Kant's *Critique of Practical Reason*. He then proceeded to explain that from the moment he was charged with carrying out the Final Solution he had ceased to live according to Kantian principles, that he had known it, and that he had consoled himself with the thought that he no longer 'was master of his own deeds,' that he was unable 'to change anything'. (136)

Eichmann thus confessed to abandoning Kant and betraying the Law rooted in the Kantian principle, claiming as his excuse that he had been "mastered" or overpowered by a force or will beyond his own. Though this admission ought to have vindicated Arendt's severe objections[29] to his describing his own ethics as "Kantian," Arendt shows some hesitancy. She weighs whether Eichmann had really "forgotten" Kant as he set to work accomplishing the Final Solution, finding "the Kantian formula . . . no longer applicable," or whether he had employed it in a twisted way. Indeed, she finds that, far from abandoning it altogether,

he had distorted it to read: Act as if the principle of your actions were the same as that of the legislator or of the law of the land—or, in Hans Frank's formulation of 'the categorical imperative in the Third Reich,' which Eichmann might have known: 'act in such a way that the Führer, if he knew your action, might approve it' (*Die Technik des Staates*, 1942, pp. 15–16). (136)

The scandal here is less that Kant's principles did not hold out against a will to transgress them, but that something in Kant's very principle seemed to an Eichmann (and a Hans Frank) to lend itself to this particular distortion.[30] At best, nothing in the structure of the law conceived on Kantian, formal lines worked to disable this particular perversion—it failed to resist the will-to-*jouissance*—not Eichmann's own, in this case, but the Führer's. (The paradox goes to the heart, as well, of the deadlock in democracy's susceptibility to totalitarianism: how can the people that rules itself with absolute freedom find itself perpetually threatened with rule by dictatorship?)

So, while Arendt details the philosophical *errors* that have permitted such a deadly misreading of the upright German idealist she also reveals how Kantianism twisted around the "fatal" weakness of democracy: its/our failure to confront the "origin" of the Laws in the democratic state:

> Kant, to be sure, had never intended to say anything of the sort; on the contrary, to him every man was a legislator the moment he started to act: by using his 'practical reason' man found the principles that could and should be the principles of law. But it is true that Eichmann's unconscious distortion agrees with what he himself called the version of Kant 'for the household use of the little man.' (136)

We have to continue to ask why an Eichmann felt not only licensed but impelled to respond to a demand to "duty" beyond the Law and to justify this sense with a distorted "philosophy." Our suspicion is that it has to do with the unbearable relation of voice to Superegoic Law, a pressure to which some of the most diligent real philosophers (like Heidegger) were not immune.[31] (What remains more inexplicable, except psychoanalytically, is why Heidegger's philosophical insight into the negative foundation of metaphysics translated at some empirical level into its opposite—an unfathomable alliance with this death drive.)

Lacan's "Kant avec Sade" and Arendt's "Eichmann" seem to me crucial first steps in the direction of incorporating the political into the body of philososphy, of setting up the need for responsibiity under democratic conditions in ways that Heidegger's work seemed to hold promise (and for his followers, like Derrida, continue to promise). For these reasons, the "case" of Eichmann, and Arendt's treatment of it, is ethically instructive. The alternative, of course, is to elaborate a philosophy of responsibility.

Administrative Massacre:
"The Altogether Unprecedented"

In this chilling, difficult, and heartbreaking report on the banality of evil, Hannah Arendt portrays Adolf Eichmann as a kind of neutral functionary, neither hero nor victim of his criminal acts. He acted in no traditional morality play. In this, she goes against the grain and accepts analytically Eichmann's self-professed normality less as an index of his mental health than of the fact of the existence, on the world scene, of a state whose norm was "thou shalt" rather than "thou shalt not" kill.

Watching without sentimentality[32] Eichmann's long, drawn out trial—tellingly, not on charges of genocide, but of "crimes against the Jewish people" and "crimes against Humanity"—unfold in Jerusalem, Arendt waits in vain for the customary theater of Justice to open a dramatization of Good and Evil in his case.[33] The dramatization of Justice doesn't catch on. Arendt grows alarmed when the traditional scene of Judgment, which places the evil doer between a judge who represents the community and the community for whom the judge speaks, does not materialize on stage. Instead, center stage is Eichmann.

A man of "rather modest mental gifts" (135) Eichmann is the man in the glass booth, whose transparency and shielding is both a metaphor for the trial itself and what places him in the typical posture of the "woman" subject, weak and on display. Arendt sees his physical position—placed below tier upon tier of judges, translators, and officials and between the prosecutors and the courtroom—as precluding the traditional work of Justice. Those who watch Eichmann ("medium-sized, slender, middle-aged, with receding hair, ill-fitting teeth, and nearsighted eyes" [5]) over the shoulders of the prosecutors form no "community" whose standards it could be said were the ones he violated. Why are the charges of "crimes against the Jewish people," and "crimes against Humanity" *separate* charges? The charges themselves err by virtue of over- or under- specificity. The result is that the "Jewish people/Humanity"—the "victims"—are not as concrete and defined as "the man in the glass booth." In fact, both "the Jewish people," and "Humanity" have a reduced, remote role, relegated to being an "audience" of literally *no one*—which means, really, they are an audience composed of everyone in the world (former victims and bystanders both). Cast as mere onlookers, peering *over the shoulders* of the prosecutors at the man who ordered and arranged for the deaths of a whole people, they can and will have their opinions shaped mainly by the physical appearance of the man, not by the standards of their "community." Under these conditions, Arendt makes clear, Eichmann is the one who looks like a victim, not an instigator, capable at best of having been an instrument but not an originator of Evil, whose source will be as inexplicable, nebulous and undefined as the "Humanity" he sinned against.

There is an Evil, though its shape is still obscure. Arendt proposes that something "altogether unprecedented" was at work in the very acts of the man who is on trial, a "new crime," for which the "prevailing legal system and current juridical concepts" (294) are entirely inadequate. What cannot be dealt with—justly—under the older forms of separation of individual guilt and group responsibility is this new crime: administrative massacre organized by state apparatus (294). And yet Arendt wants to be able to refer it to Eichmann, to his personal "judgment." She terms her work a "report on his conscience." Thus, though she is a political philosopher, Arendt, like the psychoanalyst, insists on this being an individualized *case.* She seeks not to determine a generic model but to ascertain the point at which Eichmann's will, his relation to his desire (and to the Law), was a factor in his political acts. Though her aim differs, and she will not facilitate his "cure" but only a judgment on the man, she will have reframed the question of the Law to which his drive and his desire respond (as no limit). But Eichmann himself will never be able to "reorder" the elements of his discourse, his own narration of his life, in other than precut formulaic terms.

Why is the "new crime" of "administrative massacre," which is simply the term for modern as opposed to traditional genocide, not yet able to be brought to the bar of justice? Why do those crimes committed above the "individual" level not yet have to face a *decision*, the judgment between Good and Evil? Perhaps it should be put another way: can we not mark Eichmann's original "ethical" decision (to do his "duty") as Lacan did Kant/Sade's with a *vel*—a choice made in such a way as to avoid a decision as to the good, absolutely eliminating one of the options, i.e., making it no choice at all (e.g., "Your money or your life") since without the latter one can not enjoy the former? We can, if we do what Lacan does, linking the *vel* to the *V* of the *volonté de jouir* (the will-to-jouissance). A simulacrum of judgment, the *vel's* act of absolute cutting away preempts and precludes the need for any further judgment or decision: it is a form of final solution.

Hannah Arendt makes a double argument: (1) that the escape from the area of ascertainable facts and personal responsibility that became pandemic in Germany of the Nazi years and of which Eichmann is an example is the only thing that justice can deal with and call to account—the failure to be able to decide between Good and Evil is the only moral failing. Hence her criticism of the widespread response and accusation against the trial of Eichmann ("Who are you to sit in judgment? You might have done the same in his place," etc.). All generalities ("it's Humanity itself on trial"), are for her incorrect from any standpoint that takes justice as its goal: justice is a judgment to be rendered on the deeds and misdeeds, the decisions of a person, an individual.[34]

She also knows that (2) there is, beyond the individual level, a *political* responsibility, which "exists quite apart from what the individual member of a group has done, and therefore can neither be judged in moral terms nor brought before a criminal court." (298) It is this political responsibility that she feels must be separated from the question of the *individual's guilt* or innocence, which are the only things, she tells us, "at stake in a criminal court." Whence her profound repugnance for putting a whole people, or Humanity on trial, in the showcase way that she believes Ben-Gurion is attempting to do. One can take on the "guilt" of his group's "Evil" only in a metaphorical way, and no one can be held responsible for the acts of their whole society. Conversely, no whole society can be judged "guilty," since there will always be individual members who dissented and disagreed. What the issue with Eichmann is, however, is that he felt no need to engage in the individual decision as to Good and Evil; he was "beyond" them by virtue of his being a mere executor of the will of the group, which had its own grounds for the decisions it had come to.

Thus the central structural problem—the principle and self-legislation—remains. It is even emblematized in the Eichmann case by the locale of the trial itself: Eichmann is tried not in a supreme court, but in a parliamentary building: Beth Ha'am—The House of the People is where they have installed this Beth Hamispath, or House of Justice. Arendt, of course, concludes her book as she must, by reaffirming that "the question of individual guilt and innocence are the only things at stake in a criminal court." (298) That she nonetheless felt compelled to raise the question of the guilt or innocence of "political responsibility" is telling. "It is quite conceivable that certain political responsibilities among nations might some day be adjudicated in an international court," (298) which she immediately qualifies as necessarily not a criminal court ("What is inconceivable is that such a court would be a criminal tribunal which pronounces on the guilt or innocence of individuals.") She has also shown how far Eichmann's "Kantianism" protected him from bearing responsibility for any criminality or evil to be attached to an openly expressed "political will." The question remains, then, how can the crime of genocide be adjudged a crime as such? On whose head would the guilt lie?

Despite her tremendous reluctance to consider "political responsibility" as falling within the realm of criminal justice, Arendt has, I think, actually opened a path. Her inquiry turns into one concerning the relation of genocide to written and unwritten law—the same one I proposed at the outset. And in my view, the fact that it is a woman, classically "suspicious of the signifier" (Apollon: 3) who was able first to pinpoint this problem (i.e., demanding a return of the signifier, or a kind of full speech) is what links her work to the question of feminist ethics, drive, and *jouissance* with which I opened this discussion.

Conscience and the Mother's Voice, or, Why Adolf Eichmann Was Not a Woman

For Arendt, simply having kept its Laws "unwritten"—free of content or pathological objects—granted tacit permission for National Socialism's plan of genocide. Any Law explicitly directing genocide would have already been the result of a *vel* and the expression of a specific *will-to*.[35] Single individuals were not so much loath to engage in such expressions as structurally impeded from doing so: their "will" was not "their own" as Eichmann recounted. One had to be attuned to the "principle behind the law,"[36] which should be the will of the people. But functionaries like Eichmann had no difficulty in locating the will behind the law, because they identified it with the actual, if only indirectly heard, Voice of the Führer.

For very practical reasons, of course, Hitler's genocidal program had to remain unwritten because of its "criminal" nature: international public opinion would have mobilized more quickly against it. The only language ("Officialese") to which the Nazi regime condescended to transmit its orders constituted a new kind of "discourse" framed by a "language rule" (the new *Amtssprache;* the *Sprachregelung*). This rule was to remake what once, under common civil agreements, had been called "the lie" into a form of special honorific "secret" bearing: "Those who were told explicitly of the Führer's order were no longer mere 'bearers of orders,' but were advanced to 'bearers of secrets,' and a special oath was administered to them," pp. 84–5). The "secret" therefore was, in formal communication terms, also technically "content free."

Mladen Dolar sees the primacy of *voice as such* as the "principle behind the law" operating in fascism:

> Fascism feeds on the voice, onto death. This is the case of Peter Gemeinder, who died of exhaustion, in August 1931, after a speech of two hours, preceded by 2,000 other speeches. (Dolar 1984: 42; my translation.)

Dolar continues:

> But what does this exalting voice say exactly? We don't get to know by reading the fascist reports of fascist speeches. We find a flood of words on the impressions of the reporter . . . on the atmosphere of the public, dead silences, ovations, etc. In the long poetization by Goebbels on his first encounter with the Führer we find only three specific words that the Führer speaks . . . 'honor, work, flag.' " (42)

He concludes that, "merely by emitting a voice the master becomes master, and merely by virtue of being the receiver of this voice ("his master's voice") a crowd becomes a crowd." (42)[37]

If all speech, as Lacan argued, "calls for a reply," it seeks an auditor. Where the error—in politics as in the analytic session—lies is in mistaking the call for a reply (*appel;* FE 1966: 243) for an appeal. As *appeal,* the primary emphasis is on the "feelings" of the hearer:

> If the psychoanalyst [but we could not also say political subject?—JFM] is not aware that this is how the function of speech operates ['to call for a reply'], he will simply experience its appeal all the more strongly, and if the first thing to

make itself heard is the void, it is within himself that he will experience it, and it is beyond speech that he will seek a reality to fill this void. (*EE:* 1977/66: 40).

Self-absolved from any need to *reply* (if only with silence), the unaware listener will "echo his own nothingness" in the other, and it is this "echo" that is the source of the appeal of "empty" speech: an "appeal" to the "very principle of truth," which Lacan tells us is first and foremost

the appeal of the void, in the ambiguous gap of an attempted seduction of the other by the means of which the subject has come compliantly to rely and to which he will commit the monumental construct of his narcissism. (40)

What is at stake is less "formalism for formalism's sake" in some new critical vein, but what "mere formalism" accomplishes: the *evacuation* of the pathetic content, its replacement by formal impressions and expressions, as the "response" (which is not an answer) to the insistence excess of *Jouissance* in the Other, its final Mastery over All Meanings, its being the Signified. Hence the drive to "senselessness" in the discourse of fascism without the concomitant and flexible comprehension of "form" to be found in post-Kantian thought. The fascist "meaninglessness" of words puts us, *not* on the side of the semiotic division of signifier/signified, but *into* the all-or-nothing game of a "full" meaning, yielded entirely to an Other who rewards us with the nugatory remainder, an empty "senselessness" for our being—but a senselessness experienced as a sensory impression, a certain *jouissance.*

Eichmann showed "great susceptibility to catch words and stock phrases, combined with his incapacity for ordinary speech" (p. 86). Arendt's analysis of Eichmann's speech should give us pause. According to her, the "inner voice" of conscience in Eichmann was perhaps less silent than voiced over. "Genuinely incapable of uttering a single sentence that was not a cliché," Eichmann claimed that "Officialese [*Amtssprache*] is my only language." (p. 48) At times, of course, Eichmann showed "uplift." He thrilled whenever he was able to revoice or utilize a cliché that made him feel part of the perpetual "movement of the Universe." (p. 27) Eichmann reports being "elated" when he was able to link his "mood" with its "catch phrase," (p. 62) labeling such fragments with the German term for touchstone quotations, *"Geflügelte Worte"* ("winged words," p. 48). With them, he was "in movement," (p. 43) he "lived for his idea."[39] (p. 42) That attunement with the idea had no room for "pathological" emotions:

> When he said in the police examination that he would have sent his own father to his death if that had been required, he did not mean merely to stress the extent to which he was under orders, and ready to obey them; he also meant to show what an 'idealist' he had always been. The perfect 'idealist,' like everybody else, had of course his personal feelings and emotions, but he would never permit them to interfere with his actions if they came into conflict with his 'idea.' (p. 42)

A barely perceptible thread, then, leads from the evacuation, opened by Kantian philosophy, of specific, affective content in the Law, to the absolute emptiness at the center of Eichmann's thought, the absolute void Arendt found in her report on Eichmann's conscience. Eichmann's salient "inability to speak" according to Arendt, "was closely connected with an inability to *think*, namely, to think from the standpoint of somebody else" (p. 49).

Listening to Eichmann from the "pre-Kantian," sympathetic or "pathological" posture (i.e., trying to "think from the standpoint of somebody else"), the Jerusalem judges imagined that Eichmann's perpetual recourse to "empty talk" showed the "accused wished to cover up other thoughts which, though hideous, were not empty." (p. 49) But Arendt finds otherwise. The presumption of especially savage passions is perfectly refuted by Eichmann's verbal demeanor. His clichés are purely formal. (Arendt asks, parenthetically, "Was it these clichés that the psychiatrists thought so 'normal' and 'desirable'?" pp. 48–9) Indeed, Eichmann's whole posture parallels Lacan's analysis of the sadistic pervert, who is precisely not a man filled with irresistibly savage urges, but executioner of the will-to-*jouissance* of the Other.[40]

Precisely because no written law specifically prohibited (or permitted) genocide, the command to genocide appeared as a pure function of the will of the Other. As such, it became Eichmann's duty, but not only his. It had an astonishingly immediate appeal to the state's chief functionaries, few of whom owed their careers to the Nazis, and might not have been thought reliable or responsive to Hitler.[41] Wannsee, where the Final Solution was laid out as the government's program in 1942, was a "cozy little social gathering" (113). Eichmann was secretary to this Conference of the Undersecretaries of State, and it resolved all his doubts. Arendt quotes Eichmann's deposition:

> 'Here now, during this conference, the most prominent people had spoken, the Popes of the Third Reich.' Now he could see with his own eyes and hear with his own ears that not only Hitler . . . but the good old Civil Service were vying and fighting with each other for the honor of taking the lead in these 'bloody' matters. 'At that moment . . . I felt free of all guilt' *Who was he to judge?* (p. 114)

Arendt comments, "Well, he was neither the first nor the last to be ruined by modesty" (114); but when such modesty was a function of what Eichmann himself termed a "death whirl" (p. 115) his failure to "judge" becomes obscene. His modesty instead indexes a different posture: Eichmann as the one who sacrifices his personal judgment, desires, and emotions to serve the will-to-*jouissance* of Hitler.

For Eichmann, "the death whirl" circulated around the Führer's voice. Arendt writes that the Führer's words had the "force of law" for Eichmann (Führerworte haben Gesetzkraft); which meant,

> among other things, that if the order came directly from Hitler it did not have to be in writing. He tried to explain that this was why he had never asked for a written order from Hitler . . . but had demanded to see a written order from Himmler. (p. 148)

Just what "satisfying Hitler" meant—the sacrifice or "ethical renunciation" he demanded of the German people of the 1930s and 1940s—is described movingly by Arendt. What the average German had to sacrifice was precisely his or her hard won place in the Symbolic Order, in "civilization"—he or she had to give up the symbolic modes of fending off the call of the will-to-*jouissance:*

> . . . just as the law in civilized countries assumes that the voice of conscience tells everybody "Thou shalt not kill," even though man's natural desires and inclinations may at

times be murderous, so the law of Hitler's land demanded that the voice of conscience tell everybody: "Thou shalt kill," although the organizers of the massacres knew full well that murder is against the normal desires and inclinations of most people. Evil in the Third Reich had lost the quality by which most people recognized it—the quality of temptation. Many Germans and many Nazis, probably an overwhelming majority of them, must have been tempted *not* to murder, *not* to rob, *not* to let their neighbors go off to their doom. . . . But, God knows, they had learned how to resist temptation. (150)

The "voice of conscience" called on the people to give way on their desire. After the administration and execution of Hitler's genocidal plan, justice can no longer presume a certain content or character to the "voice of conscience." In order for there to be justice based on "conscience," Arendt writes, "unlawfulness must 'fly like a black flag above . . . as a warning reading 'Prohibited!' " (148) By contrast,

in Hitler's criminal regime this 'black flag' with its 'warning sign' flies as 'manifestly' above what normally is a lawful order—for instance, not to kill innocent people just because they happen to be Jews—as it flies above a criminal order under normal circumstances. To fall back on an unequivocal voice of conscience—or, in the even vaguer language of the jurists, on a 'general sentiment of humanity' (Oppenheim-Lauterprach in *International Law*, 1952)—not only begs the question, it signifies a deliberate refusal to take notice of the central moral, legal, and political phenomena of our century. (148)

Genocide and its peculiar "call to conscience" is that "central moral, legal, and political phenomenon of our century": this we can no longer doubt, as genocidal programs increasingly dominate interethnic strife around the globe today, and as Lacan predicted, on the basis of his analysis of the pivotal role played by the *object a* (in this case, the *voice*) in the developing ethics of the drive.[42] References to "the Law" can no longer claim Symbolic status; they are no longer assumed to be delimited by the signifier. Its wounds and castrations are nowhere near as radical as those fascism (and Kant) required. Instead, they embody and support a logic of sacrifice to the *jouissance* embodied in the "principle behind the Law."

The psychoanalytic "principle behind the Law" in Eichmann's case is, as Žižek argues, the obscene ("Maternal") will-to-*jouissance* beyond the regulation of the signifier. An ethics of Drive relates to how life can be lived 'at the letter' (*petit a*), which adumbrates the Other *Jouissance*, rather than presuming the effectiveness of the phallic answer to the It. The *voice* as object *a*, the little *a* other, seems to carry this "principle behind the law"—the Thing or the "maternal" will-to-*jouissance* in its wake—together with the absolute dispossession of the subject. Object *a* performs a special kind of "balance" of the Drive (as both *equilibrium* and *remainder*, as in arithmetical division). In the equation that Lacan called *perversion*, Lacan demonstrated, with no little irony, how the solution devised by the "perverted" subject (whose connection to the symbolic mediation of excess and lack is loosened, and who thus faces the impossible "kernel" of satisfaction—the Real of Death Drive or will-to-*jouissance*) is to yield entirely to the (M)Other. More precisely, the subject *identifies itself* with the object *a*, which seems to carry the ("her") will-to-*jouissance*.[43] The subject, that is, makes itself into the *object a*, agent of the enjoyment of the Other, the object *a*, "issued" directly from the will-to-*jouissance* of the Other.[44]

Arendt's account does not psychoanalytically charge the "voice" as the "principle behind the law" with being a link to the Mother; she does, however, demonstrate the (potentially) fatal weakness in the modern state that relentlessly and remorselessly lends itself to the recurrence of genocide as the deep flaw in the origin-logic of the Laws. She does not imagine a solution; her imperturbable analysis of its Evil leaves any remedy but the supranational written Law out of play. A psychoanalytic accent ought to permit us to think the possibility of the impossibility of democracy and its perplexed relation to the Other *Jouissance*.

Feminine Sexuality and Resisting the Mother's Voice

From that very excess in femininity, something, 'a work,' can be made through a linking of that other *jouissance* sustaining the feminine subject to the symbolic and to culture. The child, upon whom the woman leaves her traces, should not be the 'work' of its mother. Today's authors, artists, physicians, and other prominent women testify to how, relying on the letter of the body where the *jouissance* of the Real is excluded but returns, they have taken it upon themselves to produce a new object of desire that sustains social life. The feminine thus reveals itself in the connection with the Real of a *jouissance* that must be inscribed in a somewhere that forcibly will be a 'no man's land.' (Bergeron, 1992:97)

Between Mother and Sister, Jocasta and Antigone, who can choose? How did the lethal "Maternal" voice, against which civilizations have for ages attempted to erect phallic barriers, come into its own in our time? That is, why does it command the ethical ground in our modern, democratic era? In the foregoing, I have tried to demonstrate how both the "principle behind the Law" (maternal *jouissance*) and its executive arm (sororal *demand*; Eichmann's "duty")[45] are, in all theoretical treatments, from deconstruction to psychoanalysis, forged in an alliance with the ultimate *jouissance*, the death drive, and hence, the Mother.

If too little has been done to remark the equation of the (maternal) voice with the central political question of our time (genocide),[46] however, perhaps too much has been made of the *parental* or *maternal* axis and not enough of the ways in which *femininity* has also always resisted the Mother, the reduction of Drive to the return slope of biological reproduction. "Femininity" reshapes, responds to, and returns from the relation to the 'Mother' (death, absolute *jouissance*). A nonmaternal "ethic of the feminine," its modality of Drive, demands to be formulated.

Not the phallic signifier alone, but its short-circuit, its bypass by a different kind of "social link" brings, for the *feminine* the insistence of the "letter" (object *a*), and woman's body (*sexuality*), to a relation to Drive. If this feminine Drive can not be articulated in *language* as such, the impossibility of its articulation can. Here I turn to the work GIFRIC has been doing with "The Other *Jouissance*" and to what Lucie Cantin has named "An Ethic of the Impossible" (1993).

Cantin follows Apollon's suggestion (1993) intensifying the Lacanian alignment of Woman with the "Other *Jouissance*," the nonphallic one. This is the *jouissance* that escapes the limits and framing proffered by time-honored masculine means, summed up as "the impossible inadequacy of language in relation to the real of the body that causes the wound of femininity." (Cantin, 1993) What distinguishes the feminine from the perverted (Eichmann/Sadique) position is that the feminine ethic accepts the "absolute requirement to find a path in the realm of the signifier and to have it recognized on the social scene." The woman here accepts an obligatory link with the Other that, Cantin argues, permits the feminine quest for *jouissance* to find "another destiny than perversion or subjective downfall." In contrast to Eichmann's need for ever emptier signifiers, purely formal, ritual repetitions as his ticket to ride on the "death whirl," or Death Drive, what Cantin is working out here is the feminine demand for "full speech," linking, "without guarantee, the letter of the body to the signifier."

In even starker contrast to Eichmann's desire for the security of institutional warrant not only for all his acts, but for the ("lawless") license to go "above the law," the traditional "lawlessness" of the woman who is de-domesticated, unhoused, or unattached to institutional settings, permits her to forgo such symbolic supports for her "full speech." Wounded by femininity she bears the brunt not, as Eichmann did, of embodying the *lack* in Drive, but its excess. Her balance is won by expressing precisely and with passion where and why the language of institutions (officialese) must fail.

Conclusion

To resume, then, the need for a written Law specifically prohibiting genocide. (1) It should by now be evident that "the pleasure principle" needs its ethical mandate, beyond the "reality principle" of a social field that can no longer be considered homeostatic and nonconflictual. The fantasmatic character of human pleasure must not only be accounted for in any ethic today, it must take primacy. Fantasy formations grows ever more central in our lives; fantasy is the support of our "reality."[47]

(2) The writing of such a Law would permit the enunciation of positively negative content, thereby reframing the Other as lacking; and it would also provide a way for the increasingly stateless "citizens" of the postmodern, "global" community, to be asked to *decide* on the necessarily paired alternatives (Good and Evil, to kill or to love) that have once again become the starkest of possibilities for them. Only this kind of decision—which is not that of the *vel*—suffers resistance to the will of the people when it is a malignant will-to-*jouissance*.

Notes

* A shorter version of this essay appeared in *Topoi* (1993) in a special issue on "Femininity and Jouissance."

1. As worked out by neo-Lacanian analysts (Žižek, 1991; Apollon, 1992; Bergeron, 1990, 1992; and Cantin, 1990 and 1992). My precedents for this coupling are GRIF, which counts Lacanian analysts on the board, a journal that devoted a special issue to Arendt; and Philippe Lacoue-Labarthe's work on both authors. Arendt's personal link to Heidegger and Lacan's interest in the German philosopher's work on language (he translated Heidegger's "Logos") make the comparison potentially fruitful. Lacan and Arendt share a similar reluctance to condemn Heidegger's political behavior explicitly, though Arendt refuses him the honor she does Jaspers, of counting him among the few persons of "conscience" who never wavered in their resistance to Hitler (p. 103–4). Recent efforts to distinguish "civilization" in the "French" senses from the more Germanic model of "culture" appear in historical perspective in Elizabeth Roudinesco (1990), and Geoffrey Hartman's (1992)

2. In *The Regime of the Brother: After the Patriarchy* (1991) I argued that national socialism and fascism were disorders or aberrations of the political form of fraternity inaugurated with modern democracy, not disorders of "patriarchy" or the Father. I recently ran across important studies by Pierre Naveau and Mladen Dolar (1984) that support this view.

I am not altogether reluctant to call "maternal" this *jouissance* in fascism, but must dissent from the more simplistic version—"the feminization of the masses"—offered by Adorno and Horkheimer (1982/68). After Lacan, feminism, and feminine artists, we can now see Woman more clearly as liberated from and resistant to "maternal" *jouissance* because she no longer needs to (nor can she) retreat to the mysterious posture in which Oedipal civilization kept her (and her Mother) safely locked away.

3. Myths, like Oedipus, are representative of such temporizations; but symbolic laws also operate as similar modes of dealing with impossible conflicts that can neither be faced nor, if experienced, remembered.

4. In tracing the start-up of *Drive*, Freud (1911/1963: 22) noted that the "first" pleasures or enjoyments in "mental" life are *hallucinatory* fulfillments of inner needs. Thus the "enjoyment" or pleasure attributed to a prior "state of nature" for any form of *mind* is already the product of desire: "Whatever was thought of (desired) was simply imagined in an hallucinatory form, as still happens to-day with our dream-thoughts every night."

5. Lacan's *Seminar IX* (1978/73:169–177) makes the Drive one of the four fundamental concepts of psychoanalysis, and he is liberal in honoring Freud's construction. Lacan explicates Freud's metapsychological concept (setting it apart from "the life force" 165) by emphasizing that it is the original break with a natural, reproductive cycle. Drive exceeds that cycle with a "partial circuit" of its own, a movement out and away from—and back to—a prior *jouissance.* What the partial circuit of *drive* is for Freud, a "hallucinated object," is for Lacan a *fantasy* object (a): breast, feces, gaze, voice. (Recall that for Freud, all human pleasure is "mental," i.e., fantasized or partially hallucinated):

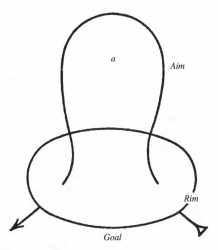

The play *in drive* is between the loss of *jouissance* (symbolic symptom) and its impossibility (the Real). Drive breaks out of, but also forms the closure of the "life" cycle. Stitch and bow string both it sutures life to what interrupts it: death. The death drive is thus fully implied by the life cycle.

6. Freud's "Thoughts for the Times on War and Death" articulated this with great clarity.

7. This partially accounts for Lacan's interest in Klein's placing "Oedipus" in the preverbal. The partial drives, anal, oral, scopic, part-object, so publicly pronounced and prominent culturally today, are not counted "regressions" by Lacan, for whom "regression" is an entrenchment rather than a dissolution of the ego. He is far from Chasseguet-Smirgel's argument in *Creativity and Perversion* (1984: 58ff.) that all collective actions have the character of "anality." If the partial drives are more "primitive" they are so only in the Rousseauian/Lévi-Straussian sense of being less veiled by symbolic orderings, and thus more starkly

facing the will-to-*jouissance*. As I argued in *The Regime of the Brother*, their prominence is a corollary of modern democracy, which is not inherently "patriarchal" or paternal in character. (Chasseguet-Smirgel sees anal/fraternal movements as a departure from democracy).

8. In his essay, "Marx et le symptôme," Pierre Naveau claims we escape the *dream* (which risks touching on the Real) into the "less burdensome" domain of fantasmatic reality, keeping us at a distance from our terrifying "meaning," which is always a *"jouissance"* (or in earlier Freudian terms, a desire-fulfilled). Naveau argues, following Kant, that the transition from the "symptôme" (which has a *pathetic* basis) to the *fantôme* (which does not), makes the fantasy the locus of "reality," reality's support.

Willy Apollon (1992:2) puts it this way: "The object is offered by the phantasm for the structuring of the drive." Apollon's study works out brilliantly the space between woman as subject of the signifier and woman as feminine object of an impossible *jouissance*.

9. See Slavoj Žižek (1989: 82–3):

> Fascism is obscene in so far as it perceives directly the ideological form as its own end, as an end in itself—remember Mussolini's famous answer to the question 'How do the fascists justify their claim to rule Italy? What is their programme?'; 'Our programme is very simple: we want to rule Italy!' The ideological power of fascism lies precisely in the feature that was perceived by liberal or leftist critics as its greatest weakness; in the utterly void, formal character of its appeal, in the fact that it demands obedience and sacrifice for their own sake. For fascist ideology, the point is not the instrumental value of the sacrifice, it is the very form of the sacrifice itself, 'the spirit of sacrifice,' which is the cure against the liberal-decadent disease. It is also clear why fascism was so terrified by psychoanalysis: psychoanalysis enables us to locate an obscene enjoyment at work in this act of formal sacrifice.

10. See Lacan's *Names-of-the-Father* seminar, tr. in *Television*.

11. J.A. Miller's argument on *extimacy* is that the cultural pressure or will-to *jouissance* is literally unbearable, since it is civilization nakedly commanding its own violation, as it were. Its unbearable nature in turn gives rise to racism: the cultural other, by apparently taking *jouissance* differently from you, incites both envy—and denial of their capacity to enjoy as you cannot. See Renata Salecl (1990).

12. I look directly to Drive as crucial in distinguishing, like Bergeron, 'maternal' from 'feminine' responses to the insistence of the real in the

call of *'jouissance'*—what Lacan called "the Other *Jouissance,*" and to elaborating an alternative feminine ethic: what Cantin calls, in relation to her reading of Teresa d'Avila, an "ethic of the impossible."

13. See Danielle Bergeron's essay on "Femininity," (1992); Slavoj Žižek (1991: 272), and Juliet Flower MacCannell, "Desire" (1992).

14. Kant, like the earlier "democratic" Rousseau and the later "liber-ationist" Freud, was said to have operated a similar awareness of the de-centering of the subject through a parallel "Copernican" revolution, bringing the human to a new being in the world. Lacan, Séminaire I 1975:16.

15. In "Kant avec Sade," Lacan points out that Sade's "republican" maxim (my right to enjoy your body and your reciprocal right to enjoy mine) is only possible where the ownership of one person by another is forbidden. *Jouissance* (enjoyment, profit) is not the same as possession.

16. In his *Seminar III* on *Psychosis,* as in the *Ethics* of *Seminar VII,* Lacan notes that all of Freud's versions of the father were adumbrations of the "malevolent super ego" of the formulations that postdate *Beyond the Pleasure Principle: Ego and Id, Group Psychology and the Analysis of the Ego,* "The passing of the Oedipus complex"—in short the formulations based on the castration complex.

17. English translation: "It is natural to have an appetite. . . . I find that it is not in good order to not always have something to eat. What a devil of an economy, men who stuff themselves on everything while others, who have an importuning stomach just like theirs have nothing to bite down on." Denis Diderot, *Rameau's Nephew,* 1966, p. 121.

18. They render incessant media parades and celebrations of third world poverty suspect. Pierre Naveau (1984) sees the fascist leader's strategy of privation for his most ardent supporters as drawing the fol-lowers to him by his *not appeasing* demand—as the paternal figure is sup-posed to.

19. "The right to *jouissance,* were it recognized, would relegate the domination of the pleasure principle to a forevermore outdated era. In enunciating it, Sade causes the ancient axis of ethics to slip . . . for everyone: this axis is no other than the egoism of happiness. It cannot be said that all reference to it is extinguished in Kant. . . ." (Lacan 1963/90: 71E; reference to English texts by Lacan hereafter are marked *E.*)

20. This was Lacan's refinement on the notion of the "partial drives" (oral, anal, scopic, genital) in Freud—finding their specific embodiment in fantasy objects. These partial drives (partial because not entirely submitted

to the Death Drive) *represent* various *jouissances* that life in society makes less unbearable than unavowable. They are not *jouissance* itself, but a particular relation to an object (a) credited with a relation to *jouissance.*

21. Recall that Lacan's *"Jouissance de l'Autre"* respected Freud's discussion of *drive* and "the two principles of mental functioning" (the pleasure and reality principles): it is always a *retrospective illusion.* The object of drive is always "hallucinatory" in character, thoroughly dependent for its image on the very *desire* (mental) that is both the product and the origin of a break with the natural circuit of satisfactions.

22. Here see Freud's essay "On the passing of the Oedipus complex."

23. The recent media dramatization of the execution of Robert Alton Harris overtly mobilized public sentiment against capital punishment, but a major side effect of it was to suppress awareness that it is a punishment disproportionately meted out to men of color.

24. I was shocked to learn that the United States has consistently refused to ratify the antigenocide treaty devised by the United Nations. If, after Rousseau, the Law is deemed less the repression of a desire than a positive form and force of the will—*la volonté générale*—the formal force of the democratic polity, it seems the "national will" must imagine itself to be Good—presumed innocent, in all senses of the term. Law that would express a will could not afford to recognize its desire.

25. See P.T. Geach (1967: 64–73): Since Kant's time peoples have supposed that there is another sort of relevant reply—an appeal not to inclination but to the Sense of Duty. Now indeed a man may be got by training into a state of mind in which 'You *must* not' is a sufficient answer to 'Why shouldn't I?'; in which, giving this answer to himself, or hearing it given by others, strikes him with a quite peculiar awe; in which, perhaps, he even thinks he 'must not' ask why he 'must not' . . . Moral philosophers of the Objectivist school, like Sir David Ross, would call this 'apprehension of one's obligations'; it does not worry them that, but for God's grace, this sort of training can make a man 'apprehend' practically anything as his 'obligations'. (Indeed they admire a man who does what he thinks he *must* do regardless of what he actually does; is he not acting from a Sense of Duty, which is the highest motive? (pp. 70–1)

26. See Žižek (1989: 82–8):

> Fascist ideology is based upon a purely formal imperative; obey, because you must! In other words, renounce enjoyment,

sacrifice yourself and do not ask about the meaning of it—the value of the sacrifice lies in its very meaninglessness; true sacrifice is for its own end; you must find positive fulfillment in the sacrifice itself, not in its instrumental value; it is this renunciation, this giving up of enjoyment itself, which produces a certain surplus-enjoyment. This surplus produced through renunciation is the Lacanian *objet petit a*, the embodiment of surplus-enjoyment. . . .

27. "The law as empty form in the *Critique of Practical Reason* corresponds to time as pure form in the *Critique of Pure Reason*. The law does not tell us *what* we must do, it merely tells us 'you must!', leaving us to deduce from it the good, that is, the object of this pure imperative." p. x, Gilles Deleuze (1984/63: x).

Žižek (1991) suggests that such exhortation denotes an absolute prohibition at work—it is the other side of "you must not!" The point is that absolute freedom to enjoy beyond the limit brings with it countless prohibitions for the little o other. "Partial" enjoyments are sacrificed, e.g., the so-called vegetarianism of Hitler, and bans on smoking, drinking, meat, loud music, free speech, noise, etc.

28. Lacan called Kant an obsessional, keeping him this side of psychosis and perversion. But he also saw how Sade would find his perverse position in a way quite parallel to Kant. As to "obsessional intrasubjectivity," Lacan also said that "the realization of full speech" began with its opposite, "hysterical intersubjectivity," (*EE* 1977/66: 46) or "femininity's" proto-discourse.

29. The question of the status of "practical reason" as woman's work, as "household" law, cannot itself be addressed here, but it should be seriously rethought. Classic political theory (Arendt does not seem to differ on the matter) claims that one must leave the "household" to become a responsible *citizen* of the polis. Psychoanalytically, however, we should make an effort to recalibrate and/or reconcile this oedipal posture with the postmodern family and household. Moreover, the "household" of Eichmann's time and place ("Kinder, Kuche, Kirche") was itself a hyperreal, artificial reconstruction, a *ghost* of the family, a retro-version of a family-time that had already passed. The reader should also look at Žižek (1989: 82–3), and Dean MacCannell (1992: 184ff.) on Nazi aesthetics.

30. Arendt was a student of both Jaspers and Heidegger, and she is aghast at Eichmann's claims to Kantian ethics: "This was outrageous on the face of it, and also incomprehensible, since Kant's moral philosophy is so closely bound up with man's faculty of judgment, which rules out blind obedience." (Arendt 1963/4:136).

31. Arendt has thus pinpointed the perverse use of Kant as agent in the process of the Final Solution. She stops at that and refuses to connect Kant's work to her argument, made only in the supplement to the first edition of the text, that genocide could possibly be made the subject of a written law—an international, if not a national, crime. She felt Eichmann should have been tried by an international tribunal, but, of course, there is no law for this. . . .

32. This question has been raised by others: On Heidegger's maternal double bind and response to the mother's "call," see Avital Ronell, 1990 and Derrida, 1985. Heidegger's case is all the more peculiar since he deeply understood the questions we raise here concerning voice and death drive. As Giorgio Agamben puts it, apropos of Heidegger's response to "negativity," If the relationship between language and death "remains still unthought," it is

> because the Voice—which constitutes the possibility of this relationship—is the unthinkable on which metaphysics bases every possiblity of thought, the unspeakable on which it bases its whole of speakability. Metaphysics is the *thought and will of being*, that is, *the thought and will of the Voice* (or thought and will of death); but this "thought" and this "will" must remain unthematized

because they can only be thematized in terms of the most extreme negativity (1991:88). It is easy to see how Lacan felt fascinated by Heidegger, who seems to have found the "maternal death drive/voice" combination, and we note in passing that Derrida remains more or less an orthodox Heideggerian in his critique of voice, full presence, metaphysics, etc.

33. Arendt follows Raoul Hilberg in utterly rejecting the long European tradition of *anti-Semitism* as the principal cause of the Holocaust and for this she has borne a great deal of criticism by her fellow Jews.

34. See Pierre Naveau's comments (1984: 20ff.) on Michelet's comprehension of the need for theater and ethics in modern democracy, as well as Mnouchkine's Théâtre du Soleil in Paris today, which is far more politically attractive than Michelet's conception. See also J. MacCannell (1991) on democracy and theater since Rousseau.

35. In working this out I have also tried to respond to the curious article I read in the infamous Belgian *Le Soir volé*'s special issue dedicated to anti-Semitism in 1942, which berated the Jews for having systematically infiltrated Europe with the vile idea of "justice."

36. Recent examples of "unwritten laws" and their connection to

modern mass slaughter are the more or less complete lapse, since World War II, in formal declarations of war whenever hostilities are undertaken as is the burial alive of "thousands of Iraqi soldiers" by the United States armed forces in the Persian Gulf war, because, as Pentagon officials explained, there was no written law against it. The Pentagon said there was a "gap" in the law (Patrick J. Sloyan, 1992:10):

Washington—The Pentagon said yesterday that a "gap" in laws governing warfare made it legally permissible during the gulf war for U.S. tanks to bury thousands of Iraqi troops in their trenches and for the U.S. warplanes to bomb the enemy retreating along the so called Highway of Death. . . . *Newsday* disclosed in September that many Iraqi troops were buried alive when the First Mechanized Infantry Division attacked an 8,000 man division defending Saddam Hussein's front line.

The Pentagon later claimed that the "heat of the battle" obscured Iraqi efforts to surrender; but no a priori constraint on the right to such mass solutions is conceded by U.S. officials. The law of war, they state, "permits the attack of enemy combatants at any time, whether advancing, retreating, or standing still."

37. Or "above the law," as in the famous quote from Oliver North's secretary, Fern Hall, justifying her illegal destruction of government records in the Iran-Contra affair.

38. French originals: "Le fascisme se nourrit de la voix, jusqu'à la mort. C'est le cas de Peter Gemeinder qui est mort d'exaustion, en août, 1931, après un discours de deux heures, précédé de deux mille autres discours." (42)

"Mais cette voix exaltante, que dit-elle au juste? A lire les rapports facistes sur les discours fascistes, on n'arrive jamais à le savoir. On trouve un déluge de mots sur les impressions du rapporteur . . . sur l'atmosphère du public, les silences mortels, les ovations, etc. Dans la longue poétisation de Goebbels sur sa première rencontre avec le Führer, on ne trouve que trois mots précis de ce que le Führer dit . . . 'honneur, travail, drapeau.'" (42)

> "C'est en émettant la voix que le maître devient le maître et
> c'est en tant que recepteur de cette voix ('la voix de son
> maître') qu'une foule devient une foule." (Dolar, 1984: 42–3)

39. Eichmann's fantasy at first is that he will "save" the Jews by his
actions. He calls himself a "Zionist": "He hardly thought of anything but
a 'political solution' . . . and how to 'get some firm ground under the feet
of the Jews'." (Arendt, 1963/4: 41) That "expulsion" under the guise of salvation inevitably turned to extermination is, however, predicted by
Eichmann's relation to *jouissance*. Since he himself only felt "elated"
when swept up as a part of the "Movement of History," Eichmann's desire
to pin the Jews to the "ground" "spares" them this "elevation" and
"movement," which he himself terms a "death whirl." The Jews would
thus go "below" and remain in "the past," reaching the endpoint of the
death drive without having to suffer its *jouissance*.

40. The true sadist, as Slavoj Žižek says, is the one who works not for
his own desire, but on behalf of the Other's *jouissance*, as its Agent or
Executioner. See "The Limits of the Semiotic Approach to Psychoanalysis" (1990).

41. Arendt reports that Heydrich was pleasantly surprised at how few
difficulties he had enlisting the active help of all the Ministries and the
whole Civil Service needed for the Final Solution. There was "more than
happy agreement on the part of the participants; the Final Solution was
greeted with 'extraordinary enthusiasm' by all present." (1963/4: 112–3)

42. See *Television* (1990/74: 32–3) for Lacan's remarks on the growth
of racism.

43. Lacan (1977: 7) "Le trait unaire nous intéresse parce que, comme
Freud le souligne, il n'a pas spécialement à faire avec une personne aimé.
Une personne peut être indifférente, et pourtant un des ses traits sera
choisi comme constituant la base d'une identification. C'est ainsi que
Freud croit pouvoir rendre compte de l'identification à la petite moustache
du Führer, dont chacun sait qu'elle a joué un grand rôle."

44. Speaking of *identification neutre*, Lacan (1977: 7) writes, "The
unary trait interests us because, as Freud emphasizes, it has nothing particularly to do with a beloved person. A person can be indifferent, and nevertheless one of their traits will be selected as constituting the basis for an
identification. It is thus that Freud thinks he is able to realize the identification with the Führer's little mustache, of which everyone knows it
played a major role." (French in endnote; my trans.)

45. Sade's Juliette rapes her mother. See Angela Carter (1978). Also

the new statistic showing the most dramatic rise in the rate of murders committed is by teenage girls.

46. See Lacoue-Labarthe (1989/88). He is noteworthy for following both Arendt and Lacan in the study of Heidegger here.

47. Note that Euro-Disney in France is restricted to only one of the "Lands" Disney's company devised for the Anaheim Disneyland: "Fantasyland."

References

Agamben, Giorgio, *Language and Death: The Place of Negativity.* Translated by Karen E. Pinus and Michael Hardt. Minneapolis and Oxford: University of Minnesota Press, 1991. (orig. Italian 1982).

Apollon, Willy, Bergeron Danielle, and Cantin Lucie, *Traiter la psychose,* Québec: Gifric, Collection Noeud, 1990.

Apollon, Willy, "Four Seasons in Femininity," *Topoi,* 1993.

Arendt, Hannah, *Eichmann in Jerusalem: A Report on the Banality of Evil,* Harmondsworth, Middlesex 1963 (rev. and expanded 1964).

Bergeron, Danielle, "Femininity," *Feminism and Psychoanalysis: A Critical Dictionary,* Oxford: Basil Blackwell, 1992.

Bracher, Mark, "On the Interpellative Power of the Discourses of Ronald Reagan and Jesse Jackson, *The American Journal of Semiotics,* 7:1/2 [1990], 89–104.

Brousse, Marie-Hélène, "Sexuality," *Feminism and Psychoanalysis: A Critical Dictionary.* Oxford: Basil Blackwell, 1992.

Cantin, Lucie, "The Feminine Thing," *The American Journal of Semiotics* 8:3 (1990) and "Femininity: From Passion to an Ethics of the Impossible," *Topoi,* 1993.

Carter, Angela, *Sadeian Woman,* New York: Pantheon Books, 1978.

Chasseguet-Smirgel, Jacqueline, *Creativity and Perversion,* London: Free Association Books, 1984.

Deleuze, Gilles, *Kant's Critical Philosophy.* Translated by Hugh Tomlinson and Barbara Habberjam. Minneapolis: University of Minnesota Press, 1984/1963.

Derrida, Jacques, *The Ear of the Other.* Translated by Peggy Kamuf and Avital Ronell. New York: Schocken Books, 1985.

Diderot, Denis, *Rameau's Nephew.* Translated by L. W. Tancock. Harmondsworth, Middlesex: Penguin Books, 1966.

Dolar, Mladen, "Prolégomènes à une théorie du discours fasciste," in *Perspectives psychanalytiques sur la politique,* Paris: Navarin Éditeur, 1984.

Freud, Sigmund, "Formulations Regarding the Two Principles of Mental Functioning" in *General Psychological Theory: Papers on Metapsychology,* New York: Collier Books, (1963/1911).

——. *Thoughts for the Time on War and Death,"* SE XIV, London: The Hogarth Press, 290–92 (1957/1915).

——. "Femininity," *New Introductory Lectures* xxxiii, New York: W.W. Norton & Co., (1963/1933), pp. 99–119.

Geach, P.T., "Good and Evil." In *Theories of Ethics.* Edited by Philippa Foot. London: Oxford University Press, 1967.

Hartman, Geoffrey, Wellek lectures (unpublished) at University of California, Irvine, 1992.

Horkheimer, Max, and Adorno, Theodor, *The Dialectic of Enlightenment.* Translated by John Cumming. New York: Continuum, 1982/1968.

Kristeva, Julia, *Powers of Horror.* New York: Columbia University Press, 1982.

Lacan, Jacques, "Kant avec Sade," *Critique,* no. 191, April, 1963.

The definitive edition appeared in *Ecrits II,* collections "Points" Paris: Editions du Seuil, 1971. English translator James Swenson, in *October 51* (Winter 1989), 55–76, with annotations from 76–105.

——. *Ecrits,* Paris: Editions du Seuil, 1966; *Ecrits,* New York: W.W. Norton & Company, 1977

——. *Séminaire I: Les écrits techniques de Freud.* Paris: Seuil, 1975.

——. "L'identification," *Ornicar?* 12, 1977, p. 7. Sem. of 16 November 1976.

——. *Séminaire II* Paris: Seuil, 1978a.

——. *Seminar IX: The Four Fundamental Concepts of Psycho-Analysis.*

Translated by Alan Sheridan. New York and London: W. W. Norton & Co., 1978 [orig 1973].

———. *Television: A Challenge to the Psychoanalytic Establishment.* Translated by Hollier, Krauss, and Michelson, New York and London: W. W. Norton & Company, 1990/74.

Lacoue-Labarthe, Philippe. *Heidegger, Art and Politics.* Oxford: Blackwell, 1989.

MacCannell Dean, *Empty Meeting Grounds.* London and New York: Routledge, 1992.

MacCannell Juliet Flower, *The Regime of the Brother: After the Patriarchy.* London and New York: 1991.

———. "Desire." In *A Critical Dictionary of Feminism and Psychoanalysis.* Edited by E. Wright.

———. "Freud." In *Oxford Companion to Women's Writing in the United States,* forthcoming.

Naveau, Pierre "Marx et le symptôme." In *Perspectives psychanalytiques sur la politique,* Paris: Navarin Éditeur, 1984.

Ronell, Avital *The Telephone Book.* Lincoln: University of Nebraska Press, 1990.

Roudinesco, Elizabeth, *Jacques Lacan & Co: A History of Psychoanalysis in France.* Translated by Jeffrey Mehlman. Chicago: University of Chicago Press, 1990

Salecl, Renata "Society Doesn't Exist," *American Journal of Semiotics* VII:1–2 (1990), 45–52.

Sloyan, Patrick J. "US Defends Burying Alive Iraqi Troops: Pentagon cites a 'gap' in international law," by [*Newsday* wire] *San Francisco Chronicle,* Saturday, 11 April 1992, p. A10.

Wright, Elizabeth ed., *Psychoanalysis and Feminism: A Critical Dictionary,* Oxford: Blackwell, 1992.

Žižek, Slavoj, *The Sublime Object of Ideology.* London: Verso, 1989.

———. "The Limits of the Semiotic Approach to Psychoanalysis" in *Psychoanalysis and . . . ,* edited by Richard Feldstein and Henry Sussman, New York and London: Routledge, 1990, pp. 89–110.

———. *They Know Not What They Do: Enjoyment as a Political Factor,* London: Verso, 1991.

Judith Roof

A Verdict on the Paternal Function: Law, the Paternal Metaphor, and Paternity Law

Contemplating the possibility of a shifting Symbolic configuration, Jacques Lacan suggests that "the oedipus complex cannot run indefinitely in forms of society that are more and more losing the sense of tragedy" (Sheridan, 310). The "sense of tragedy" attending the oedipal is linked to the "drama" of the mirror stage, a metaphorical family drama wherein the child proceeds from identification with the mother's image to imaginary mastery to castration (or separation) forced by the operation of the paternal Law that inaugurates the child into the substitutive processes of Desire. The three terms of the family—mother, child, father—provide the mise-en-scene for a tragedy that inheres in Law and Desire, not in Law's prohibitions or divisiveness nor in Desire's perpetual lack or essential insatiability, but rather in the inter-relation of the two that instigates a series of inevitably inadequate substitutions. Though operating like Fate, Law and Desire coalesce in the delusion of choice—the hingepin of tragedy. The Law affords the potential for transgression and Desire the motive, but as the parricidal sons of Freud's *Totem and Taboo* illustrate, though the Law can be broken, Desire cannot be fulfilled: together Law and Desire perpetuate the Law of Desire.

The "sense of tragedy" is understood in terms of the family: in the association of Desire with the mother and in the correlation between Law and the paternal metaphor—the Name-of-the-Father signifier that takes the part of the Law. Creating a realm of tragedy and death, the three terms of the familial configuration that host the mirror-stage drama of individuation function metaphorically as the Symbolic signifiers structuring the psyche. Despite individual family breakdowns and historical changes, the metaphorical mother and father continue to function symbolically as long as they remain in a relatively stable relation to one another even as familial functions are undertaken by others. The sense of tragedy linked to the nuclear family fades, however, when parental signifiers no longer closely attach to the three-term configuration by which the child learns Desire and loss. So that while the twentieth-century Western cultural fading of the literal father might seem to delay the function of the Law or threaten mass psychosis caused by foreclosure of the Name-of-the-Father, what Lacan suggests by the loss of a sense of tragedy is, I think, the loss of the metaphorical correlation between concrete familial terms and the structuration of Desire and Law they represent. This may happen as our "nuclear" family "form of society" gives way to other caretaking configurations (which is, perhaps, behind the cultural outcry against the family's perceived decline). Neither Desire nor Law disappear; rather their symbolization shifts as does their closely tied relation in the claustrophobic nuclear configuration that foments the intensity of tragedy.

A rising feminist consciousness that challenges the Symbolic gendering of the family drama's roles is partly responsible for the erosion of the sense of tragedy. By questioning the "natural" correlation between female and Desire and male and Law, feminist critics publicly expose what is not superficially apparent: that the gendered structuration of Law and Desire is a shaky metaphor because the "reality" of biological genders cannot sustain the Symbolic roles into which they are cast. When a scrutiny of the relation between biological gender and gender stereotype instigates legal reform, as it has in American feminist praxis, the Imaginary connection between gender and gender role breaks down, resulting in the deconstruction of familial metaphors in the realm of literal, statutory law where patriarchal authority is imagined to exist.[1] Most of this deconstruction takes the form of an ironic extension of previously gendered functions to both parents, splitting gender from gender role. In this way feminist political practice works to purge statutory law of its gender bias, hoping that changing the law will force a shift in cultural comprehensions of the value and function of gender that will effect a gender parity. That statutes are altered in ways understood to be gender-equitable suggests that the authoritarian structure of the law is malleable and demonstrates that gender ideologies are not permanent, natural, or divinely decreed. Such efforts have a political value insofar as statutory law is confused with Law—insofar as the law and the Name-of-the-Father are conflated, since revising the law's treatment of gender appears to be an assault upon the authority imagined to legislate gender value. But at the same time, the Imaginary confusion sustained between biological gender and its metaphorical function—the confusion that tends to meld the literal father with symbolic authority—means that feminist efforts to affect statutory change work within the frame of the law rather than questioning the basis and structure of legal authority itself. Statutory reform therefore never treats the idea of law or Law itself, remaining within the gendered parameters of Law and Desire and tending to reinforce the very idea of law (and Law).

Despite the political value of feminist legal reform, legislative change fails to alter underlying cultural gender ideologies that continue to inform statutory application, enforcement, and judicial interpretation and threaten constant regression into gender dualities. In fact, many of the legal reforms that appear to endow gender-equity have actually backfired, turning out to have been of more practical benefit to males.[2] One reason for this ironic return of male supremacy in the guise of gender equity is that efforts to restructure the law confuse statutory law with Symbolic Law, thus treating symptoms rather than the underlying gender drama that bifurcates and metaphorically genders Desire and Law in the first place; another is the stubborn strength of gender metaphors linked to structures of Law and Desire. It would seem, then, that any feminist attempt to alter laws would require an onslaught upon the genderment of Desire and Law in the Symbolic order; such a project must take as its focus Law rather than the law and attempt to shift the gendered metaphors that appertain to the originary drama of the mirror stage where gendered metaphors are allied with structuration. As Ellie Ragland-Sullivan maintains in her analysis of the structuring function of Desire and Law:

> The two cornerstones in the Lacanian unconscious structure of the human subject are Desire and Law. Though the specific meanings attached to the structures of Desire and Law vary according to personal experience and historical context, the structural effects are themselves Real and shape both personal trajectory and history. The 'enemy' which feminists must confront, then, is neither class structure nor patriarchy per se, but the mimetic mirror-stage processes of fusion and difference by which the human subject takes on its nuclear form between six and eighteen months of age (269).

One difficulty in confronting Law (apart from its unconscious oedipal ensconcement) lies in being able to distinguish between the Law's metaphorical appurtenances and its underlying structural function, since even our ideas of the Law are already Imaginary, i.e., gendered and metaphorical. Despite the fact that Law, as Lacan has stated, is not a hidden force moving behind the scenes, it is nonetheless difficult to approach the Law as Law; this essay itself demonstrates the tendency to represent Law in a more limited, schematic idiom. The operation of the Law can be found only by implication as it performs within and behind its veiling metaphors; as a structure, the Law is a relation determinable better in its functioning rather than in any direct representation. Only strategies that either disimbricate Law from metaphor or expose the Law's underlying functions via a shift in structural relations would tend to reveal the relation between metaphorical gender, Desire, and the Law, a revelation that might afford a potential change in the gendered metaphors of psychic structure that sustain oppressive cultural ideologies of gender. As Lacan observes, the potential for this already exists in evolving social forms as well as in the fact that the paternal function is always inadequate; he states: "Even when in fact it is represented by a single person, the paternal function concentrates in itself both imaginary and real relations, always more or less inadequate to the symbolic relation that essentially constitutes it" (Sheridan, 67).

Whether law precedes or follows such evolution, I would suggest that statutory law, as it changes in response to gender questions that directly affect social forms, reveals the operation of Law as well as the slow shift of Symbolic signifiers that may disentangle Law from its gendered associations. The disengagement of Law and paternal metaphor in American law might happen in at least two ways. One way is to create an inadvertent rift in the metaphorical relation between the law and Law, a phenomenon that has been a side effect of feminist legal reform as it attempts to introduce gender parity. The ensuing gap exposes the operation of basic kinship laws central to Symbolic Law (but still metaphorical in relation to Law) otherwise effaced by statutory formulation; their exposure makes evident the inconsistency between Law and social conditions which, if noticed, allows for a consciousness of the gendering of Law and the operation of metaphor as well as a recognition of the change in social form that creates the dissonance. Another means for disengaging Law from paternal metaphor is in the dissolution or reduction of the biological paternal function enabled by biotechnological paternal substitutions that betray the metaphoricity of the paternal. These two mechanisms operate together, often inseparably, and are evident in the texts of legal codes if such codes are read as effects of the operation of a cultural unconscious clashing with more conscious efforts to level gender inequities.[3]

Law Is to Law As . . .

That the correlation between Law and the Father might be broached either through a rift between Law and law or between Law and the paternal metaphor—the Name-of-the-Father—is possible because of the metaphorical relation between Symbolic Law and the law of statutes and legal codes. The metaphorical tie which sustains their relation—the Name-of-the Father—is the same paternal metaphor that binds Law to the metaphor of the Father. Law is to law, then, as Father is to father, and Phallus to phallus. Imbricated with Desire, Symbolic Law comes into play as that which engenders Desire by rupturing the symbiotic unity of mother and child, perpetually dividing the individual and prohibiting any Desired (re)union. This Law, connected as it is to the principle of division and difference, is thus connected to the father—to that function that permits no retreat from the tragic mirror stage recognition of separation. As Ragland-Sullivan explains, "insofar as the elemental illusion of sameness is concretely attached to the mother, primary Desire is enigmatically linked to the female; insofar as the secondary experience of difference is both abstract and attached to the father, law is linked to the male" (269). But this Law linked to the male—to the father—is linked not to the literal biological father nor to the person who might literally have interrupted mother-child symbiotic unity, both of which are initially conflated with the Law in an Imaginary confusion between the literal agent and the principle to which he is metaphorically attached. Rather, the Law is the principle that declares division in the Name-of-the-Father: "it is in the *name of the father* that we must recognize the support of the symbolic function which, from the dawn of history, has identified his person with the figure of the law" (Sheridan, 67).

In this sense literal fathers are only metonymically related to the divisive function represented by the figurative connection between Law and a Symbolic absent Father. In a discussion of *Totem and Taboo*, Lacan links this absent Father to the murdered father of Freud's tribal myth: "if this murder is the fruitful moment of debt through which the subject binds himself for life to the Law, the symbolic Father is, in so far as he signifies this Law, the dead Father" (Sheridan, 199). The Symbolic dead Father holds sway not through presence, but rather through the debt of guilt and sin provoked by the reason for his absence. The debt of guilt metonymically attaches to the Name-of-the-Father, the signifier that represents not the father, but the power of the Law transgressed. The Name-of-the-Father according to Lacan, "sustains the structure of desire with the structure of the law—but the inheritance of the father is that which Kierkegaard designates for us, namely, his sin" (*Four Fundamental Concepts*, 34). Thus, a broken law—the murder of the father—generates the Law sustained by the debt incurred in this originary transgression. Law always operates at a deficit, yet was already there to be transgressed. The Law is also linked to death, the Law that cannot be transgressed.

The paternal metaphor—the Name-of-the-Father standing in relation to the Law—represents the principle by which the individual relates to the social order: the name of the father that determines the child's lineage and place in society. "The paternal metaphor," Catherine Clément explains, "establishes the correlation between the family name—necessarily the father's name—and the subject coming into the world" (170). Thus, the paternal metaphor is also metaphorically connected to the social ordering principles of patriarchy, effecting not just a law of division but also

a law of connection to the larger sweep of the social rules of kinship exchange. "The primordial Law," according to Lacan, "is
therefore that which in regulating marriage ties superimposes the
kingdom of culture on that of a nature abandoned to the law of
mating. . . . This Law, then, is revealed clearly enough as identical
with an order of language. For without kinship nominations, no
power is capable of instituting the order of preferences and taboos
that bind and weave the yarn of lineage through succeeding generations" (Sheridan, 66).

Symbolic Law that determines social ordering, division, and
identity in any culture where lineage and names are connected is
not coterminous with the tradition of common and statutory law
by which Americans codify the relations among themselves.
Spinning through Imaginary permutations created by operations of
cultural narcissism and compromise, civil law is an Imaginary version of the Symbolic Law that disappears within its fabric. The tradition of common and statutory law, though Symbolic in its effect,
is primarily engendered in the cultural Imaginary as the narcissistic image of its jurisprudential self, composed of competing self-
interests (another narcissism), political machination, compromise,
and an image of social weal.[4] Veiled by statutory arabesques, Law
operates as an anonymous and unconscious ordering principle
whose effects only appear either as the explanation for legal gaps
and inconsistencies or in those things assumed by the law as being
incontrovertibly true (children have fathers; people die). Because
the Law forms the Symbolic order defining identity and family, it
is in civil laws that govern such matters—reproductive and paternity statutes—that the operation of Law becomes most immediately apparent.

Most state statutes treating reproduction have to do with
questions of terminating pregnancies and involuntary sterilization.
Statutes governing questions of paternity constitute the flip side,
admitting and inscribing the exact difficulty of proving the connection between father and child while providing the means to establish a connection. Because part of the current ideology of human
reproduction is that it is an absolute and completely inalienable
right even to those biologically or physically incapable of repro-
ducing, this culture would not countenance statutes that defined
when one could or should reproduce, though the state does provide
laws that set the conditions for when and how the process of reproduction can be terminated, including abortions and sterilizations.

This selective statutory coverage makes sense if reproduction is seen as "natural," and the voluntary termination of reproduction seen as "unnatural." The distribution of laws that treat certain aspects of reproduction and parenting and not others already reflects the presence of an urge toward perpetuity and immortality through undisturbed processes of mating and reproduction. In this sense reproduction is a metaphorical extension of the language of kinship and identity that forms social order, the "primordial Law" which is "identical with an order of language" and without which "no power is capable of instituting the order of preferences and taboos that bind and weave the yarn of lineage through succeeding generations" (Sheridan, 66). Human reproduction is an extension and expression of the Law and the unconscious order Lacan assigns to the Fregeian number six, "the generational number of perpetuity or lineage, referring to an immortality gained by the perpetuation of identity within family lines" (Ragland-Sullivan, 135). The kinship rules that precede and define reproduction simultaneously reproduce the Law in the form of the child who is immediately subject to that Law and who must in turn reiterate the Law, repeating the trajectory of unconscious counting from the number one (unity of mother and child) to six (Ragland-Sullivan, 133).

Legal reforms such as the ERA that codify superficial gender equity simultaneously expose the gendered effects of Law, revealing its essential lack of choice and the gendered direction of its exchange. Simple inconsistencies in reproductive laws reveal the operation of Law whose deeply ingrained gendered metaphors compete with attempts to erase gender difference. Exposed in two guises: kinship exchange principles and the interest in immortality and perpetuity reflected in property ideologies that displace the Law of kinship and social order into real estate, the effects of Law masquerade as ideologies of genetic prudence and ownership. For example, the target of legislative change by feminists, abortion statutes sometimes reveal in their self-contradictions ideologies of genetics and real property that refer to Symbolic Law. These older, pre-*Roe v. Wade* (prefeminist) statutes often betray the operation of the Law whose underlying presence is the only thing that accounts for the statutes' internal inconsistencies.[5] The differences between older statutes and "reform" statutes, which tend—in the process of gender erasure—to efface the underlying operation of Symbolic Law, expose the futility of changing law without approaching Law.

Abortion laws are already riddled with conflict—the conflict they are codified to sort out—as the interests of the mother may conflict with those of the fetus, especially when the life of the mother is threatened by the pregnancy. Already the site of displaced issues of access to women and birth control, abortion embodies the crux of the family crisis as the mother, taking on the role of the Law, threatens to separate from the child in defiance of a statutorily absent father. The premature oedipal conflict represented by abortion replays the drama of separation (the drama of Law) with the wrong characters at the wrong time. Abortion laws attempt to recast the conflict in its proper terms—mother desiring child, father protecting it and dividing it from its mother only at the proper time in his name. The interest of the fetus in abortion laws, despite its identification with the principle of perpetuity and fecundity, is not necessarily identical with the interest of either parent, but rather is identified with the interest of a social order bent on perpetuating itself—through the child, through the "correct" configuration of familial power. The dilemma of abortion, while focused on a battle between mother and fetus, is a displaced battle between an individual's desire not to procreate versus a social Law represented by the Father demanding reproduction.

This broad conflict does not really refer to the pragmatic difficulties of pregnancy nor to the plethora of social issues surrounding birth and women's health; it does, however, explain why those concerns are so easily dismissed, since they are beside the point in terms of Law. The issue of gender and Law created by the possibility of abortion is deflected in abortion laws into specific statutory self-contradictions that are related to but which also mask the Law of social order that of necessity privileges procreation. Abortion statutes generally omit mention of the father, an omission that might be seen as a progressive recognition of the woman's authority over her own body. The statutes themselves, however, treat the mother as a medium rather than as a subject with will, enforcing not a philosophy of maternal choice, but rather the authority of the state to perpetuate procreation in the name of the father, who is, of course, absent. The literal lack of reference to the father in the statute reserves the absent father's right: the Law present through the statutorily-effaced Name.

In some older abortion statutes self-contradictions symptomatic of the Law reside both in rape and incest exceptions to the prohibition against abortion and in the law's attitude toward the fetus, which is inscribed as a kind of property right in the name of the absent father instead of as a life to be nurtured and protected. For example, the Delaware statute on abortion titled "Limitation on termination of human pregnancy" (24 *Del. Laws* section 1791) makes sense only in the context of the Law of kinship exchange and its concomitant extension into property rights. The basic rule in Delaware is that "no person shall terminate or attempt to terminate . . . human pregnancy" except under certain listed conditions such as the likelihood of the mother's death or a risk of permanent physical or mental injury to her if the pregnancy continues, the "substantial risk" of birthing a child "with grave and permanent physical deformity or mental retardation;" or if the pregnancy resulted from rape or incest. In any of these circumstances a pregnancy can generally only be terminated during the first twenty weeks of gestation.[6]

The statutes's exceptions to the rule of maintaining pregnancy appear to balance the interests of the mother, fetus, and the conspicuously absent father. The primary purpose of the law is apparently to protect the fetus: the product and perpetuation of the Law. The pregnancy may be disturbed only if its continuation would kill or severely damage the mother or if the fetus itself is so damaged as to not be a fetus—as to not present the possibility of perpetuation. But despite this ostensible focus on the fetus, this abortion statute also reflects a more compelling interest discoverable through a reading of the statute's disparate treatment of the exceptions of rape and incest. Apart from health issues, the only other exceptions allowing the termination of a pregnancy are if the fetus is the creation of an illegal act upon the body of the mother: where the pregnancy is extra-Legal as in cases of incest and rape. Incest and particularly rape refer directly to neither fetus nor mother, since the fetus is a fetus no matter how procreated, but rather to the violation of some other interest during conception.

The disparate treatment of rape and incest exceptions points to the operation of a subtext linked to Law. The Delaware statute laboriously spells out the kind of rape that will permit the termination of pregnancy as one "committed as a result of force or bodily harm or threat of force or bodily harm," and cites the proof necessary to verify it: "the attorney general of the state has certified to the hospital abortion review authority in writing over his signature that there is probable cause to believe that the alleged rape did occur. . . . " (24 *Del. Laws* section 1790). If the pregnancy is a result of a physical crime and if the law is designed to protect the mother against having to bear the fruits of a crime that has presumably already been committed, why so many mechanisms to determine the actual validity of the crime in cases of rape while incest as grounds for terminating a pregnancy requires no proof at all? Though the rights of the mother to resist violent sexual abuse may be at issue in rape, those rights are not necessarily at issue in cases of incest unless incest is defined as violence *per se* or unless the incestuous act is also a rape. While we might argue that the interest of society in preventing incest and its adherently greater likelihood of genetic mishap makes incest an understandable exception, isn't rape equally heinous and equally to be prevented?

The contradiction between the statute's treatment of incest as an automatic exception and rape as a highly defended one can be explained only in reference to the Law of kinship exchange. Incest denies the exchange of women among men and thus breaks the Law by permitting the illusory fulfillment of intrafamilial Desire. The fetal product of a rape, however, is a part of the kinship exchange, though its presence threatens to subvert the order of patriarchal naming and genetic perpetuity by substituting under the name of one father the kinship line of a father with another name. The fetus of a rape can only be divested in the event that it is unfairly gotten—by violence or threat. The extra proofs required to certify violent rape refer to the confusion attending the metaphorical gendering of the Law, which appears to enfranchise all males with procreative rights over females in their associations with desire qua fecundity.[7]

What this inconsistency indicates is that, apart from any societal interest in procreation, what is at stake in the limitation on the termination of pregnancy is the vested right of the invisible father whose individual genetic investment stands in for the paternal metaphor and is protected at all cost except the life or health of the mother. The exceptions protecting the fetus—limiting abortion to only those circumstances that threaten the death of the mother or the possibility of a monster child—protect the interests of the father and through the father the interests of a social order premised upon the orderly reproduction of identifiable generations. The rape/incest exception, then, exposes the extent to which the rest of the statute is bound up with the absent father whose stake in the maintenance of the Law of kinship exchange is inscribed as a property interest—a right of ownership or control—in the fetal vestment of a right of immortality. In abortion laws the fetus is treated as a kind of property right; aligned with the state and with the vastness of social order, the fetus is inscribed not as the personal interest of what is not yet a personality, but rather as the future interest of the Law situated in the place of the absent father whose "theoretical" right in genetic perpetuity is assumed. Apart from the rape/incest contradiction that exposes kinship Law, the rest of the Delaware statute refers to the Law via the analogy of a property-like paternal right in the fetus.

Just as the literal father stands in for the Name-of-the Father, the register of property is a systemic displacement and reinscription of kinship laws. Reiterating social order, real property, like children, perpetuates the name-of-the-father, represents power and potency, and allays the certainty of mortality through the immortality of a social order inscribed in tangible assets. Among the most ancient protections in English common law, property law asserts a definitive connection between an owner and property, defining the degrees of attachment and control the owner might enjoy. Because there is no necessarily "natural" relation between an owner and (historically) his property, perhaps the most important feature of property law is that it provides an unbroken chain of title within which owners enjoy a visible, legally inscribed connection to property where none is otherwise readily apparent; perhaps its most dangerous feature, a product of legal over-compensation, is the range of property prerogatives provided to owners who zealously guard their interests through an array of remedies ranging from actions in trespass and nuisance to the assertion of interests in water and game.

In the Delaware abortion law the anxiety-allaying principles of property become the "paternal" anxieties of reproduction. Both reproductive laws and property principles focus on the property (fetus). Despite the fact that property laws make certain an uncertain connection between owner and land, property rights' attachment to the property makes the rights of ownership incidental to the thing owned. Locating the source of rights in the property itself makes those rights permanent rather than personal, producing endurance and continuity. In turn this permanence endows the owner with more potent and absolute protections in the form of nearly unassailable rights to "quiet enjoyment" and testamentary disposition. This displacement from owner to property ironically fails to affirm the connection between owner and property that is one source of anxiety. But the failure of that affirmation suggests that the source of anxiety is not only the difficulty in proving a connection between owner and land but is also some fear of the failure of continuity, immortality, and perpetuity. This second anxiety returns to ideologies of reproduction as that which will continue the "name," "the line," the genetic survival of an individual. In this way, property law intersects the Symbolic Law of kinship from which it has been displaced, revealing the hope and the failure of property law to fulfill forbidden desire through the surrogate of real property. The law that creates property is linked to the Law that dictates that one cannot own anything except a connection to the Law of social ordering, which simultaneously inscribes, immortalizes, and spells mortality.

It is in the name of the displaced property right rather than in a consciousness of kinship Law that battles over reproductive rights are fought. Not only are property rights linked to tangibility, they stand in for the operations of the Law they both occlude and enact, though the property version of the Law provides a far greater illusion of control and possible fulfillment. In this sense, property principles embody the wish forbidden by Law and Desire. The debt that effects a bond to the Name-of-the-Father in Symbolic Law is transformed in property law from a debt to the illusion of right, often, but not necessarily, premised upon a mortgage debt and existing with the threat of foreclosure. The real debt of property is not mortgage but rather the need to pass the property to someone else on death: it is an adage of property law that land can never be without an owner—the chain of title can have no break. The realizable desire of real property is full ownership represented by full payment of the mortgage; testamentary law fills in the debt of the land by reiterating kinship laws in the annals of property deeds. Real property and the laws governing its control and transference provide an illusion of plenitude and fulfilled desire with the delusion of much greater permanence than money or any other mode of exchange that might be seen as mimicking kinship exchange.

As the displaced but operative site of kinship Laws, property ideologies provide a partial explanation for certain inconsistencies in cultural attitudes reflected in laws about when life needs to be protected, whose right it is to protect, why the female is regarded legally as the blank page rather than "co-owner" of the life she carries, and why the male, whose investment is protected, is nearly invisible in statutory provisions. If part of what is at issue in reproductive legislation is the property rights of fathers, then seeing that a property interest exists reveals the extent to which much of the anxiety surrounding reproductive rights arises from the jealous assertion of property instincts that reflect Law rather than a desire to preserve or protect life (a proposition reflected in the failure of law to provide for the quality of the rest of newborn's life). The subtle presence of property also helps account for some of the hysteria that surrounds issues of abortion, birth control, artificial insemination, and surrogate motherhood. While human life issues have rarely ever been the impetus for war, the endangerment of property interests often has. Whether bellicose irrationality is perpetrated in the name of god, country, or race, encroachments on property and the protection of property interests—borders or oil—instigate battle.

Post-*Roe v. Wade* abortion statutes efface the presence of kinship Law and property ideology by delaying the "vestment" of the fetus to the second trimester of pregnancy. The Massachusetts abortion statute titled "Abortion; pregnancy existing for less than 24 weeks" plainly states: "If a pregnancy has existed for less than twenty-four weeks no abortion may be performed except by a physician and only if, in the best medical judgment of a physician, the abortion is necessary under all attendant circumstances" (112 MGLA section 12L). Gone are the rape and incest exceptions, dissolved into the category of "attendant circumstances." But curiously, the decision now rests with the physician, the arbiter and delegate of the Law, which has been displaced from property into medicine. A second Massachusetts's abortion statute, titled "Abortion; pregnancy existing for 24 weeks or more" restates the state's (father's) and fetus's interest in the continuation of the pregnancy: "If a pregnancy has existed for twenty-four weeks or more, no abortion may be performed except by a physician and only if it is necessary to save the life of the mother, or if a continuation of her pregnancy will impose on her a substantial risk of grave impairment of her physical or mental health" (112 *MGLA* section 12M).

Taking these two laws together, feminist reform has only effected a delay, given by the law, which subsequently continues its own interest with greater latitude (no rape or incest exceptions, no question of a damaged fetus) now vested in the person of the physician who represents, through ethical imperative, the interests of the State. Simply declaring the fetus a nonentity for a few months defers the alignment of the fetus with the father of the Law. But this delaying tactic that appears to depend upon definitions of when life begins invites opponents of abortion rights to affix personalty to a fetus from conception, thus sealing the realm of the Law and maintaining an unbroken chain of title—not in the name of the Father (though often in the name of god) but in the name of "life," already a self-contradictory principle. While the trimester delay shifts the balance of control over the pregnancy from patriarchal property interests to an appearance of maternal control over her own body, what it actually does is textually obfuscate the continued presence of the Law, while merely deferring its effects in relation to the fetus. While this appears to be a slight liberalization, providing some margin of choice and/or escape from the laws of social order, it does so only by delaying recognition of the personhood of the fetus that would trigger the Law, remaining strictly within the order of Law. The compromise thus merely delays both a "showdown" over the question of life, which might itself reveal the operation of Law in its self-contradictoriness (life means death), and the recognition of the Law abortion laws really represent.

The interests of the State also reemerge at different sites as these apparently straightforward statutes are undone by a plethora of corollary laws that limit the amount of government support that can be used to finance abortion procedures, restrict facilities, free physicians from any obligation to perform abortions, and require—in the reappearance of patriarchal property rights over children—parental consent for abortions performed on adolescents. The remainder or difference that exists between the earlier and later abortion statutes is precisely the apparent gap between Law and laws—between the overt operation of kinship Law stumbling through rape and incest and the veiling of that Law through delay and the proliferation of statutes that combine to reassert the Law in ways even more symptomatic of the proprietary paternal metaphor of the Name-of-the-Father.

If this is the case, then how do we balance the interests in pregnancy or dissolve patriarchal privilege in Law? In addition to the window of choice afforded by delay, the product of feminist legal reform, another effective feminist praxis may well exist in the combination of frontal assault on legislation—altering gender equity in statutes—and the apparently more indirect practice of locating Law and its gendered metaphor and exposing the connection to a cultural consciousness. Understanding the kinship basis for reproductive laws alters our conception of those laws and provides the potential for a shift in the abortion rights battle from the dismal and misleading lure of the "pro-choice" vs. "Pro-life" dichotomy into an open query about the status of reproductive laws and their relation to gender and to ideologies of perpetuity. Such conscious examination brings the relation of Law to law into open question and thereby begins to confront the authority of the law itself. If we go further to confront kinship Law with its property law displacement, the gendering of the former becomes visible in contrast with the formal operations of the latter, disimbricating Law from its gendered metaphor and revealing the nature of the social stake in Law. While there is little public forum for such analytical processes, practicing them will enable feminists to confront the law in unexpected places that may, in fact, bring to the fore more trenchant issues than those currently under discussion. Openly questioning, for example, the interest of the fetus's father (an interest that has recently emerged in abortion lawsuits that attempt to restrain the mother's legal choice to abort) situates the question of the parents' relative roles in reproduction openly as an issue of gender and parental right. In this context, the contribution of the mother is clear as is the relative contribution of both parents and the question of gender parity can be examined in direct relation to gender ideologies. Unless reproduction is approached in these terms, the rights of the father threaten to remain hidden and, thus, unassailable.[8]

Naming the Father

Abortion statutes garner the contradictory tensions of cultural anxiety about the failure of Law understood as the failure of religion, patriotism, economic strength—the failure of the advantage of world exchange—precisely because they are bound up with the Law in a way that threatens to challenge the paternal metaphor. While Stuart Schneiderman asks, "Why can feminism not just live with the idea that the function of the Name-of-the-Father is its own subversion," the Imaginary of a culture caught by questions of gender inequities schizophrenically codifies changes in gender relations at the same time that it zealously maintains—and in fact encourages—its strict, but confused notion of the Father (quoted in Ragland-Sullivan, 301). The increased incompatibility between Law and the law effects a paternal crisis: the metaphor sustaining and sustained by the Law is both eroded and aggrandized by the law, a tension that threatens to disimbricate the Symbolic Name-of-the-Father from just plain "names"—that threatens to make conscious and visible the Name-of-the-Father's self-subversion. That this might enact a desirable feminist praxis is clear; but an other, perhaps more tragic effect is to force a judgment, to bring Law and Desire into the open in a momentary impasse such as that inspired by the conscious consideration of the rights of the fetus's father.

The quiet site of this metaphorical dislocation is paternity statutes, which in broad correlation with shifts in other reproductive laws appearing to provide women more choice, reaffirm in forthright terms the relation between father and child. While reproductive laws shift to permit a margin of choice (or a suspension of the Law), paternity laws become increasingly definitive, increasing the rights of fathers as well as the certainty of the paternal/child connection. As in abortion statutes, in paternity laws the rights of the child become the rights of the State, which, in seeking support for the child, combines judicial procedures for determining paternity with procedures for affixing a burden of support on the father. Paternity statutes (formerly known as bastardy proceedings or illegitimacy proceedings, now often referred to as parenthood laws—continuing the tendency to omit the name of the father) contravene the commonly held common-law tradition that fathers bear no responsibility for the support of children born out of wedlock. Part of the rationale for that traditional principle is in response to the former impossibility of proof; part is also connected to upholding the forms of kinship Law by refusing recognition of those children born outside of the kinship order represented by marriage unless the father himself formally recognized the child as his. Common law, predictably, presumed that the husband of a woman who has given birth is the father of the child.

Paternity laws that formalize procedures for proving paternity codify a judicial search for the literal name of the father in the name of the State and in the ostensible interest of both mother and child whose financial burden is thus relieved.[9] Paternity laws, thus, reduplicate the Name-of-the-Father in their literal search for the name of the father, reducing the metaphor of social organization into the subject for microscopic scrutiny through evidentiary blood tests, tissue typing, or DNA tests. The appearance of statutes openly called paternity statutes reflects the feminist interest in gender equity by making both parents of the child equally liable for its support.[10] It also greatly reinforces a tie that previously did not necessarily exist, shifting the operation of kinship Laws from questions of exogamy (whom one marries) to the anxiety of identity (who is Dad?). The effect of this literalization of paternity is the reinforcement—doubling—of the paternal presence: the almost parodical conflation of Law and law. While Schneiderman may ask why feminists don't simply let the Name-of-the-Father subvert itself, feminists watch culture duplicate the Name-of-the-Father in a way that identifies the literal father with the Symbolic Law, forestalling its self-subversion even as it self-subverts in proliferations of paternal "proof," which obscure the difference between the Name-of-the-Father and the father's name. The debt owed to the absent father becomes the absent father's debt, reducing the paternal metaphor to a matter of social conscience, which might have the effect of reducing Law to law (the subversion Schneiderman suggests). It disengages the metaphorical connection between Law and the Name-of-the-Father by making grossly visible the state's attempt to make a literal connection between an outlaw father and his child. But this metaphorical reduction may also swerve away from the Law precisely because it is so literal, preserving the paternal metaphor in its privileged place. Paternity statutes, thus, tend to reify paternity and suggest that indeed the connection between law and the father should and can be made. Whatever subversion or disjunction is present between law and Law is recognizable only on the level of the Law. As in the reform of abortion statutes, the difficulty of feminist praxis has always been to force a separation of Law from its Imaginary effects in law.

Breaking the Phallic Bounds

Paternity statutes such as the "Uniform Law on Paternity" appear in relatively recent history, in the context not only of feminist reforms, but also in the wake of improved biotechnology that enables paternal proof. They are perhaps both symptoms and harbingers of a change in social form, attempting a last-ditch salvation of the paternal metaphor on the level of social action. This happens at the same time another threat, biotechnology, endangers the phallic function by disengaging the father from the reproductive process. As Lacan observes, "Will we have to be overtaken by the practice, which may in the course of time become common practice, of artificially inseminating women who have broken the phallic bounds with the sperm of some great man, before a verdict on the paternal function can be dragged out of us?" (Sheridan, 310). The "phallic bounds" are broken when principles of genetics become detached from acts of procreation, uncoupling the phallus from its procreative role and from the chain of signifiers attached to the Law of the Name-of-the-Father that operates without the phallus. In this context the paternal becomes literally a metaphor of the joining of genetic matter in the obverse of paternity laws that make the paternal metaphor quite literal. The paternal metaphor, when reduced to a metaphor, reveals its metaphoricity—the real emptiness at its place—which may disimbricate the paternal metaphor from Law. This is indeed the danger Lacan may see in artificial insemination, which disturbs not only phallic function but also the "social form" of the nuclear, reproductive family unit. If this is the case, then feminist reform may utilize technology to effect the breaches that shift gender metaphors in more "equitable directions."[11]

While biotechnology may threaten a shift, Law intervenes to transpose biotechnological threat into an extension of the right of the father. Given the dual potential of a need for no literal father and the possibility of a "mythical" biological father in reproductive practice, the threat to the paternal function is not surprisingly allayed by recourse to property and contract law that affix the right of control in the name of the father and absorb biotechnical products within kinship laws. Two instances of biotechnological reproductive practice—artificial insemination and surrogate motherhood—have catalyzed the rescuing operations of laws that take the place of and return the paternal function.

In the case of artificial insemination, the sperm of a man (not necessarily married to the woman who uses his sperm) is introduced extra-phallically into a woman. The insemination itself is not artificial; what is "artificial" is the means of introducing sperm as well as the family configurations such practices may create (single mother, nominal father, and biological father). The law in cases of artificial insemination, though currently evolving and unclear, reflects the differing kinship emphases behind the shifts in paternity law. For example a Washington State statute, titled, "Artificial insemination," a section of the state's "Uniform Parentage Act" states in section (2): "The donor of semen provided to a licensed physician for use in artificial insemination of a woman other than the donor's wife is treated in law as if he were not the natural father of a child thereby conceived unless the donor and the woman agree in writing that said donor shall be the father" (26.26.050). The law presents two different courses, the first, that the donor shall not be the father upholds the law of kinship ties as they relate to marriage and the orderly descent of generations under the name of the father. The second alternative, that the woman and donor can agree the donor is the father, emphasizes the genetic connections that supposedly underlie kinship order. Either case fits into a kinship scheme, though the second permits both the emergence of familial permutations—the possibility of a single mother if the donor's paternity is rejected—and a way to correct those permutations—the donor becomes the father. In the possibility of no father at all, an option implied by this statute, lies one challenge to the paternal function: the child born without a nominal father who is not illegitimate. Because of the statute's inability to close such a scission, the possibility of a "fatherless" child begotten at the will of the mother disrupts kinship Law and the paternal metaphor, at least on the level of human reproduction. In the case of voluntary single mothers, however, the name-of-the-father appears intergenerationally (unless the maternal patronym has also been changed), effecting a return to the mother's paternal line.

The other biotechnological challenge to the paternal function is the hiring of surrogate mothers to bear the genetic children of men to whom they are not married. In these situations, which are contractually defined, a woman agrees to bear the genetic child of a man for a sum of money, then relinquish all claim to the child to its father. This illustrates the conception of the mother as medium for the father's "property;" paternity becomes a enforceable contractual right. The possibility of surrogate maternity has raised the most questions about the rights of fathers, backed up as they are by contract and property ideologies. When surrogate mothers refuse to relinquish their claims on the child, law courts have generally looked to the provisions of contract to determine the mother's rights, which are sometimes perceived as merely contractual, sometimes moral and enforceable despite the contract.

Like the issue of the unborn child's father's rights over the fetus, surrogate maternity challenges the hidden singularity of the father's claim on the fetus, confronting through the disposition of the child, the Law's necessary attachment to the father. This suggests that in addition to the multiple-front challenge possible in matters of abortion, other reproductive laws also afford sites where the paternal metaphor is brought into question as an issue of the necessary right of one gender over another. Breaking the phallic bounds disrupts an entire chain of signifiers: from phallus to father to the father's name to the Name-of-the-Father to the Law. For this reason, feminist reform might profitably look at the system of law, rather than at specific laws, bringing into play the gaps afforded by artificial insemination and surrogate motherhood. In any case, the trajectory of social change, affected by increased biotechnical control over reproduction may accomplish what feminist praxis by itself cannot. Dislocating the father at the site of conception threatens to become the tragedy of tragedy. Unlike the tragedy of Oedipus whose question of identity answers society's debt for the murder of the father, the future Oedipus may locate identity and debt in a place other than the biological father whose connection to him has been mediated by test tube. At this point of tragic waning, however, when Law scrambles to shore up the father, the verdict on the paternal function is nether oedipal guilt, nor biotechnical dislocation, but a hung jury.

Notes

A portion of this paper treating the relation of concepts of property to abortion law appears in "The Ideology of Fair Use: Xeroxing and Reproductive Rights," *Hypatia* 7, 2 (Spring 1992), 63–73. That essay suggests that a similar idea of property underlies both abortion statutes and copyright laws.

1. Lacan notes in "Subversion of the subject and dialectic of desire," that "when the Legislator (he who claims to lay down the Law) presents himself to fill the gap, he does so as an imposter" (Sheridan, 311).

2. For example, in *Weinberger v. Wiesenfeld*, 95 S.Ct 1225, the Supreme Court held that "the gender-based distinction mandated by provisions of Social Security Act that grants survivors' benefits based on earnings of deceased husband and father covered by the Act both to his widow and to the couple's minor children in her care but grant benefits based on earnings of a covered deceased wife and mother only to the minor children and not to the widower violates right to equal protection secured by the due process clause of the Fifth Amendment since it unjustifiably discriminates against women wage earners required to pay social

security by affording them less protection for their survivors than is provided for men wage earners." As Robin West has pointed out, equal protection tends to come into play mainly when it benefits males.

3. Though the entire system of statutory laws in the fifty states of the United States presents no unified text, hence no sustained metaphorical "unconscious," it is possible to see the law (statutory and judicial) as a system that does, in fact, contain significant breaks and inconsistencies that are ideologically informed. Since I make no claim to read the culture of a particular state in a specific historical period (as a unified legal corpus might permit), my reading of these selected statutes is more in relation to the larger ideologies they reflect that are connected to the register of Law.

4. Lacan remarks in "Subversion of the subject" that "there is nothing false about the law itself, or about him who assumes its authority" (Sheridan, 311).

5. *Roe v. Wade* is a 1973 Supreme Court decision that basically held that "life" begins after the first trimester and, thus, the state cannot interfere until life begins.

6. It is highly likely that, if challenged, the Delaware statute as written would be deemed unconstitutional following *Roe v. Wade*. It is, thus, an example of an abortion statute that does not yet codify the first trimester "delay."

7. This gendered operation of the Law also accounts in part for the difficulties encountered in rape legislation and prosecution where despite reform rape continues to be notoriously difficult to prosecute. In rape cases, male privilege is transformed into a question of the victim's consent.

8. Even if questions of gender and parenting are discussed in those terms, such discussion threatens to create a circle where the rights of fathers become self-evident and unexamined. If any such discussion is to work it must take place within a consciousness of the constructedness of gender. As Ragland-Sullivan observes, "Language then attempts to describe the indescribable in reductionist terms of biology, archetypal myth, and the like. The father has no innate magic or intrinsic biological supremacy. It is, instead, the symbolic effect of his dividing presence to which Lacan points" (55).

9. An example of a modern paternity law, part of the Uniform Law on Paternity adopted by a number of states, reads: "Obligations of the father—The father of a child which may or may not be born out of lawful wedlock is liable to the same extent as the father of a child born in lawful

wedlock, whether or not the child is born alive, for the reasonable expense of the mother's pregnancy and confinement, and the education, necessary support and maintenance, and medical and funeral expenses of the child and for reasonable counsel fees for the prosecution of paternity proceedings. A child born out of wedlock also includes a child born to a married woman by a man other than her lawful husband" (*Rhode Island General Laws* 15-8-1). In line with abortion statutes, this statute clearly situates the child as property and the mother as the medium upon which the father reproduces.

10. The rights of the father are thus contradictory: the father has no duty or connection, but has a complete property right in the child. As noted earlier (note 3), the "overkill" effect of gender parity also appears in reformations of parenting. While such laws formally inscribe the father, they also reinforce paternal rights beyond tradition and relegate the mother to a less advantageous, almost "objective" status. In the blind zeal of gender equity legal reform, some parentage statutes include provision for an action to declare a mother and child relationship "insofar as practicable." See, for example, the Alabama Uniform Parentage Act, section 26-17-18.

11. Ragland-Sullivan observes, "The more pressing logical problem that Lacan's epistemology presents is this: if the Name-of-the-Father is an organizing principle of sexual identity and culture, which ensures societal order and psychic 'health,' how can such an effect be changed without dire consequences for the fabric of society itself?" (300). Perhaps it is the reverse.

Works Cited

Clément, Catherine. *The Lives and Legends of Jacques Lacan.* Translated by Arthur Goldhammer. New York: Columbia University Press, 1983.

Lacan, Jacques. *Ecrits.* Translated by Alan Sheridan. New York: Norton, 1977. (Referenced as "Sheridan").

————. *Four Fundamental Concepts of Psychoanalysis.* Translated by Alan Sheridan. New York: Norton, 1981.

Ragland-Sullivan, Ellie. *Jacques Lacan and the Philosophy of Psychoanalysis.* Urbana: University of Illinois Press, 1986.

the politics of mastery

Ellie Ragland

THE DISCOURSE OF THE MASTER

No discussion of Jacques Lacan's discourse theory can leave out one of his key terms: truth. In today's theoretical parlance, however, the idea of positing truth as a value (positive or negative) which is actively functional in structuring mentality, is considered laughable. Today's intellectual left in the United States takes its theories regarding truth from Nietzsche who asked: "What then is truth? A movable host of metaphors, metonymies, and anthropomorphisms: in short, a sum of human relations which have been poetically and rhetorically intensified, transferred, and embellished, and which, after long usage, seem to be fixed, canonical, and binding."[1]

Nietzsche argued that coherence theories and correspondence theories where truth supposedly finds itself mirrored in some extraneous, independently existing reality, are wrong. Truth is, rather, that dupery of language that makes people use the "hardened and congealed" metaphors of their time without any thought for the fact that no *a priori* truth, no insight as to the real nature of the world, are given there. This is so, Nietzsche maintained, because there are no such real grounds, only countless differing perspectives.[2] But what will philosophy—whose demise Nietzsche would never suppose—need to go about its task if there is no true world to be attained or described? Among other things, Nietzsche answers, a historical sense is needed.[3] Insofar as everything is basically interpretation, fiction, transcendence, or history, then following history's genealogy seems little to ask.

Although Nietzsche scholars have uncovered various categories of truth used by him, generally speaking, Nietzsche is hailed as the one who enabled philosophers to shift the course of their attention away from a Socratic aspiration to discover truths underlying appearances, or from a Kantian aim to establish particular categorical moral precepts. Richard Rorty has described this shift in emphasis as the "effort to achieve self-creation by the *recognition* of contingency."[4] Heidegger, Wittgenstein, Rorty, and Derrida are the new heroes of thought, supposedly revolutionary thought, that encourages thinkers to actively participate in deciding what to accept as beliefs and values. Taking Nietzsche as the father of this philosophical turn, Tom Ragland writes that he "admonishes us to take control of all aspects of our lives—in order that we might poetically redescribe the world through an entirely new set of metaphors."[5]

Like Nietzsche, Jacques Lacan questioned truth in his long engagement with the inadequacies of philosophy to say what truth is or is not. In his Seminar given in 1969–70, Lacan worked with the idea of the underside (*envers*) of psychoanalysis—its underweave.[6] One of the terms Lacan elaborated in the theory of discourse developed in this Seminar was truth. Actually "truth" is the only surprising term in the list of four places Lacan finds operative in any discourse: agent, other, production, and truth. Perhaps the addition of truth to the idea of discourse will make more sense if one understands that "discourse" means something different for Lacan than it does for the varying theorists who have equated it, more or less, with language.

In his *écrit* "A Jakobson" in *Encore* (*Séminaire* XX), Lacan defined discourse as that which makes "a social link, founded on language."[7] Discourse is not grammar, nor information, nor sounds made up of phonemes, then. Furthermore, the only reason anyone is fascinated by phonology, Lacan says, is because it incarnates the signifier of the phoneme (*Encore*, p. 22). Elsewhere Lacan names this primordial signifier the *dite maternelle* or the *lalangue* that flows along parasitically in grammar. In other words the phoneme is inseparable from the signifier for the mother's desire. And the language in which this primordial function of the phoneme is clearly evident is the speech the most alienated from the discourse Lacan defines as making a social exchange: psychotic speech.

The psychotic subject uses language outside the social link precisely because the paternal metaphor failed to operate on the originary repression on language. This subject's body, relatively unmarked by law, becomes a law unto itself because *jouissance* has not been put under a barrier. In consequence, the psychotic lacks the distance from his predicates to identify himself by them. Living at the level of the Other's *jouissance*, the psychotic subject retains the primordial illusion (or hallucination) of never having lost the primordial object of satisfaction. This supposition of not being subject to lack leaves the psychotic without the normal social controls in the Other that we generally ascribe to "law," taken as the function of prohibition. In psychotic speech, there is an inability to control aggression and rage. This language of insults, offense, blasphemy, and objection comes from the real, occupying the place of what has no name except the object *a* of condensed *jouissance*.[8]

Furthermore, the issue of whether the phoneme has subjective meaning or not is a political issue within university discourse where the signifier is equated with the phoneme or the alphabetical letter. And there is much ado about this. Indeed, Edgar Allan Poe, considered a pulp writer by the intellectuals of his day, would probably be amazed to find his story "The Purloined Letter" at the heart of large academic debates that have focus on the issue of whether the signifier—taken to be a letter or a phoneme—can be deferred infinitely, or not. If Derrida were right about E. A. Poe, then linguistic meaning would be indeterminate because the contexts that fix it are never stable. If Lacan is right—and this is where I stake my claims—even though the unconscious is structured like a language, not only "is it not in the field of linguistics," the signifier, although deferrable, is not easily deconstructible (*Encore*, p. 20).

Rather, the distance between linguistics and what Lacan calls *linguisterie* is the distance between love and language. But Lacan does not mean love poems. So what has love to do with discourse, much less with politics? We all know that we speak of those we love. We love those who speak well of us, who agree with us. Some of us even like speaking about love. Indeed, speaking and loving seem as intricately interwoven as affect and anxiety. Lacan called love a sign. We know that signs belong to the world of semiotics where something is represented for someone. But insofar as the semiotic concerns the realm of the visible, one must rephrase the question posed above: Of what is love a sign? It is a sign that one has changed discourse, Lacan said. In Lacan's theory of the four discourse structures—the master, the academic, the hysteric, and the analyst—one changes from one discourse structure to another, from one way of ordering desire around lack to another, when something emerges from the analytic discourse. And Lacan describes the analyst's discourse as a love discourse. "I am not saying anything else in saying that love is the sign that one changes discourse" (*Encore*, p. 21).

In calling the analytic discourse a love discourse, Lacan is, of course, referring to the transference. By talking to any analyst about one's life, an analysand comes to love something other than his or her narcissism. He comes to love the knowledge that contains the truth of his life. And he loves this knowledge, not because it is transcendant or even narcissistically appealling, but because it is the only path to change. The analysand comes to love the truth of his life because in telling it he begins to see a way out of the impasses that have held him in a death thrall. In freeing his language of the burden of lies, misrecognitions, and pretense—stories told for appearance sake—a new kind of speech emerges. This change of discourse from the realm of plaint to "well spoken" speech is not elaborate, not deceptive. It is even humble and simple.

This idea will surprise those who are steeped in poststructuralist theory. Such theory views Lacan's master discourse as commensurate with absolute, theological certainty, which they believe he alone claimed to speak. This is the end of the story for them. Actually, the story has not yet begun. We have barely begun to engage with Lacan's teaching in the United States. He teaches us to suspect the master discourse, for example, not to speak it. In the days of Socrates and Plato, of Aristotle and philosophers who came after him, Lacan points out that the slave was thought to possess knowledge. That is, the slave was the master of a certain kind of knowledge. But when Lacan uses the word "knowledge" we must be careful. He equates the "knowledge" generally associated with learning and being learned with the dessicated material of communication theories, information systems, artificial intelligence, and the like—the university discourse in brief. In his broader conceptualization of knowledge, symbolized by the matheme S2, the object of surplus value—the *petit a*—is included as well.

Something lies beyond language, something that the very use of language seeks. Each person uses language to try to attain (or maintain) the objects Lacan called the object *a*; i.e., objects we think will produce *jouissance*, taken as a logical consistency. At the simplest level, for example, we give money in exchange for objects we want. At more complex levels, we deploy our language skills to get what we want. Lacan symbolized the opaque objects one desires as elusive. The small *a* represents an excess in *jouissance* because the lure object is not really the object one seeks. The object sought falls on the side of the real, aiming at the biological organism's fundamental well-functioning (without doubt, anxiety, despair, sleeplessness, and so on). Beyond satisfaction, in other words, people seek something else. And everyone knows this, even academics and scientists who deny it. Both scientists and professors claim to be serious seekers, concerned with pinning down the truth of untruth; i.e., with objectivity. Yet their claims are based on a pretention Lacan located in the master discourse. The master takes his knowledge for truth, as a generalized formula for living that is good for one and all. Worse yet—and here is the hook—the modern master equates knowledge with conscious knowing. By believing that knowledge can be verified as true or false within the realm of the visible, even if by negatively verifiable data, the master discourse reduces knowledge itself to a discourse of opinion, to the "democratization" of thought that passes for knowledge in today's intellectual marketplace.

But partisan academics and scientists remain dupes, Lacan claimed, dupes of an intuitive (or imaginary) geometry (*L'envers*, p. 27). "The unconscious is a *savoir* which escapes consciousness," Lacan taught. "It does not denote itself any the less, however, for being exactly articulated, structured like a language: unthinkable in its effects, but also not implying just anything in a double sense—complicitous with a nature to which it is born at the same time it is, and recognizing itself in the manner by which consciousness makes one believe that there is no knowledge which does not know itself as knowing" (*L'envers*, p. 128).

Why would Lacan call the masters of knowledge dupes? What does Lacan's approach to knowledge teach, for example, when he contrasts the modern concept of knowledge with the concept of knowledge in ancient Athens? Lacan points out that in Socrates's Athens slaves were said to possess knowledge, while knowledge about *jouissance* remained the province of the masters. He takes the example of Plato's *The Symposium* where Alcibiades is described as telling those present at the Banquet of his efforts to win a sexual response from Socrates. But before launching into this discourse, he asked the slaves to stop up their ears, just as we ask children not to listen to discourse about sex. Unlike Alcibiades, Socrates hid his desire. Socrates spoke of love, not desire, to his students. When he described what sort of god Love was, referring to desire, Socrates projected the source of this knowledge onto a woman, a sibyl. Strangely enough, this split in his discourse—between love and desire—is, in Lacan's teaching, revelatory of a different relation to knowledge than Alcibiades had. Lacan suggests that Alcibiades spoke a master discourse, a discourse that imposes false unities everywhere, rejecting the splits and cracks in being. Socrates, in Lacan's view, spoke a discourse of the hysteric, a discourse in which the very split between desire and love—that is, the division of the subject between the imaginary field of love and the symbolic sphere of desire—appears at the surface of the hysteric's speech.[9]

Lacan said that Descartes gave an entirely new focus to the Western conception of knowledge by eradicating the split between the idea of knowledge as reason and knowledge as a "knowing" about *jouissance.* By equating thinking with being, Descartes prepared the way for contemporary masters of knowledge who are so sure of what they know (i.e., so obsessional, so identified with their own narcissism) that there is no longer a public opinion that attributes a special knowledge to slaves, women, or children. Lacan calls philosophy itself "this betrayal which presses the knowledge of the slave in order to obtain its transmutation as knowledge of the master" (*L'envers*, p. 14).

In an era when citizens joined enigma and the half-spokenness of truth to the words, if not the actual experience, of nonphallic knowledge, those, like slaves, who were thought to possess knowledge within the register of the *pas-tout* or "not all," tipped the prestige scale concerning what constitutes mastery. As long as the real was accorded a place of respect within the fabric of society, the worse aspects of patriarchal certainty were tempered. One might well say that the protests of feminism (always arguing that the real be, in some respect, included in the social) are a necessary consequence of the contemporary generation of masters who equate knowledge with the mind and the mind with the brain. In the early nineteenth century, Hegel asked what the *desire* of knowledge is. But he could not answer his own question. One might say that for lack of a meta-knowledge, he came up with the idea of an Absolute knowledge.

Where Hegel failed to solve philosophical problems, Marx and Freud gave political and psychoanalytic responses to the same points of impasse in thought. One might say, in memory of Voltaire's *bon mot*—i.e., that man would have had to invent God if he does not exist—that if Marx and Freud had not existed, the progressive democritization of society would have obliged us to invent them: Marx who unveiled the shame implicit in the bosses' exploitation of workers and Freud who unveiled the unconscious forces at play in the what people take to be *conscious* knowledge.

Going in the opposite direction from Hegel, relying rather on the thought of Marx and Freud in constructing a theory of desire, Lacan argued that there it is not the desire to know which leads to knowledge. With Lacan, one will always ask which knowledge is in question: academic knowledge or knowledge that bears on *jouissance*. But even academic knowledge is inclusive of desire—unconscious desire being that which pushes us to seek *jouissance*—such that desire infuses all of language. Such a theory will not, however, find support in philosophical discourses that have so vigorously reified the *logos*, whether equating it with thought or language itself, lauding the *logos* or seeking to destroy it. Lacan found his "master" in Freud whom he called a man of desire who recognized desire. And he found the source of his object *a*—the beyond in pleasure—in Marx's concept of surplus value.

As "master" teachers, teachers who recognized the split in human intentionality, Freud and Marx stand head and shoulders above the ordinary masters that Lacan's master discourse structure critiques. These masters—the blind kings—do not want to know anything about anything except what they can say and see. They do not really *want* to know about anything at all, Lacan says in *L'envers de la psychanalyse*. They simply want things to work. Lacan places what he calls a master signifier (S_1) in the position of agent in the master discourse. The master signifier denotes identification with Ideals, with the ideals of society. Such signifiers dictate what one must do to be accepted, to be "in the know," at a given moment. Thus, the master discourse is spoken in superego tones, even to the contradictory point that Lacan names: *Jouis* (You *must* enjoy!).

The master's grammatical tone is that of the imperative. In his own eyes he is the perfect individual, an autonomous, whole subject one might liken to God. What the master fails to see, however, is that one can only command another by putting that other to work to validate him (or her). The master's wish is to have himself validated as a SUBJECT OF NARCISSISM. In an Hegelian context, one might describe the master's goal as the goal to be me (m'être). One can see where Lacan is going with this thought. The master is his own slave. He puts the other to work in order to recuperate his own enjoyment as surplus value.

By adding the dimension of *jouissance* to discourse, Lacan teaches that discourse is not made up only of grammatical components. One can see that, for example, in the phenomenon of the fading of language, a phenomenon that indicates the presence of desire in language itself. And when we say that, we think we have Lacan: Aha! So that's what desire is! But Lacan never makes it so easy to pin down what he is saying. Robert Georgin, a Belgian student asked Lacan a series of questions that were first aired on Belgian radio and have since been published as *Radiophonie*.[10] Georgin asked Lacan what he heard in the master discourse. Lacan answered, the contemporary master discourse of narcissism as a mode of the superego, both ferocious and obscene. I AM = I AM KNOWLEDGE = I AM THE ONE WHO KNOWS. One might rewrite the *cogito* of the master discourse to "I am, therefore, I think." But why should one bother to care about this discourse that produces surplus *jouissance*—accumulated joy it cannot use productively, whose very excess turns into the pain of repetition for its own sake—in the quest of proving a lie: that there is no lack in that person's being. The master refuses the castration that is the inheritance of every human subject.

If one is an analyst, the answer to why one should bother about the master discourse is clinical. Masters harm those over whom they have power.[11] The analyst's discourse is the underside of the master's. Rather than denying desire, putting law in its place, the analyst places desire in the position of agent. The analyst sits in as the semblant of the desire the analysand cannot speak, evoking in the analysand the desire to know that his or her knowledge also concerns desire. That is, knowledge concerns the unconscious. The analyst knows that he or she is there to make the knowledge in the analysand's speech heard at the point where the analysand identifies with the master signifiers of others, identifications that hide this truth: When one's desire is a lost cause, lethal *jouissance* holds a subject in its thrall.

Moreover, any subject's story continually runs aground on the shoals of surplus value. At the start of an analysis, most analysands speak a kind of master discourse—that is, a discourse that divorces *jouissance* (as the cause of desire) from knowledge. If there were no consequences in divorcing *jouissance* from knowledge, there would never have been a need to take *jouissance* into consideration by any social agency, be it Socratic philosophy, psychoanalysis, entertainment industries, or Jean Genet's bordellos. But the real returns anyway in a subject's body, dreams, and fantasies, showing the loss of *jouissance* that haunts individuals with the failure of the "never done." The real of the lost cause of desire always returns into the symbolic, telling individuals as well as cultures that the *jouissance* of the Other sex, and the body of the subject that symbolizes it, is not a sign of love.

When political masters of discourse—leftists and conservatives alike—speak in order not to know about the unconscious that inhabits them, one may well wonder if their words incite others to think. Although they claim they speak in order to teach others to think, Lacan pointed to the narcissism in such speech. They speak so that others will say they are right. In this sense, *thinking is a kind of affective activity.* Thus, thinking requires that one put a little love, a little hope, a little effort into it. Lacan's radically new concept of thinking is described by Elisabeth Roudinesco in her account of his response to Noam Chomsky's question to Lacan about how thinking occurs. Lacan answered Chomsky thus: "We believe we think with our brain, but I think with my feet. It's only there that I meet something hard. Sometimes, I think with the muscles of my forehead when I bump into something. I have seen enough electro-encephalograms to know that there is no shadow of a thought."[12] Chomsky was so outraged by this answer that he dismissed Lacan as a crazy man. Even though Mitsou Ronat tried for years to explain to Chomsky the metaphorical nature of Lacan's answer, Chomsky, according to Roudinesco, remains convinced that Lacan had told MIT intellectuals that the seat of the human brain was the bone structure or phalanges of the foot (Roudinesco, p. 489).

Psychoanalysis may be called progressive, Lacan said, but only in that it defines what leftists revolt against (*L'envers*, p. 27).

The victim or proletariat consists, quite simply, of those whom the bosses or masters may consider an enemy by virtue of not belonging to the narcissistic body of "insiders." But "insiders" never realize that this label only exists at all because it refers to "outsiders" who, by definition, offer an oppositional counterpoint. Psychoanalysis is not progressive, however, in the way that today's leftist masters of theory think of themselves as doing the work of power. Yet, in a perverse way, Lacan seems radically leftwing when taken in opposition to the (theory) masters of knowledge whose certainty relies on a refusal to question the "beyond" in knowledge.

Insofar as the political requires action in order to initiate change, one may well ask what the first, or founding, act is. Lacan's answer is that of thinking. Any group that already knows, that only pretends to question, is apolitical. Worse, Lacan says, such groups define their own impotence by using their knowledge as superego dicta for others. Thou shalt not question me. Thou shalt not doubt my words. We are in the realm of the icon, the idol. Idolatry, Religion.

Jacques-Alain Miller has described the master as the "blind master." He rules *in order* not to see, as does she, his female counterpart: the *nor-mâle*. What makes the analyst different? Montaigne said of himself centuries ago that he was unlike his fellow creature only in one sense. He knew that he did not know. One could say that this was merely the narcissistic stance of the academic sceptic of old. And it was, in part. But Montaigne proved over and over in his love of citation and in his recognition of aphanisis that Narcissus was not his only master. The analyst, like Montaigne, knows that knowledge cannot remain static. That when it does, one is in the presence of the death drive. Something new must be constituted before change can occur. Moreover, knowledge must remain humble to be truthful. The one who knows knows, perhaps, only this. No person can come to know more, or know better (what is denied or repressed), unless that person first listens to the unheeded questions and doubts hidden within the forest of his or her own words. In this sense, Montaigne's stance is the correct analytic stance: *Ques Cais-je!*

The master discourse, by contrast, implies that it represents something that already exists as a natural state of knowledge. Academics veer toward the master discourse in their objects of study, be they texts, films, philosophy books, or the like. These "objects" are, in turn, interpreted for another meaning by masters who follow the latest trends in thought. As such they speak a kind of academic meta-discourse. When the object is taken as an object of investigation, one is in the territory of master signifiers where discourse strategies mean simply stopping up loss by turning away from the cuts and splits in language. The answer is preferable to any question—to the "I do not know" of the unconscious—which always opens onto matters concerning love, desire, or *jouissance.* By "object," then, Lacan is not concerned with things in themselves. Those objects merely replace the object that marks a place of loss. Thus, lure objects attenuate the effects of loss, which usher in the real of anxiety or mourning. Lacan taught that loss is not, however, an empty, negative void. It is positivized by the *jouissance* that catalyzes *repetitious* acts, whose purpose is to close out loss by anchoring its certainty in some semblance of a sure thing. So, beyond the lure objects that seem to be *das Ding,* one comes to the real of the object *a,* the object taken as condensed *jouissance.*

Although Lacan calls the *semblant* an object *a,* he does not mean that lost objects are actual objects. Rather, he refers to loss as primary and absolute, as that which de-totalizes all our perceptions and acts, introducing holes and cuts into our words and deeds. The meaning of this someThing "beyond" language is that whatever is split off from the symbolic, from conscious accounting, returns anyway in the real as *objet a,* as a surplus value. But why is this value "surplus" rather than plus? Put another way, why does the real take a bite out of the ego? How has the *effect* of trauma materialized language around *that in it* that is more than it, making of the subject itself a surplus value: that is, an object of the Other's enjoyment that has been reduced to one or more of the partial drives (the oral, anal, scopic, or invocatory)? In this context, one sees that Lacan's "beyond" refers to nothing transcendental, nothing theological. Indeed, the heterogeneous fragments that *return*—albeit unrecognizable as products of repetitions—return as pieces of the real that splinter our *jouissance* where words, names, sounds, voices, gazes have been embedded in our flesh to produce what we call affect. We are *a*-ffected, *a*-fflicted by the thrust of the drive—$/<>D—itself a demand for Being cum love.

But how can such a theory integrate itself into the academic marketplace of theories where critique is itself taken for *das Ding?* Joseph Natoli, typical of contemporary theoreticians, writes: "Critique displaces a lust for a power base, a lust for identity through the rules of the game. . . . It is the burden of the present and future to construct a theory/strategy by which cultural critique appropriates beyond the level of Marxist, feminist, deconstructive, semiotic, psychoanalytic, pragmatic, hermeneutic discourse. It appropriates science and the materialist culture, as well as those levels of worldly discourse that go on in the street, the office and the media."[13]

There is no underside of discourse for today's academic theorist such as Natoli. Everything is obvious at the level of power politics. Enemies are recognizable as patriarchs, bourgeois families, and so on. Moreover, any academic who does not speak a discourse of critique as heterology risks being branded a fascist or "true believer" in some other cause. Pointing out that a boss is a boss, whether the orientation of leftwing or rightwing, Slavoj Žižek, for one, has taken issue with the academic left. Imaginary order thinking is the enemy. Lacan placed conscious thought within the imaginary order, working as it does within the realm of the visible where things *seem* full in themselves. In this order judgments are made at face value, in a black and white sense. One might call it the order of the either/or. Still, Lacan's careful lessons regarding the EGOTISM of narcissistic (you or me) thinking have barely been heard. As early as 1969, Lacan described politics as the idea that knowledge can make a totality in the schools: And this imaginary ideal of the whole comes from our modeling of space on the paradigm of the body itself.

But left-leaning critics such as Joseph Natoli are not satisfied. A true critique will reach beyond everything, Natoli says, throw in the kitchen sink, the garbage pail and the mop, so to speak. Only that path will lead to a cultural critique of Everything by Everything. Natoli can be said to speak a master discourse in his refusal to take seriously the idea that when one stumbles over something that is not satisfying, something that makes a knot, that *thing* has its own *raison d'être*. Lacan's entire enterprise might be described as giving a logic to the knots. The master's response to the presence of the knot is to deny its presence or, at least, its seriousness: closure! click! shut! Everyone but the hysteric (who, by definition, has no choice) seeks the *jouissance* of Oneness that Lacan symbolizes by the Φ. Individuals will do anything to escape the unbearable pain of the real, whose impasses Lacan describes as knots. Indeed, most language functions in a master discourse style, manifesting the human effort to close out doubt, shut off questions, attenuate anxiety. In this the analyst's discourse is out of step with language itself, which Lacan describes thus:

> I would like to give you this rule of first approximation of the reference of a discourse: it is that it acknowledges wanting to master. But the analyst's discourse opposes itself to all desire . . . at least admitted to, of mastery. . . . I say *at least admitted*, not that it has to hide it, because after all it is always easy to recloth it in the discourse of mastery. To tell the truth, we always start from there in teaching. The discourse of consciousness . . . is taken up again every day indefinitely—also . . . the discourse of synthesis, the discourse of the consciousness which masters. How could one apprehend all this psychic activity otherwise than like a dream, when one hears thousands and thousands of times in the course of the days *this bastard chain of destiny and of inertia, of throws of the die, of false successes and misunderstood encounters which make up the running text of a human life?* Don't wait for anything more subversive in my discourse than to not pretend to have the solution (L'envers, pp. 79–80, my translation).

Nevertheless it is clear that nothing is more burning than what refers to *jouissance* in discourse. Not only does discourse originate in *jouissance,* discourse is *moved* again every time it tries to return to this origin. The result is a manifest lack of appeasement in discourse (*L'envers,* p. 80). While the Lacanian analyst uses the symbolic to work on the real of the analysand's *jouissance,* the master discourse denies the real of an obstacle, joking about it, saying it is not so, attributing it to green cheese, if it must be mentioned at all. Yet concrete obstacles were laid down piece by piece. They constitute the paths of unconscious knowledge that disrupts continuity. And because it unravels the ego, producing anxiety, people do everything to dismiss the real, to deny it at all costs.

The object *a* that Lacan places at the heart of discourse produces an impact on language that joins signifier and signified in a *point de capiton* whose punctuation comes from the "grammar" of the drives, not from the language of the signifying chain. The "Father, can't you *see?*" of the burning child dream is punctuated by the gaze, telling the dreaming father that grammar is not adequate to itself to explain the dream , nor is the image (of fire) inherently self-explanatory, nor the eye commensurate with the gaze of judgment.[14] Unlike Freud or Lacan, Joseph Natoli's paradigmatic argument typifies today's criticism of radical chic, which makes CRITIQUE of cultural critique—an endpoint. Wherein critique is an endpoint for leftwing theorists, Lacan reveals the porous materiality of language as making another kind of meaning.

Eschewing the desire that inhabits language, critics in the lineage of leftwing theorists use language in a totalizing way, creating ideologies out of *jouissance* effects. For all the lip-service paid to using language carefully, attention paid to dismantling simplistic binaries, such critics have, nonetheless, not understood the scope of the effects of language. They seem unaware of what Freud and Lacan learned in the clinic. There should be a sign on the language pack: "Use only with the warning of the Surgeon General. This could be dangerous to your health." Skating on language is skating on thin ice. Certain persons blind from birth, for example, can now be made to see by modern technology. What their doctors cannot understand is why so many of them see holes in the world, holes in trees, holes everywhere, holes that depress them. Why, say the doctors, does the gift of sight drive some of their "miracle cures" to suicide?[15]

And what, if anything, could this strange phenomenon have in common with the politics of dyslexia? I say "politics" because dyslexia is called normal when characteristic of a four- or five-year old-child, but is "diagnosed" as a brain disease when first found (or found still persisting) at age 10 or so. And this alleged brain disease goes hand-in-hand with the diagnostic category of "learning disabled" within the institutional master discourse of today's elementary schools in the United States. In the master discourse of this school system, the desire to be right about any phenomenon—to close out doubt—makes labeling more important than paying heed to the effects produced on a child named "disabled," put under the weight of this signifier and this gaze. The master discourse might be seen as a contemporary version of the evil eye, because it carves permanent wounds on young lives. For the master discourse speaks in ignorance, without knowing that the toxic effects of language are far from noxious.

Each person who learns "learns" by concentrating, by paying painstaking attention to detail. Yet, the negative side to learning is that it requires one to fill in the holes, stop up the gaps, color in the lines. But once such mastery of the symbolic order is acquired, individuals come to believe that representations are the thing-in-it-self. In fact, representations merely represent things already in-*corp*-orated in the imaginary/real body that in-*forms* Being, concrete things that make of us narcissistically defensive egos living in wounded bodies. By the time a "dyslexic" child has memorized letters backwards and learned numbers turned upside down, why should it be any easier for him or her to correct this rigidification of the signifier than for another child studying piano to learn to play octaves with the correct fingering once he or she has learned incorrectly? Or why would such learning be different in kind from learning to type correctly once one has mastered the one-finger method of typing?

Speakers of a master discourse have no interest in these concrete details of the particular, the discourse of mastery having but one goal: to be certain, to define the end point of knowledge. To be Bureaucracy, says Lacan (*L'envers*, p. 35). But equating knowing with being leaves out desire, leaves out the unconscious. Yet, Lacan says, modern masters no longer need to be masters of more than one kind of knowledge as were the philosophers of old. They need only be masters of property. Having has been equated with knowing in a capitalist discourse. Yet, everything points to the fact that "having" cannot solve the problems of being. Everything points to the real, to a palpable density returning into language from the unconscious, to indicate that there is something in meaning that lies outside the grasp of conscious understanding. In this context, the magic knight or springer in chess is neither a model for mastery or a random invention. Within Lacan's logic, the springer marks a double-bind paradox.

One might say that humans build magic or illusion into their games when they stumble over impasses in the real. One name Lacan gives to these impasses, elaborated in the third period of his teaching, is the *objet a*.[16] When the object *a* is first conceptualized as autonomous in 1960–61 in his eighth seminar on *The Transference*, he portrays it as standing in for the unsymbolized real, for truth, which Lacan describes as the little sister of *jouissance*. In its pristine state, such truth is not your friend or mine, he teaches. Rather, each subject is enslaved by unsymbolized knowledge to which he or she blindly clings, all the while telling a white-washed, idealized story intended to attenuate the pain of what he or she cannot bear to know. Such a mask, paradoxically, ensures that the real be repeated, unconsciously. But Lacan goes further. People love their pain. They reify it and dignify it, sing praises to suffering, painting it in colors of a higher and purer reality.

We must fight the bourgeoisie, say Gilles Deleuze and Félix Guattari.[17] But one wonders why they incite students to fight only the enemy without, while ignoring the enemy within. Why do Deleuze and Guattari not want to know about the harm one's nearest and dearest has subjected one to? The answer concerns the real: People cannot bear to know that the family—the beloved, enracinated familiar—is the very thing that makes one sick. So we flatten out language, praise consciousness as the god of good and embarrassedly—Lacan's *hontology*—laugh away any hint that the stuff of everyday life hurts to the quick: acts manqués, words committed that sear our flesh, the cuts of daily snubs and slights, just as quickly denied. The *jouissance* of one's accumulated scar tissue stands ready to resonate beneath the seeming solidity of one's position in the symbolic, reminding one that he or she is a subject of the cut, not just a subject with (or without) a "name."

Willy Apollon has written: "As a discursive ensemble, physics structures itself around a lack: the real, that no re-presentation gives to the discourse of physics. It [the discourse of physics] has, nonetheless, an ideal limit, both methodological and epistemological, that defines in what a discourse can belong to the body of the discourse that is physics."[18] The real in Lacan's sense is also definable. It is what gives birth to contingency. Slavoj Žižek has argued that freedom is the real in that it cannot be idealized.[19] Indeed, the real appears in language as that which puts it askew, makes it awkward, uncanny. One could describe the presence of the real as the palpability of the unbearable. Yet, insofar as we discount the condensed *jouissance* of the *objet a* that Lacan called objective, we end up trying to define limits within discourse by other means: by figures, words, concepts such as "surplus value," rather than by a serious study of the object *a* which, as a semblant, is both real and true.

The master closes out his own division and swallows his *jouissance*, thereby identifying with the death in himself that Lacan (after Freud) called the *Kern unseres Wesen*. The master will, indeed, destroy others and wage wars, rather than admit he lacks anything. Lacan is not, however, suggesting that only the meek and humble of spirit will inherit a psychoanalytic kingdom of heaven the master will never glimpse. For, indeed, the meek and humble of spirit often inherit their own deaths, faster than the master inherits his. What the master misses that will enslave him forever is the chance to change this knowledge so as to facilitate desire. Symptoms and responses to the (partial) drives mark points of limit on the body as places of impasse. The master splits these off from his or her knowledge, giving the name of the medical wisdom of the day. And, indeed, the master seems to be right. Why should one bother to gather the quicksilver dew of these moments that flee even as they appear, showing the slip of mortality and the hole in the field of language that links epistemology and ontology to desire, love, and pain.

While the master's desire is the desire of the Other—that is, unquestioned assumptions about his or her knowledge—the analyst's desire embraces the enigmatic half-speaking of unconscious knowledge (L'envers, p. 40). Beyond the truth of the real which is re-pressed, someThing presses back: the *objet a* as remainder, the leftover detritus that destroys any person's narcissistic illusion that being is a unity. But why would the analyst take up the position of standing in for this cause? To my way of thinking, the answer is political as well as clinical. The clinic enables an analysand to disentangle identifications (fantasies) that weave together imaginary and symbolic material to cover over the real. The analyst uses the symbolic to treat the real where a subject is reduced to his or her symptom whose structure is the double one of metaphor: that which hides the fact that the joy of identifying with pain—i.e., fixed positions—actually "drives" humans.

Lacan found this reality suicidal, unethical, impossible to bear. His critique of American psychoanalysis is a critique of smiling faces and good wishers who refuse to know that analysands come to analysts because they have a very real enemy within: their own death coalescing around some organ of the body, telling its story in the repressed signifiers of family history. But since repetitions are never repetitions in the identical, there is hope for change. Transference is never transference of the same material, but material repeated via a similar path.

In his *Tractatuslogico-philosophicus* Wittgenstein cogitates without collecting the fruit of his thoughts, Lacan says (L'envers, p. 67). His error is the common one of taking the grammatical structure to be the world. Deconstructive theory has pushed this idea to include the forms of the world. But where propositions generally ennunciate themselves as the facts of the world, the analytic discourse finds another sense: propositions announce nothing other than the tautology of the totality of discourse that makes up the world (*L'envers*, p. 67). While Wittgenstein sustains the world of facts as truthful propositions, Lacan reduces Wittgenstein's monumental effort to a mining of the *rien* (the nothing) he finds. And to what does such a master discourse point? To the silly tricks that rely on wanting to be the Other of someone whose desire is captivated by figures of lure. Put another way, the false sometimes implies the true. But, for Lacan, the "true" lies in implications, not in propositions. The object *a* serves as the lining of the subject. The first objects that cause desire condition language and, as such, are *a priori*. When my young daughter sees people talking to each other in a grocery store and looking at her, she says "I bet they're saying I'm cute." One might ask if, in this play of gazes, the gaze is in her or outside her? That is precisely not the point. In that moment *she* is the object-gaze: the *petit a* that Lacan called extimate, where inside and outside intersect.

Philosophers want to save truth, Lacan said, while psychotics want to know nothing of it. Yet psychotics live out the truth of *jouissance*, while philosophers want to know nothing of that. Where is the modern "philosophy" master's *jouissance* to be sought then? One hears his *jouissance* in his master signifiers and in the *petit a* his fantasy veils in discourse, but which, nonetheless, touches constantly on *jouissance*. But if *jouissance* points to veils and willed consistencies, how does a master discourse dispose of *jouissance*? By taking opaque principles or propositions as self-evidently sufficient unto themselves, the master makes closure his or her master. One might even say that any proselytizing in the name of substantives, in the name of belief systems, bespeaks a master discourse. The master has lost his way in desire and so must wait for the next signifier to reveal the next answer in a line of supposedly progressivist theories.

Lacan describes the modern master as having renounced concern with *jouissance* in exchange for putting order into his system of beliefs, without ever asking what causes his desire. The master *qua* desiring subject has become the wooden Indian outside Old West trading posts. He points upwards to the sky, blindly, dead. He is the unseeing King in the *Purloined Letter* whose only function is to ensure that the social order function as smoothly and flawlessly as an unerring guillotine. Yet the King—Créon, for example—can never be One with the law he embodies. Indeed, the murder of the father is the condition of Créon's *jouissance*, based as it is on a barrier erected between knowledge and truth, between law and *jouissance* (*L'envers*, p. 107). Today's master lives under the shadow of the real father, forbidden *jouissance*, the impossible. The master cannot, will not, admit his or her castration, will not admit that language produces this effect on being.

What does all this mean for politics? Lacan says mass media can now reproduce the master discourse of imaginary idealizations and identifications *ad infinitum*. Despite his genius, Marx has changed very little in the discourse of the master (*L'envers*, p. 175). Indeed, as revolutionaries have become increasingly unable to help workers, the master signifier that urges leftists to fight for good causes suffers identification with impotence and death. Still, Lacan gives us the hope that psychoanalysis has a small part to bring to the revolutionary of whatever stripe. If freedom comes from constituting nonidealized truths by breaking up the *jouissance* that functions as a limit to natural processes, then any group, cause, or project must ask not only what the *jouissance* is behind its narcissism, but to what *jouissance* it attaches itself in the social discourse? Not only must one interrogate one's own desire, but that of the professor, doctor, lawyer, minister, and so on, as well.

Yet today's academic discourses meant to critique the stable, normative master discourse risk becoming new master discourses—Marxist, feminist, deconstructive, semiotic, whatever—that disempower themselves by equating knowledge with the known, while leaving aside the not-known. These critics do not realize that self-evident truths are seductive and lethal, not to mention traitorous. When truth speaks as a lie based on what it tries to hide, any hope of reconstituting desire—one's own or that of cultural others—is lost. But why is truth dangerous? Why does Lacan equate it with the real and attribute it to the field of the gods? Is it dangerous because it liberates? Lacan's notion of truth goes in the opposite direction. Truth is dangerous because it hides. Altruism, "just" causes, *belle âme* sacrifices, are just a few of the guises where truth equates itself with conscious speech that liberates. Worse yet, "just causes" lie without even knowing they do so. Is this so horrible in and of itself? Yes, Lacan says, because our lies chain us to the ground and keep us in a death thrall. Lies are the stuff of everyday discourse. "I love your work. I love you. I want to be you, so I hate you. I'll destroy you because I love you and can't admit it." So many repeatings of pain, the pain of missed encounters, of lack, of loss, of denial.

Lacan takes another path than the one taken in the Bible where one is told to "Love thy neighbor as thyself." Lacan offers some hope in the place where theology loses it. "Father forgive them, they know not what they do," say the pious words of the Bible. Let them know more of what they do, Lacan says: how they are constituted, how they are beings of *jouissance*. What do we have to lose by letting our illusions of knowing fall? In the fall of the object *a* we lose our pride, the comfort of the familiar, and our symptoms. What do we have to gain? Some space of freedom to breathe deeply, some chance to change, to live, love, laugh. And maybe the chance to live beyond the first death of alienation from "within," which Lacan placed before the second animal death, or mortal one.

Notes

1. Friedrich Nietzsche, "On Truth and Lies in a Normal Sense," in *Philosophy and Truth: Selections from Nietzsche's Notebooks of the Early 1870's.* Translated and edited by Daniel Breazeale. Atlantic Highlands, NJ: The Humanities Press, 1979, 84: 79–100.

2. Friedrich Nieztsche, *The Will to Power.* Translated by Walter Kaufmann and R. J. Hollindale. (New York: Vintage Press, 1968).

3. Friedrich Nieztsche, *Will to Power,* 408.

4. Richard Rorty, *Consequences of Pragmatism.* (Minneapolis: University of Minnesota Press, 1982), 195.

5. Tom Ragland, "Nietzsche's Perspective on Truth and the Self." Honors thesis, Department of Philosophy, University of Virginia, 1988, 66.

6. Jacques Lacan, *Le séminaire, Livre* XVII (1969–70): *L'envers de la psychanalyse,* text established by Jacques-Alain Miller. Paris: Seuil, 1991.

7. Jacques Lacan, *Le séminaire, Livre* XX (1972–1973): *Encore,* text established by Jacques-Alain Miller. Paris: Seuil, 1975, p. 21.

8. Jacques Lacan, *The Seminar of Jacques Lacan, Book III (1955–56): The Psychoses.* Edited by Jacques-Alain Miller and translated by Russell Grigg. New York: W. W. Norton, 1993.

9. Jacques Lacan, *le séminaire, Livre* VIII: *Le Transfert*, text established by Jacques-Alain Miller Paris: Seuil, 1991; See also Ellie Ragland-Sullivan, "Plato's *Symposium* and the Lacanian Theory of Transference: Or, What is Love?," *The South Atlantic Quarterly*, vol. 88, no. 4 (Fall 1989): 725–55.

10. Jacques Lacan, "Radiophonie," *Scilicet* 2/3 (1970): 55–99. Excerpts of this interview are translated into English by Stuart Schneiderman in *On Signs*, edited by M. Blonsky (Baltimore: Johns Hopkins University Press, 1985), 203–6.

11. Jacques Lacan, "Sur *Le Balcon* de Genet," *Magazine Littéraire*, text established by Jacques Alain Miller, No. 313 (September 1993), pp. 53–57; Text taken from *Les séminaire, livre* V (1957-58): *Les formations de l'inconscient*, the lesson of 5 March 1958, unedited seminar.

12. Elisabeth Roudinesco, *Jacques Lacan: Esquisse d'une vie, histoire d'un système de pensée*. Paris: Fayard, 1993, p. 489; the translation is my own.

13. Joseph Natoli, "Prefacing *Future(s)*/Mediating on One Future," in *Literary Theory's Future(s)*, (Urbana: University of Illinois Press, 1989), 1–29: 19 and 25.

14. Ellie Ragland, "Lacan's Death Drive and the Dream of the Burning Child," in *Death and Representation*. ed. Sarah Goodwin (Baltimore: Johns Hopkins University Press, 1993), pp. 80–102.

15. Ellie Ragland-Sullivan, "A Writing of the Real," *Visible Language* 24.4 (Autumn 1988): 483–95.

16. Jean-Louis Henrion, *La Cause du désir: l'agalma de Platon à Lacan*, (Paris: Points Hors Ligne, 1993), pp. 102–3.

17. Gilles Deleuze and Felix Guattari, *Anti-Oedipus: Capitalism and Schizophrenia*. Translated by Robert Hurley, et al. (Minneapolis: University of Minnesota Press, 1983).

18. Willy Apollon, "La Clinique, L'Arbitraire incontournable," in *Colloque 1980: La Clinique*. Etudes et Discussions Du Reseau Simplexe. Édité par le GIFRIC (Quebec, 1980), 100: 95–116.

19. Ellie Ragland-Sullivan, from the 1987 Television conference in New York, cited in "The Eternal Return of Jacques Lacan," in *Literary Theory's Future(s)*, (Urbana: The University of Illinois Press, 1989), 70: 33–81.

literary representation

Elizabeth J. Bellamy

OTHELLO'S LOST HANDKERCHIEF:
WHERE PSYCHOANALYSIS FINDS ITSELF

The "proper place" of the "a" in psychoanalysis

When is something not a *thing* anymore? If, as Stanley Cavell has argued, tragedy is at its core "an epistemological problem" (126), then this question may be as valid a starting point as any for an inquiry into the oft-discussed handkerchief of *Othello*, a play we could subtitle "Much Ado About a Thing." We could turn for an answer to Lacan, who transformed that privileged Freudian "thing" known as the phallus into a signifier. Lacan might answer that something is not a thing anymore when it finds its "proper place." In the case of the "purloined letter" the "thing" is revealed to be not a thing, but rather a signifier that "will be *and* not be where it is, wherever it goes" (SPL, 54).[1] Or, as Derrida suggests in "The Purveyor of Truth," the "proper place" of the purloined letter is such that "[i]t cannot be found where it is to be found, or else . . . can be found where it cannot be found" (44)—and indeed the Police fail to find the Queen's stolen letter "everywhere" in the Minister's apartment. The proper place of the letter is the "ex-centric" place of the Unconscious, and one of the major lessons of Lacan's "Seminar on 'The Purloined Letter'" is that the letter is not just simply "lost" or "hidden"—like a thing—because it was never possessed to begin with. (The proper place of the letter as the place where it "will be *and* not be where it is," for that matter is the *only* way the Lacanian subject can read the allegory of the signifier, split as it is by Lacan's axiom of the displacement of the subject: "I think where I am not by thought, therefore I am where I do not think" ["Agency," 164–65].)

Derrida argues that when Dupin finds the letter in the Ministerís apartment (But where? On the mantelpiece? *Beneath* it? *Between* the legs of the woman?), he has also found the "proper place" of psychoanalysis, which, despite the elusive itinerary of the signifier, will always "find itself" in the lack, the hole, the gap that is castration. Indeed, for Derrida what is more at stake in his essay than the allegory of the letter-as-signifier is locating the way in which psychoanalysis "locates" itself, to return to the terms of the question that initiated this discussion, in the moment at which a thing (a letter) is no longer a "thing" but the signifier as pure difference, the signifier that points not to some-*thing*, but to the lack (the lack of castration) that always has its "place" such that, to repeat Lacan, it always "will be *and* not be where it is, wherever it goes." One might say, then, that the self-discovery of psychoanalysis depends on the "place" of the *accent grave* over the richest letter in psychoanalysis, the "a." To summarize Derrida's position: Do we say that the letter *"manque à sa place"* ("is missing from its place"), or rather do we say that in the letter-as-signifier, *"la manque à sa place"* ("the lack *has* its place")? With some irony we can argue that if we dis-place the *accent grave*, the piercing mark of a superscriptional castration, and claim that "the lack *has* its place," then we have arrived at Derrida's conclusion that, as he states at the outset of his essay, *"La psychanalyse . . . se trouve"* (31). Like some disciplinary *sujet supposé savoir*, psychoanalysis finds itself when a thing (like a letter, or a handkerchief) is no longer a "thing" but rather a trace of "the topos of what is missing from its place," the lack of castration that "itself is never missing" (63).

But let us suppose a psychoanalysis that "finds itself" by not finding itself. What would such a psychoanalysis entail? To begin, it would be a psychoanalysis in which a "thing" remained some-*thing* and not a lack "in place." Such a psychoanalysis would still concern itself with displacement—but it would concern the displacement of things, not the displacement of the signifier, and it would still maintain Lacan's axiom that a thing is not just simply "lost" or "hidden," but rather finds its "proper place" in displacement. If, as I will argue, anxiety is the privileged trope of displacement in *Othello*, and if, in some sense, psychoanalysis has not yet "found" anxiety, then we have the basis of a psychoanalytic hermeneutic that no longer, as Derrida would have it, "come[s] under the jurisdiction of what it itself produces" (38). Though Derrida finds psychoanalysis always finding itself in the story of castration, I would argue that no one can "find" psychoanalysis locating itself in the anxiety it seeks to trace in the displacement of a thing. In the case of *Othello*, our hermeneutic of anxiety will not, to echo Lacan, "arrive at its destination." When psychoanalysis must concern itself with anxiety, it will not fall into the trap of "discovering" itself.

The key to conceiving a psychoanalysis that does not "find" itself is to maintain the "object-ness" of a thing. This, after all, is the cue we receive from Emilia and Iago in their simple, yet resonant exchange concerning the handkerchief:

> Emilia: I have a thing for you.
> Iago: You have a thing for me? (3.3.301–2)

Psychoanalysis, like *Othello*, is frequently concerned with stories about things. Thus we are presented with stories of, for example, the cotton-reel whose loss and subsequent relocation is such a source of pleasure for Freud's infant grandson Ernst. Or, as we have seen, we have Lacan's re-presentation of Poe's "The Purloined Letter" and its drama of the letter's "theft without return."As these two stories demonstrate, we could argue that the very basis of narrative is, in some fundamental sense, not just a thing but its retroactive foregrounding in the consciousness of the ego only after the *loss* of the thing.[2] Because the existence of a thing is so closely bound up with its loss or absence (as Freud and Lacan argue, perhaps bound up with the very basis of language itself), we are left with the tendency of the thing to slip into a liminal boundary between its existence in the Real and its existence only as a (belated) representation. It then becomes possible to argue that because the child's cotton-reel inhabits the boundary between the loss and regaining of the maternal presence, and because the Queen's purloined letter takes on significance (*signifiance*) only after it has been *lost*, the deciphering of things by psychoanalysis prefers the representational status of not-*quite*-things, of things as representations.

This inevitable allegory of the thing-as-representation (as *Vorstellung*, or as signifier), I would argue, is why psychoanalysis traces a hermeneutic that, to repeat Derrida, "comes under the jurisdiction of what it itself produces." At the precise point at which the thing is viewed as a representation, psychoanalysis traces the minimal, predictable founding unit of narrative, specifically the loss of the phallus in the Oedipal story of castration. The inevitable result of the psychoanalytic ur-narrative of castration is fetishism, the reaction against the loss of the phallus, or, in the realm of the "Seminar on 'The Purloined Letter,'" the originary "theft without return." Because the fetishist knows that the object itself is lost, he fills in the gap of its theft through representations that provide compensatory satisfaction. At the point at which voyeurism joins with fetishism, creating the assurance that the gaze, the look, will always locate the object of desire, we have the point at which psychoanalysis, like the fetishist, will always find itself finding itself in the castration narrative, the retransformation of lack into a signified that inadvertently assures the object's "theft without return." The "something" does not exist, but is hypostasized as a lack "in place." This is when the thing becomes truly lost—"stolen" by a narrative whose subject can only be inevitably constituted out of an object that has been lost.

Psychoanalysis has many hermeneutic variants to this lost object of narrative, in addition to the Oedipal (and Freudian) quest to regain the lost phallus. The object can be Lacan's veiled phallus-as-signifier—or, in Lacan's own corollary of the invisible phallus, it can be an "imaginary object" that the child concedes as being literally possessed by the father—a fetish, then, for the missing maternal phallus. Or, alternatively, again following Lacan, one could claim that it is not the phallus but "the abyss of the female organ" as "the primitive object *par excellence*" (*Sem.* II, 164)—in which case, the purloined letter, less a "thing" than a signifier of lack, finds its "place" in the gap of the Minister's mantelpiece, now to be "seen," like the abyss of the female organ, as the only true object in Poe's story.

The richness, alluded to earlier, of the letter "a" in psychoanalysis also complicates the already overdetermined status of the object. We have seen how Derrida has argued that if we "purloin" the *accent grave* from the "à," what results is the essentializing of lack as a "thing" (as in, "*la manque a sa place*"). In a footnote to her essay "The Frame of Reference," Barbara Johnson argues: "The letter *a* is perhaps the purloined letter *par excellence* in the writings of all three authors: Lacan's "objet *a*," Derrida's "différance," and Edgar Poe's middle initial, *A*, taken from his foster father, John Allan" (153, n13).[3] Jacqueline Rose also comments on the status of the "a," in Lacanian psychoanalysis in particular: "Certainly there is a shift in Lacan's own usage from the small *a* as a reference to the imaginary other (*autre*) to its use as a reference to absence (the *objet petit a*)" (160, n6). (I will not comment on the coincidence of Johnson and Rose both choosing to footnote and, thereby, marginalize what I think are useful insights into the interrelationship of the "a" and the object. I will simply foreground their discussions in the body of my own paper.) And finally, we can add the appearance in Lacan's *Schéma* L and R not only of the "a" of the Imaginary Other, but also the "i (*a*)" of mirror stage identification with a paternal imago.

This shifting status of the "a" is one reason why the status of the "object" is one of the most overdetermined concepts in psychoanalysis—and, in turn, why the handkerchief is perhaps the most overdetermined "object" in all of Shakespeare's plays (if not all literature). As one of the elementary phonemes of linguistics, the "a" (as in "*Da!*") constitutes the onset of language at the expense of the "thing" itself. Thus, the "a," as the phonemic signifier as pure substitute, can point to the effacement of the object. Or it can point to, like the Derridean "a" of différance," the dissemination of the object. Or, like the "a" of the *petit objet a*, it can suspend the object in a liminal boundary between the Real and representation. It is because of this problematic "a" in psychoanalysis that we are justified in returning to the question with which I opened my discussion: When is something not a *thing* anymore?

"Ceci n'est pas un mouchoir"

There seems little question that the handkerchief, the oft-discussed "recognizance and pledge of love," is the privileged "frame of reference" for *Othello*. Unlike the play's other two-dimensional, cloth objects, the wedding sheets on which Desdemona is sacrificed and even the metonymic "thirty sails" of the Turkish fleet, the portable (and losable) compactness of the handkerchief "spotted with strawberries" is Shakespeare's stage prop *par exellence*. But the handkerchief is a "frame" that both foregrounds and obscures its status as an object. Surely the handkerchief, where psychoanalysis repeatedly "finds itself" with ease, must rank as one of the most overdetermined objects in all of literature—so overdetermined in fact that it can be viewed as a "thing," a "symbol," a "signifier," an *objet a*, or, as Lacan might argue further, a non-Euclidean "topology of knots." Predictably, psychoanalytic hermeneutics will always make short work of the "thing"—and the handkerchief is no exception.

Lynda Boose's superb study of the handkerchief stresses the significance of its strawberries as an emblem of virginal blood and of marital consummation, and a mimesis of what Othello fears are Desdemona's "lust stained" sheets (362–8). Part menstrual cloth and part wedding sheet, the handkerchief and its provocative weave of strawberries are described by Edward Snow as "a nexus for the three aspects of woman—chaste bride, sexual object, and maternal threat. . . ." (392, n11). Adding to the overdetermination of the handkerchief (but also to the self-discovery of psychoanalysis) is its complex dual origin in the Oedipal triangle, part matrilineal (given to Othello's mother by an "Egyptian charmer") and part patrilineal (passed down to the mother by the Law of the Father). These dual narratives of origin suggest to André Green that the handkerchief embodies "the Moor's desire for the mother" (*Tragedy*, 100), anticipating Arthur Kirsch's claim that the handkerchief symbolizes "the primitive world of the child's merger with the mother" (736). Green takes a further Oedipal step by calling the handkerchief a "phallic emblem" of Desdemona's castration (110), and Rudnytsky calls it "a substitute ultimately for the absent maternal phallus" (185). And it is at this point that psychoanalysis has squarely and predictably "found itself," locating the handkerchief in the lack of the castrated woman.

Both Green and Rudnytsky, however, perhaps in anticipation of or as a reaction against Derrida's charge that psychoanalysis will always "find itself" in an Oedipal allegory, also adopt a Lacanian strategy in talking about the handkerchief. In addition to calling the handkerchief a "phallic emblem," Green also refers to it as "a signifier of desire" (*Tragedy*, 125),[4] while Rudnytsky remarks that the signifier of the handkerchief, like the purloined letter, "must reside ultimately in its function and not in its contents" (184). To dismiss the contents of the handkerchief in favor of its "function"—in effect, to move from the latent to the manifest organization of the narrative—is, I would argue, to make the move whereby psychoanalysis "finds itself" more authoritatively than ever. If not in an explicitly Oedipal allegory, then psychoanalysis certainly finds itself at the point at which it guarantees that the thing is no longer a *thing*.

Although, taken together, Boose, Snow, Kirsch, Green, Rudnytsky, and many others constitute the psychoanalytic *grand récit* of the handkerchief, we might argue that the hermeneutic possibilities for interpreting it have become dishearteningly infinite, and surely we can see that no single psychoanalytic narrative is going to achieve a successful consolidation of the handkerchief's psychic collage of menstruation, virginal bloodshed, its pubic weave, its phallic "worms . . . that did breed the silk" (3.4.71), the missing maternal phallus, the absent primal scene, the Law of the Name-of-the-Father, and so on. So aggressively do all the implications of the letter "a" in psychoanalysis assert themselves into the handkerchief's topology of knots that we can no longer refer to it as a handkerchief. We cannot pursue these hermeneutic options much further without transforming the handkerchief into an emblem for the latent rebus that is the Unconscious itself, where a loose syntax of barely cathected signifiers bump against one another in uninterpretable concatenations of contradiction and illogic.

The question becomes here, how do we treat the handkerchief's over-determination while still maintaining its "objectness"? The "logical" extension of the handkerchief-as-Unconscious might be an appropriate direction to take in light of Othello's literally becoming unconscious after his epileptic seizure, just after his a-syntactic (and unsuccessful) attempt to consolidate the meaning of the handkerchief: "Handkerchief-confession-handkerchief! . . . Pish!" (4.1.37–41). But rather than allowing the handkerchief to retreat so completely into the recesses of the Unconscious, I would argue that the very fact of its overdetermination can serve as the basis for a "new" psychoanalysis that will not "find itself" where it has (and has not) already been in the past. If for Lacan the purloined letter has no meaning—if, as Derrida argues, "its flight would not have taken place if it had made sense" (42)—the handkerchief has too much meaning, an excess of meaning. I argue neither for a simplification of the handkerchief's meaning, nor for additional meanings to its growing proliferation, but rather for a foregrounding of the very *excess* of its meaning as itself mean-ingful. If anxiety is not just an excess of neurosis but also the neu-rosis of excess, then we have reached the starting point for a psychoanalysis that "finds itself" in the displacement of a "thing"—but a thing that remains some-*thing*, not just a lack "in place." The irony is painful when Othello, afflicted with a headache, shoves the handkerchief away from his head, com-plaining to Desdemona: "Your napkin is too little." Like the hand-kerchief, anxiety knows too much, not too little.

Danger: Thirty Sails

In its simplest form, anxiety concerns itself with the "loca-tion" of dangers, and thus I would argue that *Othello* is a play less, perhaps, about jealousy than about danger. Othello was never so great as when he knew his dangers—when he met and confronted them on the exotic battlefields of the Levant. His extended wooing of Desdemona in the house of Brabantio is an eloquent account of the negotiation of his many "disastrous chances" (1.3.134) through prowess, courage, and will—through the successful marshalling of physical energy into the overcoming of external threats, the as-tounding transformations of taut vigilance into the explosive con-quering of danger. And, indeed, no one is more aware than Othello that the effects of such narratives of physical peril are often in-tensely erotic: "She lov'd me for the dangers I had pass'd" (1.3.167), he admits to the duke.

But real physical danger is far removed from the battle-grounds of the Unconscious—in some ways the most "imminent deadly breach" of them all—where latent dangers, inadvertently created to compensate for anticipated inadequacies, await their re-pressed returns. Othello's past engagements in battle involved the plotting of the enemy's coordinates on the grid of the battlefield—the simple and effective military strategy of search-and-destroy that culminated once, long ago, in Othello's seizing a "malignant" Turk, a "circumcis'd dog" (5.2.355), by the throat and dispatching him instantaneously. But often dangers resist plotting, susceptible as they are to the psychoanalytic allegory of the split subject. Sometimes they trace, like the Queen's purloined letter, not a dis-cernible course, but the less palpable "itinerary of the signifier," for which concepts like "placement" and "location" are irrelevant obstacles to the confronting of danger.

One of the major themes of *Othello* is that unlocatable dangers are always a source of anxiety. Let us take, for example, the Turkish fleet, whose elusive tacking between Rhodes and Cyprus traces an indeterminate course that arouses much anxiety in the Senatorial council-chamber. Unlike the Turkish "circumcised dog" that Othello had so easily dispatched long ago, this newer version of the Turks cannot be seized. At the same time terrifying and enigmatic, the Turkish fleet, like the ghost of Hamlet's father, is neither here nor there.[5] Advancing toward Cyprus, yet at times steering a "backward course" to Rhodes, the fleet has, as one of the Senators claims, "no composition" and "in these cases where the aim reports, / 'Tis oft with difference" (1.3.1–7). Frustrating the "aim" of the Venetians, the Turks expose the outmodedness of the Venetians' military obsession with the "location" of the dangerous enemy. If metonymy is the basic condition of signification, then the Turkish fleet exemplifies the axiom perfectly. The fleet is metonymic; like the handkerchief, it is a trope of displacement in a play about displacement. We might recall at this point that Lacan's oft-cited illustration of metonymy is "thirty sails" for thirty ships, itself taken from Quintilian's example of the part-for-whole ("The Agency of the letter in the unconscious," 156). Thus we should scarcely be surprised when the Venetian messenger, announcing to the council-chamber that an "after fleet" has joined the main fleet (a sinister "supplement" to the fleet's original ships), describes it as consisting "Of thirty sail" (1.3.37). Somewhere in these thirty metonymic and tacking sails the Venetians hope to discern the destination of the unreadable and uninterpretable Turks. Enacting the privileged Lacanian trope of metonymy itself, the Turks are unlocatable, effaced in the remainder—the "difference"—of their indeterminate tacks between Cyprus and Rhodes. Although they are finally done in (lost? drowned?) by the real physical danger of a violent storm at sea, the Turks have nevertheless established anxiety as the dominant effect—or *affect*—of the play. The metonymic shifts of their indeterminate fleet have constituted less a full-fledged naval assault than, by the admission of one of the Venetian Senators, merely "a pageant / To keep us in false gaze" (1.3.18–19). Thus early in the play the Turkish fleet establishes the tenuous connection between vision and location that will come to torment

Othello. Because of Othello's later demands for using the lost handkerchief as "ocular proof" of his wife's infidelity, he must learn the hard way that you can't see a metonymy. It will always be purloined under a "false gaze" (Lacan's "glance that sees nothing" [SPL, 44]) that breeds anxiety.

As much as anything, then, *Othello* is a play about defenses and discovering the location of dangers. One function of the seeming anticlimax of the Turkish threat is to dis-*locate* the action of the play from Venice to Cyprus, an island of "displacement" that is insecure and "weakly defended" (Kernan, 78)—the very locus of anxiety itself. Like Lacan's conception of the unconscious, Cyprus is literally "ex-centric," occupying its "proper place" far out in the ocean on the edges of civilization. Even after the drowning of the Turks, danger still erupts on Cyprus in the form of a brawl on Cassio's watch. An angry Othello, interrupted in his night of lovemaking, lectures: "What, in a town of war, / Yet wild, the people's hearts brimful of fear, / To manage private and domestic quarrel?" (2.3.213–5). In his anger, Othello seems almost embarrassed by the brawl, registering his sheer distaste that a drunken riot has intruded on the sanctity and solemnity of Cyprus's anxious vigil. But despite Othello's contempt for "private and domestic quarrels," these are precisely the new dangers he will have to face. Cyprus's vigil, of course, is for the Turks who continue to pose danger for Othello long after their defeat by drowning. We should recall that back in Venice it was, among other things, the threat of the Turks that interrupted Othello's and Desdemona's first night of lovemaking—and, as we shall see, this very interruption becomes Othello's new danger. Stranded in Cyprus without a conventional enemy to combat, Othello must face a new "enemy" in Desdemona, both a new bride and, in his own imagination, a "fair warrior"—an oxymoron that forces an uneasy combination of the military and the erotic.

It has often been noted that the soldier Othello is in over his head in a society where anxiety (the anxiety of husbands who worry about their adulterous wives, and the anxiety of wives who, in Iago's words, strive to "keep't unknown") is a routine way of life, merely part of the "discreet charm" of the Venetian bourgeoisie. For Othello, Desdemona's "displacement" from Venice to Cyprus becomes the convergence of the locus of Desdemona's own self-confessed "downright violence" (1.3.249) in marital love—a danger that is no less real for being less palpable. "Farewell . . . to big wars," as Othello will later lament to Iago, for the dangerous "hour of love" awaits. In "weakly defended" Cyprus, where danger lurks not only in petty theft but also, more figuratively, in displacement, Othello feels anxiety for the first time.

The "false gaze" of thefts without return

Any narrative of a "theft without return" will always be a narrative not just of desire but also of anxiety. As Freud's grandson Ernst came to learn, what is here (*Da!*) and possessed can always be there (*Fort!*) and lost. Possession is always caught up in a dialectic with loss. Othello (with his preoccupation with monogamy as property) fears this, and it is a source of anxiety for him. In his essay "*Othello:* An Essay to Illustrate a Method," now almost forty years old but still uncannily rich in its suggestiveness for psychoanalysis, Kenneth Burke has emphasized the importance of the concepts of property, ownership, and possession in the story. The play virtually opens with Iago's crude taunting of Brabantio: "Thieves, thieves, thieves! Look to your house, your daughter, and your bags! Thieves, thieves!" (1.1.79–81). The almost capitalist sense of ownership—its fetish for commodities—that pervades the play is summarized by Burke in a marvelous anticipation of post-structuralist perspectives:

> [A]dd the privacy of Desdemona's treasure, as vicariously owned by Othello in manly miserliness (Iago represents the threat implicit in such cherishing), and you have a tragic trinity of ownership in the profoundest sense of ownership, the property in human affections, as fetishistically localized in the object of possession, which the possessor is himself possessed by his very engrossment. . . . The single mine-own-ness is thus dramatically split into the three principals of possession, possessor, and estrangement (threat of loss). . . . *La propriété, c'est le vol.* (166–7)

No one is more aware than Othello of how easily things (people, daughters) can be stolen from possession. Much like the Minister in "The Purloined Letter" who so deftly steals the Queen's letter in her own watchful presence, Othello steals Desdemona (embodying, in Burke's terms, "the tensions, or mysteries

of property" [199]) from Brabantio in the bourgeois privacy and presumed safety of the old father's own home. But unlike the Queen
who alertly, if helplessly, witnesses the horror of her theft,
Brabantio does not know of the theft of his precious property until
Iago's piercing, belated cry of "Thieves!" Thus Brabantio is less
like the Queen in "The Purloined Letter" than the King, less a full-
fledged character than, as Lacan argues, the "'place' that *entails
blindness*" (SPL, 69), the "place," like the old men of farce and fa-
bliaux who are robbed unknowingly, that marks the site not of
blindness-as-insight, but of blindness-as-castration. This blindness-
as-castration is contagious, for so much of the rest of the play is
concerned with Othello's preoccupation that he will inherit the
"place" of blindness-as-castration, his fears that he already inhabits the liminal boundary between possession of Desdemona and
her theft. As Green argues, "He wanted the father's place: he has it.
This is as much to say that he puts himself in a position to lose it"
(*Tragedy*, 93).

    If the King in "The Purloined Letter" is "dead" (Derrida, 79),
then so also does Othello in some sense "die" when he is forced
into the circuit of the handkerchief. Because *Othello* is a performance and not a story, like "The Purloined Letter," the play's audience occupies the place of the Queen: that is to say, we see the
theft of the handkerchief but must remain silent as the "non-seer"
destroys himself over its function as "ocular proof." It is at this
point that we too, like so many of the play's characters, are implicated in the circuit of the handkerchief—and it is in this sense that
the circuit of the handkerchief becomes literally performative.
Perhaps the audience should blame *itself* and not Emilia for
Othello's not knowing the circumstances of its theft. Perhaps
every audience of *Othello* is slightly sadistic (not to mention
voyeuristic). As Lacan argues in his "Seminar on 'The Purloined
Letter,'" ". . . we might soon begin to wonder whether . . . it is not
this impression that everyone is being duped which makes for our
pleasure" (46). What if the "visual pleasure" for any audience of
Othello is watching the duping and subsequent torment of the
"'place' that entails blindness"?

    All of which is to say that Othello needs the wisdom of the
Queen. By definition, theft occurs, except in "The Purloined
Letter," where one does not *see* it. What makes the Queen so intriguing is that she may be the only character in literature who
does see the place from which the Other is looking at her. She

knows, after all, that the Other (the Minister who steals her letter) knows that she knows of the theft. This does not save her from anxiety, but, unlike Othello, her knowledge of the Other means that she at least *knows* that she suffers from anxiety. She knows that the subject is never the (only) one looking.

Moreover, if, as Jacqueline Rose argues, the voyeur (like psychoanalysis) "is always threatened by the potential exteriorisation of his own function" (156), then Othello, like psychoanalysis, needs to learn that he cannot see what he wants to see. *Othello*, we can argue, is a play based squarely on the act and importance of seeing—all of which brings us back to the over-determination of the handkerchief. Whereas the letter is stolen and hidden by the Minister, the handkerchief is stolen and *planted* as evidence, meant to be seen by Cassio and, eventually, Othello. (In this sense, the handkerchief, unlike the letter-as-signifier, *does* return to its origin.) But Othello suffers what Lacan calls "the realist's imbecility," the delusion that he will "see" what he is looking for. As Green claims, "Othello wants to see, as Oedipus wants to see. But neither of them has any ideas of what he is looking for" (127).

Perhaps even more significant for *Othello*, a corollary of the "realist's imbecility" is not just that you think you will "see" what you are looking for, but that you think that what has been lost, like the purloined letter, was once "possessed." But did anyone ever "possess" the handkerchief? Did it originate with the "Egyptian charmer's" gift to the mother? With his father's gift to his mother? With Othello's gift to Desdemona? With Cassio's gift to Bianca? If, like the purloined letter, the handkerchief has no possessor but displacement itself, then can Othello lose what he does not have?[6]

For that matter, what does it mean to say that the handkerchief has been lost? Green notes that the handkerchief takes on meaning only belatedly—that Othello "forecloses" the existence of the handkerchief only until it is lost (*Tragedy*, 125), forcing us to conclude that loss may be the site/sight of representation itself.[7] If Othello has "foreclosed" the existence of the handkerchief, then we should return to the circumstances of its "loss," Othello's headache that Desdemona attempts to bind with the handkerchief. At this point, the stage direction, deceptively simple, reads: "He puts the handkerchief from him, and it drops." (Again, we must wonder, has Othello, in some sense, *ever* seen the handkerchief?) The absence of human agency in the phrase "it drops" calls into question the very concept of "loss" itself.[8] (If the Queen at least knows when she has lost the letter, Othello cannot *remember* when the handkerchief was lost.) After its "loss," Emilia "steals" the handkerchief for her husband. But has it really been lost—and has it really been "stolen"? I would argue that herein lies one of the textual elegances of Shakespeare's version of the itinerary of the signifier. Whereas the purloined letter experiences only a literal theft prior to its circuit, the handkerchief inhabits a liminal boundary between loss and theft. Neither fully "lost" nor fully "stolen," it has never occupied a "proper place" either in Othello's psyche (in the history of his ego) or in the play itself. It is due to the narrative genius of Shakespeare that the pseudo-comedic pedantry of determining whether or not it is "lost" also constitutes one of the most painful moments in the play:

> Othello: Is't lost? Is't gone? Speak, is it out o' th' way?
> Desdemona: It is not lost; but what and if it were? (3.4.80–3)

If, as Cavell argues, tragedy is "an epistemological problem," then we are at the heart of the crisis in *Othello*. Although the location of the handkerchief is indeterminate, Desdemona's response indicates that she has missed her chance to tell Othello that you can't pin a meaning on the handkerchief (by claiming that it is "lost" or "possessed" by another).

This why we can begin to argue that *Othello* is a tale not of desire, but of anxiety. The Lacanian object of desire "isn't a question of recognizing something [some-*thing*] which would be entirely given" (*Sem*. II, 229). The object of desire is not *entirely given*; it is not something that would have already been there in the beginning. This object of desire "not entirely given" opens up the space of lack (the lack—not of the object—but the lack of *manque-à-sa-place*) that sustains the narrative of desire and deferral. But it can by no means be desire that induces Othello to look for the handkerchief. Othello "knows" his lack insofar as— through Iago—he comes to know that the handkerchief *manque à sa place*. It is not a case of its being "not entirely lost"—or rather, it is lost just enough to torment Othello that its return might not provide relief.

Narratives of repression and desire entail keeping something away from consciousness. But the handkerchief, on whose fragile, two-dimensional weave so much of the narrative depends, is an object under continual pressure to be *seen*, to be available to Othello's consciousness on demand. Like the Lacanian phallic signifier, which comes into play to achieve signification only if it is veiled and invisible, the handkerchief achieves prominence (is foregrounded in Othello's consciousness) only after it is lost and hidden from view. But unlike the phallic signifier, the handkerchief (and Othello knows this) has the simple capability of being *found* and being seen again. Though its loss (like the letter or the phallus) is structured around its lack, the lack is Real. Unlike the cotton-reel that embodies the dialectic between presence and absence, the handkerchief may come as close as anything in literature to an object that signifies itself. Neither an object of repression, nor an object of desire, nor an object that embodies the pure difference of presence and absence, the handkerchief *exists*—but less in its loss than in Othello's demand for "ocular proof." The fear that what you have you will lose and that what you have lost is a source of danger *is* the preservation of the thing *as* a thing—and it is the site of anxiety.

"It is the cause, it is the cause. . . ."

There is no-*thing* that causes anxiety—which is why, as we shall see, anxiety itself has no "proper place." This is not to say that anxiety does not displace itself throughout the itinerary of the thing—that it does not require the thing to evidence its psychic drama. But it also requires the body and the mysteries of its affects for its displacements. The difficulty, then, lies in locating the "proper place" of the link between symptom and object as part of our own anxiety of interpretation.

As I have suggested earlier, *Othello* is not a narrative of desire because we desire only what we lack.[9] Othello is rather a subject who, we could say, lacks (in the handkerchief) what he does not desire—or what he fears to desire. For Lacan, narratives of desire begin with representations of primordial objects, specifically with the attempt to recover the lost (m)Other through the *objet a*, which is never a "thing" itself, but what Green has referred to as a "structure of transformation" ("Logic," 185), lying somewhere between the Real of the mother and the Imaginary of the infant's signifying system. Thus narratives of Desire do not concern themselves with a particular object, but are structured around a lack that is the aftereffect of the subject's (long repressed) attempts to replace the *objet a.* "The loss of the object," argues Green, "is of no importance as long as desire survives and extends it" ("Logic," 177). But the loss of the object is precisely the crux of interpretation in *Othello,* and to call the play a narrative of desire (and, hence, of repression), is to run the risk of overlooking the "objectness" of the handkerchief, its palpable existence in the Real.

Moreover, because "lack" as a structuring principle has no economy, any effort to view *Othello* as a narrative of desire must contend with Shakespeare's foregrounding of Othello's physical affect in the play, his consistent charting of the link between symptom and emotion. As we have seen, Othello's prowess as a soldier has already made us aware that he used to be a man of physical power, presence, and sheer muscularity—a man whose physical readiness precluded the easy signalling of emotions. That Othello did not always exhibit such a volatility of bodily affect is evidenced by Lodovico's remark after Othello strikes Desdemona, "Is this the nature whom passion could not shake?" (4.1.265).

But Othello is a changed man following his marriage. After he is reunited with Desdemona in Cyprus, Othello experiences a "content, / . . . that is too much of joy" (2.1.196–7)—an excess of feeling that, as will become clearer later, could be described as unrelieved sexual tension. And when he is moved or angry, his violence is like the excess of the "Pontick sea" itself. Othello's fury after Cassio's and Montano's brawl on the watch is so intense that he warns, "Now by heaven, / My blood begins my safer guides to rule. . . ." (2.3.204–5). Following Iago's initial accusations of Desdemona, Othello's facial and bodily reactions are so readily observable that the ever-viligant Iago has no difficulty interpreting his misery: "I see this hath a little dash'd your spirits" (3.3.214), and "My lord, I see y' are mov'd" (3.3.224), and "I see, sir, you are eaten up with passion" (3.3.391). Despite Othello's clumsy denials, his feelings are an open book for such an astute interpreter as Iago, and thus Iago is able to judge his own successes simply by looking at Othello's face.

Ironically, it is the easy readability of Othello's bodily affect that draws the handkerchief into the play, making it such an object of prominence and assuring its fateful association throughout the play with Othello's physical agitations. (It might be appropriate at this point to make the obvious but necessary point that any handkerchief is meant to serve the purpose of absorbing the minor traumas of affect.j If the letter, as Barbara Johnson has noted, is known "only in its effects" (139), then the handkerchief, we can argue, is known only in its *a*ffects. It is the headache afflicting Othello after Iago's initial treachery that Desdemona tries to relieve by binding with the handkerchief. Iago's lie to Othello that he "did to-day / see Cassio wipe his beard" (3.3.437–8) with the handkerchief is an explicit linking of the handkerchief with the body; and Iago's image of (postcoital?) perspiration on Cassio's beard may have been on Othello's mind when he tells Desdemona that her hand is "Hot, hot and moist" (3.4.39). Bodily affect and the handkerchief are again associated in the renowned confrontation between Othello and Desdemona over its loss. Othello's affliction of "a salt and sorry rheum" (3.4.51) is the reason he demands the handkerchief that Desdemona cannot produce. The handkerchief also haunts the most violent outburst of affect in the play, Othello's epileptic trance, embedded as it is in Othello's raging doggerel just prior to his loss of consciousness: "Handkerchief-confession-handkerchief! . . . Pish! Noses, ears and lips. Is't possible? Confess? Handkerchief? O devil!" (4.1.37–43).[10]

Though the reader must operate in the absence of explicit stage directions, one can speculate that to a large extent the grim effectiveness of Iago's deadly magic is facilitated in its momentum by the sustained onset of Othello's bodily agitations, disturbances of libidinal economy—whatever one chooses to call them. We can imagine such readily visible (and highly theatrical) reactions as perspiration, hyperventilation, rolling eyes, stammering—all instances where Othello's bodily trauma might actually be working to serve not as a release from but as a physical cause for the further heightening of his emotions.

All of which leads us to return again to the question of what causes anxiety and the reasons why the handkerchief is, as Thomas Rymer would have it in his "A Short View of Tragedy," no "mere trifle" taken out of all proportion. Why does it elicit, in Rymer's words, "so much stress, so much passion"? Why does it elicit such an anxiety of interpretation—in both Othello and in the reader?

For Freud, anxiety has its roots in bodily affect, specifically a build-up of sexual tension seeking release. And Laplanche characterizes anxiety as "an affect in which nothing [no-*thing*] remains but the quantitative aspect" (*Life and Death*, 56). But this affect cannot be said to constitute an "origin" for anxiety in the

Unconscious. When Laplanche and Pontalis argue that "the affect cannot become unconscious in any strict sense" (393), they are emphasizing the fundamental gap in the psychoanalytic experience between body and representation. Thus anxiety, unlike repression, is not caused by a particular object (which, in the mechanism of repression, would be submerged and abandoned in the Unconscious), but is a state of physical agitation that lies in waiting for an ideational representative (like a handkerchief) to which it can attach itself. In short, anxiety lies in waiting for the opportunity to displace itself.

We would do well at this point to heed Jacques-Alain Miller's caveat that "affects are strangely coded" (28)—and so we should tread lightly in any effort to pinpoint the "cause" of Othello's anxiety. In the realm of psychoanalysis, affects are hard to read, as is evidenced by Desdemona's inability to discern the cause of Othello's headache. And it proves to be a fatal misreading that introduces the deadly handkerchief into the circuit of the play, rendering it not a forgotten memory in the Imaginary, but a Real "object" of danger.[11] Thus, the handkerchief, like anxiety itself, is the point at which repression *fails*. Again, Othello's headache is a key case in point. As a somatic conversion of Othello's fear of Desdemona, the headache cannot speak for itself. As a result, Othello's anxiety becomes a trauma, the "imminent deadly breach" that itself elicits an anxiety of interpretation, a resistance of its own identification.

To repeat, then, anxiety is the (unreadable) *failure* of repression. Specifically, I argue that Othello is not suffering from repression because the act of coitus with Desdemona has not perhaps occurred and is neither fully representable, nor fully repressible.[12] Othello's lament, "Why did I marry?" (3.3.246), is perhaps a more resonant question than he can possibly know. In the absence of inwardly cathected representations of sex, Othello is left to suffer the "quantitative aspect" of his physical agitation, a discharge of excitations that, like his experiencing the "too much of joy" upon his arrival in Cyprus, is always in excess of its own representation. Anxiety is such a radically different neurosis from repression that, as Samuel Weber argues, "anxiety calls the very process of cathexis itself into question" (50). Despite his protest to Iago to the contrary, it is all too easy for Othello to "make a life of jealousy, / . . . with fresh suspicions," because this is the very path of uncathected anxiety.

Thus in *Othello*, the independence of idea and affect is demonstrated by the way in which for Othello the "idea" of sex with Desdemona goes unrepresented—or as Laplanche might describe it, "perfectly decathected" and "rendered inaccessible" (56) in the wake of the quantum of affect. Insofar as the handkerchief could be viewed as a representation throughout the play and not an object, it is the means by which Othello unsuccessfully attempts to represent what is for him the unrepresentable: to echo Lacan, for Othello there is no "rapport sexuel"—only a handkerchief. It is ironic that *Othello* is a play replete with Iago's representations of the "beast with two backs"; he thrives on vivid *Vorstellungen* of coitus between Othello and Desdemona, as when he taunts Brabantio that "an old black ram / Is tupping your white ewe" (1.1.88–9). No one is more aware than Iago that Othello has no vision of coitus in his "mind's eye." The vulgarity of his demanding of Othello, "Would you, the supervisor, grossly gape on? / Behold her topp'd?" (3.3.396–7), seems designed less to exploit Othello's jealousy than to goad him into an unwanted cathexis onto the very idea of coitus—in effect, to force Othello's participation in a (belated) primal scene.[13]

All of which leads us back to the centrality of the concept of danger in *Othello*. Put simply, anxiety needs to pose an external danger—and, as we have seen, Othello's ego can only be constituted out of danger.[14] Insofar as Othello suffers a threat throughout the play, it is the trauma not of a real danger (like the aborted danger posed by the drowned Turkish fleet) but of an inability of the excess of his physical energy, his "too much of joy," to cathect on to a representation. In short, for Othello the act of coitus (again, like the drowned Turkish fleet whose anticipated danger also, in some sense, goes unconsummated) is a danger—and it is a danger on two "fronts": he is both afraid that consummation will not occur and afraid of it as a situation that must be avoided. It was one thing to conquer Desdemona with his narratives of physical danger; in Brabantio's house, after all, she is scarcely more than, as Green describes her, "a fortified place to be captured" (*Tragedy*, 109). But it is another to face the unknown "danger" of conquering her on the bridal bed. Although Othello could be certain that Desdemona loved him for the "dangers he had passed," he cannot now be certain that he can "pass" the dangers posed by the bridal bed and its staging of the "hour of love."

Thus the excitations that characterize anxious trauma are

always excessive—and in Othello's case the excess of energy, the "too much of joy," that is anxiety means that, as in the old days of combat, he must be in a state of preparedness for danger. Freud argues that anxiety arises when the psyche "feels itself incapable of fulfilling, through the appropriate reaction, a task (danger) *emanating from without*" (*S.E.* 3, 112). That danger "emanating from without" will become, for Othello, the handkerchief—less a symbol of jealousy, less a reminder that Cassio, its presumed "possessor," is cuckolding him, than it is a symbol that Othello has failed where Cassio has succeeded, failed to consummate his love for Desdemona. As Othello insists to the witnesses of his murder of Desdemona, ". . . but yet Iago knows/That she with Cassio hath the act of shame/A thousand times committed" (5.2.210–12). *This* is the "danger" lying latent in the handkerchief that Othello must react against. And the handkerchief is the "ideational representative" that Othello's physical agitations have been lying in wait for. The charge by past readers that, given the temporal claustrophobia of the action on Cyprus, it strains credulity to think that Cassio and Desdemona could have committed "the act of shame" even so many as ten time is irrelevant. Anxiety requires very little time to develop. As Lacan reminds us, "Anxiety is always defined as appearing suddenly. . . ." (*Sem.* I, 68). Thus anxiety is perfectly suited for the tight temporal unity of a play like *Othello*.

Othello's trauma of unrepresented coitus evacuates itself onto the handkerchief, ensuring that the trauma can only be experienced in displacement. What we as spectators see, however, is the handkerchief itself as the play's privileged trope of displacement, taking on meaning insofar as it absorbs an anxiety that can only manifest itself in displacement. Othello's anxiety is activated by the handkerchief, not an object of repression, but an *angstsignal* that takes on significance only belatedly—only because it is the displacement, the *entstellung*, of a coitus that cannot be represented. Rymer notwithstanding, the handkerchief is no mere trifle. It is a source of danger, whose loss is a threat that Othello must confront. As Weber argues, anxiety requires a "place" for its displacement. It requires an object to displace "outwards and forwards, . . . literally, something that is *placed-out-in-front*, spatially as well as temporally" (54). This is why the handkerchief is such an effective stage prop for theatrical presentation—and why anxiety is such a grimly appropriate psychic affliction for Othello. As a soldier, he is used to dangers that occupy a "place out in front"—a place *on* the battle front that renders the enemy easily locatable. But the problem remains for Othello that the handkerchief, though a thing, occupies, like the Turkish fleet, the place of dislocation, of *entstellung,* an object of danger in its very displacement.

Anxiety, then, becomes the expectation of its own trauma, its own danger. To echo Emilia on jealousy, the anticathexis of anxiety is "born on itself" (3.4.162)—and we are not to consider anxiety "for the cause" (160), for Othello is anxious because he is anxious. As the reaction against its own danger, anxiety is tautological, or, as Weber puts it, anxiety "has no proper place" (58). Or maybe it does—but only if its "proper place," like that of the purloined letter, "will be *and* not be where it is." This is what makes Othello's story of anxiety perhaps a more elegant narrative than "The Purloined Letter," our other privileged story about a "theft without return" and the anxious feelings of helplessness induced by the loss of an object. The theft of the letter initiates a fear in the Queen that is eliminated when Dupin returns it to her. Even though the letter, as Lacan stressed, has no meaning or content, there is something in the letter's return that can provide immediate comfort to the Queen. But even had the handkerchief been found (other than in Bianca's hands) and returned to Othello, he would still find it a source of danger because he can never be sure that he ever (like Desdemona) "possessed" it. In some ways, for Othello the handkerchief is perhaps less threatening in its continued loss. As long as anxiety enacts the trauma (drama) of the uncathected, he inwardly hopes, despite his plea for "ocular proof," that, like the drowned Turkish fleet, it remains lost. We can recover a lost object through a compensatory *Vorstellung,* but the displaced object of anxiety defies such recovery, even when it is "found."

An(X)iety:
Where psychoanalysis does not "find itself"

If the *objet a* is not a representation but, as Ellie Ragland-Sullivan has argued in her essay, "Lacan, the Death Drive and the Dream of the Burning Child," the primal lack in representation— i.e., the loss of the (m)Other whose gap must be compensated for through representation—then we could view the handkerchief-as-object as not the *limits* of representation, but the *excess* in representation that renders the handkerchief, as we have seen, not an object of repression (like the *objet a*) but an object of confrontation, or, as Freud would call it, the "nodal point" of anxiety (*S.E.*, 16, 373). The handkerchief constitutes the excess that is beyond representation—beyond representation as having a "proper place" in the psychic history of the ego. If the *objet a* is the loss that can only be repressed, the lack that touches off the signifying chain of desire, then the handkerchief is the danger that must be confronted—a "dangerous" exteriority that derives its danger from the excess that *is* displacement.

Where does psychoanalysis "find itself" in this discussion of Othello's handkerchief? Does the story of *Othello* enact the loss of the handkerchief as a trope for displacement (as I have been suggesting up to now)—or does it enact, in some larger sense, the displacement of displacement as the trope for anxiety? If we view the handkerchief as a trope for displacement, then we have merely recapitulated the story of "The Purloined Letter" as what Barbara Johnson has referred to as the "allegory of the signifier" and its prescriptive rule that the displacement of the signifier is displacement itself. For Poe's story, in the beginning was the letter, an object whose itinerary eventually tropes its way into becoming a signifier of displacement. But in *Othello*, in the beginning is the handkerchief as a symbol of displacement (an aftereffect of anticathexis) that paradoxically tropes its way into becoming an object. In *Othello*, in the beginning we are already presented with anxiety-as-displacement. If Poe's story builds into a narrative that only in the end demonstrates the trope of neurosis (of "neurosis" as the "realist's imbecility" that believes one can actually "hold" or "possess" a signifier), *Othello* is always already a narrative not of the trope of neurosis, but of the *neurosis of trope*, the psychic affliction of displacement-*as*-displacement, the psychic affliction of an anxiety that resists its own identification. In "The Purloined Letter," we can watch the letter being displaced, but in *Othello* we cannot watch anxiety resisting its own identification through its displacement onto the handkerchief.

But to pose the question again, where does psychoanalysis "find itself" in any discussion of anxiety? If, as Weber points out, anxiety was not a term introduced by psychoanalysis (48), then isn't anxiety an unlikely diagnosis for psychoanalysis to "find itself"? Freud, never fully succeeding in pinpointing the "danger" to which anxiety reacts, designated its quantum of affect as an "X," marking the spot of the displacement of anxiety. As Weber argues,

"This 'X' marks the spot to which psychoanalytical thinking is constrained . . . to return, a spot that is impossible to occupy because it is impossible to locate" (59). But I would argue that this "X" marks the spot not of the "constraining" but of the enabling of a psychoanalytic hermeneutic of anxiety.

If, as we have seen, the "a" of psychoanalysis has always been where psychoanalysis "finds itself," where, as Derrida charges, psychoanalysis "come[s] under the jurisdiction of what it itself produces"—or if the "a" (as in *objet a*) always marks the *limit* of representation, the limit where psychoanalysis finds itself in the phallic allegory of a thing that is never quite a *thing*—then I would argue that the "X" is a more enabling letter for psychoanalysis, marking, as it does, the point at which psychoanalysis "finds itself" in displacement, i.e., "finds itself" by, in effect, *not* finding itself in the thing as a thing. A hermeneutic of anxiety dictates that interpretation does not "arrive at its destination."

The resistance of anxiety to its own identification is the "X" where, Derrida notwithstanding, psychoanalysis resists "finding itself." If the handkerchief cannot be found on the Minister's mantelpiece, if it cannot be found between the legs of Desdemona, if it cannot even be found in the recesses of Othello's unconscious, then neither has psychoanalysis found the "proper place" of anxiety. Barbara Johnson has argued that psychoanalysis is "the repetition of a *trauma of interpretation*" (142). Or rather we should effect a simple reversal and say that psychoanalysis (at least wherever anxiety is concerned) is the *interpretation of a trauma* that will always be in excess of its own representation. Just as the handkerchief can always be "found" in the dislocation of the anxious excess of Othello's psyche, so also can psychoanalysis be "found" in the "X" of anxiety, the unlocatable e*X*cess of displacement. Most enabling for a psychoanalytic hermeneutic of anxiety is its glance toward the long-neglected Lacanian Real. Not surprisingly, Ellie Ragland-Sullivan describes the Real as "an algebraic x, inherently foreclosed from direct apprehension or analysis" (*Jacques Lacan*, 188). As an "algebraic x," the Real enables us, at least, to *infer* the existence of a Real object (not a lack) that structures the narrative of anxiety as displacement. A hermeneutic of anxiety, then, is just such a manipulation of the "algebraic x." Existing somewhere between Freud's "nodal point" of anxiety and Lacan's Real, the "X" of anxiety both traces the "realist's imbecility" that is the anxiety of interpretation, while at the same time vindicating the "realist's imbecility" that some-*thing* is "out there" in the Real. If narratives of desire are structured on a lack that always knows too little, then we may say that anxiety is structured on an excess (on the "X" of excess) that knows too much. Because anxiety always knows too much, a hermeneutic of anxiety will never arrive at its destination. In the alphabet of psychoanalysis, anxiety finds its "proper place" not in the "a" but in the "X."

Notes

1. Peter Rudnytsky's perceptive essay "The Purloined Handkerchief in *Othello*" first suggested the purloined letter of Poe's story (and the subsequent continuum of Lacan-Derrida-Johnson on the letter-as-signifier) as a useful analogy for understanding the circuit of Othello's handkerchief. But what is primarily at stake for Rudnytsky in applying this analogy is his argument that the handkerchief is the missing maternal phallus of Desdemona as the site of castration. It will become apparent, especially in the next section of my paper, that my use of the metaphor of the purloined letter is very different from Rudnytsky's.

2. This is perhaps why, as Jonathan Culler has argued, narrative is "the preferred mode of explanation for psychoanalysis" (178). As I will eventually argue, a hermeneutic of anxiety neither traces nor requires a narrative in any conventional sense of the term.

3. I would argue further here that if the purloined letter exists somewhere between Poe's story in English and Lacan's analysis of it in French, then so also can the phenomenological status of the handkerchief be determined somewhere between the French letter "a" as an unsignifiable remainder, and the English indefinite article "a" as the designation of a thing.

4. In another essay, "The Logic of Lacan's *objet (a)* and Freudian Theory," Green makes a brief but suggestive case for the handkerchief as the Lacanian *objet a*, "ultimately revealing to Othello his desire" (184).

5. The Lacanian dis-*place*-ment of the metonymic ghost of Hamlet's father, like that of the Turkish fleet, is nicely summarized by Rainer Nägele: "the ghost of Hamlet's father is here and everywhere. But he is never there, where Hamlet stands and speaks. . . . But he speaks for Hamlet, in his place. Hamlet speaks there, where he is not" (5).

6. The play is resonant with the confused echoes of the question of

the ownership of the handkerchief. Bianca demands of Cassio, ". . . whence came this?"—and, later, "Why, whose is it?" Cassio can only reply, "I know not, neither" (3.4.180–7). When Bianca throws the handkerchief at Cassio in anger, Othello exclaims with no small measure of uncertainty, "By heaven, that should be my handkerchief!"⁴ (4.1.157), and later, almost literally enacting the "'place' that entails blindness," he asks of Iago, "Was that mine?" At the end of the play, Othello asks Cassio, "How came you . . . by that handkerchief that was my wive's" (5.2.319). The tragic flaw of Othello is that he never comes to realize that no one "owns" the handkerchief except the Law of anxiety. This "Law" is never more authoritatively exemplified than in the fact that, despite Emilia's and Cassio's wishes, the "work" of the nonmimetic handkerchief (unlike the purloined letter) cannot be "copied" and cannot be exchanged.

7. In her essay, "*Sir Orfeo:* The Representation of a Return to the Repressed" (forthcoming in *Assays 8*), Ellen Martin argues, "We can only continue to have, we can only trust, what we un-have through representation. When we lose something, we do miss it and mourn for it, but if it had never come into a mediating imaging of itself, we would never have had it to lose. . . ." We could say that Othello "trusts" in the handkerchief only in its loss. But, as I will later argue, Othello never really formulates "a mediating imaging" of what the handkerchief comes to represent. (Although I do not link anxiety with repression, I am indebted to Martin's paper for its intriguing connection between anxiety and the representation of loss; and throughout my paper I am indebted to her focus on the concept of interpretation as anxiety.)

8. If we go back almost a century ago to A.C. Bradley's lectures on *Othello,* we can detect one of the earliest efforts by Shakespearean critics to preserve the loss of the handkerchief in a kind of "realist's imbecility" of logical positivism. In the course of his analysis, Bradley makes several illogical assumptions, demonstrating that the concept of "loss" will often escape scrutiny. First, Bradley assumes that Desdemona drops the handkerchief (147); but, as we have seen, the stage directions do not permit the assumption that *either* Othello *or* Desdemona is responsible for its loss. Furthermore, we can move at this point to Bradley's own footnote (again, the marginalization in the footnote of what is often most interesting), where he argues that when the handkerchief drops, "neither she nor Othello observes what handkerchief it is. Else she would have remembered how she came to lose it, and would have told Othello [during their later confrontation]" (147, n3). Somewhere in Bradley's syllogism is an embedded assumption that mars his logic. For Bradley, the remembrance or forgetting (repression?) of the loss of something seems to hinge on whether or not the object is especially treasured in some way: if Desdemona had known that she had lost the treasured handkerchief, then

she could have told Othello. Bradley's embedded assumption, then, is that the loss of something that is treasured enables us to reconstruct (belatedly?) its origin in loss. Although Bradley's argument depends on a tautology, in its own way it reenacts the repetition compulsion of psychoanalysis to find an origin—in Bradley's case, the "primal scene" of loss—through a narrative. And, after all, at virtually the same time as the publication of Bradley's Oxford lectures, Freud, in Vienna, was attempting to do the same thing for the Wolf Man. Bradley, like Freud, threatens to make loss (and its reconstruction in memory) the primal scene it seeks.

9. In his essay, "The Sound of O in Othello," Joel Fineman makes a brilliant case for Othello as a narrative of desire, arguing that Othello is "absent to the self that bears his name [which is the name of desire itself]" (84). Fineman's essay privileges not the letter "a" of psychoanalysis, but the letter "O," what he calls the play's "abject O's, which I . . . associate with Lacan's objet a, . . . the occasion of desire" (88). Much of Green's essay, "Othello: A Tragedy of Conversion," is also an extended analysis of desire as the key structuring principle of the play.

10. It is worth noting that the two people who attempt to minister to Othello's pains—Desdemona, when she attempts to bind Othello's headache early in Act 3, and Cassio when, entering soon after Othello's epileptic seizure, he attempts to "Rub him about the temples" (4.1.52)—are the two people most entangled in the itinerary of the handkerchief.

11. It is Othello's anxiety then that makes the handkerchief more than simply a kind of anaclitic object-choice, a token of parental nourishment and protection. Although its anaclitic value makes it an appropriate target for the free-floating energies of Othello's anxiety, I will argue that parental memories are not nearly so threatening to Othello as the absence of a representation of coitus.

12. The possibility that Othello is suffering from sexual anxiety is argued by Stanley Cavell, Edward Snow, and Stephen Greenblatt. Cavell views Othello as "horrified by human sexuality, in himself and in others" (137). Snow claims that Othello harbors a "post-coital male disgust with the 'filthy deed' of sexuality itself," (388) while Greenblatt argues that the cause of Othello's sexual anxiety is "his buried perception of his own sexual relations with Desdemona as adulterous" (233). My argument has no particular stake in maintaining the allegory of misogyny that pervades these accounts of Othello's sexual anxiety. My argument is simple: Othello fears (and probably has not had) sex with Desdemona. The energies of my argument are concerned not with tracing Othello's misogyny but with a careful maintaining of Othello's sexual anxiety as *anxiety*, and with preventing the term from slipping into discussions of repression. Snow contends that Othello's anxious jealousy is because of "unconscious

pressures" and "unconscious scenarios" (394), while Greenblatt, as we have seen, speaks of "buried perceptions." But I am suggesting that anxiety, if it is to remain *anxiety*, must be kept separate—or at least further apart than either Snow or Greenblatt would allow—from repression.

Much of my argument draws out the implications of Stanley Cavell's provocative suggestion that Othello and Desdemona head into Act 3 never having really consummated their love. If, as Cavell claims is possible, Othello and Desdemona are interrupted in their bridal bed by angry shouts in the street (or perhaps, more significantly, by the impending Turkish threat), and if they are again interrupted in Cyprus by the brawl on Cassio's watch, then they may quite literally have indulged in scarcely more than *coitus interruptus*. (See Cavell, 131–2). In addition, André Green asks, "Who can say what took place during their wedding night. And one may well wonder what Othello means when, weeping over Desdemona's corpse, he remarks: 'Cold, cold, my girl! Even like thy chastity'" (*Tragedy*, 110). And most recently Joel Fineman argues that "Othello never consummates his marriage until the climactic moment in which he strangles Desdemona, when the marriage bed . . . becomes the death bed" (92)—all of which is another way of arguing that Othello achieves orgasm (a kind of spiritual death) only through the murder of his wife.

13. Snow argues that Iago's vulgar insistence that Othello observe the act of sex between Cassio and Desdemona "implies a displacement of sexual desire onto the act of looking, knowing—where it becomes intrinsically unsatisfiable, a kind of perverse anti-sexuality or death-drive" (396). Of particular usefulness to me in my argument is Rudnytsky's claim that in *Othello*, "the 'absent thing' is in one very concrete sense the sight of Desdemona engaged in intercourse with Cassio" (175).

14. Lacan argues that the object of anxiety mirrors for the subject "the very figure of his dehiscence within the world" (*Sem.* II, 166).

Works Cited

Boose, Lynda E. "Othello's Handkerchief: 'The Recognizance and Pledge of Love.'" *English Literary Renaissance* 5 (1975): 360–74.

Bradley, A.C. *Shakespearean Tragedy.* New York: St. Martin's Press, 1969.

Burke, Kenneth. "*Othello:* An Essay to Illustrate a Method." *Hudson Review* 4 (1951): 165–203.

Cavell, Stanley. *Disowning Knowledge in Six Plays of Shakespeare.* Cambridge: Cambridge University Press, 1987.

Culler, Jonathan. *The Pursuit of Signs: Semiotics, Literature, Deconstruction.* Ithaca: Cornell University Press, 1981.

Derrida, Jacques. "The Purveyor of Truth." Translated by W. Domingo et al. *Yale French Studies* 52 (1975): 31–113.

Fineman, Joel. "The Sound of O in *Othello*." *October* 45 (1988): 76–96.

Freud, Sigmund. *The Standard Edition of the Complete Psychological Works of Sigmund Freud.* Translated by James Strachey et al. Edited James Strachey. London: The Hogarth Press, 1953–74.

Green, André. *The Tragic Effect.* Translated by Alan Sheridan. Cambridge: Cambridge University Press, 1977.

———. "The Logic of Lacan's *objet (a)* and Freudian Theory: Convergences and Questions." Translated by Kimberly Kleinert and Beryl Schlossman. In *Interpreting Lacan: Psychiatry and the Humanities*, 6. Edited by Joseph H. Smith and William Kerrigan. New Haven, Conn.: Yale University Press, 1983.

Greenblatt, Stephen. *Renaissance Self-Fashioning.* Chicago: University of Chicago Press, 1980.

Johnson, Barbara. "The Frame of Reference." *The Critical Difference: Essays in the Rhetoric of Reading.* Baltimore: Johns Hopkins University Press, 1980.

Kernan, Alvin. "*Othello*: An Introduction." In *Shakespeare: The Tragedies.* Edited by Alfred Harbage. Englewood Cliffs, N.J.: Prentice-Hall, 1964.

Kirsch, Arthur. "The Polarization of Erotic Love in *Othello*." *Modern Language Review* 73 (1978): 721–40.

Lacan, Jacques. "Seminar on 'The Purloined Letter.'" Translated by Jeffrey Mehlman. *Yale French Studies* 48 (1972): 38–72.

———. *The Seminar of Jacques Lacan. Book I: Freud's Papers on Technique.* Edited by Jacques-Alain Miller. Translated by John Forrester. New York and London: Norton, 1988.

———. *The Seminar of Jacques Lacan. Book II: The Ego in Freud's Theory and in the Technique of Psychoanalysis.* Edited by Jacques-Alain Miller. Translated by Sylvana Tomaselli. New York and London: Norton, 1988.

———. "The Agency of the Letter in the Unconscious." In *Ecrits: A Selection.* Edited and translated by Alan Sheridan. New York and London: Norton, 1977.

Laplanche, Jean. *Life and Death in Pyschoanalysis.* Translated by Jeffrey Mehlman. Baltimore: Johns Hopkins University Press, 1976.

Laplanche, Jean and J.-B. Pontalis. *The Language of Psycho-Analysis.* Translated by Donald Nicholson-Smith. New York and London: Norton, 1973.

Martin, Ellen. "*Sir Orfeo:* The Representation of a Return of the Repressed." Forthcoming in *Assays* 8.

Miller, Jacques-Alain. "A and a in Clinical Structures." In *Acts of the Paris-New York Psychoanalytic Workshop.* New York, 1986.

Nägele, Rainer. "The Provocation of Jacques Lacan: Attempt at a Theoretical Topography apropos a Book about Lacan." *New German Critique* 16 (1979): 5–29.

Ragland-Sullivan, Ellie. *Jacques Lacan and the Philosophy of Psychoanalysis.* Urbana: University of Illinois Press, 1986.

———. "Lacan, the Death Drive and the Dream of the Burning Child." Paper delivered at the Conference on Representations of Death. Harvard University, November, 1988.

Rose, Jacqueline. "The Imaginary." In *The Talking Cure: Essays in Psychoanalysis and Language.* Edited by Colin MacCabe. New York: St. Martin's Press, 1981.

Rudnytsky, Peter. "The Purloined Handkerchief in Othello." In *The Psychoanalytic Study of Literature.* Edited by Joseph Reppen and Maurice Charney. Hillsdale, N.J.: The Analytic Press, 1985.

Rymer, Thomas. "A Short View of Tragedy." In *The Critical Works of Thomas Rymer.* Edited by Curt A. Zimansky. New Haven, Conn: Yale University Press, 1956.

Snow, Edward A. "Sexual Anxiety and the Male Order of Things in *Othello.*" *English Literary Renaissance* 10 (1980): 384–411.

Weber, Samuel. *The Legend of Freud.* Minneapolis: University of Minnesota Press, 1982.

Bruce Fink

READING HAMLET WITH LACAN[1]

*Je te demande de refuser ce que
je t'offre puisque ce n'est pas ça.*

Lacan's reading of *Hamlet* constitutes a kind of encounter—
though perhaps not exactly a chance encounter or an instance of
τυχή. Lacan was working on a number of problems when he took
up *Hamlet,* among them the following: how desire comes to be
constituted and what is involved in symbolic castration. Few
people approach literary texts looking for insights concerning such
subjects, and that may account in part for the apparent strangeness
of the way Lacan goes about exploring this Shakespearean text.

Lacan does not set out to analyze the author of the play—
Shakespeare himself—as have other psychoanalytic interpreters.
He adopts a rather different approach here, as in his work on "The
Purloined Letter" and in Seminar VIII, *Transference,* where he
takes up Plato's *Symposium.* His intent is not simply to read into
poetic works psychological structures that have already been identified but also to seek new psychoanalytic insights in poetic works.
He says that the latter *engender* psychological creations more than
they reflect them. There is, nevertheless, a sense in which Lacan
simply applies his "graph of desire" to the play, showing how

Hamlet, the character, can be situated on it; but his reading takes him beyond a simple application of his own preexisting notions.

His intent is thus not so much to interpret the play as to learn from it. The play, he says, teaches us something about human desire and something about the phallus: it at once illustrates for us the passing of the Oedipus complex through the intervention of castration (a notion Freud had already developed in his paper "The Passing of the Oedipus Complex") but also—and herein lies its originality—how something comes to be equated with symbolic castration and serve the same purpose as the latter in a case in which it had not taken place (at the age at which it is generally considered to take place).

This very particular equation or substitution allows Lacan to develop a theory of how such substitutions are generally possible. As always in psychoanalytic work, "the particular is what has the most universal value."[2]

Substitution is a fundamental concept in Lacanian psychoanalysis, and it is related in some sense to notions like compensation and supplementation. Consider Lacan's view of the treatment of psychosis: the latter is defined by Lacan as a problem with the symbolic order as a whole—something is said to be missing therein, which leads to a skewing thereof. The symbolic thus needs to be shored up: something has to be used to compensate for the deformed workings of the symbolic, something has to be found that can hold some semblance of structure together (structure here consisting of the three intertwined orders: symbolic, imaginary, and real) when an essential link that should be there is not. Some other register must be developed in such a way as to cover over the hole in the symbolic and keep the three registers functioning together.

In the treatment of psychosis, one of the analyst's primary goals is to make the imaginary register serve as a prop or even as something of a stand-in for part of the symbolic order—a sort of building up of one order around another that is defective or failing in some respect.

In the case of neurosis we could make out the claim, on the basis of what Lacan says about Hamlet, that one way or another *symbolic castration must come about if the "problem of desire" is somehow to be resolved,* if, that is, the neurotic's desire is to be somehow "freed" from the Other's desire. Thus the two questions Lacan was puzzling over before devoting himself to a sustained reading of *Hamlet*—how desire comes to be constituted and what symbolic castration is all about—become intertwined in the course of his reading.

He focuses in particular on two exemplary scenes, and without wholeheartedly endorsing his interpretation of them as concerns the letter of the Shakespearean text, I nevertheless think he successfully isolates two crucial moments in the development of the play and of Hamlet, the character.

I

"What Hamlet is faced with [. . .] is a desire [. . .]. This desire is far from being his own. It is not his desire *for* his mother, but rather his mother's desire."[3] Lacan thus begins his reading by stressing that it is not Hamlet's *own* desire that is a problem, but rather another person's desire *insofar* as it has been incorporated by Hamlet, yet never assimilated, subjectified, or made his own.

While most critics seem to have emphasized the stasis or knots in Hamlet's desire or will, Lacan shifts ground, pointing to how *Hamlet is captivated by his mother's desire:* in a certain sense her desire constitutes a space within which his movements are confined.

Lacan points to the scene following the one in which the traveling troupe of actors has enacted a murder. Hamlet goes to see his mother in her "closet" as it is called in the play (act III, scene IV). By this time, Hamlet has not only the word of his father's ghost but also Claudius's reaction during the play within the play to convince him of Claudius's guilt. His intention now is supposedly to kill Claudius. And yet, summoned by his mother, he decides to work on her:

> "... Soft! now to my mother.—
> O heart, lose not thy nature; let not ever
> The soul of Nero enter this firm bosom:
> Let me be cruel, not unnatural:
> I will speak daggers to her, but use none;
> My tongue and soul in this be hypocrites,—
> How in my words soever she be shent,
> To give them seals never, my soul, consent!"

Then, to his mother he says:

> "Come, come, and sit you down; you shall not budge;
> You go not till I set you up a glass
> Where you may see the inmost part of you" (act III, scene IV).

He decides to lecture her and to thereby try to bring her back into the fold. He sings the praises of her former husband, upon whom

> every god did seem to set his seal,
> To give the world assurance of a man;
> This was your husband.—Look you now, what follows:
> Here is your husband, like a mildew'd ear
> Blasting his wholesome brother. Have you eyes?
> Could you on this fair mountain leave to feed,
> And batten on this moor? Ha! have you eyes?
> You cannot call it love; for at your age
> The hey-day in the blood is tame; it's humble,
> And waits upon the judgement: and what judgement
> Would step from this to this?

Despite her protestations to the effect that he is killing her with his remarks, despite her entreaties for him to stop, culminating in her exclamation, "O Hamlet, thou hast cleft my heart in twain," he continues,

> O, throw away the worser part of it,
> And live the purer with the other half.
> Good-night: but go not to mine uncle's bed;
> Assume a virtue, if you have it not.
> That monster custom, who all sense doth eat,
> Of habits devil, is angel yet in this,—
> That to the use of actions fair and good
> He likewise gives a frock or livery
> That aptly is put on. Refrain to-night;
> And that shall lend a kind of easiness
> To the next abstinence: the next more easy;
> For use almost can change the stamp of nature,
> And either curb the devil, or throw him out
> With wondrous potency.[4]

His whole sermon seems up until this point to aim at convincing her to leave behind her sinful lust, to let good judgment regain the upper hand, and little by little to turn Claudius, the usurper, out of her bed, her heart, her life. All along his mother has been protesting, saying stop, enough, please, I can't take any more, but—after this whole lesson in morality and Hamlet's profuse demand that she try to rectify, to however small an extent, what has been done—when Hamlet says

> So, again, good-night.—
> I must be cruel only to be kind:
> Thus bad begins and worse remains behind.—
> One word more, good lady.

The queen suddenly replies, "What shall I do?"

The queen suddenly acquiesces, in a sense, to Hamlet's demand: she seems to give in and request his counsel as to the course of action she should follow. What does Hamlet do?—he backs down.

Lacan, while emphasizing the reversal in Hamlet's attitude, does not pinpoint it in this exact passage (at the end of scene IV), suggesting instead that it is the ghost's earlier intervention in the scene that brings on the about-face in Hamlet's approach. The ghost tells Hamlet to

> step between her and her fighting soul.—
> Conceit in weakest bodies strongest works.—
> Speak to her, Hamlet.

and Hamlet begins anew lecturing his mother on how she should behave in a fashion befitting a queen. Lacan thus attributes the turnaround to the dead father's appearance on the scene, but Hamlet can also be seen as backing down at the very moment at which his mother says, "What shall I do?"

Whereas Hamlet has been insistently demanding that she clean up her act, thrust aside lust, and "assume a virtue, if [she has] it not"—in a word, that *she give up on her desire*—he suddenly backs down. He seems to do so at the very moment at which he senses her acquiescence, and no doubt precisely because she seems to be acquiescing.

Hamlet makes a demand upon her—"throw the toad out"—
and yet as soon as she begins to yield, he says 'forget it.' In response to her "What shall I do?", he replies: "Not this, by no means,
that I bid you do."

Shakespeare here provides us a fine illustration of Lacan's distinction between demand and desire. Hamlet makes a quite explicit demand on his mother, *his desire being for her to say no to
his demand.*

- His *demand*: throw the bugger out, agree to my request, give in.
- His *desire:* say 'no.'

Hamlet could not bear for his mother to assent to his demand.[5] For that would give him the lion's share of space in his
mother's desire. He would become the main focus of her desire,
the main occupant of her heart,

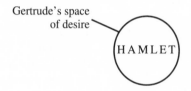

FIGURE 8.1
Hamlet's Place in Gertrude's Desire

meeting with untimely success in his Oedipal struggle. There is
never any suggestion here that Hamlet's "development" is so
stunted that he could actually "return" to a mother-child dyad,
willingly assuming all of the space of his mother's desire.
Alienation,[6] that first operation of symbolic castration, has clearly
taken place for Hamlet as speaking being. What Lacan does claim
is that Hamlet's submission or subordination to his mother's desire remains very great, overpowering, in fact, until he is able to
construct for himself something that can complete his castration—
and I would suggest that this constructing involves a form of separation.

Lacan refers to this moment in the play as "a time of oscillation"; Hamlet's appeal to his mother "fades and vanishes as he
consents to his mother's desire. He lays down his arms before this

desire which seems ineluctable to him, unmovable" (*Ornicar?*, V. 25, p. 21). Consider this in relation to the graph of desire. A child's "needs" (associated with the small triangle at the point of origin of the arrow) must be interpreted and recognized or consented to by the Other, or mOther in this case ("A" on the graph) in order to take on any kind of social existence. Need has no existence in the world of speaking beings until it has been translated, assimilated, and absorbed into language and thus into the Other as language or linguistic Other (as we might translate Lacan's *"l'Autre du langage"*). Need thereby becomes something foreign and alienated, loosely speaking.

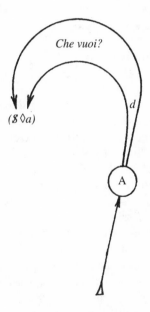

FIGURE 8.2
Utopian Moment of the Graph of Desire

There is a sense in which desire is conceived of here—in Lacan's Seminar VI, *Desire and Its Interpretation*, of which his reading of Hamlet constitutes seven lectures—as something that goes beyond the alienation inherent in the absorption of need into the symbolic order. It may be viewed as a sort of utopian moment wherein one somehow gets beyond subjugation or domination by the Other (illustrated by that part of the graph that rises above and beyond the circle containing the Other). And yet the very dictum Lacan repeats again and again, "man's desire is the Other's desire,"[7] tells us that desire itself can be alienated in the sense of not being one's own, being instead some foreign extraneous thing grafted upon a living being—or, to use Bergson's metaphor, "encrusted upon the living."

But in Lacan's discussion of Hamlet, there seems to be something more redeeming about it: "full-fledged" desire is endowed with the ability to get beyond the Other, to break on through to the other side, as it were, and become autonomous or free from the Other's clutches.

At the very next stage of the graph of desire, however, a complex kind of loop seems to develop, closing off this "utopian" escape from the circuit. Jacques-Alain Miller has shown that the graph of desire can be derived from group theory diagrams, and that it is a fairly direct spin-off of the $\alpha,\beta,\gamma,\delta$ Network found on p. 57 of the French *Écrits* (Seuil, 1966), that network representing the autonomous functioning of the symbolic order in the unconscious. The graph indicates that there is but a limited number of permutations possible, and thus only certain directions allowed in running through the circuit. While there seems to be an out, an exit, an opening toward freedom at the *Che vuoi?* stage of the graph, it seems to evaporate when Lacan proceeds to the next stage of the graph (two short pages later in "Subversion of the Subject and Dialectic of Desire" in *Écrits*).

Why does that utopian moment, designated by the placing of fantasy ($\$\lozenge a$) at the end of those hopeful arrows in the *Che vuoi?* diagram, vanish? As a first attempt to explain why, we might consider the clinical observation that, after a longer or shorter period of analytic work, analysands are often able to remember fantasies that had clearly been unconscious, and are terribly dismayed to realize that they correspond detail for detail to fantasies recounted by their parents and/or other relatives. They are even more likely to be outraged and disgusted[8] at the realization that not even their "innermost" fantasies are their own. Their sense is that these important others (incarnations of the Other) have been so invasive as to attack even their "own" most "personal" fantasies. Not even repressed fantasies are really one's own: they too are colored or tainted with otherness.

Desire and fantasy are thus brought back into the circuit, the circuit of the complete graph of desire, corresponding, in some sense, to only those permutations and combinations allowed by the symbolic order.

The move beyond the Other illustrated by the *Che vuoi?* arrows amounts, according to Lacan, to the real question a child asks its parents. The child's questions, "What do you want?", "What do you want from me?" can be translated as "What is my place in all of this?" Hamlet's "question,"[9] and Lacan views this question as being posed in Hamlet's long tirade to his mother in act III, scene IV, is "Where do I fit in?"

Lacan's gloss here seems to imply that there are essentially two kinds of answers the neurotic can receive to that question. In other words, the Other or mOther can respond in two different ways. Graphically speaking, she can respond at a higher or a lower level, she can elevate or bring down her neurotic child. According to Lacan—and this is one of the points in his interpretation with which I do not agree, but that nevertheless illustrates the working of his graph of desire—the *"response"* provided by Hamlet's mother to Hamlet's "why don't you throw the toad out" is as follows: "I just can't, I'm a sex maniac—that's just the way I am, I need a man all the time."[10] Lacan situates that response at the level of s(A), the signification of the Other (or the mOther's meaning): an explanation provided by the mother about herself. Gertrude's response, as Lacan sees it, does not concern Hamlet—she does not, for example, say, "Why don't you mind your own business?!" or "You are not enough for me, I cannot live without someone else in my life"—but rather simply describes Gertrude herself: "that's just the way I am."

According to Lacan, however, Hamlet was for once seeking an answer at some other level, or even no response at all. Lacan puts forward the notion that the neurotic must be confronted with the fact that there is in the Other no signifier that can answer for (*répondre de*) what he or she is.[11] That *"répondre de"* has to be understood quite forcefully. Suppose that a number of French-speaking people are involved in a conspiracy to kill the president, and one of them mentions that if they don't bump off the vice-president at the same time, the situation will be even worse than it was at the outset. Another of the conspirators then turns to the group and says, *"je réponds de lui."* It will be immediately understood that that conspirator is taking upon himself or herself the responsibility of putting the vice-president six feet under. He or she is telling them, "I'll take care of him," "I'll take responsibility for that particular detail." Similarly, when Lacan says that there is no signifier in the Other that can *répondre de* what I am, he doesn't simply mean "answer for," but "account for," "take responsibility for." It is not simply a signifier that tells you what you are but one that takes you under its wing, defines you, protects you, and constitutes your *raison d'être*.

There is no such signifier, but not every mother allows her children to realize that. Some mothers lead their children to believe that there *is* such a signifier and that it's called mom. When, according to Lacan, Hamlet surreptitiously slips Gertrude the question, "what's my place in all this," she doesn't say, "damned if I know, and anyway you're old enough to figure it out for yourself." Hamlet's mother never answers his questions with a "how should I know"; instead she says, at least these are the very words Lacan puts in her mouth, "I am what I am; in my case there's nothing to be done, I'm a true genital personality—I know nothing of mourning" (*Ornicar?*, V. 25, p. 23).

The point is that the mOther's discourse here has to do with herself, her own identity, her own characteristics. It concretizes something about the mOther—and it's plain to see that it concerns lack: according to Lacan she says she has to be "getting it" all the time. But the answer is incommensurate with the question as Lacan understands it. If you ask your mother what you mean to her, and she answers by saying she loves petting cats, and every time your discourse is a fairly transparent cover for the same what-do-I-mean-to-you type question she answers in the same general way, talking about herself, she gives a particular kind of meaning to your question, and meaning is always determined retroactively. You may think your questions are about some sort of larger life-related issue, but the type of response you receive may prove them to be "about" something else. Your mOther here decides the meaning of the question you formulated, using the code made available to you by the Other as language; your statement comes into being as some particular message on the basis of her response. Thus, according to Lacan, Hamlet's mother converts Hamlet's discourse, Hamlet's repeatedly expressed desire to know where he fits in, into demand pure and simple, i.e., into a demand for attention/love. All demands are ultimately, according to Lacan, regardless of their apparent content, demands for love. By converting Hamlet's desire into demand, Gertrude flattens it out, bringing it down to the lower level of the graph.

Some other kind of response might have been able to bring Hamlet face to face with the signifier of the lack in the Other, finally separating him from the symbolic order, i.e., from the Other as language. This signifier of lack in the Other, S(Ⱥ), can, for all intents and purposes here, be considered equivalent to the signifier of (the Other's) desire, Φ, lack and desire being coextensive. Hamlet looks to the Other for an answer about who and what he is. Instead of being given an answer at the level of meaning (as in the case in which Gertrude, according to Lacan, responds by talking about the kind of woman she is), he would, in the best of all possible worlds, be led to encounter the signifier of desire that just is—having no rhyme or reason, no explanation, justification, or *raison d'être.* The burgeoning desire (d) that we see precariously perched on the "ladder" leading to the upper level of the graph would become full-fledged due to its encounter with Φ as signifier of desire, i.e., as signifier of the Other's desire. And a type of *jouissance* would become possible that is correlated with symbolic castration (see the upper horizontal arrow in the complete graph).

The concept of Φ, the phallic signifier or signifier of desire, in Lacan's work is related, at least in part, to triangulation: the need for a third term if the danger inherent in a dyadic mother-child relationship (potentially leading to psychosis) is to be obviated. That is one of the greatest dangers from the Lacanian vantage point. There must be a third term in what the mother says, i.e., in her discourse: not necessarily a real husband, boyfriend, lover, or what have you, but a place, a term reserved for someone else, someone other than herself and her child.

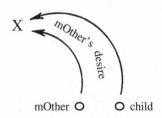

FIGURE 8.3
Man's Desire Takes the Other's Object As Its Own

Now since man's desire is *the same* as the Other's desire, it adopts as its object the same object desired by the Other, mysterious as that object may be (assuming there is some such object, that is, some third term in the mother's discourse). If we refer to that object as an X, an unknown, we see that a child's desire mimics his or her mother's desire.

In such a case, there is a third term that simultaneously occupies the space of the mother's desire in which the child has come into existence as barred subject. Try as he or she might, the child cannot occupy the whole of that space.

Hamlet's mother does not, according to Lacan, make mention of that third-term place holder. Hamlet can thus be understood to remain caught within her space of desire. Alienation has clearly taken place: Hamlet *has* entered the Other's world (something autistic children do not do, or just barely) and assimilated the Other's language and the desire with which it is ridden, but separation has not occurred. Momentarily associating that X, that unknown object of desire, with object (a) instead of Φ, we can see that Hamlet (as barred subject) has yet to split off from the Other, taking object (a) with him, as it were.

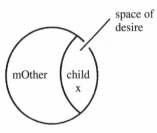

For separation is not simply a breaking away from the mOther but a decompleting of the mOther (signified by A̶) as the child comes to be in relation to an object that functions independently, in some sense, from the mOther. Whereas that object may have been intimately related to the mother's *desirousness* at the outset, through separation it takes on a life of its own, in a manner of speaking.[12]

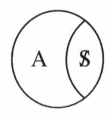

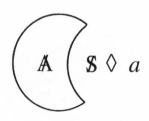

FIGURE 8.4

What Lacan refers to in his work on Hamlet as accession to the upper level of the complete graph—an encounter with the signifier of the lack in the Other—translates in his later terms as the advent of object (a) and the subject's separation. No longer *"à l'heure de l'Autre,"*[13] subjugated by the Other's will, swept along by the Other's every whim and fancy, and unable to initiate any action of his own, Hamlet, when he finally reaches this stage (which he does, according to Lacan), is able to act.

II

In his classes on *Hamlet*, Lacan attempts to account for Hamlet's acts, his ability to bring on symbolic castration resulting in the passing of his Oedipus complex, and his reincorporation of Ophelia as object of desire, all on the basis of his rivalry with Laertes. This may seem rather odd, at first, as after all it is Lacan who tells us that rivalry of this kind is indicative of specular/imaginary relations, and that imaginary relations *interfere* with symbolic ones, one of the goals of analysis being, in a sense, to clear away or deflate these imaginary antagonisms and relations, and establish ever clearer symbolic ones.

But Hamlet by no means undergoes analysis and must make do with the means at hand. Lacan sustains that it is thanks to his rivalry with Laertes that Hamlet is able to catapult himself beyond the lower half of the graph, that half associated with alienation. This construction seems, at first sight, to bear an affinity to work with psychotics, where one seeks an imaginary support with which to prop up the symbolic order. But whereas the imaginary relationship between Hamlet and Laertes is clearly the catalyst here, the process is closer in kind to that at work in the three-prisoner problem Lacan lays out in his article "Logical Time and the Assertion of Anticipated Certainty,"[14] involving a *precipitation of subjectivity through an accumulation of temporal tension.* Just as, in that article, the prisoners are forced to subjectify the situation, due, of course, to the logical constraints of the situation but also to the specular nature of their reciprocal relations, so too Hamlet is led, owing to the course of events and his rivalry with Laertes, to become the subject of his fate.

Laertes is clearly depicted in the play as Hamlet's equal in many respects—they are both excellent fencers,—and Hamlet himself tells us that he sees Laertes' as very like himself:

> For by the image of my cause I see
> The portraiture of his. . . .

In the cemetery scene, Hamlet competes with Laertes in the expression of grief over Ophelia's death. In act V, scene 2, Hamlet agrees to fence with Laertes in fulfillment of a bet made by Claudius—i.e., in fulfillment of another person's demand (indicating that he is still *à l'heure de l'Autre*). At another's behest, he willingly accepts to be a pawn in Claudius's wager. And Lacan says here that "This encounter with the other is there to allow Hamlet to at last identify with the fatal signifier." "The instrument of death can only be given him by an other" (*Ornicar?*, V. 26–27, p. 26).

The "fatal" or "lethal" signifier is a term advanced in the course of Lacan's first interpretation of Hamlet's shift at the end of the play, which seems to rely on a very Freudian view of the phallus. This first interpretation begins with a play on words (Ibid.):

> Hamlet: ". . . Give us the foils; come on.
> Laertes: Come, one for me.
> Hamlet: I'll be your foil, Laertes; in mine ignorance
> Your skill shall, like a star in the darkest night,
> Stick fiery off indeed."

The pun here is on the word "foil," meaning rapier or sword, but also a setting for a jewel: the mount or hole in which a jewel is set; a foil-leaf is placed in the setting to set off the polished stone and make it shine still more. The foil here is a reflector—it reflects back Laertes's skill and prowess. Or at least that seems to be the most obvious interpretation, given that Hamlet says to Laertes, "Your skill shall, like a star in the darkest night, stick fiery off indeed," in other words, be set off to best advantage.

According to Lacan, however, "In this pun there is, in the final analysis, an identification with the lethal phallus" (Ibid., p. 27). But apart from Hamlet's association of himself with a foil, the arm or weapon Laertes will use against him—that aspect of the pun that leads Lacan to speak of an identification with the lethal phallus—it seems to me that many of the connotations lead in a rather different direction: "I shall be my own undoing, I'll do the work for you, I'll be the best reflector of your talent, I'll be the setting, the foil-leaf in the hole in which you will be set, mounted, and displayed in all your glory." Hamlet seems to me to be adopting the position of setting in which Laertes will be placed to be shown off to his best advantage.[15]

Clearly, there is a sense in which Hamlet, in saying "I'll be your sword" is identifying himself with a phallic-like symbol. It is, however, a double-edged sword, in that it is a phallus that is weak compared to Laertes's, Hamlet claiming that he is bound to lose, and thus his sword will bend or yield beneath Laertes's blows, before Laertes's prowess. (There are no doubt further possible meanings, such as "I'll be your undoing.")

A second interpretation is, however, forthcoming by the end of Lacan's seventh talk, according to which it is Laertes's evocation of the hole created by Ophelia's disappearance that brings on a mobilization of logos in Hamlet; here Φ finally comes forth for Hamlet as the signifier of the lack in the Other, allowing him to identify the phallus beyond the King and act.

Stated somewhat differently, the emphasis placed by Laertes on Ophelia's disappearance amounts to an insistence upon the lack in the Other, a lack in the symbolic order.[16] That insistence leads Hamlet, due to the rivalry between he and Laertes generating a great deal of subjective tension, to a mobilization of logos around this lack, and the eventual surfacing (surgissement) of Φ, the advent of Φ as the signifier that can signify the lack in the Other and that, qua signifier, need not be identified with any particular warm or cold body ("The King is a thing. . . .").

Time seems to play an important role in the mounting of this subjective tension:

> Laertes: It is here, Hamlet: Hamlet, thou art slain;
> No medicine in the world can do thee good;
> In thee there is not half an hour of life;
> The treacherous instrument is in thy hand,
> Unbated and envenom'd: the foul practice
> Hath turn'd itself on me; lo, here I lie,
> Never to rise again: thy mother's poison'd:
> I can no more:—the king, the king's to blame.
> Hamlet: The point envenom'd too!—
> Then venom to thy work. [Stabs the King]

Faced with the certainty of death, Hamlet can finally act—certainty seems to elude him throughout the play, but finally emerges due to the immanence of death. Hamlet is here faced with a kind of "now or never" situation where, already partly separated from life itself, he is at last able to separate from the Other and enact his *own* will.

Separation is ultimately what analysis with neurotics is all about, i.e., symbolic castration has never been *thoroughly* effectuated in the case of most neurotics. Apart from all the symptoms neurotics present—whether psychosomatic or "purely" psychical—due to identification with parents, relatives, and friends, which must obviously be worked through, a large part of the work with neurotics revolves around the completion of separation. Psychoanalytic techniques such as punctuation and the variable-length session were developed for precisely that particular job.

An implication of Lacan's discussion of *Hamlet* is that life/history may create the circumstances necessary for the kind of precipitation of subjectivity that is orchestrated under "controlled" conditions within the analytic setting. The timing of those circumstances, when fortuitously orchestrated by life itself, may, however, leave a great deal to be desired.

I do not entirely agree with Lacan's conclusion that Hamlet does take the leap in the end:[17] it is not at all clear to me that Hamlet is ever able to act in any full sense of the term. Consider one of his last passages:

> I am dead, Horatio.—Wretched queen, adieu!—
> You that look pale and tremble at this chance,
> That are but mutes or audience to this act,
> Had I but time,—as this fell sergeant, death,
> Is strict in his arrest,—O, I could tell you,—
> But let it be.—Horatio, I am dead;
> Thou liv'st; report me and my cause aright
> To the unsatisfied.

"Had I but time": Hamlet's time never comes—now he is *à l'heure de la mort*. He remains as neurotic as ever, his time is never now, he cannot speak his piece, someone else must speak for him and plead his cause before the world. He is forever constrained, never free. The neurotic never acts in the present, living instead in the past or but for posterity—posthumously.

Notes

1. This paper presents a number of the themes developed in a series of talks at the University of California at Irvine, organized by John Smith and Julia Lupton, which were subsequently condensed for a lecture given in the context of Ken Reinhard's course on Lacan at UCLA.

2. *Ornicar?*, V. 24, p. 12; all translations of Lacan's work provided here are my own.

3. *Ornicar?*, V. 25, p. 20.

4. Hamlet expresses here decidedly behavioristic views!

5. And there is a sense here in which *the content of demand is irrelevant:* The question at issue is whether or not the other person, the person to whom the demand is addressed (in this case the mOther), will accede, will give in.

6. See Lacan's discussion of the your-money-or-your-life paradigm in Seminar XI, *The Four Fundamental Concepts of Psychoanalysis,* where he first introduces the operations of alienation and separation. Cf. my article, "Alienation and Separation: Logical Moments of Lacan's Dialectic of Desire," in the *Newsletter of the Freudian Field,* V. 4, 1990, for a long and detailed exploration of these two operations.

7. Cf. bottom of p. 814 in the French edition of *Écrits: "le désir de l'homme est le désir de l'Autre ... c'est en tant qu'Autre qu'il désire."*

8. Their disgust is a confirmation that the fantasies in question were repressed, disgust being, as Jacques-Alain Miller has so aptly pointed out, a sure sign of repression.

9. And to Lacan's way of thinking, desire is essentially a question.

10. I fail to see exactly where Gertrude says or implies any such thing.

11. *"[I]l n'y a dans l'Autre aucun signifiant qui puisse dans l'occasion répondre de ce que je suis," Ornicar?,* V. 25, p. 32.

12. For a more complete and precise account, see my article on "Alienation and Separation," op. cit.

13. *Ornicar?*, V. 26–27, p. 14.

14. *Écrits,* Seuil, 1966; English translation by Marc Silver and Bruce Fink in *Newsletter of the Freudian Field,* V. 2, No. 2, 1988. See my detailed commentary thereupon, "Logical Time and the Precipitation of

Subjectivity," in *Reading Seminars I & II: Lacan's Return to Freud*, eds. Richard Feldstein, Bruce Fink, and Maire Jaanus, Albany: SUNY Press, forthcoming.

15. Lacan, however, takes the other meaning of "foil" to be *écrin* or jewelry box (not mount or setting), a false lead, to the best of my knowledge, perhaps suggested by one of the French translations of *Hamlet* Lacan was consulting at the time.

16. Lacan refers to it in 1956 as a hole in the real, but as we know from his later work, the real is smooth and unrent; only the symbolic order can be characterized as having a hole or as lacking something, e.g., a book on a library shelf is missing because it has a place in the Dewey decimal system, not because there is a real space for it on the shelf.

17. Nor with many other of his conclusions, e.g., that Gertrude does not make mention of a third term, etc.

Maire Jaanus

KUNDERA AND LACAN:
DRIVE, DESIRE, AND ONEIRIC NARRATION[1]

I

In the realm of totalitarian kitsch, all answers are given in advance and preclude any questions. It follows, then, that the true opponent of totalitarian kitsch is the person who asks questions. *A question is like a knife* that slices through the stage backdrop and gives us a look at what lies hidden behind it. In fact, that was exactly how Sabina had explained the meaning of her paintings to Tereza: on the surface the *intelligible lie;* underneath the *unintelligible truth* showing through.[2] [my ital.]

Like Lacan, Kundera opposes truth and knowledge. Truth has to do with the unintelligible, the nonsensical, the mute—with cutting, surgery, and questions—whereas knowledge is about answers, the requirement of coherence in discourse, intelligibility, and, for Kundera, totalitarian kitsch. Knowledge is a form of systematization, bounded and inert; truth, by contrast, is coextensive with origination, invention, and birth. "In all knowledge once constituted there is a dimension of error," writes Lacan, "which is the forgetting of the creative function of truth in its nascent form."[3] Truth belongs fundamentally to the unconscious and to the obscure origins of psychic reality whereas knowledge is allied to political, social, and academic life. If the state and the university are not particularly interested in psychoanalysis, it has to do with their desire for sense, meaning, the verifiable, and objective—for a knowledge that has power precisely because it claims, erroneously, to be synonymous with truth.

By Kundera's definition the novel is a genre that asks questions.[4] Questions, traditionally, are an opening, akin to the unknown and possibility, while answers are the known, the definite, connected to closure and a limit. *The Unbearable Lightness of Being* opens with a strange query: was Parmenides correct or not when he identified lightness as positive and weight as negative? "That is the question," quotes Kundera (6), echoing *Hamlet,* and with it all the weight of the ambivalence of that play, which he makes reverberate through his own highly ambiguous "meditative interrogation."[5]

Kundera links his characters to an unintelligible core, to their dreams, to a question. A question is, as Lacan said, what constitutes a subject.[6] Unanswerable questions direct us toward the unconscious. The question for Tereza is: what is the link between my soul and my body? Or as the text says:

> Then what was the relationship between Tereza and her body? Had her body the right to call itself Tereza? And if not, then what did the name refer to? Merely something incorporeal, intangible? (139)

Tereza names her heifer "Marketa" and her dog "Karenin," but she is not able to name herself. A name unifies the spirit and the body, but Tereza wonders whether in her case it refers only to her spirit. The corporeal part of her being is at once too terrifying and too common to bear the individualizing and unifying mark of a name. Thus, her unnamed, and hence unowned, body lacks that first distance from the organism, which Freud called the "bodily ego," the ego centered on an image of the whole body.[7] This first "image ego"—born of the surface of the body or taken like a photograph of its exterior, and wholly imaginary—initiates a narcissistic, mirror self-servitude, but it operates also as a defense against the fragmented body in pieces left behind.[8]

Tereza is torn between her desire for a body *image* and a terrified sense of her real, "rumbling," and fragmented *organism*. From girlhood on, Kundera tells us, she has stood before the mirror looking for her bodily ego—a face, distinct from that of her mother—on the surface of her body, away from its interior.

> She would stare all the more doggedly at her image in an attempt to wish them [her mother's features] away and to keep only what was hers alone. Each time she succeeded was a time of intoxication: her soul would rise to *the surface of her body* like a crew charging up from the bowels of a ship, spreading out over the deck, waving at the sky and singing in *jubilation.* (41) [my ital.]

She wants the mirror image to eradicate her sense of herself as a "mere resounding soulless mechanism," (57) or an animal organism, dehumanized and automated. Whenever the mirror does reflect her desire, there is cause for jubilation.[9]

> . . . She forgot she was looking at the instrument panel of her body mechanism; she thought she saw her soul shining through the features of her face. She forgot that the nose was merely the nozzle of a hose that took oxygen to the lungs; she saw it as the true expression of her nature. (41)

Even if images are "our animal weakness," as Lacan once said,[10] we need the specular image to protect us against our organism and to mediate the physically real. A visually objective self institutes a cut that allows the body to become an *object.* An object that we can *see* assures us of existence. The body image seems to be real and to guarantee entification even if it is only a virtual, paradoxical, and untouchable reality. It has evidential force and the power of authentification. It is as Roland Barthes said, "a certificate of presence."[11] But Tereza, who wants to obliterate duality rather than to accept division, cannot steadfastly see her bodily ego before her as an *object* that could, narcissistically, be loved. For her there is no libidinal rebounding of form or the shelter of an imaginary identification. Not being a fully split and castrated subject—

one secured in images fastened to words—she depends on Tomas to make not only her soul but her body unique and present for her by the force and exclusivity of his love. She wants him to confirm the indivisibility of her body and soul.

Given her intense desire for a stable self-image and her unconscious hatred of her mother as well as of Tomas [as emerges in her dreams (15)], it is not surprising that she finds fulfillment, briefly, as a maker of images, a photographer, in the Prague Spring of '68 when she takes photographs preserving "the face of violence for the distant future" (67) out of "passionate hatred" (71).

Tereza was an unwanted child, born because a doctor refused to perform an abortion (42), "born of the rumbling of a stomach" (39) rather than of the desire of a man and woman. This beginning puts her in conflict with her organism and its "ventral voices" (39) all her life. Her striving is to separate not only her bodily ego, but more fundamentally, her very organism, from that of her mother, haunted as she is by the sense that she is still organically bound to her mother's insides, to her stomach, the site of primary connectedness for all of us.[12] She is mortified that her stomach rumbles when she sees Tomas, given that she was especially concerned with keeping *her* face, i.e., her soul before her body on this day, so as to be represented by something other than her animal organism.[13]

> During the journey, she made frequent trips to the toilet to look in the mirror and beg her soul not to abandon the deck of her body for a moment on this most crucial day of her life. (53)

Unsure, unstable, unsymbolized, without a body image or ego to uphold and protect her, and lacking language, she is left with an hysterical and violent body, nervous, graceless, and helpless, caught in desperate dreams and vertigo.

> Several hours after the decision [to obey Tomas and not visit her mother] she fell in the street and injured her knee. She began to teeter as she walked, fell almost daily, bumped into things or, at the very least, dropped objects.
>
> She was in the grip of an insuperable longing to to fall. She lived in a constant state of vertigo. (61)

Her hands and feet tremble; she falls, stumbles, teeters. She can't walk properly. She drops things. She is like the child in a state of motor helplessness, lacking muscular coordination, fragile and fragmented. Her mother robs her of her access to the imaginary and the symbolic, but without her mother she has no hold on life at all. She falls. Her vertigo is a not a fear of falling but a desire to fall, to return to the archaic maternal corporeality that she was able to leave only because her mother never spoke to her in a "loving voice" (60). Her mother never talked to her. She "talked no baby talk. She did not talk at all" (42).

Tereza is infected by her mother's somatophobia, her extreme hatred and disrespect for the body:

> Tereza stood bewitched before the mirror, staring at her body as if it were alien to her. . . . She felt disgusted by it. It lacked the power to become the only body in Tomas's life. It had disappointed and deceived her. (139)

Her mother became disappointed in her own body when it failed to deliver to her the love, satisfaction, and power that she thought her due as a desirable, young, and nubile women, "a beauty" in whom her grandfather had seen "the image of Raphael's madonna" (42). In a revenge that turns itself on her own flesh and that of all others, she diminishes the carnal to the level of the worthless, the merely animal, and traps Tereza in an abysmal bodily humiliation.

> 'Tereza can't reconcile herself to the idea that the human body pisses and farts,' she [the mother] said. Tereza turned bright red, but her mother would not stop. 'What's so terrible about that?' and in answer to her own question she broke wind loudly. (45)

Tereza's mother is a prisoner of the instinctual body, the body of the inner organs and their raw, grinding processes. She is unaware of the body of the drives, proposed by Lacan, that other body developed from the erogenous zones, in connection with the demand of the other.[14] The drives move within the open surface zones of the body and not within the interior organism, but Tereza's mother is concerned with bringing forth the interior. Belching, burping, breaking wind, pissing, blowing her nose—these noisy processes and *sounds* become means by which the mother oppressively asserts the identity of the human and animal organism, or of the instinctual body and the drive body. She wars for the triumph of an unbearable physical coarseness—degenerate and degrading—that would testify to the truth of her own felt, subjective experience of having been subjugated and defeated by the bodily real. She blocks Tereza's desire to find both a face and a voice and to become a named, symbolized *human* body.

> When she lived at home, her mother forbade her to lock the bathroom door. What she meant by her injunction was: Your body is just *like* all other bodies; you have no right to shame; you have no reason to hide something that exists in millions of *identical* copies. In her mother's world all bodies were *the same* and marched behind one another in formation. Since childhood, Tereza has seen nudity as a sign of concentration camp *uniformity*, a sign of humiliation. (57) [my ital.]

A concentration camp is the systematic subtraction of all that is human about humans, previous to their total erasure in mass graves. It is an unrelentingly cruel and brutal tearing off of the coverings of clothes and culture, the annihilation of the imaginary-symbolic environment that protects humans against their fundamental nothingness and sameness. By a bold analogy Kundera makes the concentration camp experience a psychic reality for this child kept uncovered by her mother. Tereza's mother is naked herself and demands that Tereza be naked as well.

> At home, there was no such things as shame. Her mother marched about in the flat in her underwear, sometimes braless and sometimes, on summer days, stark naked. (45)

Tereza's mother denies her the right to privacy and to cover her nakedness with differentiating images and words. Tomas says of her that she came to him "uncovered" (209).

Tereza yearns for what is *beyond* the body (49), for voice (Tomas's), for music (Beethoven), for language (she carries with her *Anna Karenina*), for images (the mirror, photography), but she is unable to leave behind the indelible, traumatic inheritance from her mother, centered on the abject body, which continues to mark both her life and her dreams. Her dreams have all to do with ferocity, with being literally hunted by others as if she were an animal, ever on the verge of imminent annihilation. Executioners stalk and dominate her in her nightmares, demanding her extinction. She is not able to pass beyond the organism of her mother, an instinctual representation of the body that makes her want to die.

Tomas, her libertine husband, leads her right back to the female *organism*, close up to it, forcing as if her very face into the vagina of another woman. "All . . . night she . . . had to inhale the aroma of another woman's groin from his hair" (139). She is subjugated by smell, the most primitive and animal of the senses, by the real of sexual odor.

Like everyone in the book, she is caught in what Lacan in the 1950's called "the fundamental disorder of the instinctual life of man,"[15] as she is unable to maintain the distinctions between need, drive, and desire. Given her demoralizing impasse and Tomas's infidelities, she attempts an affair, the solution of the flesh, and has an intense experience of the body's independent orgasmic will—its power for excitation and arousal. But while her body discharges in pleasure, and ecstasy "flow[s] through her veins like a shot of morphine," (156) she spits in dismayed revolt in her lover's face.

The shock of pleasure that the encounter with sexuality and the real brings is objectionable, giving no lasting satisfaction nor an answer to her question. The encounter foregrounds her body, bringing it to prominence, ["her own body, newly discovered, intimate and alien beyond all others, incomparably exciting" (161)], but as an organism, in which little human remains, nearly annihilating the bit of ego and soul that she has. The undesired orgasm—the violently voided discharge, that comes, as do her spit and her feces, from her insides with unstoppable force—is simultaneously blissful and disgusting to this woman of the unsymbolized body. It is for her a shocking encounter with the inner organic self, with the real, and an affirmation of her mother.

> She was sitting there on the toilet, and her sudden desire to void her bowels was in fact a desire to go to the extreme of humiliation, to become only and utterly a body, the body her mother used to say was good for nothing but digesting and excreting. . . . Her soul . . . had retreated deep into the body again, to the farthest gut, waiting desperately for someone *to call* it out. (156–7) [my ital.]

Her sexual experience leaves her with "a feeling of infinite grief and loneliness" (157). She has become the utterly worthless piece of feces, the unwanted fetus, to be expelled, as her mother wished to expel her in an act of abortion. The anal universe where all differences are abolished reclaims her.[16] She is nothing but imageless, unformed flesh again, producing particles of interchangeable and chaotic fecal matter. She has betrayed her soul. Drive and desire collapse back into mere need. Need is a reduction to the self-preservative processes of digestion and excretion. She has returned to the mother, the merely animal. She approaches a state of dejection close to death.

Thereafter, all that she can unconsciously think of doing with her body is to bury it, to cover it up with earth, the only *cover* left for her. Burial, which Vico called one of the founding rites of civilization, is the rite that grants *another* status to the body than that of animal. The idea, no doubt, comes to her when she tries to rescue a near-dead crow, cruelly buried alive by some children, because her own exposed, "concentration camp" body seems to her even less covered and less civilized than a properly buried corpse.

She dreams that she has already been buried for a long time and lies sleeplessly waiting for Tomas to come and knock on her grave (a macabre version of Sleeping Beauty), so that she can come out. He wipes the dirt from her eye sockets, while she says, "I can't see any way. I have holes instead of eyes" (228). But as his visits become less frequent, and she sleeps less and less waiting for his return, and grows more and more ugly to behold, she puts her disappointing self out of sight into a grave. She can no longer be looked at. The passive fantasy is, at the same time, a form of active exhibitionism and an importunate, merciless, and exacting seduction.

Her body is the organ by means of which she makes her demands and hysterically discharges her deflected, self-destructive matricidal drives, but her fantasies of doing so grow ever more perilous. The drive in her eyes, her desire to make herself be seen (*se faire voir*),[17] is close to extinction. She has also lost her own voice; she no longer screams, but only grimaces in a painful and absent manner, when making love (226) whereas before, Tereza, to indicate her most important feeling, her love for Tomas, had screamed. Kundera points out that her scream is not an expression but a negation of sensuality (54), its banishment in favor of a divisionlessness of body and soul. The nonsensual scream, unformed and unstructured, bespeaks her desire for Tomas, who represents for her all that she knows of the imaginary and the symbolic. For her he is "the signifier of signifiers;" he is the phallus to which she clings.

Whenever Tomas abandons her, she clings even more. Her dream of execution ends with her sobbing for a phallus to be given to her from the depths of time:

> Her whole body racked with sobs, she embraced the tree as if it were not a tree, as if it were her long-lost father, a grandfather she had never known, a great-grandfather, a great-great-grandfather, a hoary old man come to her from the depth of time to offer her his face in the form of a rough treebark. (151)

This dream, the architectural center of the book, as Scarpetta has pointed out,[18] posits Tereza between what Lacan called the primal, alienating and anxiety-provoking division of being and meaning. To make a "being" in language means *not* to be on another level.[19] It is an agonizing life and death choice.

> The symbols' emergence into the real begins with a wager. . . . The wager lies at the heart of any radical question bearing on symbolic thought. Everything comes back to *to be or not to be*. . . .[20]

Tereza dreams of the very wager that determines the symbol's emergence for the subject, but she cannot bear the castration that would leave her a mere witness to the absence of the phallus. Thus, she plays with the phantasy of her own death and proposes herself to Tomas as a vanishing, dematerializing object of desire in order to remain with the primordial form, the phallus.

Tereza is the main dreamer in the novel. Unable to speak, she dreams. Wordless, she is in the grip of images. She "speaks" oneirically, holding Tomas with "the hypnotic spell cast by the excruciating beauty" (59) of her bewitching unvoiced desires. She dreams of Tomas's voice.[21] She wants only to hear Tomas's knock on her grave and his voice. "All her eagerness for life," Kundera writes of Tereza, "hung by a thread: Tomas's *voice*. For it was Tomas's *voice* that had once coaxed her timorous soul from its hiding place in her bowels" (55) [my ital.]. Love for her has to do with voice, the "loving voice" her mother lacked. Love, she says, is born when a "woman cannot resist the *voice* calling forth her terrified soul" (160) [my ital.]. Even with the engineer, she feels that she could recover her soul and fall in love with him "if he spoke to her in a soft, deep *voice*" (157–8)[my ital.].

The encounter with the voice of another human being is *as necessary* as the encounter with one's own image in the mirror. And Tereza has neither. For the humanization of an individual, speech has to enter the body and designate it as a resounding and desiring body, a body with voice. The body image unifies the fragmented body and hides it. The human voice dominates and binds up the organism's sounds and noises. It triumphs over the natural sounds, these mere indistinct, unpatterned, and unregularized sounds that her mother liked to emit, creating around the human another, new, orderly, and rhythmized sound pattern of music and language. The capacity to respond libidinally to acoustical order and harmony distinguishes the human body from the organism in nature. It is to the musical and linguistic order that the human infant is able to link a part of its initially chaotic bodily and affective experience. This auditory experience is as jubilatory as is the discovery of form in the mirror.

But more important, the voice of *the other*, cuts into the cycle of needs that is the organism and institutes a relation of demand and desire. Demand subjugates, masters, and directs us, whereas desire may ultimately free us from the other and reveal them to us in their own mystery and lack. Humanized, we are the relation of desire to desire. But just as Tereza's mother does not help her attain a bodily ego or image so she does not inaugurate her daughter in the intersubjective relationship of desire, treating her only as an object of her own most selfish and brutal demands. Desire makes possible desexualized love, disembodied, verbal love. This is what Tereza wants. She is willing to die to find out whether she is desired.

Tereza is, paradoxically, possessively desired and therefore not particularly wanted by Tomas. She hooks into what Kundera calls Tomas's "poetic memory" (209), his buried, unconscious store of infantile memories and metaphors, particularly those pertaining to the mother and maternal care. She links up to his representations of being and meaning and less so to his sexual demands. She brings out his "rescue fantasies" (along with a need for *her* fidelity), which Freud relates to a man's tender feelings for his mother and his conviction that she needs him (whereas he once needed her).[22] Freud speaks of the child's desire to repay the gift of life, by giving the parent a child, really himself as a child. Freud writes:

When in a dream a man rescues a woman from the water, it means that he makes her a mother, which . . . means that he makes her his own mother. When a woman rescues someone else (a child) out of the water, she represents herself as the mother who bore him, *like Pharaoh's daughter in the Moses legend.*[my ital.][23]

Tomas's first and primary fantasy in relation to Tereza is that she is "an abandoned child" (11)[24] sent to him on the river to be rescued, as Pharaoh's daughter had rescued Moses.

. . . it occurred to him that Tereza was a child put in a pitch-daubed bulrush basket and sent downstream. He couldn't very well let a basket with a child in it float down a stormy river! *If the Pharaoh's daughter hadn't snatched the basket carrying little Moses from the waves,* there would have been no Old Testament, no civilization as we know it. How many ancient myths begin with the rescue of an abandoned child! *If Polybus hadn't taken in the young Oedipus, Sophocles wouldn't have written his most beautiful tragedy!* (10–11) [my ital.]

In the light of Freud's commentary (which it seems likely that Kundera knew), it becomes clear that Tereza is a mother surrogate for Tomas. She elicits signifiers having to do with a mother and child. She brings out his maternal impulses both toward himself as a child and toward her. She is the child that connects him to the one he once was. She is Tomas's fantasy of being a child with his mother as well as of being a mother himself, a woman who gives birth to a child (namely himself) that he can then give back to his mother as a gift, and that is why she is for him different from all other women, the unique one, the all-encompassing, absolutely desired one.

Thus, Tomas really is another Oedipus who sleeps with his mother and doesn't know it. And it is in connection with writing about Oedipus that he is entangled in the political web that ends up costing him his life's meaning and mission, his career and position as a surgeon. He pays as did Oedipus for approaching the realm of the mothers, which opens up his fantasies, also the one of being Polybus, the father, who took in Oedipus. He fantasizes watching over Tereza, protecting her like a father (139). He identifies her with all that he unconsciously knows about loving, the maternal, the paternal, and the child, that part of himself that needs rescuing and protecting. Tomas's conscious drive is to cut and to know, but his unconscious fantasy is to rescue and to protect as well as to be rescued and protected.

Because Tereza is able to evoke his infantile and maternal memories, or in Kundera's terms his poetic memory, she is the only woman he loves, the one he desires to be with beyond sex. She is the cause of his desire rather than what he desires to enjoy. Tomas *enjoys* women and is driven to be with them, but he *desires* Tereza. Tomas finds his freedom from the slavery of Don Juanism by affirming Tereza, by affirming some other desire within himself, which she represents for him and which is beyond phallic satisfaction. Only Tereza has what Roland Barthes called "punctum" for Tomas; only she can "wound" him or penetrate his being.[25] He has compassion for her. He "sleeps *with*" other women but only with Tereza is he actually able to sleep and to dream.

Despite his womanizing, Tomas himself does not actually like *bodies* and has a touch of somatophobia of his own: "waking in the middle of the night at the side of an alien body was *distasteful* to him, rising in the morning with an intruder *repellent*" (14) [my ital.]. He refuses—as the extreme vocabulary ("distasteful," "repellent") indicates—everything about the body of his mistresses but their sex, and sex, as he understands it, does not lead to any kind of unity (15). Unity can only be achieved in sleep. With Tereza he sleeps. Sleep, however, is a prefiguration of death that supreme obstacle to love but therefore also the supreme goad and incitement. Desiring Tereza is dangerous because it evokes at once the craving for an unobtainable unity with another and the death drive. First he shares sleep with her (as he once did with his mother in the womb) and then death.

Thus, with Tereza and her exclusively, Tomas is also Tristan, the excessively faithful, bound, and monogamous lover, the original child-lover of the mother, who desires one woman only, absolutely and unerringly. He is identified with her nighttime masochistic suffering and her wounded and bleeding oneiric body. He kisses imaginary drops of blood off her fingers when she dreams of hysterically jabbing needles under her fingernails to shift her psychic pain to a physical level (16).

By contrast, his mistresses have little part in his fantasies and none in his unconscious desires. He is aware only of their sexual being.

> Of each erotic experience his memory recorded only the steep and narrow path of sexual conquest. . . . All else he excluded (almost pedantically) from his memory. (207–8)

Sexual pleasure satisfies Tomas's obsessional desire to possess and control an object, but it is a fulfillment neither of drive nor desire whose objects are elusive and lost. Tereza, by contrast, hooks into his unconscious metaphoric structuration, his elemental scenes and fantasies, as well as his signifiers of desire. She is the "first word," the first love bond he forged with another in an act of desire. Thus, she, his love, is born, not in the conscious word, but as an unconscious signifier. She is part of the nonsensical constellations of meanings that underpin his conscious use of language.

> . . . *metaphors are dangerous. Love begins with a metaphor.* Which is to say, love begins at the point when a woman enters her *first word* into our *poetic memory.* (209) [my ital.]

Metaphors, for Kundera, are a type of coincidence or fortuity, an attempt to make a connection between seemingly unrelated events. A metaphor is a contingency or it can be kitsch, but in it we assert a connection, no matter how irrational, nonsensical, or bizarre, and, for this reason, it is a step toward love, an assertion of connectedness in a universe where everything ultimately is unconnected.[26] Tereza, his love, is his only connection to something more primordial: the child Moses in the basket and Pharaoh's daughter.

Although metaphors hide or occult something in the act of substitution, they keep the hidden present through a metonymic connection. Thus, as a form of condensation, they produce a thickness, a more solid mass, a sense of being. Tereza arrests him and annoys him because she hinders his lighthearted collection of sexual curiosities. She stops the ongoing sexual metonymy. But she gives him psychic weight and being. Thus, at the end of their lives, he is able to say to her: to be obsessed with missions and meaning is to be unfree, and to love and desire, though a weight, is to be happy (313). Therefore, though he repeatedly calls her a child, she is for him, if we follow Freud's argument in "The Theme of the Three Caskets," the women who is at once the mother, the one who bore him and cared for him (the Paraoh's daughter); the wife, with whom he shares bed and board; and the destroyer, mute, silent death, and Mother Earth.[27]

Tereza is for Tomas the acknowledgment of death: "Yes, that is death," Tomas thought," Tereza asleep, having terrible night-mares, and he unable to wake her" (228). But he has to attempt to deny death in a reaction-formation of intense love. He substitutes love (choice) for death (necessity). "No greater triumph of wish-ful-fillment is conceivable," said Freud. "Just where in reality he obeys compulsion, he exercises choice; and that which he chooses is not a thing of horror [i.e., death], but the fairest and most desir-able thing in life."[28] Thus Tomas thinks: "Love is our freedom. Love lies beyond 'Es muss sein!'["it must be"] or necessity" (236). Yet, in the structure of the novel, it is clear from the beginning that she is his necessity, the object that he cannot avoid, the object of weight, coming to him with her "enormously heavy suitcase" (13,10) as well as his destined death, drawing him back to nature and ultimately under the weight of the overturned truck that crushes them both to a pulp (122).

Tomas unconsciously recognizes Tereza as the harbinger of his death at the very beginning of their relationship when he sud-denly fancies that "she has been with him for many years and was dying. He had a sudden clear feeling that he would not survive her death. He would lie down beside her and want to die with her" (7). This abrupt and irrational fantasy, signifying something of his un-conscious desire, calls on him to change his exuberantly promis-cuous, but fundamentally lonely, life. It is this first, Tristan-like scene that makes him love, compelling him by its beauty. It be-longs to the "most beautiful moments he had ever experienced" (8). The heightened sense of ineffable beauty at once both an-nounces and veils the unconscious truth, some already-lived re-ality that anchors and destines his being.

Through Tereza, we can say, as Freud says of Lear with Cordelia, Tomas "make[s] friends with the necessity of dying."[29] She brings forth his Tristan side, the side of the infantile lover ever faithful to the mother, the originally beloved. But in evoking his primal desires for fusionary identification, she also provokes his desire to die and the release of the ancient Tristan love-death complex, which acknowledges that the ultimate price of perfect fusionary identification or symbiosis is loss of self or death.

Freud speculated that human beings never encounter death, except in confrontation with the death of a beloved since the deaths of others matter not at all to our narcissistic selves. But the death of the loved one, whom we have made a part of our being and to whom we have lent some of our narcissistic love, awakens us to reflections that force us to split the body from the soul. We let the body go (together with that bit of unavoidable hatred felt even toward those we love) while keeping the soul, verifying the memory we inevitably have of them, or even postulating a reunited afterlife.[30] The mind-body split, or more essentially, the language-body split, the fundamental castration, initiated in Tomas in part by old age, the tiring of his aging organism, and his stomach pains and in part by Tereza's dreams, enables him to start dreaming himself and to see that a phallic athleticism that ends up turning its head in a woman's groin is not such a great thing.

Tomas's adventure with the "giraffe-stork woman" is also for him an experience of transgression, as was Tereza's affair with the engineer, in that it also involves a passage beyond the drive zones toward the "asexual real," for us the unbearable domain. For to go beyond the rimlike orifice of the drive, as Lacan said, is to go back into the organism and to get effects and reactions that are not erotic but real.[31] Tomas and Tereza each go beyond the erotic zone of the drive into the instinctual, desexualized zone from whence come reactions of hysterical disgust—"he hated [the storkwoman] now" (235). In order to return to the drive and to desire from there, Tomas and Tereza have to dream.

It is finally only dreaming that enables them to surmount the crisis and impasse of their relationship and to turn from the body, the seat of the instinctual life from which develop the confused and disorderly montage of drives and demands, to a recognition of their fantasies and desires that allow them a momentary contact with the impassible peace of the symbolic. Thus, as the novel is closing and his characters have to die, they live more and more within oneiric speech and narration,[32] the only domain where their thwarted lives and baffled love can find mute expression and where truth and desire still operate together, knotted up with an unspeakable real. Tereza's harrowing dream of execution on Petrin Hill, which is the very naval of the novel, disappears in a vast, incommunicable, and originative anxiety, the emotion that for Lacan announces the ultimate real of death.

By the end, they have lost their professions, their place in social, political, and legal reality. They have left only their link to nature, to Karenin, just barely to each other, and each to their own unconscious. Nearly destroyed and silenced by their sexual encounters in the real; alienated in the Imaginary, where, neither quite lives up to the other's ideal image; their fundamental truth and humanity is restored in the dream, by means of contact with the unconscious. Kundera's oneiric narration does not serve a psychoanalytic interpretative purpose but is his way of giving space in novelistic art, and beyond it, to the unconscious and the psychoanalytic dimension of life.

The dream is between the desire to sleep (the absence of stimulation, inertia, indistinct union, and death) and the desire for fulfillment (wish, drive, life, and love). But in the dream, as Lacan says, desire is for nothing. The fulfillment of the wish in dreams that Freud speaks of can only be a "metaphorical fulfillment." It is a fulfillment of the *recognition* of desire and of the desire for recognition.[33]

Jouissance concerns satisfaction; *desire* only concerns realization, recognition, or avowal. The oneiric is the domain in which desire can at least be realized although not satisfied.

> There are indeed desires which will never find any other satisfaction than that of being acknowledged, that is to say avowed.[34]

Thus the book ends with oneiric narration because this brings us to the indestructibility of human desire *and* to its acknowledgement: its only possible fulfillment.

Love is in part the ego relation in the Imaginary that leads always to an assertion of the ego and to demands. Love is also in part a drive that would like ultimately to capture life itself in the guise of a beloved, but runs ever in a circle, returning ever to itself, unable to grasp either the other or even the remnant or memento of its own once complete being: the lost *objet petit a*. Desire wants to speak and seeks an answer to the riddle of its meaning but is never able to express what it wishes to say and discovers that meaning without being is inadequate and painful.

Tereza's dog, Karenin, by contrast, whose death Kundera introduces near the end, lacks any such knowledge of love and desire. He has to begin with no body ego or body image. He looks at himself in the mirror "vacantly, with incredible indifference" (296). He is not Narcissus, but Adam.

> Adam, leaning over a well, did not yet realize that what he saw was himself. He would not have understood Tereza when she stood before the mirror as a young girl and tried to see her soul through her body. Adam was like Karenin. (296)

Karenin is not concerned with himself, not narcissistic or self-reflective, but moves in a circle of known people, routines, and objects: his breakfast rolls and daily walks. The human sense of time runs ahead in a straight line, but Karenin's turns in a circle; therefore, Karenin is in paradise, says Kundera. For paradise is not an "adventure" or the "unknown," but "mov[ing] in a circle among known objects" (295).

Karenin's life is a repetition, which he experiences as a recurrence. Kundera does not explicitly draw a distinction between repetition (the same) and recurrence (a repetition experienced as if it were a first occurrence), but I believe it is implicit in his novel. For Karenin, life is not a repetition but a recurrence—a same, an identical—that he experiences as ever fresh and original. For him the *same* breakfast roll every morning is ever new and delightful, and he leaps at it with the same enthusiasm every day. Kundera says: "That is why man cannot be happy: happiness is the longing for repetition" (298). I would add: it is the longing for repetition, experienced as a *first* occurrence, as pristine and unfamiliar.

For the animal, life recurs. It is a recurrence, not a repetition, and that is perhaps why Nietzsche at the onset of his psychosis embraced the horse and burst into tears. Perhaps, at that moment Nietzsche understood the significance of the eternal return: that it was what the animal has: an unquestioning, unambivalent desire for life, life, not as a dull repetition, boring and unbearable, but life as eternal freshness and newness, unendingly desirable. The life in which the answer to "the question in each and every thing, 'Do you desire this once more and innumerable times more?'" would be:'Yes'.[35]

Kundera thinks of the episode of Nietzsche with the horse while he is thinking of Tereza and her dog. He interprets

Nietzsche's madness as a break with the Descartian conviction of man's mastery over nature, a particularly virulent lunacy issuing from the imaginary ego (290). Nietzsche, instead, in embracing the animal, embraces paradise, unselfconsciousness, freedom from the division and pain caused by consciousness. He may very well at this "psychotic" moment be *in* paradise, in the idyll, *with* the animal. At this moment, it may be that he too *is* Adam. The price, however, of this idyll is the loss of human consciousness and language. As Kundera says, "The longing for paradise is man's longing not to be man" (296).

What Tereza thinks as she embraces Karenin before his death is that the love that exists between humans and dogs is better than the love possible between men and women, given that we have egos and cannot avoid power plays. Her love for her dog is without questions and needs no answers. She has loved Karenin reasonlessly, without trying to change him and without demanding that he love her in return. At the same time she realizes how she has manipulated Tomas and how she has demanded to be loved by him instead of herself actively loving.

> Perhaps the reason we are unable to love is that we yearn to be loved, that is, we *demand* something (love) from our partner instead of delivering ourselves up to him *demand-free* and asking for nothing but his company. (297) [my ital.]

She has loved Tomas in the Imaginary. She has displayed her suffering and used her weakness aggressively. She has made him retreat and capitulate, wishing him to be old or a mere rabbit, strengthless, in her arms (310). Now, for a moment, she is able to see beyond demand and to recapture a more innocent, nonpossessive, and selfless way of loving. She has sight of an ineffable state of desire where each lives isolate and alone but in the proximity and "company" of the other. Momentarily, Karenin because he is not expelled from paradise (298), as animals are not, returns her with Tomas, a rabbit, in her arms, to her childhood home, to her grandparents, with "faces as wrinkled as the bark of a tree" (306), far from Petrin Hill and safe from any execution.

Thus she turns her aggressive demand *to be loved* into a desire *to love* and accedes to the drive, ever futile, to make herself be looked at, the drive necessary for the desire of the other and thus for her own fulfillment. She puts on a pretty dress for Tomas. They go out dancing. They go up to their hotel room. There is a lamp. And "up out of the lampshade, startled by the overhead light, flew a large *nocturnal butterfly* that began circling the room" (314) [my ital.]. This nocturnal butterfly represents once again the unbearable lightness of being. The nocturnal refers to the night, their imminent death, to suffering, being, heaviness, and weight: the unbearable. The butterfly refers to the lightness and flight of movement and meaning, the weightlessness of time, language, concepts, and images: equally unbearable.

The nocturnal butterfly, an image of monumental time and unending life dependent on death, circles the room, reminding us of the theme of the eternal return, of repetition, and recurrence that are at the core of this novel. This final image reminds me as well of what Lacan, citing a fragment of Heraclitus, called the dialectic of the bow: "*to the bow [Biós] is given the name of life (Bíos,* the accent being this time on the first syllable) *and its work is death.*"[36] The bow is our body and our life and the way we bend our organism to live is a form of archery: "the movement outward and back in which it is structured." The aim of archery and of the movement of life, which emerges out of the body with immense tension, is somehow to make a hit, to have satisfaction. The aim is a path, the challenge of succeeding in that one and only opportunity given us to have joy. The aim, no matter how difficult or impossible or how circuitous the way to it, as Lacan says, is not the dead bird, but an objectless experience of bliss.

II

Kierkegaard celebrated Mozart's Don Giovanni as the most perfect expression of the pure power of sensuous drive. Don Giovanni *is* the life force, "the genius of sensuousness," the ever-ready energy, "the exuberant joy of life," nonreflective and languageless, "powerfully and irresistibly daemonic," an affirmation of sexual pleasure and power such as only music can express.[37] Don Giovanni seduces others by his drive, not by language. He conquers by the power of pleasure. He is never rejected; he is always victorious.

For Kierkegaard, the Don Juan who speaks is already in contradiction with Don Juan, the principle of sensuous immediacy because the purely sensuous has no need for words at all. It has also little use for the social, legal, ethical, or aesthetic. When Don Juan is given language, says Kierkegaard, as he is in Tirso de Molina, Molière, and Byron, he becomes a seducer, one who gains his aims by persuasion, hypocrisy, or lies, and not by the force of sheer drive.

If we look at Molière's *Don Juan,* notions of truth and falsehood as well as of right and wrong are indeed irrelevant when the issue is pleasure or nonpleasure. Molière's *Don Juan* is an Alexander of the flesh. His sense of being a conqueror is a byproduct of pleasure, which gives a feeling of superabundant power. Driven by the power of pleasure, Molière's *Don Juan* violates the sixth commandment and the marriage vow. He steals Elvira from a convent. Religion and God mean nothing to him, nor does filial duty. He lies to his father and he kills for sex. He is indifferent to God, truth, language, and the law. Hence, because he can no longer be stopped by law or religion, he has to be stopped by death. But because life and anarchic sensuous enjoyment are all that he understands, death has to come in a kind of Pygmalion fantasy, as an oxymoronic, *living* representation of death: art come alive in the form of the moving and objective statue of the commander.

Kierkegaard's interpretation of Don Giovanni is an example of the nineteenth-century celebration of the sensuous-sexual body as the pure will to life, as libido, found in Whitman, Nietzsche, and D.H. Lawrence, among others. But this kind of a unified, powerful sexual body synonymous with life itself is, as Lacan says, a myth:

> It is the libido, *qua* pure life instinct, . . . immortal life, or irrepressible life, . . . simplified, indestructible life, . . . [which] is precisely what is subtracted from the living being by virtue of the fact that it is subject to the cycle of sexed reproduction.[38]

Indestructible life is what the human species lost when it became a sexed biological being. We are not a fragment of the immortal life instinct, separate but identical in essence to life as such. We are sexualized life. And the price of sexed life (and birth) is death. The pure life instinct is *before* sexualized reproduction, and therefore, in a sense actually the asexual. We do not have access to the "lamella" (Lacan's name for the myth of immortality)[39] except through the partial drives. The human species as such has never had a taste of immortal *jouissance,* but only of mortal *jouissance,* and mortal *jouissance* is only the possibility of a sequence of partial pleasures rather than any kind of totality.

Instead of Kierkegaard's Don Giovanni, or even Molière's *Don Juan*, Lacan's *démontage* and partialization of the drives makes possible only a womanizing window washer, running breathlessly between assignations with his circa two hundred women (198), whose faces he cannot even remember (225) and of whose anatomies he recalls only parceled privy parts and pieces. A postmodern Don Juan is necessarily himself an object of the partial drives, as Tomas is with the storkwoman, pursuing the chimera of the *objet petit a*, the absent object, lost piece of our own substance, "fallen" from our body, that we fantasize would make us whole, by filling once again the broken, open orifices in our body.[40]

Drive has no definite object because it is our break with need. It institutes the fundamental cut between our erotic and animal nature. Circling continuously around an absent object, drive is only concerned with making sure that the movement produces pleasure, no matter how. The drive's indefinite object entails a degree of freedom allowing the drive in the course of its path to veer away either in the direction of sublimation or perversion. Perversion would signify not giving up the real objects or the fantasy that the lost and prephallic objects are real and can be obtained whereas sublimation means relinquishing the real object for the symbolic substitute.

Drive courses beneath desire, resisting language and the demand of the other even though it hears them. Drive resists language because it is in search of the obscure object, not the signifier and meaning. Given the lack of the absolute object, drive in a sense concerns approximation, almost a blind, intuitive guessing at what that elusive, missing object might be. It plays the complex game of what Lacan called *se faire:* making oneself be seen, or heard, or shitted, etc., which involves the other but not as a speaking being. "The drive," says Lacan, "is a radical structure—in which the subject is not yet placed."[41] The speaking, desiring subject (the *je* or I) is placed in the word. But the living human being, lacking its being, is announced in the circling of the drive which never culminates in any kind of real possession except that of a momentary pleasure. Thus, drive touches on the unappeasable.

All of Kundera's characters live fundamentally on the level of drive. They are as if a mute quartet, debarred from expressing their desire, but seeking their pleasure.

$$\frac{S_1 \rightarrow S_2}{\$ \quad a}$$

They live beneath the bar of unconscious meaning ($S_1 \rightarrow S_2$): as improperly split subjects ($\$$) of the surreal drive and its object (a). They are all inadequately castrated, slightly hysterical, preoedipally seeking their fulfillment in nonsignifying *jouissance* rather than in signifying *jouissance*.[42] They make each other the objects of their drives and they mistake each other for the cause of their desire. They are in search of impossible satisfaction and of being more than of meaning.

Tomas is the fundamental pleasure seeker, representing all of them, the libertine, derived, ironically, from the Latin *liber* meaning free, and signifying originally: "made free from slavery," a free man; then, free of religion, a free thinker; free of moral scruples; then, dissolute, licentious. Kundera shows him to be unfree, enslaved. Belatedly it occurs to Tomas that "his womanizing was . . . an imperative *enslaving* him" (234) [my ital.].

Kundera makes Tomas the epic womanizer for whom an objective world to conquer and to explore really exists: the other sex, women as another sexual reality, objectively separate from himself. The epical Don Juan is supposedly nobler than the lyrical Don Juan precisely because more objective. The lyrical womanizer seeks his own inner and unchanging dream of a woman in all women (201). This ideal woman, according to Freud, would be the mother, but she is in the past and can never be gotten. She is, however, the hidden, unconscious cause of desire, the reason for the inconstancy, the disappointment, and the continual infidelity and substitution of one woman for another. As Freud says, "the pressing desire in the unconscious for some irreplaceable thing often resolves itself into an endless series in actuality—endless for the very reason that the satisfaction longed for is in spite of all never found in any surrogate."[43]

As the epic Don Juan, Tomas answers the old question: "Isn't making love merely an eternal repetition of the same?" (199) in the negative. Thus he avoids sexual kitsch. For him every woman is drastically unique and different, albeit *only* in her sexuality. He tries to get his mistresses to acquiesce in "minor perversions" (207), and the anus, a zone of the mother (as is the mouth), is his favorite part of the female anatomy (205). Tomas enjoys cutting into bodies, using his phallus like an imaginary scalpel, opening "the surface of things and looking at what lies hidden inside" (196). He likes to do with female bodies what Sabina does with her canvases and for similar reason. His sexual pleasure is an obsessional desire for possession exclusively of the unimaginable part of each woman's sexual reality (200) and a surgical desire to make a breakthrough somewhere in the general dissimulation, the exasperating insidiousness of surfaces, covering up a violent real.

His obsessive search for sexual dissimilarity makes him, ironically, end up as a sexual "curiosity collector" (201), embroiled in the comparative deadness of collecting things and confronted with the perverse "storkwoman," who mirrors precisely all he does and gives him his own "strip-command,"[44] thereby turning *him* into a thing, into *her* sexual object. Her demand questions his drive. The mirror, able only to reflect back the self enigmatically, retains a disruptive power. Kundera's Don Juan, closer to Byron's than to Mozart's, lives merely in an imaginary epic reality.

Tomas's epic womanizing, his need to possess an unending string of partial objects, with its traces of perversity, is an obsessive compulsion signifying a failure of the sublimation of his drive that leaves him straddled between weight: his painful, metaphoric connection to Tereza, and lightness: his constant metonymic need to change mistresses.

III

The Unbearable Lightness of Being is structured, to paraphrase Lacan, like language. Metaphoric and metonymic signifying chains course through the novel and become attached to each of the characters in different ways, but nonetheless so absolutely that the human quartet constituted of Tereza, Tomas, Sabina, and Franz is inexorably bound together by its very play of identities and differences, opposites and contraries (to put it in semiotic terms),[45] or by variation, interval, counterpoint, and restatement, to put it in musical terms as Scarpetta aptly has.[46] Each of the characters is also represented by what Kundera calls "key words" or signifiers which provide the clue to their existential problem or code.[47]

> . . . making a character 'alive' means . . . getting to the bottom of some situations, some motifs, even some words that shape

him. . . . A theme [or motif] is an existential inquiry. And increasingly I realize that such an inquiry is, finally, the examination of certain words, theme-words. Which leads me to emphasize: *A novel is based primarily on certain fundamental words.* [my ital.][48]

Metaphors are a contingent link, being, love, or weight. Metonymy is lightness, becoming, movement, or promiscuous sexual adventure. Like desire, metonymic movement is the constant disemburdenment of having or possessing, as the movement of Sabina is—an assertion of lack, forever en route to fathomed being or meaning. Metonymy connects by a continual erasure of the past whereas metaphor maintains a hidden link with the substituted. Metaphor is more stubborn. It doesn't let go. It adds, it marries, it couples, clandestinely. Each character tries for a different type of dissociation of the fundamentally nondissociable metaphoric and metonymic chains, while Kundera keeps them bound in his novelistic network that is, as he says, an experiment with the taking to extremes of various, unrealized possibilities in himself.

Each one has crossed a border that I myself have circumvented. It is that crossed border (the border beyond which my own 'I' ends) which attracts me most. For beyond that border begins the secret the novel asks about. The novel is not the author's confession; it is an investigation of human life in the trap the world has become. (221)

For Kundera bad art or kitsch is art unaware of the metaphoric and metonymic ground of language and meaning. Kitsch is whatever denies the radical originality and specificity of human drive and desire as well as the infinite significatory power and polysemy of the sign that allows it to become art. Kitsch is part of the "crisis of European humanity," which Heidegger called the "forgetting of being" and which for Kundera specifically entails the forgetting of the human subject by modern politics and science:

Once elevated by Descartes to 'master and proprietor of nature,' man has now become a mere thing to the forces (of technology, of politics, of history) that bypass him, surpass him, possess him. To those forces, man's concrete being, his 'world of life' (*die Lebenswelt*), has neither value nor interest: it is eclipsed, forgotten from the start.[49]

Sabina's old bowler hat is a sign weighted down with a multiplicity of intimate significations, based in her own lived experience, inventiveness, originality, and her genealogy. It is like a "riverbed" through which a "semantic river," bringing ever fresh and contrary meanings, flows (88). "Riverbed" is at once stasis and flow, metaphor and metonymy, the place where a river is bedded, as Tomas is with Tereza, the only woman he can bear to let stay in his bed. Like the sign in a poem, the bowler hat accrues meanings while generating its own contraries and negations as well as the negation of its contraries. With the passage of years, the hat becomes "a recapitulation of time, a hymn to lost time, a Proustian object" (88), heavy with metaphorical weight, but only for her, as it retains its quality of being nothing but a hat, utterly lacking in meaning or having merely the impersonal meaning that Barthes called "studium," for anyone else.[50]

The hat, classically a symbol of the detachable phallus, (as Freud made clear in his essay, "A Connection Between a Symbol and a Symptom,") suits Sabina, who knows so well how to be the phallus for men, mainly because she castrates herself all the time, forever disengaging and removing herself from everything to which she is attached: her inheritance from her family, her country, even her own biography. Thus, when in a showing of her art in Germany, the catalogue represents her face with a barbed wire across it and describes her paintings as "a struggle for happiness" against injustice, she protests:

> 'My enemy is kitsch, not Communism!'. . . From that time on, she began to insert mystifications in her biography, and by the time she got to America she even managed to hide the fact that she was Czech. It was all merely a desperate attempt to escape the kitsch that people wanted to make of her life. (254)

She effaces and betrays her very origins to avoid having the account of her life turned into an unbroken, coherent, meaningful narration, with a strong cause-effect dramatic line, out of which a positive good must come and "happiness"—a story without any room for doubt, skepticism, and uncertainty, utterly unlike

Kundera's paradoxical and complex musical narration, arranged in the manner of Greimas semiotic square, in which narration disappears into unintelligible dreams.

Her radical metonymy of betrayals, her refusal of all libidinal bonds, however, makes her burden that of the unbearable lightness of being (122). At bottom, like everyone, she is fleeing the anxiety of death: those cemeteries where the graves are covered with stones, and the dead can no longer get out (123). It is the contrast between the stony graves of Paris and the garden graves of her native Bohemia that enable her for one moment to understand Franz's unsentimental definition of a graveyard as nothing but a "bone and stone dump" in his Dictionary of Misunderstood Words and to miss him (124). But still, she has to flee further away, never turning back, "because were she to die here [Paris] they would cover her up with a stone, and in the mind of a woman for whom no place is home the thought of an end to all flight is unbearable" (125).

When Sabina puts on the hat for Franz, he has no idea how to play with it, (85) fundamentally because he sees it only as a meaningless hat. For him it is like a dead word, one more sign in The Dictionary that prevents Sabina and him from forming a lasting connection. Also he does not know what to do with the hat because unlike Tomas, Franz (who would be a lyrical womanizer if he were one) searches in all women, Sabina included, for the same idealized mother, whom he worships, and with whose body he does not know how to play because he is not properly castrated from it. The hat as the detachable phallus, symbol of the reality of primary castration, the cut of the flesh and the word, as well as of the division of the sexes that is the precondition for their mutual erotic desire, is what is refused in different ways by all the characters.[51]

By contrast, Tomas knows instantly what to do with the hat. He immediately puts it on his head, and then on Sabina's. They make mad love. When they meet later in exile, Sabina greets him with the bowler hat on her head, and both apprehend instantly what it now signifies: the painfully pleasurable reality of ever-lost, inaccessible satisfactions past and the indestructible desire to attempt to enact them, to recapture them, once again (87–8).

Only much later in the novel are we told what else was entailed in the original scenario of lost pleasure with Tomas that Sabina is unable to retrieve with Franz (86). It was a climax brought on by a fantasy of Tomas seating her on the toilet in her bowler hat and watching her void her bowels. Suddenly her heart began to pound and, on the verge of fainting, she pulled Tomas down to the rug and immediately let out an orgasmic shout. (247)

Human pleasure is that peculiar, bizarre, and unique. By what means drive achieves its satisfaction can never be predicted. No ideology can dictate or ever surmise individual happiness, given its specificity to each individual and its rootedness in unconscious fantasy. The high moment in Sabina's love life is for Tereza a moment of utter debasement and despair. For Sabina the fantasy of defecating is highly erotic (247), for Tereza it is a abasing reality: "Nothing could be more miserable than her naked body perched on the enlarged end of a sewer pipe" (157). Thus, even the common act of voiding one's bowels—to which Kundera boldly submits both the heroines but, noticeably, not the heroes of his work—is radically idiosyncratic in its significatory potential. Within the lethally leveling reality of excrement there is excitement as well as disgust.

The fantasy and act of defecation is part of Kundera's novel because kitsch is among other things "the absolute denial of shit" (248). Western theology, which tried to make accordant the symbolic and the flesh, the word and the real, "resolved the damnable dilemma," in the works of the great Gnostic master Valentinus, "by claiming that Jesus,'ate and drank, but did not defecate'" (246). Our need to sublimate the nonaffirmable, nonpalatable aspects of human life produced a God incompatible with shit, which the child Kundera decided is a lie, for it must be that either man is created in God's image and therefore God shits or God doesn't and therefore we are not like him (245).

> Spontaneously, without any theological training, I, a child, grasped the incompatibility of God and shit and thus came to question the basic thesis of Christian anthropology, namely that man was created in God's image. Either/or: either man was created in God's image—and God has intestines!—or God lacks intestines and man is not like Him. (245–6)

The question is: why did we create a God who does not shit? Why did we create a theology without excrement, which does not take into account our abasement and full human reality? Given that God does not shit neither can therefore art, philosophy, or the state. However, since they all do, we lie. That lie is called kitsch. In opposition to kitsch, Kundera puts his heroines on the toilet. Thus his novel insists on the exposure of anal matter while also condemning it because the one who keeps the bathroom door unlocked is Tereza's mother. The real of the body is an unmasking and demystifying force and at the same time it is the ultimately nonrepresentable and impossible. It is part of the anxiety of the real into which the text passes at its structural center where Tereza's dream of execution flows seamlessly into the narration of her infidelity, her identification with the anal object, the feces that she voids on the toilet, and her desire to die.

Idealization is kitsch, but kitsch is inescapable because life is unbearable. When idealization fails, devaluation often takes its place and tries violently to prove that something (e.g., the body in the case of Tereza's mother) is worthless, meaningless, no better than excrement, and worthy therefore only of destruction, but the effort is defeated by the fact that even excrement can be exciting, erotic, and valued, as Tereza is valued by Tomas. Lacan says about the anal drive (*se faire chier*):

> It is quite wrong to separate it [the scabala, i.e., the constipated feces of the obsessional neurotic] from what it represents, a *gift* . . . and from the relation it has with soiling, purification, and catharsis. It is wrong not to see that it is from here that the function of oblativity emerges. In short, the object, here, is not very far from the domain called that of the *soul.* [my ital.][52]

Tereza comes to the riverbank of Tomas's bed as a gift that he cannot refuse, and she becomes his access to a sight of love and soul.

Kundera's rather Bovaristic point that he stretches across the entire structure of his novel is the ineluctable proximity of the polar opposites of the scatological and the romantic, the real and kitsch.[53] Idealization and sublimation are our primitive defenses against transitoriness, our animal origins, and death—associated with anality,[54] the zone of the body toward which Kundera directs us with sonorously singing signifiers.

Kundera's scathingly ironic logic only spares those who recognize their own kitsch and do not presume to prescribe it to anyone else. Thus, Sabina's fantasy of the white clapboard house, "ruled by a loving mother and wise father" (255) is kitsch, but she knows it.

> As soon as kitsch is recognized for the lie it is, it moves into the context of non-kitsch, thus losing its authoritarian power and becoming as touching as any other human weakness. For none among us is superman enough to escape kitsch completely. No matter how we scorn it, kitsch is an integral part of the human condition. (256)

Kitsch is part of the imaginary repertoire that each one of us cannot avoid positing but we can refrain from imposing it on others. Certain, quite banal images, such as that of children running on the grass, bring us to tears. That is the individual crying over kitsch. It is when one image insists on being *universal*, the cause of tears in *everyone*, that kitsch becomes authoritarian. It is the second tear, which says "how nice to be moved together with all mankind, by children running on the grass," to which Kundera objects (251). For him, as for Sabina, the "dictatorship of the heart" is as intolerable as the dictatorship of the state (200).

What we do not wish to acknowledge is that our very desire for kitsch, sublimation, and transcendency points, simultaneously, to our capacity for repressive terror, negation, and denial. Our highest ideals are linked to our deepest anxieties and cruelties. Idealization, as Freud explained in *The Ego and the Id*, involves desexualization and therefore a disintegration or defusion of the normal erotic-aggressive unity:

> After sublimation the erotic component no longer has the power to bind the whole of the destructiveness that was combined with it, and this is released in the form of an inclination to aggression and destruction. This defusion would be the source of the general character of hardness and cruelty exhibited by *the ideal*—it dictatorial "Thou shalt'. [my ital.][55]

Idealization, which we all adore and practice, is, in fact, dangerous. The higher and the more impossible the ideal the greater the danger of the emergence of destruction, terror, and death. An overblown superego, in the grips of what Freud called "a pure culture of the death instinct,"[56] is how Kundera reads communist totalitarianism.

The ultimate ideal, for which Kundera reserves his deepest scorn, is the Grand March. The Grand March signifies hope in the actualization of all imaginable possibilities: the possibility of the good material life for everyone as well as the ultimate unification and brotherhood of man. It is the faith Herbert Spencer once put succinctly into a single sentence: "The telos of human life is the practical and continuous amelioration of the material, social, and moral conditions of the Human Organism—the unity of the Brotherhood of Man on this planet."[57] Lacan, by contrast, introduced the category of the impossible as "an absolutely radical one" in the foundation of the Freudian field.[58] It is the category of the impossible which absolutely separates Hegel—the great philosopher of the possible, of self-realization and self-actualization, the true originator of nineteenth-century ego psychology—from Freud and Lacan, and from the psychoanalysis and art of the twentieth century.

The Grand March is the Stalinist misunderstanding and distortion of eighteenth- and nineteenth-century enlightenment-romantic ideals of socio-economic-political development and self-realization. It is romantic notions of organic growth and development perverted into the nightmare of forced concentration labor and totalitarian production. It is the arrogant, deadly triumph of a "belief" in the revolutionary "making" and "changing" of history, ignoring all limitations, obstacles, and impossibilities. It is Marx's eleventh thesis on Feuerbach, one of the most devilish theoretical sentences ever written, put brutally and hastily into practice by cruelly barbaric means: "The philosophers have only *interpreted* the world, in various ways; the point, however, is to *change* it."

The Grand March represents whatever enforces categorical agreement by political terror and turns what was once the Yes of God, His sevenfold, beneficent affirmation: 'it is good,' uttered after each day of creation, into a savage and sadistic law of deadly conformity and uniformity.

Kundera's justified hatred of the inhuman deeds and soul-killing deceit of communist totalitarianism make him interpret even Genesis with suspicious doubt as a text false in its fundamental premise and, therefore, potentially sadistic and evil in its consequences:

Behind all European faiths, religious and political, we find the first chapter of Genesis, which tells us that the world was created properly, that human existence is good, and that we are all therefore entitled to multiply. Let us call this basic faith a *categorical agreement with being.* (248)

God affirms that creation is good, and we have to agree. There is to be no doubt, no criticism, no skepticism, and no irony.[59] The founding law is one of affirmation.[60] Negation and the ten negative commandments are secondary. If Franz's death is nearly as violent and awful as that of Stalin's son and even less meaningful and if the meaning and interpretation of his life is then given over to final distortion by his wife, it is because he signifies the mindless collusion of Western liberal ideology with atrocity that deserves at least poetic punishment.

Kundera's discussion is reinforced by an overall drive of inner destruction built into the very structure of this, formally, most Flaubertian of novels—caustic, cruel, cold, bitterly cynical, but ravishingly beautiful. A raging but impotent hatred, directed at the unspeakable crimes of communism, expends itself also in the representation of the gratuitous destruction of bodies: ripped to pieces by a mine on the Cambodian border (265); beaten senseless and unconscious (Franz) (275); auto-electrocuted on a fence (Stalin's son). Accused by British prisoners of not knowing how to shit properly, Stalin's son hurls his body at the electrified barbed wires in revolt against that which is unbearable to *him*—his reduction, given that he is almost a god, to shit (244). In terms of the degrees of satisfaction that can be gotten out of the sublimation of sadistic impulses, Kundera's structuration of this mini-tale of an ending, must have given him, the anti-Stalinist, a high yield of pleasure.

An implacable fate still exists for each subject, even if the classical gods who used to direct our destinies have disappeared. Both drive and desire are themselves a testimony to a fundamental barrier. The totalitarian nonrecognition of barriers produces the absolutist desire with its authoritarian terror, perversion, and desperation. Against the betrayal by politics, art tries to reestablish the *truth* of the lived experience of the subject, but in so doing reveals not only the subject's implacable limits but those of art as well: the limits of representation.

What limits representation, making it nearly impossible, is the fact that "the truth," as Lacan most radically put it, "has a

structure of fiction because it passes through language" and language itself "has a structure of fiction. It can only be half said."[61]
The unconscious truths that are real cannot be said at all. "We can
be sure," said Lacan, "that we are treating or dealing with certain
things of the real only when it has no longer any meaning whatso-
ever. It has no meaning because it is not with words that we write
the real."[62]

Fictionality, however, allows the insertion of beauty. Because
language is structured like fiction we can compose our lives by
"the laws of beauty." It is the singular advantage of having a life
with language. Fictional truth is beautiful whereas the real is not.
As Kundera says, referring to the perfect composition that Anna
Karenina's tragic life is: "Without realizing it, the individual com-
poses his life according to the laws of beauty even in times of
greatest distress" (52).

We, the reality of the sexualized, are forced to exist between
two poles of the asexual: between asexual, but beautiful and fictional language and the nonsexual, anxiety-stirring real (i.e., the instinctual outside the erogenous zones of the drives). Our existence
is between two impossibilities: beauty and anxiety.

By 1975, the time of the Kanzer Seminar at Yale University,
Lacan no longer accentuated the opposition of truth and knowledge, but posited the opposition of truth (fiction) and the real. This
opposition is the most fundamental one for Kundera as well. Given
that all languages—scientific or literary—have the structure of fiction, the *language* of the unconscious does too, but the real, which
provokes anxiety rather than enjoyment, does not. Kundera's art
makes contact with that anxiety.

Notes

1. A shorter version of this paper, titled "Kundera and Lacan: Don
Juan, Desire, and Oneiric Narration," was delivered at the Conference on
Lacan, Culture, and Sexual Identity at Kent State University on 26 May
1990. For an incise political reading of Kundera see Robert Boyers,
Atrocity and Amnesia: The Political Novel Since 1945 (Oxford, 1987).

2. Milan Kundera, *The Unbearable Lightness of Being*, trans.
Michael Henry Heim (New York: Harper & Row, 1984), 254. Future references in the text will be to this edition.

3. Jacques Lacan, *The Seminar of Jacques Lacan: Book II The Ego in Freud's Theory and in the Technique of Psychoanalysis 1954–1955*, editor Jacques-Alain Miller, translated Sylvana Tomaselli (Cambridge: Cambridge University Press, 1988) 19. For the elaboration of these distinctions see especially chapt. 1 and 2.

4. "A novel does not assert anything; a novel searches and poses questions. I don't know whether my nation will perish and I don't know which of my characters is right. I invent stories, confront one with another, and by this means I ask questions. The stupidity of people comes from having an answer for everything. The wisdom of the novel comes from having a question for everything. When Don Quixote went out into the world, the world turned into a mystery before his eyes. That is the legacy of the first European novel to the entire subsequent history of the novel. There is wisdom and tolerance in that attitude. In a world built on sacrosanct certainties the novel is dead. The totalitarian world whether founded on Marx, Islam, or anything else is a world of answers rather than questions. There, the novel has no place. In any case, it seems to me that all over the world people nowadays prefer to judge rather than to understand, to answer rather than to ask, so that the voice of the novel can hardly be heard over the noisy foolishness of human certainties." "Afterword: A Talk With The Author by Philip Roth" in *The Book of Laughter and Forgetting*, trans. Michael Henry Heim (New York: Penguin Books Ltd., 1985) 237. See also Milan Kundera, *The Art of the Novel* (New York: Grove Press, 1986).

5. Milan Kundera, *The Art of the Novel* (New York: Grove Press, 1986) 31.

6. Jacques Lacan, *Écrits* (New York: W.W. Norton, 1977), 86.

7. Sigmund Freud, *The Ego and the Id* (New York: W.W. Norton, 1962) 16. Kundera writes: "Ever since man has learned to give each part of the body a name, the body has given him less trouble." *The Unbearable Lightness*, 40.

8. Lacan, *Écrits*, 1–7.

9. Given this scene, but particularly the last sentence quoted above, it seems evident that Kundera is familiar with Lacan's ideas on the Mirror Stage.

10. Lacan, *Seminar II*, 88.

11. Roland Barthes, *Camera Lucida: Reflections on Photography*, translated Richard Howard (New York: Hill and Wang, 1981) 87.

12. Later, it is Tomas who has stomach problems. Tereza is able to persuade him to move to the country when *he* is suffering from a bout of pain, i.e., when he is troubled by his connection to the maternal (310).

13. The body-soul struggle is first of all a war between the bodily interior and its surface. Even babies when breast-fed, look at the mother's *face*, not at the breast. See Michael Eigen's discussion of the necessary distinction to be made between the face and the breast in "Instinctual Fantasy and Ideal Images," *Contemporary Psychoanalysis* (1980) 16:130.

14. For a development of the distinctions between the instinctual body and the body of the drives see Maire Jaanus, "The *Démontage* of the Drive," a paper delivered at a scientific workshop of the NPAP on 14 February 1992, in Bruce Fink, Richard Feldstein, and Maire Jaanus, editors. *Reading Seminar XI: Lacan's Four Fundamental Concepts of Psychoanalysis,* (SUNY, 1994).

15. Lacan, *Seminar II,* 177.

16. See Janine Chassequet-Smirgel, *Creativity and Perversion* (New York: W.W. Norton, 1984) 2–6.

17. Jacques Lacan, *The Four Fundamental Concepts of Psycho-Analysis* (New York: W.W. Norton, 1981), 178 and passim.

18. Guy Scarpetta, "Kundera's Quartet," *Salmagundi* (no. 73, Winter 1987) 113.

19. Lacan, *The Four Fundamental Concepts,* 210–5.

20. Lacan, *Seminar II,* 192.

21. By voice here I do not mean Lacan's anacoustical object a.

22. Freud, "Contributions to the Psychology of Love," *in Sexuality and the Psychology of Love* (New York: Collier Books, 1963) 52, 56.

23. Ibid., 57.

24. That she is a child for him is repeated over and over again: "she seemed to him a child" (6); "she was neither mistress nor wife. She was a child . . ." (7) etc.

25. Roland Barthes, *Camera Lucida,* 25–7.

27. Sigmund Freud, "The Theme of the Three Caskets" in *Character and Culture* (New York: Collier Books, 1963) 78–9.

28. Ibid., 76.

29. Ibid., 78.

30. Sigmund Freud, "Reflections Upon War and Death" in *Character and Culture* (New York: Collier Books, 1970) 126–30. See also Maire Jaanus, "Viivi Luik: War and Peace; Body and Genotext," in *Journal of Baltic Studies* (Fall 1989) 277 and passim.

31. Lacan, *The Four Fundamental Concepts*, 172–3.

32. For Kundera's comments on his use of oneiric narration as compared to Novalis and Kafka, see *The Art of the Novel*, 80–2.

33. Lacan, *Seminar II*, 211–2.

34. Ibid., 213.

35. See Nietzsche's definition of the eternal return as "the greatest weight" ["*das größte Schwergewicht*"] in *The Gay Science*, translated Walter Kaufmann (New York: Vintage, 1974) 273.

36. Lacan, *Four Fundamental Concepts*, 177.

37. Soren Kierkegaard, "The Immediate Stages of the Erotic or The Musical Erotic" in *Either/Or*, vol. I, translated David F. Swenson, Lillian Marvin Swenson (New York: Anchor Books, 1959) 98–100, 106.

38. Lacan, *The Four Fundamental Concepts*, 198.

39. Ibid., 197.

40. Ibid., 198.

41. Lacan, *The Four Fundamental Concepts*, 181-2.

42. For the distinction between signifying and nonsignifying *jouissance* see Jacques-Alain Miller, "A and a in Clinical Structure" in *Acts of the Paris-New York Psychoanalytic Workshop*, 24–5.

43. Freud, "Contributions to the Psychology of Love," 53.

44. The playful, light sexual "strip-command" echoes with the sinister nakedness of Tereza's dreams and the sadistic, perverted command of the concentration camps.

45. I am thinking here of A. J. Greimas's well-known semiotic square:

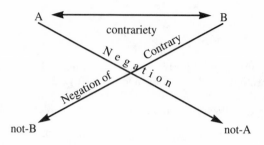

46. Scarpetta, "Kundera's Quartet," 109.

47. Kundera, *The Art of the Novel*, 29.

48. Ibid., 35, 84.

49. Kundera, *The Art of the Novel*, 3–4.

50. For an excellent (studium) history of the bowler hat see Fred Miller Robinson, "The History and Significance of the Bowler Hat: Chaplin, Laurel and Hardy, Beckett, Magritte and Kundera," *TriQuarterly* (Spring/Summer 1968).

51. The relative distance from the maternal, as Scarpetta first noticed, is homologous here with each character's distance from ideological kitsch, from which Franz is the least free. "Kundera's Quartet," 113. The possible negative political consequences of caption in the maternal, the source of the ultimate archetype of the good and the utopian, is also noted by Kristeva in "Woman's Time," *The Kristeva Reader*, editor Toril Moi (New York: Columbia University Press, 1986) 204–5.

52. Lacan, *Four Fundamental Concepts*, 196.

53. Kundera said of *Madame Bovary* that it "never fails to enchant us," for among other reasons because Flaubert "unmasked the mechanisms of sentimentality, of illusions; he showed us the cruelty and the aggressiveness of lyrical sentimentality." quoted in Jordan Elgrably, "Conversations with Milan Kundera," *Salmagundi* (Winter 1987) 4, 6.

54. For an excellent discussion of anality, also in Kundera, by a non-lacanian, see Leonard Shengold, *Halo in the Sky: Observations on Anality and Defense* (New York: The Guilford Press, 1988) 72–3.

55. Sigmund Freud, *The Ego and the Id* (New York: W.W. Norton, 1962) 45–6.

56. Ibid., 43.

57. Quoted in the OED, 3253.

58. Lacan, *Four Fundamental Concepts,* 166–7.

59. "The world of one single Truth and the relative, ambiguous world of the novel are molded of entirely different substances. Totalitarian Truth excludes relativity, doubt, questioning; it can never accommodate what I would call the spirit of the novel." *The Art of the Novel,* 14.

60. For a commentary on affirmation in Genesis see Maire Jaanus Kurrik, *Literature and Negation* (New York: Columbia University Press, 1979) 2–5.

61. "Elle a une structure de fiction parce qu'elle passe par le langage et que le langage a une structure de fiction. Elle ne peut que se mi-dire." "Yale University, Kanzer Seminar," 24 Novembre 1975, *Le Seminaire de Jacques Lacan, XXIII Le Sinthome,* Texte établi par Jacques-Alain Miller.

62. "Nous pouvons . . . être sûr que nous traitons quelque chose de réel seulement quand il n'a plus quelque sens que ce soit. Il n'a pas de sens parce que ce n'est pas avec des mots que nous écrivons le réel." *Ibid.*

Elisabeth Bronfen

Fatal Conjunctions:
Gendering Representations of Death

In his famous and infamous poetological essay "The Philosophy of Composition," Edgar Allan Poe makes one of the most important basic statements for an aesthetic rendition of feminine death: "The death . . . of a beautiful woman is unquestionably the most poetical topic."[1] If one sees a direct, binding, and unbroken relationship between an artistic depiction and any actual, historical feminine reality and thus grants literature the power to form and determine the woman reader's conceptions of self, her expectations, and her actions in a direct and unambiguous way, then Beth Ann Bassein's criticism of Poe seems valid. She maintains that, by depicting women in what she conceives as an extremely passive state, namely that of death, he has done damage to generations of female readers.[2] Although it may seem appropriate to read Poe literally and draw a direct parallel between his texts and concretely lived reality, such a strategy would lead one to reduce all works dealing with this subject to an expression of necrophilic misogyny. I, however, believe that the poetic coupling of femininity and death has far-reaching and multidimensional resonances beyond the sadomasochistic charm Mario Praz[3] finds in these texts. I therefore don't want to withdraw immediately from this charm but would like to take it seriously in order to question the presuppositions underlying Poe's claim. What does it mean to maintain that the death of a woman is the most poetic topic? Why a dead, why a beautiful woman? Where does the erotic and aesthetic fascination lie? And above all, why the *most poetic* topic? I will thus speak of a word—the superlative—and add to this another central question: the most poetic for whom?

The aesthetic coupling of woman and death presents us with a strange and trenchant contradiction, which is further enhanced by the popularity of the theme. This motif is not limited to the works of the eccentric outsider Poe; rather it appears as a popular though diversely utilized thematic constant in literature and painting from the age of sensibility to the modern period. The contradiction can be formulated in the following way: in reality (or rather, in the colloquial understanding of femininity) woman is primarily connected with the domain of life, with life-bringing and nourishing nature. If she dies, commits suicide, or is killed, this is not beautiful, and it also endangers the survival and procreation of her race. On a conceptual level, furthermore, the combination of beautiful and dead seems a contradiction in terms; either a denial of the Real of death, which is the decomposition of forms, the breaking of aesthetic unity, or a denial of beauty, which, as Lacan will have it, can be understood as an occultation of death, its antithesis. Why, then, the reversal of this colloquial understanding in art, where it is precisely the death of a woman that guarantees the survival of a family, a clan, a community, or brings about the production of an artwork? The list of questions could be extended. Let us instead look at Poe's argumentation somewhat more closely.

Poe himself justifies his choice of the superlative only conditionally. It is his goal to work out the general effect of a poem, and, in the course of doing so, he maintains that Beauty is the supreme atmosphere and essence, the sole legitimate province of the poem. For "that pleasure which is at once the most intense, the most elevating, and the most pure, is, I believe, found in the contemplation of the beautiful."[4] By "Beauty" Poe means an effect rather than a quality; to be exact, "that intense and pure elevation of *soul—not* of intellect, or of heart." To this he adds that sadness and melancholy are the most legitimate of all poetic tones. Since he is concerned with the supreme expression of the lyrical, with the sublime and the perfect, he concludes that death is the generally accepted superlative of the melancholic domain, and that his melancholic subject is the most poetic when it is intimately connected with Beauty. The coupling of "death" and "beautiful woman" thus offers him the necessary, universally acknowledged highest degree of his basic principles "Melancholy" and "Beauty." And he adds a point that will prove essential to our inquiry: "equally is it beyond doubt that the lips best suited for such a topic are those of a bereaved lover?"

Why a male speaker? Is the reference to a male viewer arbitrary or is it a male viewer, a male cultural norm, that is always implied and for whose benefit, for whose view, the female death is aesthetically staged? Since in his argument Poe is primarily concerned with the description of the perfect poem, we must further ask: why is the loss of the object of erotic desire especially fascinating? When death and the beautiful woman are coupled in art, where the erotically desired object is absent (existing only as an imagined body) or, in the case of the decoratively exposed corpse, present only as a dead and thus unavailable body, what does this suggest about traditional images of women? When one begins to compare texts from this thematic corpus, one realizes that in literature and painting Woman is often used metonymically—and not only when dead—to represent other semantic areas (which would include death, art, beauty, but also purity, innocence, chaos, and demonic eroticism, to name some paradigms), so that one must further ask: what ideas and values come together in the poetic image of the beautiful dead woman? What condensation and displacement, in Freud's sense, are at work here? And what functions do individual depictions or discussions of female death serve within the text as a whole? In her death, the woman not only serves as the motive for the creation of an artwork and its object of representation; by dying she also sometimes becomes an art object or, as a dead body, is compared with an artwork. In this sense she marks the point of self-referentiality, the *mise en abyme* of the text. What cultural and aesthetic norms are debated on the grounds of this topos? In what sense is the coupling of femininity, death, and art an attempt to break taboos and conventions? In what sense does it mark the place where norms are affirmed, stabilized, and secured? If one is willing to understand the corpse as a representative of Lacan's order of the Real, which Ragland-Sullivan defines as "that which is minus its representation, description or interpretation," as the site "before which the Imaginary falters, and over which the Symbolic stumbles," how stabilizing can representations of feminine death be for the narcissistically informed self-presentations of an artist or a culture?[5] Or, put another way, is it death that is ultimately articulated in these images or is death in fact recuperated back into the stabilizing, even if illusionary economy of representations? Is it the failure of representation when faced with the Real of death that is at stake?

Poe's choice of the superlative "most poetic" suggests that the literary depiction of feminine death need not be limited solely to the thematic level; rather it also refers to the poetic quality of a text. Some texts dealing with feminine death are, beyond their beauty and their elevating qualities, also "the most poetic" in the sense that they refer to their own artistic nature. They explicitly thematize what Roman Jakobson calls the poetic function of a speech utterance.[6] That is, they privilege the self-referentiality of the sign or utterance and stress least the reference to a world outside the text. And this happens when the depiction of female death on the content level, which expresses an objectification, depersonalization, and sacrifice of the woman, is coupled with a poetological statement. For then feminine death figures as an analogy to the creation of an artwork, and the depicted death serves as a double of the aesthetic quality, a double of its formal condition. As Lacan puts it, "the symbol manifests itself first of all as the murder of the thing, and this death constitutes in the subject the eternalization of his desire. The first symbol in which we recognize humanity in its vestigial traces is the sepulture."[7] Not without reason does the word *corpus* refer both to the body of a dead human or animal and to a collection of writings.

Thus, from the mid-eighteenth century on, diverse conceptual strands cross in the motif of the aesthetic staging of feminine death, and these strands cannot always be kept apart. First of all, the depiction of feminine death can serve as an epistemological discussion about how one can appropriate the world through the act of seeing and how the spectacle of another's death may impart knowledge about one's own death, or about the world beyond death. The motif can also serve an aesthetic discussion about the conditions of artistic creation, about the fascinating dangers involved in translating living nature into art, about the ambiguous demands of art to transform animate material into inanimate form.

Seen from this point of view, the beautiful corpse explicitly sheds light on the threshold between death and art production, on their mutual interdependence. Since all corpses are, strictly speaking, the same, the woman as corpse, as pure body without soul, is semiotically speaking, a figure—that is, a rhetorical figure without any distinguishing facial traits of her own, an arbitrary, empty, interminable surface for projections, purely a mirror. Lacan's question of the absence of any sexual relation seems in this case to take a peculiar turn. Reformulating Lacan one could say, faced with death biological sexuality is obliterated, the corpse defines a position of a sexual nonrelation. And yet in representations this erasure is depicted through a gendered body, the feminine corpse.

Second, the motif of the beautiful corpse, as victim of society or as a lover, serves in a discussion of cultural norms. Because Woman is semanticized as "the Other" (Simone de Beauvoir), she always represents the extremes in Western cultural discourse (yet another superlative): the extremely good, pure, and helpless or the extremely dangerous, chaotic, and seductive; the saint or the whore; Mary or Eve. As the outsider per se she also stands for a negation of the existing norm,[8] and as such she furthers a dynamization of society that must end with her effacement. The norm is confirmed and secured, whether the depicted sacrifice of a too virtuous woman serves as a superficial social critique (in that she is, in a profane manner, an embodiment of Christ and through her death reveals that the pure cannot survive in this world, while at the same time she takes on the sins of others), or whether the sacrifice of a dangerous woman reestablishes the order that was momentarily suspended due to her presence. Presenting Lacan's formulations, Rose defines courtly love "as the elevation of the woman into the place where her absence or inaccessibility stands in for male lack" and her "denigration as the precondition for man's belief in his own soul." As Lacan puts it, "for the soul to come into being, she, the woman, is differentiated from it . . . called woman and defamed."[9] Furthermore, the image of the beautiful dead woman can be used to show how love is connected with the fatal taking possession of the loved one but also how the mediated love for a no longer attainable woman is privileged over the love for a physically available and as such imminently dangerous woman. In representation the dead woman as object of desire is, one could say, an explicit rendition of Lacan's formulation that the "whole of his realisation in the sexual relation comes down to fantasy."[10] Rose explains, "as the place

onto which lack is projected, and through which it is simultaneously disavowed, woman is a 'symptom' for the man."[11]

In order to impose a clarifying though not exclusive analytic
structure on this complex set of questions, I will divide my discussion of the beautiful corpse into three parts, each of which will be
filled out with consideration of some trenchant examples. I will
discuss the beautiful dead woman (1) as a poetic function, in order
to show that these depictions are extremely self-reflexive and serve
a metapoetical discussion, (2) as pleonasm, whereby I will argue
that woman and death belong to the same paradigm, and (3) in her
function as threshold, since paradoxes, disparities, and contradictions come together in this literary topos to form a situation of
mutual dependence.

The Superlative; or the Artist, Scientist, and Lover As Vampire

In Richardson's epistolary novel *Clarissa* (1748), the heroine
gives up her life willingly after a long series of attempts to elude
her rapist, Lovelace. After her death, the rake's friends can only
barely prevent Lovelace from an insane undertaking: he wants to
steal Clarissa's corpse, take out the heart, and mummify the body
in order to postpone its decay as long as possible and thus also
maintain his possessive claim to her. "Whose is she dead, but
mine?" he explains.[12] As though she had a presentiment that as an
object of sight she would become a fetish, Clarissa explicitly states
in her will that Lovelace may not see her dead body. In death she
believes, her situation will be comparable to that in which he
raped her. Only on condition that he simultaneously read a text
she has prepared will she allow him to view her body. In this text
she emphasizes that the woman he once ruined died happy, and
that she wants him to interpret her dead body as a *memento mori:*
"See what thou thyself must quickly be—and REPENT!"[13] By thus
superimposing Christian values of repentance and atonement onto
her dead body, she tries, with the last resource available to her, to
divert the interpretation of his act of seeing away from erotic satisfaction and usurpation.[14]

Superficially the death of Clarissa has the function of ac-
cusing both the free mores of the libertines and the double standard of the rising bourgeoisie. The visit to her dying and dead body

is meant to provide her family with the opportunity for remorse and forgiveness. Yet at the same time, though only in asides, a very different component of feminine death is discussed. The emphasis placed on the beauty of Clarissa's corpse—the charming peace, the exquisite smile—as well as the fact that only in death can she be completely at the disposal of her relatives' wishes and expectations, points to a coupling of self-validation, satisfaction, and usurpation with the death of the desired object, a coupling that Lovelace heightens. Only in a state similar to death could he take possession of her. Yet that time she was at his disposal for only a short period, since upon awakening she fled from him. His second attempt to take possession of Clarissa no longer aims at any direct bodily contact. He wants to see her, and this wish—to possess her by observing her—is made possible not only through her death (since, dead, she can no longer flee from him): by also mummifying her, he wishes to reach the "highest degree" of satisfaction—to transform her into an almost eternal object of his usurping gaze. How unusual is the fantasy of this perverted libertine, whom his author clearly condemns, not least through the choice of a name that is a homonym for "loveless"?

Not all that unusual, if one considers, for example, the written version of the folktale "Snow White," offered seventy years later by the brothers Grimm. The fantasy of Lovelace has been realized— the body of a beautiful dead woman lies in a glass coffin on top of a hill "so that it can be seen from all sides."[15] That is, the contents of the coffin not only can be viewed from all sides, but due to the prominence of its position, the body virtually offers itself to the gaze of others, draws this gaze onto itself. Now, in his study on death Philippe Aries[16] points out that a beautiful staging of death— an understanding of the lying in state and surveillance of the corpse as an aesthetic event, much like a visit to a museum in its encouraging and elevating effects—is an invention of the early nineteenth century. This coupling of death and aesthetic viewing, which has its roots in cultural history is, however, significantly intensified in the Grimm tale. For on the coffin in which Snow White lies, the dwarfs have written in gold letters her name and her heritage. Laid out ceremoniously, Snow White resembles an art object exhibited in a labeled frame. And the prince, the privileged male viewer, demands of the dwarfs not Snow White but rather the coffin. His life, he claims, depends on being able *to see* her dead body displayed under glass, on being able to honor and worship her "as his loved one."[17] The erotic desire for the beloved is shifted to the level of viewing. The act of seeing means possession and pleasure.

Lacan suggests that "the interest the subject takes in his own split is bound up with that which determines it—namely, a privileged object, which has emerged from some primal separation, from some self-mutilation induced by the very approach of the Real, whose name . . . is the *objet a*."[18] The fascinatory element introduced by the gaze is connected to this separation (constituting the subject), in that it attempts to arrest another living body into the position of the *objet a*, in an illusory recuperation of the lost object, and thus articulates the very separating it attempts to occult. Yet the woman best fulfills the conditions of this desire in a deathlike state, when she has become totally body and is at the same time preserved from decay, when she unconditionally represents the mortal frame without soul or self: pure, unfading materialization.

The thematic proximity of an embalmed woman to an art object, made explicit by virtue of the fact that they are both a fetish, is taken up in various metapoetical stories about creation and art production, where the transformation of living material into dead form is problematized. In Poe's "The Oval Portrait" the narrator is so deeply moved by the lifelike expression in a young woman's portrait that he reads about her past in a volume discussing the painting. The story reveals that she was unhappily married to a painter, that she was jealous of his "other" wife (namely his art), and that he in turn was obsessed with the desire to transfer his living wife into his other wife: into art. The portrait sittings became the scene of a transfusion, the "tints which he spread upon the canvas were drawn from the cheeks of her who sat beside him." When the last stroke has been completed, the portrait seems to be "Life itself," but his wife lies dead beside the canvas.[19]

Creation or transformation can be understood as a transposition of sign systems, whose genesis Julia Kristeva describes as the "destruction of the old position and the formation of a new one."[20] What is interesting, however, is that the aesthetic victims I am concerned with, the blood donors, whose destruction is the starting point and the condition for the creation, should so often be female. A story by Poe's contemporary Hawthorne presents some explanatory suggestions. In "The Birthmark,"[21] the scientist Aylmer is obsessively irritated by a small, handlike mark on the cheek of his wife, Georgiana, for he sees it as a flaw in her otherwise perfect appearance, sees it as a symbol for her "liability to sin, sorrow, decay and death." He forces her to undergo an operation to obliterate this sign of earthly imperfection. To eliminate this mark means to remove any reference to her mortality, but the mark is as deep as life itself and leads directly to the heart. A removal of the reference to the indirectly absent death can only be replaced with the presence of death itself. As in Poe's story a transfusion takes place. To the same degree that the red taint of the birthmark pales in Georgiana's face, her breath also fades away, until both vanish simultaneously. Her soul flies to heaven, and next to Aylmer lies the now perfect woman—an empty form. In order to understand this act of creation, one must ask: Why did Aylmer feel so compulsively threatened by this mark? Why does its effacement become such an obsession?

Not only does Aylmer's love for his wife rival his love for science to such an extent that both must be interwoven; as a scientist he feels himself to be in direct competition with nature. His attempt to create Georgiana a second time, to render the almost perfect masterpiece of nature immaculate through his art, is an expression of the desire for some proof that he not only ultimately controls but can also surpass nature. This attempt reveals Aylmer's aspiration to become like God. Not only does he presume to imitate God's creation by undertaking the operation, but he directly assaults the mortality designated by God—the temporary and finite—with his efforts to transgress these given barriers of imperfection and mortality. This blasphemous act proves fatal, possibly an indication of Hawthorne's implied criticism. Yet even if the woman's body serves to secure the Christian world order and the blasphemer is punished by degradation, it is she who ultimately pays.

There is, however, another dimension to the question of why the mark must be removed at all costs, for it is also a sign of Georgiana's erotic charm. Her lovers see the mark as a token of her magic endowments to "sway over all hearts." Removing this "charming" mark also means terminating Georgiana's erotic fascination for others. Above all, the mark opposes Aylmer's mania for perfection by virtue of its essentially incalculable nature. At times present, at times absent, dark crimson when she turns pale, vanishing "amid the triumphant rush of blood" when she blushes, it is a sign for the movement that constitutes life, for inconstancy, for the never entirely ascertainable. As a result its constant alternation between flaring up and extinguishing, this mark can be understood as an instable mark in Lacan's conception of *aphanisis*, a constant interplay between appearance and disappearance, presence and absence. As Lacan repeatedly demonstrates, the subject's entrance into and exchange with language, his mastery over the soma, is contingent upon acknowledging the splittage it undergoes due to its fading before the chain of signifiers: "the subject appears first in the Other, in so far as the first signifier . . . emerges in the field of the Other and represents the subject for another signifier, which other signifier has as its effect the *aphanisis* of the subject. Hence the division of the subject—when the subject appears somewhere as meaning, he is manifested elsewhere as 'fading,' as disappearance."[22] The fateful logic seems to be that if a mark, which explicitly stages this process of *aphanisis* (a process inscribing all human existence) can be effaced, then by extension, one's own splittage, one's own fading may be overcome. Yet an ego stability gained by procuring, as object of its gaze, a body whose vacillation has been arrested in a mortified figure, is precarious. Though it successfully denies that aspect of death's drive, articulated in the instable play of absence and presence, it acknowledges the other aspect of death— the inevitable return to an inanimate immobility, which, in turn, by implication comes to reflect the psychic stasis of the survivor and his gaze. It thus becomes evident that the desire for a transparency of the sign, containing no divergence or difference, no opacity, no movement, is fatal. An obsession with perfection, with the immaculately pure, proves to be an expression of the death wish.

Having up to now spoken only of women as passive objects for reification, I want now to discuss a case in which a woman's death functions as a consciously desired act of setting a mark. An episode in Tennyson's version of the Arthurian legend, "Idylls of the King,"[23] describes the tragic love of Elaine of Astolats for Lancelot, who rejects her because he has sworn constant faith to Queen Guinevere. On her deathbed, Elaine makes a strange request: shortly before she dies, someone must place a letter she has written into her hand and close the hand upon it. She then must be placed on her bed, decked out like the Queen, with all her riches. A barge draped in black is to take her, in this apparel, to the Queen. And since she is convinced that "surely I shall speak for mine own self, and none of you can speak for me so well," she wishes to be piloted by a mute old man alone. Thus she floats down the river, a dead body rowed by a mute, in her right hand a lily, in her left a letter, a golden blanket covering her to the waist, all dressed in white, her bright hair streaming around her.

The staging of this voluntary death concerns, on a superficial level, what Margaret Higonnet has written in general about feminine suicide:[24] it is a woman's attempt to use her death to project an image of herself—both in order to have an aesthetic effect (everyone notices her beauty) and to purposely provoke a certain interpretation of this act. Elaine wants the truth of her love for Lancelot to be proclaimed forever; she wants compassion, sympathy, and understanding. To put it another way, the dedication that she adds, not unlike Clarissa, to this suicidal act allows her to manipulate the lives of the survivors and her own obituary, by making herself into her own text. What is interesting about this act of creation is that with her death, the woman in this case is not transformed into an artwork nor is she destroyed in favor of an artwork; rather, she becomes an author and, simultaneously, the object of her own authorship.

Seen semiotically, something else is also at work here, because in this staging of her own death, in which the body becomes the vehicle for an expression, the woman makes herself into a pure sign. If one understands the lingual sign as something that takes the place of an absent object, then we have here the reversal. The present object takes the place of the lingual sign, becomes so to speak the sign itself, the text. Her body is not only the place for a lingual sign but also the realization of the sign, a condition that cannot really exist. It is her intention that the body (as expression, as signifier) be congruent with the meaning of her death (the content or signified); that they form a transparent relationship—without any deferment or shift in the meaning, without the difference inherent in language. That is, what she attempts to stage in this instance is the literal realization of the sign, a materialization of the symbolic, made possible through her death. Death here is conceived as a moment, where the normally distinct realms of soma and sign are allowed to collapse. But Elaine, attempting to get out of the contradictory relationship of representation and body, only reconfirms this contradiction through her fatal staging. For any signification is always such that the body functions as a signifier whose signified and whose referent is inevitably gliding and whose materialization is never complete and at the same time, the body, especially the dead body, belongs to the Real outside representation and can only be re-presented and figured, but never presented in its material presence. Thus, even as she seeks to fall out of the symbolic order (with its supplements and slippages of meaning) through the insertion of Real death, Elaine is convinced that it is this form of utterance that is perfectly appropriate for expressing her intention, and so remains inscribed within the economy of representation. The attempt at a materialization of the symbolic through death is coupled with the superlative; again a woman reaches the "highest degree" of a desired effect through the aesthetic staging of death. But the process of signification is maintained, for the staging implies an identification on the part of its actress with an ideal audience. The materialization of the symbolic continues to mean, always remains within the interplay of necessary supplementation in the sense of Lacan's object a—a double displacement, involving the mixed paradigm of "feminine and death" that offers a compensatory substitute for the always already lost object. We are left with the question—for whom is this aesthetic staging of death superlatively effective?

The Pleonasm; or the Sacrifice and Effacement of the Desired Feminine

I have spoken up to now about the aesthetic sacrifice of woman, using examples in which feminine death and artistic innovation, renewal, and change are mutually interdependent. Now I want to turn to the question of woman as a victim of society and discuss how feminine death is the requirement for a preservation and a reestablishment of the old, how it is used to depict a connection between confirmation and guarantee of the order that represents the homogeneous, ruling norm. Recalling Lacan's formulation of the symbol as the murder of the thing, Julia Kristeva employs a discussion of the sacrifice ritual to elucidate her distinction between the semiotic and the symbolic. She describes this process as "this violent act puts an end to previous (semiotic, presymbolic) violence, and, by focusing violence on a victim, displaces it onto the symbolic order *at the very moment* this order is being founded. Sacrifice sets up the symbol and the symbolic order at the same time, and this 'first' symbol, the victim of a murder, merely represents the structural violence of language's irruption as the murder of soma, the transformation of the body, the captation of drives."[25] At the corpse of the victim, the semiotic force receives a signifier and can by virtue of this representation be detained and admitted into the symbolic order. The essential point is, however, not only the fact that society is founded on the basis of a collective murder but also that at least an imitation of this process can be found in diverse discourses. Above all, cultural discourses repeatedly depict and stage this process. That is to say, the semiotic chora, a concept Kristeva uses to designate the interminable, heterogenous, presymbolic force, must be transferred and incorporated into the symbolic order of society, even if this occurs in the form of displacement or suppression, in order for it thus to be preserved in a mitigated form. In this order, the chora voices itself as a pulsating force, in the form of contradictions, insignificance, ruptures, silence, breaks, evasions, and ellipses. For the stability of this order depends on being dynamized by this Other, by the Semiotic, and yet in the end also on obliterating this "disruptive force."

The question now is: what position does the sacrifice of femininity occupy? "In dreams," Artemidorus explains, "a writing table signifies a woman, since it receives the imprint of all kinds of letters."[26] In her book, *Monuments and Maidens*, Marina Warner discusses in great detail how a multitude of abstract concepts like freedom, truth, wisdom, justice are attached to a depiction of the female body. Interesting for us is that woman can in various ways also stand for the realm of death, so that in the depiction of female death we have an accumulation of words that are semantically the same. Woman can be depicted as an allegory for death or she can be conceived as a substitute for the chaotic—more precisely as the erotically and rationally dangerous being, the potential death-bringer. As Ragland-Sullivan explains, representations of femininity are not only the source of man's pleasure and truth because the feminine body here functions as a symptom of his belief in a mystic, universal Woman. In cultural discourses Woman is also perceived of as alien and dangerous because she functions, in her semantic proximity to the maternal, as a reminder of our psychic Otherness; her "void . . . symbolizes the loss that becomes the unconscious."[27] One could say, culture's double inscription of femininity is such that it both masks and reveals a loss or gap.

Second, the literary motif of the beautiful dead woman performs a representation of the first primitive sacrifice. Whereas for the dying woman the invasion of death means complete stasis, a reduction to a selfless form, for the surviving family or community it means purification, fertility, a life-effecting transformation. What is essential, then, is not just that the normative affirmation is discussed over the body of a woman. It is equally important to define the position occupied by this body (which can be seen as a moment of excess and disruption), as it is used to argue innovative or restorative tendencies, and to determine the position from which the discourse representing this sacrifice speaks.

From the position of the patriarchal norm, the imagined woman marks the borderline between symbolic order (in which woman, according to Lacan, has a negative place of her own, points out the lack fundamental to human existence, the nonbeing of the sexual relation and so pervades its discourses and representations with *aphanisis*) and the imaginary, with its link to the soma. For Lacan to argue "Woman doesn't exist" is to say that woman is defined purely against man, and thus to point to the fact that such a definition is always a fantasy, which makes woman into a symptom, a supplement of the lost object, *objet a*. Explicating Lacan, Miller writes "just one symbol for the libido, and this symbol is masculine, the symbol for the female is lost. . . . The absence of the signifier "woman" also accounts for the illusion of the infinite, which arises from the experience of speech, even while that experience is finite. . . . The passion for things symbolic has no other source. Science exists because woman does not exist. Knowledge as such substitutes for knowing the other sex."[28] Yet the "not all" that Lacan suggests Woman metonymically represents within the culture refers also to the fact that any system of representation is not all, and thus refers to its vanishing points, to the limitations that it must acknowledge even as it attempts to deny them. This borderline position, which femininity occupies, both protects and shields the symbolic order from the imaginary and the real, yet seems at the same time to be part of this disorder, and thus metonymically to represent it. Marking this unsymbolizable position, this moment of excess and impossibility, femininity has been both vilified by culture as representing darkness and chaos and at the same time venerated as representative of a higher and purer nature. The essentialism thus attributed to the feminine body corresponds to the essentialism of male fantasy, where woman is man's symptom, securing, as stake, the validity of his belief. In either case, these projections are necessary stakes to guarantee the security of the normative concept of the world, a security that consists in a dissociation from the too good as a virtuous example and from

the chaotic as danger. Woman is thus the Other that has only an instable, nonplace in the norm, that must, however, be designated so
that the norm can define itself *ex nihilo* by virtue of this demarca-
tion. Woman is that position in the patriarchal system against
which the norm is defined in reference to a visible difference and a
forbiddance against the male subject's identification with the maternal body. As Rose explains, "the system is constituted as system
or whole only as a function of what it is attempting to evade, and it
is within this process that the woman finds herself symbolically
placed. Set up as the guarantee of the system she comes to represent
two things—what the man is not, that is, difference, and what he
has to give up, that is excess," in Lacan's own terms, sexual difference and the renunciation of *jouissance*.[29]

In the course of this argument it becomes clearer wherein the
particular charm of female sacrifice might lie: in this depiction,
she who metonymically represents the realm of death is secured as
a dead body; her dynamizing force is averted or exorcized, overcome in favor of the normative order. That is, she marks a dual position of power—the semiotic force, which penetrates the symbolic
order, rupturing this order for a short period of time, is here
forcibly transferred into a signifier, a sacrificed body, in Lacan's
sense a *point de capiton*, momentarily arresting the gliding of the
signifieds under the bar of the signifier. In addition to the already
discussed interdependence of death and art production, the image
of the dead woman thus marks a further boundary situation,
namely between chaos and order, and again the image is meant to
effect a self-reflexivity, an accumulation of the same, the superlative. The construction of the hierarchical order over chaos, which
is played through in the representation of such sacrifice, is further
heightened by the fact that the object of this sacrificial representation issues from the paradigm death (so that what is staged in a
sense is a triumph over death). Thus, the image of the beautiful
dead woman contains a reference to that chaotic, dynamizing force
that disrupts the order, but is also necessary to this order. At the
same time it serves as a confirming mirror that guarantees the stability of the normative (patriarchal) construction of the world. It is
a representation of excess, that dispels the disruptive quality even
as it renders it, for the combination of beauty, death and femininity covers the castrative aspect of sexual difference and fatality
in a seemingly unified image, so that the male viewer can, in confrontation with this *figure* or *image* of sexual difference and death

have the illusion of avoiding an apprehension of lack, momentarily frozen in place.

Countless examples could be give to illustrate how the corpse of a woman, the gift of her body, her blood, her life, helps regenerate the order of society. The pattern remains more or less constant, even if the values that are connected with the dead woman and that are discussed in connection with her death vary. If motifs of the atoning Christ or the legends of the martyrs serve as model for the narrative, then the death of the innocent, virtuous woman, as we saw in the case of Clarissa, serves a superficial critique of the norms and mores of society. Because these women tend to be figures of redemption and salvation, taking on the sins of others— that is, giving up their selves for others (and Dickens's Little Nell or Goethe's Othilie would be cases in point)—their death appears both inculpatory and at the same time edifying and soothing to the spectators who undertake a pilgrimage to the dying body. The potential for change is shifted away from oneself onto the signifier of the sacrificed body and can thus be transferred into the existing order without fundamentally changing it. The same applies to the innocent woman, who represents a danger in the sense that she cannot be domesticated, that she is, for example, too close to nature, to the irrational, that she cannot or will not comply with the normative behavioral roles assigned to women. She is punished and sacrificed in favor of a preservation of order—one need only think of narratives that operate with allusions to witch hunts. This dangerous innocent woman may also submit to the conventions of her society and sacrifice herself, like Maggie Tulliver in George Eliot's *Mill on the Floss*; after Maggie's death in a flood, peace and fertility return. A further variant would be such women who consciously incur guilt, who break with conventions, and who must be punished in exemplary fashion for this offense—most trenchant depictions are those of women who have committed infanticide or adultery. In some cases a woman's desire to commit a crime, which must end in her death, or her direct choice of suicide, can be understood as her first step toward becoming subject of her history rather than just a passive object of fate, as a first attempt to assume authorship for her own destiny. Although it would be necessary and worthwhile to analyze a number of examples, I must limit myself at this point to stating that the image of the dead female body is used to debate cultural and social norms and that both the position from which the narrator speaks and the position toward which the meaning of this death is directed are decisive for determining whether these depictions are revolutionary or norm affirmative.

I would like, here, to bring another aspect into the discussion. Annicke Jaulin (in continuation of Lacan) speaks about a dual female death: "There is a death before death . . . known above all to women. It makes no difference whether one calls it silence, cleavage, usurpation, or death. In any case it signifies that here is not the right place for one who has no place."[30] This symbolic death before death is expressed not least in texts of the nineteenth century that thematically emphasize the objectification of women. Again the dividing line between a critique of this predominant condition and an apology of it cannot easily be drawn. What is problematized in any case is that the woman (as John Berger, speaking of the social implications of the equation between woman and art, explains) must turn herself into an object of sight for the male viewer.[31] She must kill herself into an art object in order to please the master on whom she is dependent.[32] Many texts illustrate how a woman is exhibited like a commodity on the marriage market, how she is traded or sold. Furthermore, these texts imply that the socially required roles are inadequate, stifling—in short, a kind of murder in themselves. Certain vampiresque traits are attributed to society and its proponents, since they suck at the autonomous forces of the woman and let her become a half-dead being, a commodity, a being who may not determine her self independently. In these texts, the depiction of feminine death is also a pleonasm in the sense that death, whether endured or actively sought, is only an elucidating intensification of the woman's true condition, or rather of the condition that has been delegated to her from the start. To put it another way, death proves to be the woman's apotheosis.

Tolstoy describes the first love scene between Anna Karenina and Vronsky in the following strange and, at the same time, revealing way: "He felt what a murderer must feel when looking at the body he has deprived of life. The body he had deprived of life was their love. . . . But in spite of the murderer's horror of the body of his victim, the body must be cut in pieces and hidden away, and he must make use of what he has obtained by the murder. Then, as the murderer desperately throws himself on the body, as though with passion, and drags it and hacks it, so Vronsky covered her face and shoulders with kisses."[33] Why does one wish to kill the being one loves? Wherein does the mutual interdependence of erotic desire and death wish lie?

One of the most popular motifs for the linkage between an erotic desire and death is the variously transformed story of Carmen. It is significant that Merimee prefaces his narrative with the following epigraph from Palladas: "All women are like the gall bladder, but they have two good hours: one in bed, the other their death hour."[34] It is equally significant that his story is commonly interpreted as being about a man's ruining himself for a woman who is beneath his dignity,[35] rather than about a jealous husband killing his wife, who seeks freedom and self-determination.

The tragic conflict lies less in Carmen's faithlessness (for her gypsy nature is by definition fickle, inconstant, promiscuous) than in her different understanding of the word "faithfulness." Carmen understands the word to mean changeability, freedom, mobility, a diverse cultivation of her own pleasure, and an interchangeability of the object of her desire. That is, she equates faithlessness with a life comprising displacement of the erotic object of desire, with a constant deferral of erotic fulfillment. Jose, on the other hand, cannot bear the uncertainty of the arbitrary and the changeable. He wants permanence and steady rules,[36] for Carmen, as object of his desire, is not only supposed to reflect his world of durable and stable order; she can only fulfill this requirement if she is completely constant, completely immobile, completely his possession. For Jose, the inability to control her means that with every move Carmen makes she threatens not only *not* to reflect his world adequately but also to endanger it. To demand faithfulness of her means, as he explains, "to be sure of her."[37] Yet to demand of someone that he or she offer you a surety and guaranteed certainty can also mean turning the other person into a token, a pledge, a security—that is, making the other into a static body, an unambiguous and thus transparent sign that lacks all difference. Jose's fantasies about strangling Carmen in order to attain such security, fantasies that he later acts upon, are thus only consistent with what Carmen is meant to be from the start—a sign mirroring exclusively him and his world, that is, a dead sign.

If one spins Carmen's tale a bit beyond Merimee's ending, one could say that in Carmen's corpse Jose has found the perfect fulfillment of his desire. For possession is connected with an unfortunate paradox: to possess something opens up the possibility of losing this object, triggers the fear that one can never fully, never eternally own something. At the same time, this fear keeps the desire alive, makes up a fascination that must constantly be overcome. Any doubt about the exclusivity of one's possession is naturally only heightened (and thus the desire for it increased) when the concerned object is animate, because it thus resists any bondage and seeks to express its own conception of self in conflict with the expectations of the other person. In the state of total objectification, as a dead body, as an image that one creates in one's memory, however, possession and desire are secured. Desire is forever preserved, for it has now been indefinitely deferred, never fulfilled, but at the same time will never be deceived by faithlessness. If one understands desire as the desire for the desire of the Other (Lacan), then any surmounting of faithlessness, at least from Jose position, means that Carmen's desire is now directed exclusively toward him in the sense that it can be directed at no one else. Lacan calls true envy "the envy that makes the subject pale before the image of a completeness closed upon itself, before the idea that the *petit a,* the separated *a* from which he is hanging, may be for another the possession that gives satisfaction."[38] It also means an overcoming of the danger that Carmen might flee the parameters of the image designated to her and thus no longer securely reflect his world. What is ultimately secured, however, is the instability of desire provoked through Carmen. Not unlike Hawthorne's birthmark, her "faithlessness" sketches the movement of *aphanisis,* a trajectory of appearance and disappearance. What Carmen, as object of his desire, signals to her lover is that as a desiring subject, he must necessarily also subject himself to the economy of desire, within which he is forever split and forever fading. Her corpse thus functions as the illusionary arrest of an exchange of desire, that perpetually articulated this lack of wholeness and self-stability. But the fulfillment that the death of this instable and destabilizing object of desire, that the arresting of her vacillation seems to afford, can only be seen as a displaced signifier for the impossible. What is at the core of this image is the illusory triumph over the vacillation of the desiring subject, whose status is not only that of a surviving but also of a dying subject.

Another case in point is the narrator of Stendhal's *La Vie de Henri Brulard,* who likewise prefers his lover to be dead rather than faithless. Julia Kristeva explains that in the course of this idealization of the female lover as a dead being, the woman loses her attributes of being other, another sex, and merges with the desired force of her lover to the point of obliteration. As a dead body she has become objectified and at the same time infinite, to the highest degree reified and at the same time in a realm beyond. "The dead woman," says Kristeva, "by virtue of being untouchable is . . . jouissance as nostalgia, within reach and forever lost, impossible. . . . These dead lovers remind us that phallic idealization edifies itself on the pedestal of the female body put to death."[39] But, she asks further, "Who dies . . . the lover or the femininity of the lover?"

At the dead body of the woman the semiotic Other receives its signifier. Regardless of whether this signifier is identified as dangerous chaos, as innocent purity, or as the fear of losing a privileged object of desire, each of these values is connected with femininity. Through this act, the necessary, dynamizing Other can be mitigated and transferred into the normative order, in fact becomes the privileged signifier of the security of this order.

The Paradox; or the Death of the Woman As Gathering Threshold

The fact that in the cultural modeling of the world women are often designated as half-dead suggests yet another reason for the fascination with this topic, for women thus represent the intersection between material and dematerialized world. Whether demonic or angel-like creatures, these women, as Gubar and Gilbert put it, "simultaneously inhabit both this world and the next,"[40] the world beyond, which they metonymically represent. This function of bringing together two worlds is further heightened in the depiction of their concrete death. It is generally believed that in the spectacle of a dead body one can concretely observe the threshold between life and death. Whereas the body is now totally in the material world, the soul is already in the world beyond, in the realm of the absolute. The body, now completely surface, a figure without any distinguishing traits, seems to refer to the beyond. An attempt to artificially preserve this border situation is an expression both of the desire to negate or surmount mortality and to create a bridge with the world beyond, in order to experience the Other, which can never be known to the mortal in a vicarious manner. Vampire narratives, like Bram Stoker's *Dracula* (in which Lucy is artificially kept alive in this intermediary state by the blood of her suitors) and also narratives about spiritualists and artists, where a dead woman is meant to be reanimated (through metempsychosis, as in Poe's "Ligeia," or through artificial representation in the form of portraits and poetry), illustrate how the woman can be used as a medium in order to set up contact with the realm of the dead. Since one cannot gaze at God directly without being punished, one looks at the dead woman, who seems to be in the presence of God. She thus serves as a protective shield between the viewer and the absolute. In Lacan's words, "It is in so far as her *jouissance* is radically Other that the woman has a relation to God greater than that stated in ancient speculation."[41]

But whose mortality are we concerned with? What is the reference point of this knowledge? Even in respect to our death, the viewer's death, the female corpse functions as a confirming mirror. By looking at it, we are imagining our own death as well as the realm beyond, which we can never know. We see our conceptions of the Other, not the Other itself. I have already stated that the woman is the shielding borderline between the symbolic order and chaos, which she in part represents. I can now add to this statement that, as an observed dead body, the woman is in exactly the same sense a shielding borderline between life and the absolute.

In a similar manner one can supplement the foregoing discussion of how the body of a dead woman serves to fix the object of desire and defer eternally a fulfillment of this desire. An artificial conservation of the state of death serves to fix the state of transiency, the invalid corporeality, serves in fact to emphasize the meaning of corporeality in connection with a knowledge that the actual, material body will soon no longer exist. This heightened corporeality, on the basis of which one hopes to decipher the realm beyond, onto which, however, one only projects one's own conceptions and expectations, this corporeality that marks the intersection between the here and the beyond, allowing one to surmise the divine while being entirely of this earth—this corporeality receives its special fascination from the fact that it is positioned as close as one can get to death and at the same time as far from the desired absolute as possible. In the same way that the woman, once dead, can no longer be reached, marking the place of eternal deferral of erotic desire, she—and with her the realm of death—cannot be known. She represents an enigma that one holds onto, a possession which is not a possession, which marks the place of deferral of the desire to know death. To witness the death of another means to expect an explanation or a revelation in the highest degree, and this desire is disappointed in a superlative manner, both in the sense that it cannot be fulfilled and in the sense that it is exposed as an illusion of one's own conceptions.

But also poetologically speaking, various discourses and levels of discourse come together in the motif of the beautiful dead woman. In these texts a cross occurs between a discussion of social victimization and art production, because the body of the beautiful dead woman points to the mutual interdependence of death and art creation (text production), of sacrifice and the establishment or preservation of the normative order. These texts, however, also present the highest form of contradiction (which is generally true for literary depictions of death), because the immobile female body, which I understand as a transparent sign precluding difference, is the condition, catalyst, and object for a text, for the transforming opaque, open signifying process. Thus, the dead woman functions for a viewer implied by the text as an object of desire, which mirrors his world and thus secures it. As the same time, she represents that which is Other to the norm, the semiotic *chora,* which receives a signifier at her dead body, and is thus the condition for language, for memory, for narration. She is "the most poetic subject" because she marks the position of a metapoetic self-reflexivity, of an accumulation and doubling of the semantically related areas "Femininity," "Death," "Art." What it means for our culture that these areas form semantically related paradigms, and that an intensification of these concepts produced by their linkage leads to the supreme expression of sublimity and perfection, opens up a very different question.

Notes

1. Edgar Allan Poe, "The Philosophy of Composition," *Essays and Reviews* (New York: Library of America, 1984), p. 19.

2. Beth Ann Bassein, *Women and Death: Linkages in Western Thought and Literature* (Westport, Conn.: Greenwood Press, 1984), esp. the chapter on Poe.

3. Mario Praz, *The Romantic Agony* (Oxford University Press, 1973). See also Nina Auerbach, *Woman and the Demon: The Life of a Victorian Myth* (Cambridge, Mass.: Harvard University Press, 1982).

4. Poe, "Philosophy of Composition," p. 16.

5. Ellie Ragland-Sullivan, *Jacques Lacan and the Philosophy of Psychoanalysis* (Urbana: University of Illinois Press, 1986), p. 188.

6. Roman Jakobson and M. Halle, *Fundamentals of Language* (The Hague: Mouton, 1956).

7. Jacques Lacan, "Function and field of speech and language" in *Ecrits. A Selection* (New York: Norton, 1977), p. 104.

8. Hans Mayer, *Aussenseiter* (Frankfurt: Suhrkamp, 1975).

9. Jacqueline Rose, *Sexuality in the Field of Vision* (London: Verson, 1986), p. 72f.

10. Jacques Lacan, "A Love Letter" in Jacqueline Rose and Juliet Mitchell (eds), *Feminine Sexuality* (New York: Norton, 1985), p. 57.

11. Rose, *Sexuality in the Field of Vision*, p. 72.

12. Samuel Richardson, *Clarissa*, vol. 4 (London: Dent, 1951), p. 376.

13. Ibid., p. 417.

14. Ibid.

15. "Schneewittchen," in *Kinder - und Hausmaerchen*, collected by the brothers Grimm (Munich: Winkler, 1973), reprint of the 1819 edition, p. 306. My translation.

16. Philippe Aries, *L'homme devant la mort* (Paris: Seuil, 1977), p. 466.

17. "Schneewittchen," p. 307.

18. Jacques Lacan, *The Four Fundamental Concepts of Psycho-Analysis* (New York: Norton, 1981), p. 83.

19. Edgar Allan Poe, "The Oval Portrait," in *Poetry and Tales* (New York: Library of America, 1984), p. 481–4.

20. Julia Kristeva, *Revolution in Poetic Language* (New York: Columbia University Press, 1984) p. 59.

21. Nathaniel Hawthorne, "The Birthmark," in *Tales and Sketches* (New York: Library of America, 1982), p. 764–80.

22. Jacques Lacan, *The Four Fundamental Concepts of Psycho-Analysis*, p. 218.

23. Tennyson, "Lancelot and Elaine,: in "Idylls of the King," *Poetical Works* (Oxford: Oxford University Press, 1971), p. 368–87.

24. Margaret Higonnet, "Suicide: Representations of the Feminine in the Nineteenth Century," *Poetics Today* 6, nos. 1–2 (1985): 104.

25. Kristeva, *Revolution in Poetic Language,* p. 75.

26. Artemidorus, *Oneirocritica,* quoted in Marina Warner, *Monuments and Maidens: The Allegory of the Female Form* (London: Weidenfeld and Nicolson, 1985), vii.

27. Ragland-Sullivan, *Jacques Lacan,* p. 288f.

28. Jacques-Alain Miller, "Another Lacan," quoted in Ragland-Sullivan, *Jacques Lacan,* p. 297.

29. Rose, *Sexuality in the Field of Vision,* p. 219.

30. Annicke Jaulin, "Avant-Propos," in *La Femme et la Mort,* (Toulouse-Le-Mirail: G.R.I.E.F., 1984), p. 7.

31. John Berger, *Ways of Seeing* (Harmondsworth: Penguin, 1977), p. 47.

32. Sandra M. Gilbert and Susan Gubar, *The Madwoman in the Attic: The Woman Writer and the Nineteenth-Century Literary Imagination* (New Haven, Conn.: Yale University Press, 1979), p. 14.

33. Leo N. Tolstoi, *Anna Karenina* (New York: Norton, 1970), part II, chapter XI, p. 135ff.

34. Prosper Merimee, *Carmen et autres nouvelles,* vol.2 (Paris: Livre de Poche, 1983), p. 181.

35. Ibid., p. 178.

36. Ibid., p. 216.

37. Ibid., p. 221.

38. Jacques Lacan, *The Four Fundamental Concepts of Psycho-Analysis,* p. 116.

39. Julia Kristeva, *Histoires d'amour* (Paris: Seuil, 1983), p. 442ff.

40. Gilbert and Gubar, *The Madwoman in the Attic,* p. 24ff.

41. Jacqueline Rose, *Feminine Sexuality,* p. 153.

graphic representation

Hanjo Berressem

DALI AND LACAN: PAINTING THE IMAGINARY LANDSCAPES

Introduction

Parallel to the topography of the *Imaginary*, the *Symbolic* and the *Real*, there are three nodal points between Jacques Lacan and Salvador Dali. The first is a photo that shows the two together in New York in 1975. Apart from this visual proximity, there is a discursive one: in the first issue of the surrealist magazine *Minotaure*, an article by Salvador Dali is followed immediately afterward by an article written by a certain Dr. Lacan. Finally there is their real meeting in 1932.

In his *Seminar II* Lacan reminds his listeners to

remember in the society's inaugural lecture. What I talked to you apropos of the symbolic, the imaginary and the real. I was using these categories in the form of small and capital letters.

iS—imagining the symbol, putting the symbolic discourse into a figurative form, the dream.

Si—symbolizing the image, making a dream-interpretation.[1]

With this differentiation between the dreamer's position (iS) and that of the analyst (Si), Lacan describes the two directions within which psychoanalysis is defined: the regressive movement inherent in the creation of dream-images by the dreamer and the complementary progressive re-translation of these images into their symbolic, verbal "originals" by the analyst.

In the following, I will counter Lacan's emphasis on the *Symbolic* (which also denotes the analyst's position) with Dali's emphasis on the *Imaginary*, on the dream-images and on their relation to the dream navel. What interests me in this juxtaposition is the possibility to read each position in the light of the other.[2]

Miraginaire

Within psychoanalysis, the differentiation between the word and the image is expressed in the Freudian notions of "word-representations" and "thing-representations," and, more recently, in Jacques Lacan's topography of the *Imaginary* (the visual scene), the *Symbolic* (the realm of language) and the *Real* (that which is neither *Imaginary* nor *Symbolic*), the threefold grid within which the Lacanian subject is suspended and defined.

It is in dealing with the *Imaginary* that Lacanian psychoanlysis comes to deal at length with visual perception and the way in which it structures the subject, with the visual "grammar" into which the subject is inscribed and last but not least with the general relation between the image and the word.

Very roughly, Lacan's notions of the *Imaginary*, the *Symbolic*, and the *Real* refer to the way in which the subject is related to its images, its language, and its body, respectively. In the same way in which for Lacan language and its structure are the blueprint of the *Symbolic*, the visual scene provides the underlying structure of the *Imaginary*. It is inaugurated in and during what he has termed, in a 1936 article: *"The mirror stage."*[3] This concept describes the formation of the *ego*, defining it as an essentially "fragmented," (*E* 4) hallucinated entity connected to a "function of misrecognition that characterizes . . . [it] in all its structures." (*E* 6)

In the article, Lacan describes the visual structure within which the child (before the acquisition of language) develops the instance of the *ego*—the image it has of itself. Because of the specifically human "prematurity of birth," (*E* 4) the confrontation

with his mirror-image can never lead to a perfect mapping. It results rather in an always "alienating identification" (*E* 128) that inaugurates the *double* simultaneously with the *ego*. In fact, it inaugurates the ego *as* the double, a twofold dynamics that is the
reason for a specific "ontological structure of the human world
that accords with [Lacan's] . . . reflections on paranoiac knowledge" (*E* 2). For Lacan, the ego is ontologically ruptured and split.
Within the *Imaginary*, the mirror functions as the plane along
which this split is executed.

Apart from this initial concept, Lacan develops another, more
elaborate structuration of the visual field in his *Seminar I* in which
he traces the way in which instinctual/bodily agencies are represented within the perceptual apparatus developed during the
"mirror stage" and conceptualizes how libidinal forces affect the
visual arena as well as in how far visual space is itself invariably libidinal.

Within this discussion, the asymmetry of the ego's body-
image (the *imaginary* identification of the mirror stage) and its instincts is modeled into a schema that is itself a "visual metaphor".
In a decisive move Lacan states that visual phenomena can not be
taken as "substantial, nor epiphenomenal in relation to . . . the apparatus itself. Hence they should be interpreted by means of an optical schema."[4] The visual, Lacan is saying, has to be treated on its
own, visual terms.

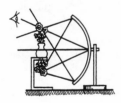  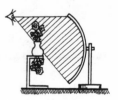

FIGURE 11.1
"The experiment
of the inverted
bouquet" (*I*, 78).

FIGURE 11.2
"The experiment
of the inverted bouquet."
The shaded area designates
the space of the *Real.*

FIGURE 11.3
"The experiment
of the inverted bouquet."
The shaded area designates
the space of the *Imaginary.*

In this first model, the box stands for the body, the vase for the
body-image, the flowers for the body's instincts and desires, the
mirror for the cortex and the eye for the subject (which is, strictly

speaking, only the retroactive "effect" of the procedure). This structure is divided into an *imaginary* space (the space visible to the eye) and a *real* space (that part of the apparatus excluded from sight). [Figures 11.1–11.3] Lacan uses this schema to show that the real objects, "although they inscribe themselves as residue or 'traces' . . . are not *perceptum*, for they offer no specular image or alterity."[5]

The image the subject sees consists of the mapping of the real, that is objective[6] "*imaginary* vase" (*I* 79) and the real (objective) image of the phantasmal "*real* flowers," which are mirrored into the perceptual apparatus from the *real* space forever excluded from it and which create within the *imaginary* space an "imaginary bouquet" (*I* 78). The oscillation between the image of the *imaginary* vase and the *real* flowers, strongest at the seam between the top of the vase and the stems of the flowers, denotes the basic split of the *Real* and the *Imaginary* on the visual plane.[7] The flowers are both *imaginary* and *real*, precisely because they cannot be present as such within any system of registration (because they are part of the *Real* of which Lacan had said that absolutely nothing can be said about it and that it is "without fissure" [*II* 90]). Their inexact representation, caused by the fact that the rays of this real image produce a mere "approximation" (*I* 78), denotes their oscillating instability within the perceptual apparatus. The completed mapping of the two planes results in an "illusion of reality, a real illusion." (*I* 109) The important point is that although the *Real* is not accessible in any direct way, it is mirrored into the perceptual apparatus where it has specific effects—the effects of instinctual and libidinal agencies within the structure of the subject's visual scene.

This setup functions only, however, if the eye is "within the cone" (*I* 80) so that the relation between the *Imaginary* and the

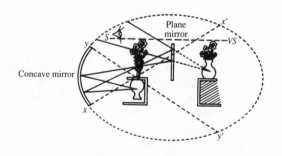

FIGURE 11.4
"Simplified schema of the two mirrors" (*I*, 139).

Real is ultimately dependent on "the position of the subject." (*I* 80) This position is, in turn, dependent on "its position within the *Symbolic* world" (*I* 80), the realm of language. In these schemata, another mirroring effect has been added to the one between the *Imaginary* and the *Real*, showing the transfer of the real image-system into a virtual one. [Figure 11.4]

The subject can now be positioned *outside* of the *imaginary* field and still be "capable of seeing . . . [the image] in a mirror, as a virtual image." (*I* 140) The split between the body-image and the desires that inaugurates the instance of the *ego* is thus repeated again along another axis; that of the plane mirror. This split creates from the *ego* a *"virtual subject"* (*I* 140). Together, these two splits mark the ruptured form of the human arena.

A small movement of the plane mirror would obviously have immense effects on the visibility of the image. These secondary movements, Lacan sees as "commanded by the voice of the other." (*I* 140) It is here that Lacan introduces language, which leads the subject out of the visual scene. In the same manner in which the meeting between the *Real* and the *Imaginary* was executed along the plane of the stems of the flowers and the vase, the transition from the *Imaginary* to the *Symbolic* (from the *moi* to the *je*) is executed (still within the visual scene) along the mirror-plane of the second mirror. With this second mirroring Lacan also describes his contention that after the entry into the *Symbolic*, *symbolic* structures dominate the *Imaginary*, because they potentialize the refractions of the initial mirroring. The *Imaginary* and the *Real* operate on "the same level," (*I* 141) because their interplay engineers the—more or less successful—optical mapping of the external images of the world and the *ego's* internal images of the world.

Think of the mirror as a plane of glass. You'll see yourself in the glass and you'll see the objects beyond it. That's exactly how it is—it's a coincidence between certain images and the real. What else are we talking about when we refer to an oral, anal, genital reality, that is to say a specific relation between our images and images? This is nothing other than the images of the human body, and the hominisation of the world, its perception in terms of images linked to the structuration of the body. The real objects, which pass via the mirror, and through it, are in the same place as the imaginary object. The essence of the image is to be invested by the libido. What we call libidinal investment is what makes an object desirable, that is to say how it becomes confused with this more or less structured image which, in diverse ways, we carry with us. (*I* 141)

Throughout his discussion, Lacan's objective had been to prove the impossibility of the unity of the subject. This impossibility results from its inscription into a specific visual structure. There can be no pre-reflexive *ego*, because it is a reflection that inaugurates the *ego* in the first place. It is not the *ego* which structures the visual scene; it is rather the visual scene that structures the *ego*, its structure being the matrix in whose structure the "I is precipitated in a primordeal form." (*E* 2) The *ego*, then, is a mirror-effect.

This impossibility of unity is also pre-programmed within the *Symbolic*. Because of the bar between signifier and signified, every encounter with the *Real* within the *Symbolic* must by needs also be a missed encounter: "It goes wrong. That is objective."[8] In relation to the speaking subject, Lacan talks of a "gliding . . . within the chain of signifiers" (*EN* 55) and the impossibility to pin a signified to a signifier once and for all: "the subject is always punctual and fading, because it is a subject only because of another signifier and for another signifier." (*EN* 155) In the same way in which the *ego* is a mirror-effect, therefore, the subject is an "effect of the signifier."

Lacan, however, introduces a further asymmetry into the *Imaginary*, that between the *eye* and the *gaze*. This asymmetry is isomorphic to the one between signifier and signified, with the gaze standing for the subjective position within the objective "visual apparatus," the eye:

> in our relation to things, in so far as this relation is constituted by way of vision . . . something slips, passes, is transmitted, from stage to stage, and is always to some degree deluded by it—that is what we call the gaze.[9]

This incessant "oversight" is especially obvious in dreams, in which the gaze also always misses (the primal scene), and thus it comes to symbolize a structural lack within the visual field itself: "in the final resort, our position in the dream is profoundly that of someone who does not see." (*FF* 75) This *Imaginary* "missed encounter" is described within the visual field by what Lacan calls the *stain*.

With the differentiation between the *gaze* and the *eye*, Lacan plays out the subject of the gaze (*desidero*: the subject of desire) against the subject of the eye (*cogito:* the self-conscious subject) and physiological against physical space. Linked to the *eye,* "consciousness, in its illusion of 'seeing itself seeing itself'" (*FF* 82) is forever subverted by the *gaze.* In yet another visual metaphor Lacan uses the anamorphosis in Holbein's painting *The Ambassadors* (which shows quite literally a "stain" on the pictorial plane) to describe these dynamics, giving a reading of the painting in which he stakes the anamorphosis and the gaze against the central perspective and the eye.[10]

For that project, Lacan goes back to the time of the "invention" of the central perspective by Brunelleschi and Alberti in the first half of the fifteenth century, which brings about the geometrization and mathematization of visual space. With Dürer's optical apparatus, which is based on the premises of this new mathematization, one can project three-dimensional space onto a two-dimensional surface with the help of a system of coordinates. Lacan uses the apparatus to show that what is at issue in geometrical perspective is "simply the mapping of space not sight." (*FF* 86) Its strictly geometrical image-system can be visualized even by a blind man and is in no way dependant on physiological factors. The apparatus also shows the two prerequisites on which the system of the central perspective is based: a fixed point of view and a theory of projection.[11] Although initially a means to simulate the "correct" perception of reality, the structure of the apparatus can also be reversed in order to obtain quite different effects:

> If I reverse its use, I will have the pleasure of obtaining not the restoration of the world that lies at its end, but the distortion, on another surface, of the image that I would have obtained on the first. (*FF* 87)

Because it is based on and operates within Cartesian space, the central perspective is based on a vertical cut through the visual cone. This characteristic is completely *inherent* in its underlying systematics and cannot be explained by physiological arguments or, in fact, any arguments from *without* the system, such as arguments from within systems based on "spherical" space. Within Cartesian space, the vertical cut through the visual cone is the most simple and most elegant form of projection and therefore has become the norm. Other cuts produce images that are mathematically and geometrically well-defined distortions of this vertical norm. These images can be re-translated into "correct" images by a well-defined shift of the viewer's point of view that counterbalances the initial distortions and reinstates the vertical norm. The normal position (the position from which the projection originated) is thus only one (although a privileged one) of many, structurally equal cuts through the visual cone; it is ultimately the *relation* between viewer and image that produces the visual effect. Every position of the eye in relation to geometrical space being structurally equal, anamorphic distortion can be defined as a mathematically and geometrically well-defined aberration from the vertical norm. In structural terms, however, *every* point of view has to be understood as a distortion, because all are based on the general abstractions underlying the system of the central perspective. This structure is in many ways reminiscent of the Freudian notion of "distortion" [Entstellung] inherent in the transposition of the latent dream-thought into manifest representations, which is also dependent upon the abstractions underlying the system of representation and has to follow "considerations of representability" [Rücksicht auf Darstellbarkeit].

It is important to realize that in both anamorphoses and the central perspective the point of view has to be fixed, and that both follow the same underlying rules: the rules of the *eye.* The movements and shifting positions of the subject *within* this geometrical space, (the *relation* between Holbein's anamorphosis and the "representative" part of the painting) however, are defined by the *gaze.*

Lacan has a specific reason to deal at such lengths with optical space: Having in "The mirror stage" defined the *ego* within a visual scenario and as an effect of its insertion into a specific visual structure, he can now compare visual distortions of images within the system of the central perspective to the distortions caused by "libidinal agencies" within psychic space. Visual distortions can thus serve as a (visual) metaphor of psychic distortions; the effects of the interference of the libido within the perceptual apparatus.

In Holbein's case, geometrical space is punctured by an anamorphosis. As both are mathematized image-systems with fixed points of view, the resulting effect is dependent upon the subject's change of position *vis-à-vis* the painting. Normally, anamorphoses are used to create geometrically "correct" images on "distorted surfaces," such as cylindrical or conical anamorphoses, or to simulate a "distorted surface," as in Pozzo's anamorphoses in S. Ignazio in Rome, where it is used to simulate a copula.

Yet there are also paintings in which *both* points of view create readable, although different, images, in such a way that one image-system is incorporated into the other one so as to become almost invisible. This strategy was sometimes used to hide secret messages within seemingly "innocent" images, in a similar way in which the latent dream-thought is coded "invisibly" into the dream-images.

In Holbein's case, the two image-systems are superimposed onto each other without being legible simultaneously. When the spectator puts himself into the central, geometrically correct position in front of the painting, (the point from which the projection of the image originates) "the eye" sees the image, and the anamorphosis as a stain. But, while turning around to walk away from the painting—an effect carefully engineered by the specific position of the painting within the room in which it was originally hung—it sees in the last moment, in the last "gaze" that it casts back, the anamorphosis and, consequently, the image as a stain. Holbein's painting flattens these two points of view onto one image-plane with the explicit aim to make them exclude each other, an effect De Chirico produces by using two diverging perspectives within one pictorial system.

In terms of content, what the eye sees, after it has (in looking at the painting) secured itself of geometrical space and of itself within this geometrical space, is a scull. The subject (itself) as "annihilated." Ironically, the scull serves simultaneously as that part of the painting that makes the painter immortal, because it is a visual correlative of his signature ("Hohlbein," meaning "scull" [hollow bone] in German). The relation of the subject to death is taken up by the vanitas symbols within the pictorial representation but more importantly by its optical structure itself, in which the stain denotes the "blindspot" of geometrical space, the central perspective as "annihilated."[12] Death and the subject are related to each other like the painting and the stain, or like the central perspective and the anamorphosis. Where the one is, the other is not, yet one cannot think the one without the other. The mutual exclusion of the image and the anamorphosis thus has to be seen as an artistic strategy that mirrors and repeats the "subject" of the painting. The painting, and Lacan with it, thus play out the central perspective (the visual grammar) against its distortions:

distortion may lend itself . . . to all the paranoiac ambiguities . . . from Archimboldi to Salvador Dali. I will go so far as to

say that this fascination complements what geometral re-
searches into perspective allow to escape from vision. (*FF* 87)

A first difference between the eye and the gaze is thus that the eye
denotes the abstract geometrical structure of space as defined by
the central perspective, while the gaze denotes the subject's position and movement(s) within this space. A second differentiation is
that while the eye *projects* space and the central perspective is
based on a theory of projection, the gaze is defined by the way in
which images are *taken in* and is based on a theory of introjection:
"unlike the gaze which is *in* us, the eye is outside (and) works as a
principle of law and judgement" (*FF* 95).

Within geometrical space, the subject-of-the-eye sees everything, but has to pay for it by being a mere optico-mathematical
ideal: "that punctiform being located at the geometral point from
which the perspective is grasped" (*FF* 96). Against this "objective"
subject, Lacan evokes the subject as "the depth of field, with all its
ambiguity and variability, which is in no way mastered by me" (*FF*
96). This depth-of-field is *inherent* in the geometrical system and
vice versa. And again, as in the Holbein painting, although on a different level, it is a position that denotes the system's *lack*. Yet this
lack is part of a dialectics: the subject of the eye—being "pure
spirit"—has no "body." Being "nothing" but a pure abstraction, it
cannot incorporate a "lack." The subject of the gaze is "a body,"
and it is as such that it is implicated by "lack."

These two orientations make out the subject's complete visual topography. The structure of the subject-of-the-eye is superimposed by the structure of the subject-of-the-gaze. The clear, projec-
tion-image of the eye is overlaid with an "opaque" (*FF* 96) screen.
While the eye is situated *outside* of the image-system, being the
point from which it is projected, the gaze describes the subject

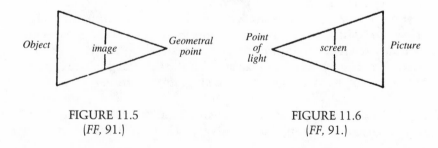

FIGURE 11.5
(*FF*, 91.)

FIGURE 11.6
(*FF*, 91.)

within the image-system. It denotes its shifting positions within visual space[13] as well as the specific mode of the perception of images defined by that part of the eye (as an organ) that makes out its "surplus" to being a purely geometrical apparatus. [Figures 11.5–11.6] While the first cone depicts geometrical space and its projection, (the point of light is on the side of the objects in cone #1), the objects look, in "the spectacle of the world," (*FF* 73) at the subject in the same manner in which the subject looks at them (cone #2). Their images enter what Dali calls "the canvas of . . . [the] mind"[14] *through* the gaze. The overlapping of these two orientations defines the complete visual topography into which the subject is inscribed. [Figure 11.7] It is precisely by the play and relation between the *gaze* and the *eye* with which the artist amazes, especially in *trompe l'oeil* painting, which is a "triumph of the gaze over the eye" (*FF* 103). It is the play with the doubly defined screen that art is all about. Because reality is always "approached with the apparatus of desire" (*EN* 61), reality as such is "marginal" (*FF* 115) and functions only as the underlying materiality on which the artist's play is based. It is within this play that desire precipitates itself, when, "by a mere shift of our gaze, we are able to realize that the representation does not move with the gaze" (*FF* 112).

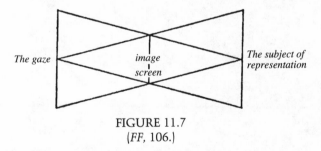

FIGURE 11.7
(*FF*, 106.)

It is thus never geometrical space as *against* the subject's position in it but their interplay with which art deals. Giacometti's object "Pointe à l'oeil" (1931) [Photo 11.1] illustrates this double movement. Within its play with the systems of projection and introjection it depicts the anamorphotic and libidinal softening of the visual cone, the element of agressivity inherent in the structures of the *Imaginary* and defines every distortion as a distortion of a strictly geometrical form. With Giacometti and Lacan, the visual one "melts with desire."

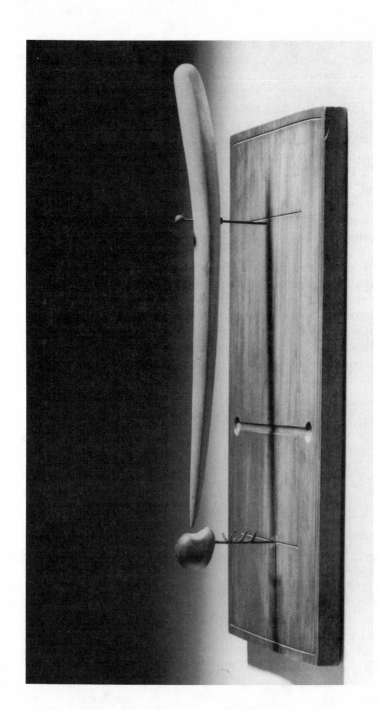

PHOTO 11.1
Alberto Giacometti: *la Pointe à l'oeil*, 1932.
Musée national d'art moderne Centre Georges Pompidou, Paris.

Lacan/Dali

I am because I hallucinate, and because I hallucinate, I am.[15]

In one of his numerous autobiographies, Salvador Dali describes his meeting with a "brilliant young psychiatrist"[16] who had read Dali's article on "The Inner Mechanisms of Paranoiac Activity" (SL 18) and who wanted to come and discuss the theses Dali had put forward in this article. This young psychiatrist was none other than Jacques Lacan.[17]

The meeting was memorable not only because it was conducted with Dali "unconsciously" still having a piece of paper attached to the tip of his nose that he had put there while painting the portrait of the Vicomtesse de Noailles (which would date the meeting to 1932) but also because it brought together two people who had separately developed a redefinition of the status of paranoiac systems and processes. While Lacan had been looking for an *explanation* of specific psychic states, however, Dali had been looking for a theoretical *proof* of both the results of his self-analysis and the artistic theory he had developed from them.

Dali and Lacan thus came to think about paranoia from quite opposite directions. Unlike the true paranoiacs with which Lacan dealt, Dali always considered himself a sane madman, a paradoxical position that he expressed by stating that "the only difference between me and a madman is that I am not mad."[18] He always understood his paranoia as a simulated one and a specific artistic strategy. Within this simulation, Dali positions himself into the ambiguous position of a "critical dreamer," while Lacan (the analyst) is always a "critic of dreams." Both, however, were looking for a way to understand the paranoiac hallucination not as a gratuitous, unordered collage of mental images, which one *then* sets out to interpret, but as an inherently systematic scene. It is this "structuralist" approach that especially fascinated Dali about Lacan's theses, and in his article on "The Angelus," Dali mentions Lacan as the person who has for the first time explained paranoiac hallucinations themselves as a specific, active "form of interpretation" (GW 201).

Lacan has brought the light of science into a phenomenon which had been a secret for most of the contemporaries—the term paranoia—and has given it its real meaning. Before

Lacan, psychiatry had made a grave mistake, in that it claimed that the systematization of the paranoiac delirium was a belated action and this phenomenon had to be taken as a "thinking madness." Lacan has proven the opposite: the delirium itself is a systematization. (SD 155)

In his 1933 article on "Le problème du style et la conception psychiatrique des formes paranoiaques de l'expérience," (an article that very much bears the stamp of his meeting with Dali) Lacan, in turn, states that paranoiac hallucinatory systems are "symbolic' expressions" (GW 355) with their own "original syntax" (GW 356) and judges them as *"on the same level as the inspiration of the greatest artists"* (GW 355, emphasis added).

Contrary to earlier, materialistic explanations, Lacan sees paranoiac hallucinations as an "interpretative disturbance of the perception," (GW 360) a disturbance that is oriented away from the "reality-principle" and toward the "pleasure-principle" (GW 75)—and thus from geometrically coherent space to anamorphoses—and that translates instinctual systems, such as "aggressivity,"[19] (GW 361) into "symbolic images." (GW 361)

On the one hand the field of perception of these subjects presents an imminent and "personally meaningful" (a symptom called interpretation) frightening character. . . . On the other hand, the strong change in space-time preception modifies the significance of their conviction of reality. (GW 355)

Lacan shows that the images and symbols within this paranoiac scene follow certain mirror-structures of repetition, doubling and multiplication, exactly these "more and more paralyzing, vast concentric . . . hallucination(s)" (II 169) that a *symbolic* mediation could "unfreeze."[20]

For Dali, as well as Lacan, the "symbolic language of the unconscious is the only truly universal language" (GW 74).[21] Within this language, Dali defines paranoia as an "interpretative hallucination of associations with a systematic structure," (GW 273) and his method as the "spontaneous method of irrational cognition, which rests on the critical interpretative association of hallucinatory phenomena" (GW 273) in which the "critical apparatus" interferes only as a mere "developer" (GW 273) that "objectifies" (GW 274) the initial hallucinatory images without interfering with their structuration. This objectification finds its painterly, visual correlative in *trompe l'oeil* painting, which makes the "representational images of the concrete irrationality" visible with a "bossy precision" (*GW* 271). Dali compares this process to photography, describing his paintings as "snapshot(s), handmade color-photograph with the help of fine, adventurous . . . deluding, hyper-normal, mentally retarded images of the concrete irrationality" (*GW* 271).

Dali, however, sees in these images not only the result of a madman's subjective, free, libidinal and intensified production of hallucinatory image-systems. They are merely a specific variant of the "normal" hallucinatory system; the hallucination of reality: "even the real intuitive images are dependant upon the degree of our paranoic faculties" (*GW* 132). Lacan describes precisely this as the fundamentally paranoiac structure of human knowledge and the phantasmatic structure of reality.

Within the hallucinatory system, specific, libidinally regulated obsessive images [*Zwangsvorstellungen*] manifest themselves through the mapping of two (or more) images, in such a way that the obsessive image manifests itself in the *secondary* image. The elaborate technique of the mapping is the result of the "interpretative cunning" (*GW* 132) of the paranoiac system itself, which creates

> a double image, which means the representation of an object, which, without any figurative or anatomical change is simultaneously the representation of another, completely different object, which is also free of any distortion or anomaly. (*GW* 132)

This structure shows close links to Lacan's theory of metaphor, which follows rules similar to that of the double image, only within a verbal scenario, because

> The creative spark of the metaphor does not spring from the presentation of two *images*, that is, two signifiers equally actualized. It flashes between two signifiers one of which has taken the place of the other in the signifying chain. (*E* 157, emphasis added)

It is this flashing effect that is also operative in Dali's double images, and this structure might be a link between the realms of the word and the image. [Figure 11.2]

PHOTO 11.2

Salvador Dali: *Paranoia*. (1935–36) Oil on canvas. 15 x 18 1/8 inches.
Collection of Mr. and Mrs. A. Reynolds Morse. On loan to The Salvador Dali Museum,
St. Petersburg, Florida. Copyright © 1994 Salvador Dali Museum, Inc.

Within psychoanalysis, images are basically understood as "retrospective signifiers." This contention becomes especially striking in Lacan's treatment of the Freudian dream-rebus, in which he interprets the dream-images as "always already" translations of verbal, symbolic structures:

> So the unnatural images of the boat on the roof . . . are to be taken only for their value as signifiers. . . . the value of the image as signifier has nothing whatever to do with its signification. (*E* 159)

Yet although the dream-images are signifiers, these signifiers in turn are—in their retranslation—metaphors, that is: verbal images.

Played out, then, is the *signifier* against the *form* (the contour): in the same way that every image is a signifier, every signifier is an image. While Lacan stresses the verbal image in the reconstruction of the dream-thought (the latent content) from the manifest dream-content in a movement of extrapolation, Dali emphasizes the visual image in the regressive movement from the manifest dream-content toward the latent dream-thought and the "navel of the dream." His reconstitutions provide not a *symbolic* explanation, but an image "which becomes every instant clearer and more enigmatic" (*GW* 154).

The emphasis on the primary process brings Dali constantly into the proximity of the *Real*, which Lacan also links to the phantasma (hallucination) and the *Imaginary*, because Lacan sees the *ego* as

> a mechanism of regulation, of adaption to the Real, which enables the organism to refer the hallucination . . . to what is happening at the level of the perceptual apparatus. (*II* 144)

The structures within this apparatus mediate the hallucination (the primary process), which is itself an image "reproduced by stimulation," (*II* 141) so that it can only be seen through the images superimposed upon it by the image-repertoire of the dream. The initial, invisible, and veiled image is related to the navel of the dream, that which within the dream is forever excluded and escapes, the unconscious, (as the *real* space within the mirror structure) another space (or scene) where the *Real* is experienced "without any mediation, whether imaginary or symbolic" (*II* 225).[22]

Interestingly enough, Lacan also relates this unmediated experience not to something verbal but to specific images—to a scene in which mirroring is again a predominant motif:

> The Medusa's head . . . is the revelation of that which is least penetrable in the real . . . the essential object, which isn't an object any longer, but this something faced with which all words cease and all categories fail, the object of anxiety par excellence. (*II* 164)

Within the hallucination—the confrontation with the image—the subject fades completely. It is, to stay within Lacan's image, "turned into stone." And again, it is by a trick involving a mirror, (by looking at the Medusa in the mirror of his shield, and thus "filtering" the image), that Perseus succeeds in overcoming her.

In *Encore*, Lacan describes this passage from the *Real* to the Phantasma, which he had defined visually in his optical schema and which also describes the passage from the outside to the inside, in a linguistically revealing way, defining the *Real as* a phantasma:

> a Real which has nothing to do with traditional theories of cognition, and which is not what they thought it was, reality, but exactly a phantasma. (*EN* 141)

This paradoxical statement has exactly the structure of a verbal double image. The *Real* and the phantasma are mapped onto each other in the same way in which Dali grafts images onto each other. Lacan, however, is ultimately more interested in the subject's symbolic reconstructions of the initial image, whereas Dali is trying to (re)produce if not the *Real* as phantasma, then the phantasma as *Real* by projecting not simply images from the outside, but showing the "paranoiac correspondence" between images projected by the subject and "real," objective images.

> One day one will have to admit officially that what we have baptized reality is an even greater illusion than the world of dreams . . . reality is epiphenomenal, a by-product of thought. . . . The true reality is within us, and we project them to the outside via the systematic use of our paranoia, which is an answer and reaction to the pressure—the negative pressure—of the cosmic emptiness. (*SD* 158)

The link between the anamorphosis—which I read as a visual pun—and the pun—which I read as a verbal anamorphosis—is developed along these lines. In Dali's paranoiac images, as in the pun, two (or more) signifieds share one signifier or contour. They are the utopia of an anamorphic universe and present a double anamorphosis, in which every contour is seen as absolutely distorted from the position of the other contour; an anamorphic *concetto*, in which the spatial movement of the spectator is changed into a movement of perception within the apparatus of registration itself. Unlike in Holbein, where a spatial movement was still necessary, Dali's double images function from one spatial position. Dali specifically inserts his theory of visual anamorphoses into a scenario of libidinal space and compares the visual to the psychic anamorphosis: "The conic anamorphon: the plane re-creation of a distortion mirrored in a very smooth cone" (*GW* 241) to the "psychic anamorphon: short re-creation of a desire which is distorted by the refraction within a cycle of memories" (*GW* 241). Ultimately, Dali is interested in the detachment of the "image of desire" from its psychic bonds and its symbolic mediations, which, while they assimilate the image also distort it. His double images show distortion as the normality of every form and every perception as anamorphic.

Narcissus

In 1936, the year in which Lacan writes "The mirror stage," Dali writes his poem *Narcissus*[23] and paints the canvas of the same name. The fact that already the original myth contains the motifs of visual mirroring (Narcissus) and linguistic mirroring (Echo) is taken up again by Dali in the fact that he treats the subject both in a painting and a poem.

In *The Metamorphosis of Narcissus* [Photo 11.3] Dali takes up the subject that had already served Freud as the ultimate model for the psychic system of narcissism and the one into which Lacan had inserted the structures of the *Imaginary*. It is also the painting he took to his meeting with Freud in 1938.

In this earliest of mirror-stages the separation of self and non-self is executed along the mirror formed by the water, which effects the first doubling of Narcissus. The image of the *ego* and the image of the outside (the *ego as other*) are separated as well as superimposed

PHOTO 11.3
Salvador Dali: *Métamorphose de Narcisse*
Tate Gallery, London.

via this natural mirror. Dali, however, does not stress so much this initial doubling as the new image the two doubles create as a whole, the hand:

> If one looks at the hypnotic, motionless form of Narcissus for a while from a little distance and with a certain "distracted fixedness," it slowly vanishes and finally becomes invisible.
>
> Exactly in this moment the metamorphosis of the myth takes place, because the appearance of Narcissus suddenly is transformed into the appearance of a hand, which emerges from its own mirror-image. This hand carries in its fingertips an egg . . . from which the new narcissus is formed—the flower. Next to it, one can see the plaster-sculpture of a hand, the hand of the water turned to stone, which holds the . . . flower. (*GW* 280)

Everything on the left side of the painting is defined by mirrorings, a motif that creates a "dizzying space of mirror-images." (*NA*) By again doubling this image he represents the youth and his mirror-image as "their own interpretation," prolonging the *internal*, vertical partition between Narcissus and himself into a *spatial*, horizontal one, which in itself becomes a new image. He underlines the second partition by the color-scheme, which contrasts a warm, reddish-brown part with a colder, blueish-green one. The result is a subjective-figurative zone and a theoretical, objective-monumental one, a differentiation that is again taken up by the juxtaposition of the "heterosexual group" (*NA*) on the left and the statue on the chess-board on the right.

The first doubling of Narcissus in the water denotes the *internal* structuration of paranoia. (In this partition, the section of body and water is also formally a "golden section"). With the specific pose of Narcissus, whose face is not visible, Dali stresses that he is ultimately concerned with an interior, self-reflexive process.

The right part of the painting, which is formally quite literally a displacement of the right half is a *secondary* "doubling of the doubling" that takes up the metamorphosis of the left part, theoretizing as well as monumentalizing it.

It is thus not quite correct that, as Jose Pierre states, one is confronted "not with a 'double image,' but with a 'doubled image.'"[24] The plaster hand is rather the doubled image of the double image, a monument of the inner system that repeats the structure of objectification by visually objectifying the image and turning Narcissus' body into stone—respectively plaster—in the same way in which Narcissus was "turned into stone" by his mirror image, a motif that recalls once more Lacan's confrontation with the head of the Medusa.

Dali's painting is thus both a specific interpretation of the myth of Narcissus as well as a theoretical treatise on his "critical-paranoiac method." The image evokes all the narcissistic tropes: mis-identification, death, aggression and regression. Narcissus, the Gods, as well as the heterosexual group with its "latent morphological atavisms" (*NA*) regress: "The human returns to the flower." (*NA*) Dali thus not only presents the narcissistic image per se, he simultaneously presents the visual structure of the theory of which the image itself is an effect, the "systematic and interpretative ordering of the 'sensational' unconnected and narcissistic surrealist raw-material." (*GW* 273) The exactness of this visual treatise shows the visual possibilities of structuring the visual scene, as well as the precision of such a visual language. Dali's objectifications explicitly attempt to transcend subjective, psychoanalytically legible image-systems and define the initial obsessive image as utterly inexplicable and unconscious: "The intuitive images of the concrete irrationality are the really unknown images." (*GW* 271) For the reception, this implies that the painting's structure can be (and must be) analyzed with the utmost precision, but that its content remains enigmatic, because it lacks "sense." In this context the shadow on the right side of the painting, which again forms a stain on the image-plane, becomes important. It is the "hole" on the canvas that prevents it from ever being read completely, because one part of the image is forever hidden. This shadow without figure makes it impossible to read the painting without "the shadow of a doubt." As a reminder of the other scene that lies "behind" the figurations of the *Imaginary* and the *Symbolic*, it stresses the ontologically enigmatic character of the unconscious and turns the painting into an "objective mystery."[25]

Against the verbal reconstructions, Dali's images ultimately attempt to re-produce and "portrait" the *Real* (as a phantasma): "Without mercy I comb through the Real and see in its shining objectivity with astonishment the emergence of a universal diagram from a hyper-subjective phenomenon." (*GW* 167) His shift from the dominance of the *Symbolic* over the *Imaginary* to the dominance of the image over the word has to be understood as a first step in his attempt to show the phantasmatic structure of what we call *reality:*

PHOTO 11.4
Caravaggio, Michelangelo Merisi da: *Narcise.*
Roma, Galleria Nazionale d'Arte Antica, Palazzo Barberini.
Archivo Fotografico Soprintendenza per i Beni Artistici e Storici di Roma.

But this gives rise to a new fear. Because we got rid of the old phantoms, which secured our inner peace only too well, we have to look upon the world of the objects, the objective world, as the true, obvious content of a new dream. (GW 167)

His program to "paint realistically according to irrational thinking" (GW 271) and the shift from the interpretative paranoia within perception to the paranoia of perception itself is ultimately the attempt to give a proof of the inherent paranoiac structure of *reality* as such. The paranoiac images thus function as the "true translations" of the primary, illegible image.

One question has remained open until now: if Dali's theory is applicable to his own paintings, then the "unknown image" of the "double Narcissus" should have a correlative in the "real," which would form the invisible background to the visible obsessive image. In the case of Narcissus, this trigger is itself *another* painting of Narcissus; a *further doubling:* Caravaggio's *Narcise,* [Photo 11.4] in which Dali only "displaces" the right arm and its mirror-image to the right, where it completes the form of the hand. This painting, in turn, prefigures Dali's scenario of alienation, because the face Narcissus looks at in Caravaggio's version is also that of "another."

Impressions of Africa

If Dali had predominantly dealt with the visual, narcissistic aspect of paranoiac images, and the node of the *Imaginary* and the *Real* in *The Metamorphosis of Narcissus,* in *Impressions of Africa,* [Photo 11.5] he creates a complex interference-pattern of the *Imaginary* and the *Symbolic,* taking as a "trigger" a text rather than an image and thus combining the visual and language in an especially striking way. The text is Raymond Roussel's *Nouvelles Impressions d'Afrique.* Dali, who was one of the chosen few mentioned in Roussel's testament to receive a copy of his *Comment j'ai ecrit certains de mes Livres,* was fascinated by Roussel's work, which in his opinion showed "highly obsessive constants" (GW 180) and whose "wonderfully devalued metaphors skim the borders of mental debility" (GW 180).[26]

Like that of *Nouvelles Impressions d'Afrique,* the subject of the painting is the construction of visual puns. Rather than a description

PHOTO 11.5
Salvador Dali: *Impressions d'Afrique.*
Museum Boymans-van Beuningen, Rotterdam.

of "Africa," the painting presents a psychic landscape. It is a "post-card from the other scene," this equally dark and unknown conti-nent. In fact, Dali's description of the painting's subject is an exact parallel to the structure of the unconscious and its endless transcriptions of an illegible text: "it was astonishing how many memories I had of a place I have never been to."

The painting's double images show again the subject's aban-donment to the visual and language material and the projection of paranoiac images into formal modules but also, read in reverse, the creation of paranoiac images from these very modules. The defini-tion of the painter by the "painterly signifying chain" but also the play of its manipulation.

Roussel's text and Dali's painting are perhaps the closest one can get to an approximation and convergence of the visual and lan-guage. While Roussel's texts always show the *imaginary* aspect of the *Symbolic*, Dali's painting shows how much the *Imaginary* is in complicity with and complementary to the *Symbolic*.

Michel Foucault has shown that Roussel constantly explores "imaginary," narcissistic tropes, creating a literary rebus or a "word-image."[27] His starting position, "The infinitesimal but im-mense distance between . . . two phrases," (*DL* 14)[28] which is then bridged by a complex story, is in fact a precise verbal equivalent to Dali's double images, which, like Roussel's juxtapositions are a *concordia discors* that bring about "the unexpected meeting of the most distant figures of reality" (*DL* 14).

Like Dali, who explicitly states that the primary images are completely inexplicable, the motif of the "double" in Roussel's work "has the function . . . of filling the void with an enigma that it fails to solve" (*DL* 23). It can never solve this enigma, because the "question" itself is illegible. All the artist can do is ceaselessly repeat the mechanism of "translation," a process Dali symbolically recreates in his painting *The Endless Enigma*, in which six para-noiac images are superimposed upon each other.

It is the paranoiac system itself that installs itself as the un-bridgeable gap between these doubles and functions as a mirror-plane. It is for this reason that both Roussel's and Dali's mappings are ultimately "a joining of beings which carry no lesson" (*DL* 84).

Both Dali's double images and Roussel's starting sentences are defined within the twofold dynamics of repetition and differ-ence, or better: repetition *as* difference. They present two terms "so intricately linked . . . that it's not possible to distinguish which came first" (*DL* 24). The notion of the double connects both concepts in a singular manner, denoting both the duplication as well as the "otherness" of the duplicate. It is ultimately the difference *within* repetition, the flaw "by which a mask denounces itself as only a mask," (*DL* 118) which inaugurates the recursive space of the constant "mappings." This dependence upon "precursors" is the reason for Roussel's "refusal to be original" (*DL* 45) as well as for Dali's "triggers."

In "The agency of the letter in the unconscious or reason since Freud" Lacan had stressed the fact that language is inevitably "polyphonous" (*E* 154) and that "the structure of the signifying chain discloses . . . the possibility . . . to use it in order to signify *something quite other* than it says." (*E* 155) Lacan's psychoanalysis as well as Roussel's texts gain their final meaning from "the fact that the same word can designate two different things and the same sentence repeated can have a different meaning"; (*DL* 165) Dali's paintings gain their meaning from a similar structure within the visual. If Roussel's *Impressions of Africa* show the "proliferating emptiness of language," (*DL*) Dali's *Impressions of Africa* show the "proliferating emptiness of the visible."

Conclusion

In Lacan, the *Imaginary* is defined as a site in which the subject is *passively* confronted with images, which he then confronts and assimilates *actively* within the *Symbolic*. Dali's imaginary scenes show how much the visual arts might be seen as a site in which active forms of interpretation and assimilation can be staged. This re-evaluation of the visual would have to go hand in hand with research into a "visual language," of which Dali's images are a striking example.

Apart from the obvious connection between the fragmented body-image of the mirror-stage and the "corpes morceles" of Dali and the surrealists,[29] Dali's critical-paranoiac method describes the relation of the *Imaginary* to the *Real* as well as to the *Symbolic* from within a visual grammar. His images provide a perfect "text" for a visual approach to Lacan's topology, an approach that balances Lacan's own emphasis on language and its metaphoricity, with an emphasis on the image itself. It might thus be seen in many ways as a mirror-image of Lacanian theory, which shows both the divergences but also the interrelatedness of an *imaginary* and a *symbolic* approach. As such, Dali's critical-paranoiac method—an instance of a pre-Lacanian Lacanianism—might lead to further interest in an visual, imaginary reading of Lacan and his psychic landscapes.

Notes

1. Jacques Lacan: *The Seminar of Jacques Lacan Book II The Ego in Freud's Theory and in the Technique of Psychoanalysis 1954–55*, Cambridge: Cambridge University Press, 1988, 196. In the text abbreviated as *II*.

2. For a recent interpretation of Dali's paranoiac-critical method see Naomi Schor, *Reading in Detail*, New York, Methuen: 1987.

3. Jacques Lacan, "The Mirror-Stage" in: Jacques Lacan, *Ecrits*, New York: Norton and Co., 1977. In the text abbreviated as *E*.

4. Jacques Lacan, *The Seminar of Jacques Lacan Book I. Freud's Papers on Technique 1953–54*, Cambridge: Cambridge University Press, 1988, 160. In the text abbreviated as *I*.

5. Ellie Ragland-Sullivan: *Jacques Lacan and the Philosophy of Psychoanalysis*, Urbana and Chicago: University of Illinois Press, 1987, 22. In the text abbreviated as *PP*.

6. Lacan here plays with the double meaning of real/imaginary and real/virtual. Within optics, there are *real* as well as *virtual* images (with *real* images, the reflected rays actually meet in a real room, so that the image can be projected onto a surface, with *virtual* images, only the "rearward extensions" of the rays meet. Generally, *real* images are *in front of the mirror, virtual* images *within* the mirror). There are also *real* rooms (the room in which the mirror is situated) and virtual ones (Alice's wonderland). Lacan links the *virtual* image to the subjective realm, the *real* image to the objective (which is in accordance with optical theory), but simultaneously points to the interplay between these two realms, which is what his image is all about: "When you see a rainbow, you're seeing something completely subejctive . . . it isn't there. . . . But nontheless, thanks to a camera, you record it entirely objectively. . . . We no longer have a clear idea, do we, which is the subjective, which is the objective. Or isn't it rather that we have acquired the habit of placing a too hastily distinction between the objective and the subjective in our little thought-tank? Isn't the camera a subjective apparatus? . . ." (*I* 77)

7. This shift from the *real* flowers to the real image of the *real* flowers also denotes the one from "materialism" to "structuralism."

8. Jacques Lacan, *Encore*, Paris:1, Editions du Seuil: 1975, 64. In the text abbreviated as *EN*.

9. Jacques Lacan, *The Four Fundamental Concepts of Psycho-Analysis*, New York: Norton and Co., 73. In the text abbreviated as *FF*.

10. For further references, see my "From the Canvas to the Page: Rhetorical Movements in the Discourse on Art," *Subjects/Objects*, Brown University, 1985.

11. For further references to the system of the central perspective see: A. Flocon and André Barre: *La perspective curviligne*, Paris:1, Flammarion, 1968, Erwin Panofsky: "Die Perspektive als 'symbolische Form,'" in: *Aufsätze zu Grundfragen der Kunstwissenschaft*, Berlin:1, Bruno Hessling, 1974 and Rudolf Arnheim, *Art and Visual Perception: A Psychology of the Creative Eye*, Berkeley: University of California Press, 1974.

12. Such a blind spot is also operative within the organ of the eye. The place at which the optical nerve is attached to the eye is "blind." Within visual perception, this blind spot is "automatically" filled in, in the same manner in which one "fills in" the space covered by the anamorphosis in *The Ambassadors*.

13. see Flocon, 68 ff.

14. Salvador Dali: *Gesammelte Schriften*, München:1, Rogner und Bernhard, 1974, 304. In the text abbreviated as *GW*. All English quotes are my translation from the German.

15. Salvador Dali: *So wird man Dali*, Wien-München:1, MTV Molden-Taschenbuch-Verlag, 1973, 155. My translation. In the text abbreviated as *SD*.

16. Salvador Dali: *The Secret Life of Salvador Dali*, London:1, Vision Press, 1948, 18. In the text abbreviated as *SL*.

17. It is certain that Dali could not have known of Lacan before 1932, the year in which Lacan published his dissertation *De la Psychoses paranoique dans ses Rapports avec la personalité*, and that their meeting took place before Lacan's publications in Minotaure of "Le problème du style et la conception psychiatrique des formes paranoiaques de l'expérience" (Minotaure, no. 1, 68–69) and "Motifs du crime Paranoiaque" (Minotaure no. 3–4, 25–28.) Dali himself had already developed his critical-paranoiac method in a number of articles (Posició moral del surrealisme, (Hélix

no.10, p. 4–6, 1930) and in "La femme visible" (1930) and had already used it in the painting *The invisible man*, which he painted in 1929, the year he himself mentions as the year in which he first developed his method. He first mentions Lacan's disertation in: "Interprétation paranoiaque-critique de l'image obsédante 'L'Angélus' de Millet' Prologue" (Minotaure, no. 1, 65–66) as an "admirable treatise" (*GW* 200).

18. Salvador Dali, *Diary of a Genius*, London:1, Picador, 1964, 21.

19. In "Aggressivity in psychoanalysis," (*Ecrits* 8–29) Lacan defines imagos as matrices which underlie the more "transcient images" (*E* 11). From these underlying imagos he especially singles out the "imagos of the fragmented body" (*E* 11) with their aggressive tendency. This aggressivity underlies the *Imaginary* arena, and is mediated only by the *Symbolic:* "In order for the system not to resume a general concentric, more and more paralyzing hallucination, in order for it to run, a regulating third has to intervene." (*II* 216) It is the Oedipal identification "by which the subject transcends the aggressivity that is constitutive of the primary subjective individualization." (*E* 23) Exactly the differentiation between the initial imagos and the ego's "alienating identification" with the object allows for (paranoiac) knowledge to appear, a knowledge which is, however, affected by the initial "mirror projection . . . that gives human space its originally 'geometrical' structure, a structure that I would be happy to call *kaleidoscopic*" (*E* 27). This fractured space describes "the most general structure of human knowledge: that which constitutes the ego and its objects with attributes of permanence, identity, and substantiality . . . with entities or 'things' that are very different from the Gestalten that experience enables us to isolate in the shifting field, stretched in accordance with animal desire." (*E* 17) This aspect of "premanence" is "where the symbolic relation sets in. The power to name the objects structures perception itself. The percipi of man can only hold itself within a zone of naming. Via the naming, man gives a specific consistency to the objects. If these only stood in a narcissistic relation to the subject, they would only be perceived in an instantaneous way. The word, the word which names, is the identical." (*II* 217)

20. See also: "The hallucination is very fruitful in producing cyclically repeated mirages, constant multiplication, an endless, periodic return of the same happenings in doublets or triplets. . . . These intuitions [Anschauungen] are obviously related to constant processes of poetical creation" (*GW* 355).

21. For Dali, this language is based on "the sexual drive, the death instinct and the bodily experience of space as a mystery" (*GW* 74).

22. Lacan describes this impossible transition from the outside to the inside not only in a spatial but also in a temporal paradox: "What we see in the return of the repressed is the effaced signal of something which only takes its value in the future, through its Symbolic realization, its integration into the history of the subject. Literally, it will only ever be a thing which, at the given moment of its ocurrence, will have been" (*I* 205).

23. In: *GW*, 280–285. All quotes are my translations from the German. In the text abbreviated as *NA*.

24. *Salvador Dali: Retrospective 1920–1980*, München:1, Prestel Verlag, 1980, 140.

25. In the context of the basic "senselessness" of the network of signifiers see also Lacan's categorical statement that "The signifier is stupid" (*EN* 25).

26. "We consider the *Nouvelles Impressions d'Afrique* as an oneiric travellogue of new paranoiac phenomena" (*GW* 181).

27. Michel Foucault: *Death and the Labyrinth*, Berkeley: University of California Press, 1987, 114. In the text abbreviated as *DL*.

28. In this case "Les lettres du blanc sur les bandes du vieux billard" (The white letters on the cushions of the old billiard table) and "Les lettres du blanc sur les bandes du vieux pillard." (The letters of the white man about the hordes of the old plunderers.)

29. Peter Gorsen, "Der kritische 'Paranoiker'" in: Salvador Dali: *GW*.

musical representation

Peter Widmer

ORPHEUS AND EURYDICE: MUSES OF MUSIC[1]

"*Alles, was irdisch, muß endlich vergehn, Musica bleibet in Ewigkeit stehn!*"—Everything mortal must pass away, but music is eternal, as a German song from the seventeenth century puts it. Transcendence is unmistakably part of the essence of music. Music is a realm beyond human limitations, and music, by transcending them, makes them all the more distinct. The Greek myth of Orpheus and Eurydice depicts this beautifully.

Orpheus, the singer and kythara player, loses his young wife Eurydice when she is bitten by a snake. His grief and his seductive music convince the gods to permit him access to the underworld in order to bring his wife back to the world of the living. The gods grant his request under one condition: while departing from the underworld, the realm of shadows, he may not turn around or look at Eurydice. Orpheus fails. He loses Eurydice a second time, this time forever.

The figure of Eurydice is fundamentally associated with the music of Orpheus. It is not by his power or by his words but by his music and singing that he gains access to worlds closed to mortals. He breaks down the resistance of the gods, overcoming their misgivings. His music reaches to the place of the lost, represented by Eurydice. Through music he would have torn her away from the underworld, were it not for his backward glance that attempted to discover what was happening unseen behind him.

In this Greek myth, then, music is associated with the invisible, with the shadow realm of Hades, but association is also established through language, for Orpheus is a singer. Here language is not so much conceived as a mediator of the visible but as a call to the gods, poetry capable of addressing the divine. With his poetry Orpheus emphasizes the divinity of language, but even that would have proved insufficient; his melody and the playing of his kythara were needed as well. Music thus transcends language, even the poetry of language. In harmony with language, music finds access to the shadow realm of the underworld. The dimension of the gaze, of the visible, of the imagination of the conceptual is opposed to the music of Orpheus. When he slips back into this dimension, he again loses Eurydice.

This leads us to the interpretation of the myth. Orpheus and Eurydice embody man and woman as opposites. The realm of shadows is the realm of the invisibility of the essence of woman. Orpheus as male is capable of reaching the lost female, whose sojourn in Hades can be understood as a metaphor for the invisibility of her essence. Into this realm of darkness Orpheus journeys, repudiating any sense of orientation or certainty. He must totally rely on his voice and his music. Eurydice symbolizes the embodiment of music—an invisible body. The prohibition against seeing her conceals the fact that she is invisible by suggesting that she would be visible if he were *allowed* to see her.

The myth may also be understood as a representation of two principles: that of the visible and that of the invisible. Orpheus embodies both; Eurydice is thus his female, invisible side. Of course one could also say the reverse: Orpheus represents the visible side of the invisible Eurydice; thus Orpheus would be the embodiment of Eurydice. However one views it, we conclude that the female "side" belongs to the invisible, the male to the visible. The myth addresses the question if these two categories can ever meet. The female side does not remain lost and inexpressible, as happens with the common man, but can be revealed through music. The myth unequivocally answers the question about the joining of the two categories: they are not complementary, but rather exclude one another. The gaze, instead of reassuring him of Eurydice's presence, leads to her loss. Only when Orpheus relies on his female side, the equivalent of the dark and the invisible, does he reach Eurydice. Here is a clear either/or: either the male gaze or the female invisibility, either the male imagination or music. The fascination of this myth lies in its idea that this indissoluble opposition can be overcome, that language, music, and the gaze are capable of rescinding the loss that each person suffers through the effects of language.

The motif that has reverberated through the ages is that of the intimate relation of music to the female. Numerous allegories—from the figure of Venus and the goddess harmonia to the medieval *Frau Musica*—represent music as a female figure or closely associate it with femininity.

Music and the Ecstatic

What is the power of music? Why can music open doors that would otherwise remain locked? Music pours into the gaps and voids torn open by abstract language. The mind of music reaches for the ecstatic, for that which is lost in abstract language; it reaches for the lost object, which is immediacy and presence. In this sense an inexpressible object belongs to music. Where language divides, music wishes to unite. Do we not recognize in this the relation between the unconscious and music? And does not the myth of Orpheus and Eurydice suggest the extension of these essential connections to the female, which is that unnameable being who does not cease to be the mover of culture and whose invisibility even more stubbornly refuses the appearances of science when science relies on the eye rather than on the ear. The music of Orpheus feeds the hope of finding what is lost through the medium of the accoustic; it feeds the hope of finding and being Eurydice. That would be the ecstasy of language: Being without having (having is based on the imaginary and the gaze). It would also be pure pleasure. Probably Chopin's search for the *note bleue*, the sound that so distinctively marks his music and for which perfection he sought indefatigably, signifies a similar goal. In Bloch's utopia of the plentitude of the moment it is recognizable as well. In that moment time would stand still, and the dark core of the historic would manifest itself.

But this ideal has its reverse side. The purer the music the less it should be possible to know it. Knowledge reestablishes a relation with Having, nonidentity, which precisely music wants to overcome. The realm of perfect music would be the realm of unknowing but also of the fullness of Being. Like the unconscious in Freudian psychoanalysis, music would be identical with itself; only through division can it enter the dimension of the knowable. In listening to music one experiences the tension between complete immersion in the music and the intermittent desire to reflect upon it. Who has not experienced being so totally caught up in music that one forgets oneself? The possibility of such an experience can be perceived as a threat; the intruding thoughts that divert one's attention from music are a response to the fear of being totally enveloped. Conversely, a more disinterested hearing, one that seeks neither separateness from nor unity with music, allows for a realization of earlier motifs and musical associations. The effort to accomplish this prevents the listener from "forgetting" himself and the ecstatic experience remains limited.

The Dependence of Music on Language

Even the purest music cannot forget its earthly origins or shake off its linguistic dimension and thus cannot leave behind the realm of human imagination of the real and of Being. Or to say this differently, music cannot attain its lost immediacy, a state external to the experience of time, it remains bound to the human. In transcending language it carries with it the structures of language. This can be shown in composition itself. Music and language are articulated and can—up to a certain point—be written and read. The linguistic sentence relates to the tonal phrase, the writing of letters to the writing of notes, grammar to the principles of composition, the human voice to the voice of the instrument. In the dimension of language, literature consists of genres such as poetry and prose, the novel, the documentary, theater, and so on. In music similar genres like chamber music, church music, symphonic music, and vocal or instrumental music can be distinguished.

All of this does not mean that music can be reduced to conceptual language. The latter divides what was originally whole, fragments and tears apart the world of the subject, and turns that world and its people into an object by naming it. Language confronts the subject with itself and assigns it its solitude. It orients itself by such criteria as the lie and the truth. Language results in creating objects that become lost, which then must be sought again. Music transcends these linguistic realities, but music also presupposes them while promising liberation from these limitations: from concept, finiteness, meaning, truth, lie, and the lost object. Music removes boundaries, opens the space of pure pleasure. And yet we must remember that the absolute fulfillment of the desire of music, even in the myth, is impossible.

Translated by Harold and Lynne-Marie Schweizer.

Notes

1. The chapter is from Peter Widmer's *Die Lust am Verbotenen und die Notwendigkeit Grenzen zu überschreiten* (Zürich: Kreuz Verlag, 1991) 148–53.

filmic representation

Danielle Bergeron

ALIENS AND THE PSYCHOTIC EXPERIENCE

The axis of psychoanalysis is the relation to the Other. For all subjects, the foundations of this relation are laid during one event—the subject's meeting with the lack in the Other at the time that s/he enters into language. For the subject, this meeting constitutes a traumatism to the extent that to compensate for lack, s/he believes s/he is constrained to fulfill the requirements of the Other according to the particular manner in which s/he enters into language. In neurosis, fantasy is what structures this response to the lack of the Other. In perversion, a scenario of denial plays this function. In psychosis, the subject's response to the lack of the Other is articulated in the form of a delusion or an acting out. Each subject elaborates a particular way of relating to the Other; it takes the structure of a primary traumatism giving meaning to his or her life.

The Oedipus signifies that the father as the representative of legal authority sets a limit and a prohibition to respond to the lack of the Other in terms of *jouissance*. This enables the subject to situate him or herself in the problematic of desire, that is, to establish a link with an object identified as the cause of his or her desire. In fantasy, the object articulates the subject to the Other's lack. As stated in the Lacanian algebra, the matheme of the neurotic's fantasy places a subject, barred by the law of the father, in relation to an object ($<>a).[1] In the hypothesis that the fantasy of the psychotic may be formulated in a matheme, we posit that the fantasy is to be an object articulated to the nonbarred Other, the real Other (a<>O).

In both the first and second *Aliens*, the producer, no doubt without realizing it, scripts a psychotic fantasy—the position of a subject who has become an object delivered up to the all-powerful Other that demands entire satisfaction of its needs. The subject landing on the territory of settlers, LG4-26, in a land occupied by the Creature, is placed in the position of a psychotic. Clinical experience makes it quite plausible that *Aliens* could also very well be, in a sense, the transposition of a psychotic's delusion as the frames of a film.[2]

the symbolic in question

Ripley experiences psychotic solitude when, after returning from her wanderings in the interstellar void, she gives her account of the expedition to the scientists who simply do not believe her. They consider her crazy and treat her accordingly. She is discharged from her position as flight officer and moved to a subordinate post. It would seem too much money had been invested in the project to believe that something not even represented in the symbolic order of the society could become a possibility. Ripley speaks of a creature "never recorded once in over 300 surveyed worlds," and everything she says about this Beast has no reference. In Lacanian terms, it is the symbolic, the order of language, that determines the imaginary and what may be represented by it.[3]

Ripley tries to explain the truth of her experience to the Company members, but because she is the only survivor, her farfetched adventure is perceived as a delusional conviction. The Company knows that the settlers have been living with their families for many years on LG4-26, which has "supposedly" been invaded by a terrifying Beast, but for all that the base has remained quite sound. Furthermore, other than the nightmare that leaves no tangible traces on her body that can be analyzed by the scientists,

Ripley brings back nothing—no specimen of the Thing, no hint of aggression, and no wounds as evidence of struggle. Nor can she prove the Truth of her discourse. From the company members, Ripley experiences skepticism and blunt refusal.

Recently Mr. Fox, a schizophrenic, told of his difficult position during the forty years he spent in a psychiatric ward: "I am a clear-headed man. Here's what happened to me. A secret power has been hypnotizing me ever since I was a little boy. When I am quietly sitting down it makes me act and do negative things when I want to do positive ones. There is no proof of what I'm telling you about the hypnosis and the strange things that are happening in my body, but it's true, I'm experiencing it." All his life Mr. Fox had to face the same skepticism and the same blunt refusal from the people around him as Ripley experienced from the members of the Company. His long stay in hospital is evidence for that.

But while in a delusional situation, Ripley is not psychotic. She still believes in the social link, and it is the symbolic order that governs her desire in her relationships with her peers. She is not believed, and she finds herself alone with her tale; she is thought to be crazy, but she continues to stay with the men. She does not draw into an imaginary world, give up social life, or kill herself as a psychotic could do in an ultimate gesture of affirmation before the Other. She accepts a menial task, which in her last combat will save her from the Beast. When working for her living, Ripley learns how to operate a metallic robot—the steel Beast.

When Berk, the Company man, suggests that she "get out and face the Thing," giving her his word of honor that the purpose of the mission is to exterminate the Beast, Ripley has faith in his word. This belief in the human word enables her to redirect her life around a given word.

a psychotic fantasy:
being delivered up to the jouissance of the Other

In *Aliens* the symbolic order governs human relationships as long as the subjects stay on Gateway Station. Once on the territory that has been invaded by the "xenomorph," nothing is the same. Everyone grapples with the absence of A—father[4] as intermediary and therefore confronts the real of the Thing. In the empire of the real, in the place occupied by the Other who demands *jouissance*, in this area in which the Creature has conquered the human, the symbolic fails to provide markers for meaning. These holes in the symbolic order are exemplified by the holes in the metallic structure of the colonial base that the soldiers discover on their first reconnaissance mission.

In this Fatherless and lawless space where the human is of interest to the Creature only as a body for its reproduction, a controlling power replaces the rules of the game. A state of war exists between the Creature and the men. The Beast invades everything, is ungovernable by any law and resorts to every possible means to achieve its goals. As a third party governing relationships of good faith, the father there is inoperative and nonexistent. This is where Berk lays down his card and bares his hand. We then learn that he could be perverse. First, we realize that he is not a man of his word because he took aboard an android and "omitted" telling Ripley. Then he organized the staging of the capture and the fecundation of Ripley and Newt by the Creature so he could take their fecundated bodies back to earth. He thus becomes an ally to the *jouissance* of the Beast that he believes can be mastered. He denies castration and refutes the Law of the Father to achieve his dream of prestige and to exact the maximum for himself. But to play Russian roulette with the death drive is to tempt the Devil, and in the end he dies for it.

In psychosis, where Oedipus has not implemented the Law of the Father, this absence of representation of authority to limit *jouissance* delivers the subject up to the Other. A psychotic sees him or herself therefore as an object meant to satisfy the Other, the object that completes and maintains him or her as nonlacking.[5] Once landed in the colony, everyone is placed in the psychotic position of being objects delivered up to the *jouissance* of the xenomorph, a fantasy providing each person with a meaning for every minute of their lives. It could be said that *Aliens* stages the relation of the psychotic to the Other.

Two complementary aspects of this capture by the Other in psychosis are revealed in the film.

(a) The first is the overwhelming of the subject by terrifying impressions, unchained drives caused by the unpredictable wandering of the Thing.

Ripley left with a mission to fight an Evil, to kill the Creature threatening humanity. It is the same type of mission for the delusional psychotic who seeks out some Evil in the world and then invests him or herself with the task of eliminating it. For example, believing himself St. Michael the Archangel, one psychotic leads his present "public" life as a dilettante, always ready for the day when the world will come to an end and he will have to fight Satan to save humanity, and especially the women, from destruction: that is his mission.

The unchained drives attack the psychotic's body, causing strange impressions, presentiments, and panic confusions that prevent the managing of time and space; he attributes them to an Evil in the universe caused by a malevolent Other ravaging his life.

Just as wandering drives from the Other persecute the psychotic, the Creature in *Aliens*, avid for human beings, attacks from all quarters and violates the body. In the beginning it is indeterminate and multiple. It arises out of nowhere and can foresee strikes against it; its movements nearby can be tracked on a detector yet it remains invisible, and it seems to be aware of everything going on because it can hear all conversations. It is even able to shut off the power. And when one finally is killed, another one takes its place. Sometimes it is hidden outside the body, sometimes within. It occasionally allows movement within its interior, as shown in certain scenes in the film where the soldiers appear to be inside the Creature's claws, in the extensions of its body. The unforeseeable nature of the Thing causes a complete disorganization of the soldiers' lives, dispossesses them of their means, and constantly threatens their integrity.

One psychotic clearly reveals this possession of his being by the Other. Terry states that, "for the benefit of science, NASA has for years put me into an integrated process of testing my physiology, manifested by hormonal friction and physiological tension between organs, which stop functioning to let others act. It is the most painful process that a human person can suffer. A total abdication of oneself." In *Aliens*, the embryo's incubation period in the human body corresponds to that horror.

Terry continues, "All of my organs and glands were subjected to testing, which kept me in bed several times a week. But how do they know the times of my meetings with you? The night before we are to meet, they do all sorts of things to keep me from sleeping, like using jack-hammers, turning off the power, having men whisper homosexual propositions at my door and having the dogs howl. The neighbors often act out horror scenes in the halls and yell obscenities." He concludes by saying, "It is obvious the aggression comes from the Other." Like the settlers at LG4-26, Terry is the place of experiments conducted by others.

In the same way that the psychotic's life is determined by the Other who manipulates him or her at will ("ferociously and cruelly" as Lacan would say) the way people in the film act is determined by the Creature. As the film progresses, the mortal grip this Other has on them tightens. Even the artificial man that everyone thought was shielded from the terror of the real is sensitive to the xenomorph's intrusion. In leaving on a mission, he says, "I might be synthetic but I'm not stupid."

(b) The second point demonstrates that the subject's interpretation of his or her position as an object is essential to the survival of the Other.

"NASA needs me," says Terry. "Sometimes, what happens inside my body is like a classical symphony." Being overwhelmed by the Other provides meaning to the psychotic for an otherwise wasted life. "They love their delusion as themselves," wrote Freud about psychotics. Being the object delivered up to the full enjoyment of the Other is what in the eyes of the psychotic justifies his or her dramatic and painful existence. This is expressed in *Aliens* particularly by the strange means of reproduction enabling the Creature to survive.

The families of the settlers, the soldiers, and all the crew are at the mercy of the instincts of the Beast who doesn't have any bad or good feelings about them. It just needs them in order to reproduce. Without them the Beast would be lacking. Being the object filling the lack of this Other is what links the life of the humans to this Thing. The image of the Creature using the bodies of kidnapped men and women to reproduce itself is a restatement of the question posed in relation to the absence of the Father or of the failing of the signifier in the occupied territory. As Lacan put it, "what does being father mean . . . The question is that the sum of these facts—copulating with a woman, the carrying of something in the womb for a certain length of time, the product finally ejected—will never be able to constitute the notion of what it is to be a father."[6]

The excerpt from Lacan's writing enables us to express what the settlers experience in relation to the Beast; there is copulation of sorts, then they carry the Beast's embryo for some time before it is eventually ejected. All the Beast does is set in place a process of fecundation and reproduction that uses the other against his or her will. Just as a woman cannot impose paternity on a man who has not committed his desire for it, there is no father for the Beast's offspring. This is another expression in the film of the absence of the father in psychosis.

a treatment process

Newt was especially marked by the intrusion of the Creature in her childhood. Her struggle for survival against the Beast was determinative for her and is inscribed in her body. When Ripley discovers her, she no longer behaves like a human but reacts like a tracked animal. She no longer speaks. She had believed her mother, who told her that monsters don't exist, but this word from the parental Other watching over her life as a child and acting as Father for her could no longer be sustained once the Creature came into her daily reality. Her parents, brother, the other settlers, the scientific experiments in progress, her relationship with Gateway—everything that maintained for her the symbolic Other and on which her existence as a little girl was based, was destroyed. Newt's face was one of terror and fear brought on by the dramatic overwhelming of her life by an Other who swept away and voided her symbolic markers. Newt is traumatized. Her life now has only one meaning, that of being an object delivered up to the *jouissance* of the Other. Alone against this real Other on the deserted base, she finds herself in a psychotic position. She no longer smiles. She is expressionless. There is only the Creature's presence that makes her scream.

In a process similar to the treatment of psychotics, Ripley restores Newt to the position of a subject. In the little girl's refuge, Ripley first looks for signs that will give access to Newt. And Newt does not remain indifferent to this adult who is looking for her name so that she can be called, as a subject. In relying on the army, the scientists, the sophisticated equipment, and even on her own desire to know more about the knowledge inscribed in Newt, Ripley reintroduces a symbolic framework. Ripley also decides that the Beast can be eliminated, that this Other has a weakness, that it is not all-powerful and that its *jouissance* can be fractured. And she ensures Newt that she will not be left alone in the clutches of the Thing. All these measures create a mechanism of compensation for the deficiency of the symbolic Father, open a space torn from the

Other's *jouissance,* and enable Newt to engage in the process of stalking the Beast. Having expressed her doubts before Ripley about the ability of the soldiers and their heavy equipment to protect her, and hiding under the bed to sleep, Newt nonetheless leans on Ripley's word. She tells her doll, "don't worry, everything will be all right." She supposes a knowledge to Ripley.

In assessing the traumatic knowledge acquired by Newt about the Beast's habits, and in relying on what is inscribed in the body of Newt as remaining evidence of the struggles with the Beast, Ripley returns with Newt to where the traumatic events took place. What marked Newt's body in childhood as witness to the Other's *jouissance* becomes the tool essential in her reappropriation of her life and history. In demanding that Newt speak from this knowledge marked in letters of death in her body, and with the aid of maps, weapons, and the whole gamut of symbolic logistics, Ripley frames, in a signifying logic, her rendezvous backtrack with the Beast in its cave. The transference with Ripley becomes truly evident only at the very end, when Newt says to Ripley, "I always had confidence." It was this transference that made it possible for Newt to accompany Ripley to stalk the Other.

The psychotic's treatment consists in providing a means of support in the passage from the relation to the nonmediated Other that structures the fantasy of being the object of the Other's *jouissance* to the position of subject linked to an object representing the lack in the Other. For that to take place, the internal object ravaging the psychotic's life must be externalized. But, what in *Aliens* represents that "externalization of the object" that Apollon holds as the determinative step in the process of separation securing the psychotic's treatment?[7] The embryo's Beast, developing within the bodies of the captive humans was an internal object for Newt and the entire crew. The steel Beast, dressed and animated by Ripley, externalizes the object; on the outside it is akin to the Beast on the inside. It is what determines the Creature's death, its limit and its lack. This metallic human-made structure, a product of the symbolic, separated from the body, positions Newt differently in the fantasy; thanks to the steel Beast used by Ripley to destroy the terrifying Beast, Newt is no longer the plaything of the Other, subjected to its demands and its whims, but is a subject relating to an external object, an imperishable witness to the Other's limitation. The steel Beast is what determines the "death" of the all-powerful Other.

At the end of treatment, the psychotic will have found an object palliating for the absence of the Father and operating for him as a support for the symbolic. Ripley's epic struggle with the Creature directed from within her metallic robot ends with the Beast being propelled into the interstellar void. Its projection into the void and the closing of the human place confirms the essential separation of places of meaning from places of *jouissance*. The film leaves us to think that it is the ultimate gesture of closing the space shuttle's door that ensures the Beast will never come back and removes once and for all the power it had.

All are reassured by the closing of doors opening onto the void, a bit like the symbolic order set down and represented by the Father that creates a universe in which *jouissance* is limited, placed out of bounds, shared, divided, and where everyone may live. But just as the symbolic order is not founded, being only a consensus, so the reassuring framework of the space shuttle is based on nothing; it is itself a totally arbitrary structure moving through the universe—it offers no permanent solidity. Moreover, this "reassuring" framework shielded from any attack by the Beast, by *jouissance* as death drive, refers to another framework, another social structure equally as fragile—that of Gateway Station.

This time Ripley will not be alone in speaking of the terrifying Creature. But while the others may be able to imagine this Thing from outside, Ripley, Newt, Hicks, and even the android will remain permanently marked by the nonmediated relation to the Real of the *jouissance* of the Other inscribed for them in the letter of the body as an indelible knowledge.

Notes

1. Lacan, Jacques. "The Subversion of the Subject and the Dialectic of Desire in the Freudian Unconscious," in *Ecrits: A Selection*. New York: Norton, 1977: 292–325.

2. In this paper I will refer to *Aliens*, the second film produced in 1986 by James Cameron.

3. Lacan, Jacques. "Le séminaire sur "La lettre volée," in *Ecrits*, Paris, Seuil, 1966: 11–61.

4. ———. "On a Question Preliminary to any Possible Treatment of Psychosis," in *Ecrits: A Selection*. New York: Norton: 217.

5. For clinical examples of this Lacanian theoretical position, see Bergeron, Danielle, "The Lost Body of the Schizophrenic," a lecture given at the San Francisco Society for Lacanian Studies, 2 May 1992, Wright Institute, Berkeley, California.

6. Lacan, Jacques. "Le Séminaire, livre III, Les Psychoses," Paris, Seuil, 1981: 329.

7. Apollon, Willy. "Psychoanalytic Treatment of Psychosis," in *Lacan and the Subject of Language.* Edited by Ellie Ragland-Sullivan and Mark Bracher. New York: Routledge, 1991: 137.

Lucie Cantin

ALIENS OR STAGING THE TRAUMA

In this analysis we will consider two characters, the protagonist Ripley and the young girl, Newt. Our working hypothesis is the following one. In the first film Ripley witnesses the collapse of her rational world, which is shattered by the irruption of the real. This is represented by the sudden appearance of the Thing (portrayed as both a thing and an animal), against which the scientist's knowledge and the soldiers' most potent weapons fail. The Thing cannot be identified; it doesn't have a name. It is outside the realm of significant representation. Ripley's being is then fractured by the irruption of the Other's *jouissance,* represented by the Beast. The *jouissance* returns in its death-bearing the unbreachable form. The first film stages this trauma, which leaves on Ripley the indelible marks of an experience that changes forever her relationship to meaning, the phallus, and science. The first film presents the staging of the trauma, after which Ripley finds herself absolutely alone.

The second film opens with the portrayal of that solitude. Ripley and the cat are the only two witnesses left. A special knowledge keeps her apart from the others. Alone, she cannot hide from that knowledge that is now apart of her. Although she withdrew and let fifty-seven years go by, Ripley must still live with the memory she can't repress. The nightmare she has at the beginning marks the point of no return in confronting that knowledge. Once the trauma is passed, the unconscious attempts to organize and to arrange for its return in a way that will be bearable. But the sequence of nightmares reveals that Ripley is devastated by the *jouissance* that, as Lacan says, "endlessly remains unwritten" ("ne cesse pas de ne pas s'écrire"). She faces the following dilemma: to die as a subject or to go back and confront the Thing, which will take a more precise form as the film goes along. The second film shows that confrontation. It presents the staging of how Ripley manages to distance herself from the *jouissance* of the Other, symbolized in these films by the Beast.

According to Willy Apollon, the *jouissance* stemming out of the "lack in the Other" is an insisting *jouissance* for which an object must be found. In the nightmare scene at the beginning of the second film, we see Ripley impregnated by the Other and possessed by a Thing that is destroying her. But as the film progresses, we see her dealing with an external object becoming increasingly delimited. In the nightmare sequence, she is pregnant with something she could not be *delivered of*; later in the film, she returns with a young girl she has adopted after saving her from the Beast. In this regard, the second film is the "*theatralization*" or representation of the Trauma. The film sets in place the building up of *obliviousness* in Ripley; this is represented by setting the Thing at a distance and its delimitation. The Beast becomes a thing more and more limited and contained in a space increasingly small. It is broken up in smaller parts (by everything it is fed: bullets, fire, grenades, etc.), and, at last, it is expelled from the spaceship and falls into emptiness.

the advent of the trauma and
the return of jouissance

We define trauma as a subject being confronted with the *lack in the Other*. This definition is expressed in two different ways in the film. On the one hand, Ripley is faced with the lack in the Other when science and the protective systems set up by the Army fail. The scientist's knowledge is incomplete, but above all inefficient; it is useless, as are the soldiers' weapons. What had been used to fill in this lack in the Other—namely the authority of the Law, science, and the world of meaning governed by the signifier— falls apart. Ripley faces the inadequacy of what acted as the Name-of-the-Father and served to repress the void in the Other, and she must now confront that void. Part One stages that blow.

On a second level, Ripley is confronted with a *jouissance* for which she can only be an object. The recurrent nightmare brings her back to that *jouissance,* night after night. The Beast is using Ripley's body to live; it is living off her body. In the nightmare, Ripley becomes the object that corresponds to the lack in the Other, to the lack left by the parasitic Beast that needs a body to develop. Ripley is the object of the Beast's *jouissance.*

The breaking of the barrier of meaning and the effraction of the real are well staged in the first film when the Beast enters the ship. It starts when some men take off in the direction of the call they have intercepted. On returning to the ship, they find that one of the men has a living, unidentified organism on his face. So Ripley, the commander, forbids the soldier from entering the ship and quarantines him, as the rules require in order to prevent contamination. It is the breaking of the quarantine rule by the scientist who wants to study the specimen brought back by some members of the crew, contrary to Ripley's order, that allows the Beast in as the eighth passenger. The law is the Law of the Signifier, which protects the authority of language and which in turn produces and maintains meaning. The law blocks the way to real *jouissance,* which aims at being total and immediate. That barrier has now collapsed; the Beast is on board.

As we said, from a psycho-analytic point of view, trauma is the subject being confronted with the lack in the Other. It puts the subject in contact with the return of a death-bearing *jouissance,* the Death drive described by Freud. It is important to define clearly the status of that returning *jouissance.* Human beings, because they have language, are cut off from any real *jouissance.* Such *jouissance* is made inaccessible because we have language, because we can speak and must therefore rely on the Other for the satisfaction of our needs. The law forbids that real *jouissance.* The trauma is the return of a *jouissance* that comes back "despite" the barrier of the law. It threatens the very basis of the law. The resurfacing *jouissance* is beyond the limit; it actually comes back through a breach in that limit. Everything Ripley goes through in the two films illustrates that movement. The first film is the experience of the trauma; it shows how the signifier fails to contain the *jouissance.*

Before that experience, Ripley is portrayed as a woman who is very much at ease among the men with whom she works. She holds a position of authority for which she has been trained, and she has friendly relationships with those men based on the meaning of the word. She is well integrated in the world of the signifier and of the symbol. That world will be shattered when she encounters the Thing.

the failure of the signifier: the nightmare

The second *Aliens* opens on the exposition of Ripley's symptoms: she cannot sleep, her life is not the same anymore, she is harassed and haunted by nightmares. Her whole life is disturbed. Freud has described how dreams are elaborated and how they are "triggered," so to speak, by an element from the preceding day that activates something the subject has repressed. Starting with something that cannot be assimilated because it is part of a real *jouissance,* the unconscious, through dreams, orchestrates a meaning in order to integrate the meaningless element into the field of representation.

It is important to remember these details on dream work as we examine Ripley's nightmare. It is indeed through that nightmare that the trauma she has experienced is repeated and maintained. According to Freud, a nightmare is a dream that has failed to reach its objective. The dreamer's awakening finalizes that failure. The point at which the dreamer wakes up is the dream's umbilicus where the *jouissance* that the dream has failed to mask is revealed. The nightmare is due to Ripley's maddening compliance to the Beast's demands, the Other, who possesses her and whose *jouissance* negates her existence as a subject. Ripley gives her body so that the Other may live. Therefore, the point at which she awakens—where the *jouissance* of the Other would be revealed—is where she would give birth to the monster that she now bears.

The trauma has left a mark on her, written on the body a knowledge of an experience that has shattered the barrier of meaning for her. It is what keeps coming back in the nightmare in which she cannot be delivered of the Thing. The object remains in her and literally continues to eat up her life.

In *Beyond the Pleasure Principle,* Freud touches on the repetition of the recurring traumatic element in the nightmare. What is at play in the compulsive repetition is the Death Drive, the capture of the subject by a *jouissance* that is always the *jouissance* of the Other, which is always insistent and to which the subject complies. Ripley's nightmare continuously recurs; she cannot escape from it. It is anxiety, a moment of vertigo where she vanishes as a subject, grotesquely handed over to the Thing as prey. That moment and another, when she wakes up in a panic, is the limit of what can pass into the unconscious from the Id. We have called that point the "rock of *jouissance*" which cannot be represented because it is outside of meaning, beyond the limit imposed by the law and the symbols that govern the world of meaning. The recurring dream brings Ripley back to the frightening point where she complies to the ferocious demands of the Beast, which represents the Other. She awakens just before the point of no return, when she would find death, that is, just before the realization of the fantasy staged in the nightmare. At this point we can turn to Willy Apollon's definition of fantasy: "the staging of the trauma's structure," is "what repeats, preserves and maintains the trauma." Ripley complies with the *jouissance* demanded by the Other by offering it her body. That response of the subject, which aims at making the Other complete, is entirely alien, or as Apollon suggests, "is against the logic of organic life."

the exteriorization of the Thing

In the first film Ripley experiences the trauma. In the second *Aliens* the elements of that trauma are organized into a new representation. Ripley decides to go back and face the Thing. Burk swears on his honor and the commander assures her that he will "guarantee her safety," but she remains skeptical. Ripley cannot believe all those promises, as if nothing could heal the wound that has eroded in her the power of meaning. The "rapport" with the world of symbols and the signifier that used to govern her whole life seems to be irreparably damaged. The Marines spread out their weapons and boast, full of narcissistic self-conceit, certain of being invincible. But Ripley echoes her doubts, "I wish it were as easy as that."

She assumes the same position as Newt, the little girl who no longer believes in storybook explanations she was given to explain existence. When Ripley tries to reassure her, she answers: "I know they can't be as strong as they say." The next scene shows the scientist Bishop studying the Beast the men have found, while the soldiers study the map of the colony complex. The scene is written to show that the knowledge shared by Ripley and Newt is the opposite of that of the scientist and the armed soldiers: on the one hand, we have the *jouissance* of the Thing; on the other, the symbolic order, what is supposed to make that *jouissance* impossible. The *jouissance* of the real is impossible for the soldiers and scientists as long as they haven't been confronted by it.

the discovery of what is unfounded

Ripley asks the lieutenant in charge of the crew how many missions he has undertaken. "Two," he answers, "the thirty-eight others were simulations." This fact, acknowledged in front of the crew, kindles a first doubt in the men: the authority of the officer in command is based only on semblance.

The dispersal of the lieutenant's authority materializes in the panic when he sees his men die one by one, abandoned to the Beast. The horror is personified in the face of the woman who, engulfed in resin, opens her eyes and begs to be finished off. This scene replicates the film of the nightmare taken to its conclusion. It becomes the equivalent of the nightmare for the soldiers. At this point, the lieutenant loses his command. He is injured, but above all, he loses his authority over the men who have seen and know. The display of the weapon's power loses its effect. Something has changed in the Marines. They can no longer be under the command of a man who has no knowledge of the Thing.

As for Ripley, it is through the video screen that we watch the representation of her nightmare. The screen puts a distance between her and the Beast. It also brings back the image of horror. From then on she is no longer alone. The soldiers are with her. In the film, this moment is a turning point. From the passive position that they all shared, under the power of a still imaginary being about which Ripley could not speak for fear of being considered insane, they all go on facing an object that slowly takes shape. We see here the "joint" that links the trauma to the fantasy, which proposes an object in the place of the nameless *jouissance* that activates the trauma. This turning point is well represented in the scene where Ripley sees herself as the woman who gives birth to the Thing. The vision wakes her up, as if the representation of the nightmare had the same distancing effect that the telling of a traumatic event has for the patient undergoing analysis. At this point, she takes up command with Hicks and prepares a strategy to attack the Beast, which has been exteriorized.

the staging of the Thing

In trying to limit the *jouissance* of the Thing, the signifier, as well as scientific knowledge and the power of weapons have proven insufficient. The rest of the film shows what could be called the constitution of the object, which takes two forms. It is first represented as a Thing that has limits and can be circumscribed, which later becomes more and more circumscribed and identifiable. The Thing becomes something external that exists outside the body. This array of objects—weapons and machines of all kinds that the men feed to the Beast instead of their own bodies—also serves to fragment the Thing, to delineate its shape and reduce it to its ultimate form, the Mother Beast that lays its eggs.

Although it slowly takes shape and is more and more limited in space, the Object still cannot be tamed. Throughout the film we see the Beast passing through every possible barrier put in its way. Even when it is fragmented, it keeps resurfacing. It is only when it is expelled, in other words, when it is put at a distance outside the ship, that it finally falls into oblivion. It doesn't die; it is cast aside.

Trauma is the inscription in the subject of bits of reality, shattered pieces of memories, words overheard, ambiguous sentences, looks, silences, gestures, in short, everything that has failed to be represented in the subject's world of meaning but has nevertheless left its mark. The trauma confronts the subject with something that escapes meaning; it emphasizes the failure of the signifier in stopping the *jouissance* of the Other when it creeps through a crack in meaning. *Jouissance* is always the Other's *jouissance,* to which the subject feels obliged to comply. The compliance is what causes the subject to disappear; it deprives the subject of his or her being as a subject. It is this aspect, so well represented in the film, that is associated with the Beast.

The question then becomes how can the subject divert a part of the death-bearing *jouissance* and turn it into a life-giving process? How does Ripley pull away from the *jouissance* of the Thing by which she is possessed in the nightmare?

In the place of what cannot be contained by the Law or become an object of scientific study, the film offers the theatralization of a process—the distancing of the Other's *jouissance*, not by eclipsing it, but rather by diverting it from its objective. This distancing is based on the knowledge gained from the trauma, from the mark, the inscription left by a real on the subject's body, as opposed to scientific knowledge based on signifiers. That opposition is well developed in Ripley's and Bishop's respective positions. In the first film, the scientist shows his fascination and admiration for the Beast, which he sees as an object for study and which he endeavors to understand and analyze. Faced with the strangeness of something different, Bishop tries to relate it to something he knows. His knowledge comes from books; it is based on tradition, on analyzing something familiar. He tells Ripley, "The molecular acid oxydates. When the creature dies, the acid neutralizes." To which Ripley replies, "That is all very interesting, but it doesn't help us. I need to know what we are faced with."

What will guide Ripley's actions is the knowledge gained from what has left marks on her. All her reasoning and inferences are supposed to lead her to a decision and an action. We therefore see all the tactics she thinks of to face the Beast, the thing that resists reason, scientific knowledge, and military might. She no longer tries to relate to Truth, but rather aims at finding something that will work and allow her to escape from the Beast's domination.

An important scene illustrates that behavior, which is based on the knowledge she has gained from her experience with the Thing. Confined with the survivors in a small closed space toward which the Beast is approaching, Ripley quickly accepts a suggestion from Newt, who reveals to her the existence of an underground passage to an airstrip. During their escape through the tunnel, Ripley repeatedly asks Newt which way to go, until the girl starts leading the way for the soldiers. The action is based on the letter and not on the signifier. The tunnel was not on the maps; it is in Newt that the directions are to be found.

conclusion

Aliens stages the manifestation of a death-bearing *jouissance*, which springs up through a Thing, a xenomorph that the phallic limit and the order of meaning cannot contain. The incompleteness of the system of reason to which the scientist refers leaves him powerless against that real, indomitable *jouissance* that defeats his knowledge.

It is at that breach that experiencing the Thing has opened in Ripley that she bases her strategy to break free from the *jouissance* of the Other in which she is caught. She decides to face the Thing without negating its irreducibility in a battle where she allows herself to be guided by the knowledge inferred from the wound left in her by the trauma.

The thing is not subjugated; it is put at a distance. It is "externalized," as Willy Apollon would say, in an object that is more and more circumscribed and diverted from its path. The Thing can now fall into oblivion. "Now we can dream," says Ripley to Newt as she tucks her in.

References

Apollon, Willy. Psychanalyse et traitement des psychotiques, in *Traiter la Psychose*. Edition du GIFRIC, Collection Noeud, Québec, 1990.

———. *Séminaire clinique*, Année 89–90, Inédit.

Freud, Sigmund. *Beyond the Pleasure Principle*. New York and London: Norton, 1961.

Lacan, Jacques. *Le Séminaire, Livre XX, Encore*. Paris: Seuil, 1975.

cross-genre representation

Catherine Portuges

LOST OBJECTS:
DURAS'S MINIMALIST CINEMA OF REMEMBRANCE

> *I wanted to tell you that if I were young, if I were*
> *eighteen, if I knew nothing yet of the separation*
> *between people and the nearly mathematical certi-*
> *tude of this separation between people, I would do*
> *the same thing as I am now doing, I would write*
> *the same books, make the same movies . . . if I had*
> *died yesterday I would have died at eighteen. If I*
> *die in ten years I would also have died at eighteen.*
> —*Marguerite Duras*, Les Yeux Verts[1]

In 1979, Marguerite Duras published three "textes" titled *Aurélia Steiner*, as well as two films, *Aurélia Steiner, dite Aurélia Melbourne* and *Aurélia Steiner, dite Aurélia Vancouver*. The text of *Aurélia Steiner, dite Aurélia Melbourne* closes with the spoken words of the unseen subject:

> My name is Aurélia Steiner.
> I live in Melbourne. My parents teach school.
> I am eighteen years old.
> I write.[2]

In this, one of her most formalistically experimental, minimalist films, the desire for reparation with a lost love is meshed with the phantasm of the holocaust, implicating the spectator as both voyeur and eavesdropper by means of the director's sustained use of a woman's speaking voice. An encounter between word and image (joining to the same incantatory and hypnotic effect initiated by

Hiroshima mon amour), *Aurélia Steiner, dite Melbourne* takes place—if indeed one can speak of it in such narrative terms—on and around a river, just as *Hiroshima mon amour* is both linked and divided by the temporal crossings of the Loire River in France and the Ota Estuaries in Japan, and *L'Amant* is marked by the young girl's passage on the delta ferry. A woman's voice (Duras's own, in the original French version) reads letters to her imaginary (or lost) lover, object of her impossible desire, while the camera records the varying moods of the Seine as a boat makes its way from Bercy to Passy, under vaulted bridges and changing skies. This disembodied voice speaks from that nameless place where image, voice, text, and memory converge:

> I write you all the time, always, you see, nothing but that, nothing. Maybe I will write you a thousand letters, give you letters, give you letters about my life now. And you will do with them what I expect you to do with them, by that I mean exactly as you please. That's the way I want it. That it should be meant for you. Where are you? How can I reach you? How can the two of us draw ourselves nearer to that love and erase the illusory fragments of time that separate us from each other?

In this zone of visual and auditory pleasure and pain, that privileged terrain that is also the space of autobiography, both subject and reader/spectator may experience what Lacan called "correct distance," and Winnicott "potential space," the safety of apprehending the desired object without fear either of the suffocation of excessive closeness or the detachment of too wide a separation.[3] Through these words echo those of *Hiroshima mon amour*: "Tu me tues, tu me fais du bien," the oppositions of pleasure and anguish, and the process of reconstruction in time and space that is the occasion of cinema.[4] Of the making of *Aurélia Steiner, dite Aurélia Melbourne*, Duras writes:

> I think there is no hiatus, no blank between the voice and what she speaks. In a sense, when I am speaking, I am Aurélia Steiner. What I pay attention to is less, not more. It is not to convey the text but rather to be careful not to distance myself from her, from Aurélia, who is speaking. It demands extreme attention, every second, not to lose Aurélia, to say with her,

not to speak in my own name. To respect Aurélia, even if she comes from me.[5]

This fusion of speaking subject with writing self is familiar enough to readers of Duras and to viewers of her films. To experience pleasure, the viewer of women's personal films must establish in relation to the visual text a locus of receptivity that encourages the integrity of her own identificatory process. Duras enables this dynamic to take place not, as more conventional directors might, by drawing in the viewer through illusionistic cinematic strategies, but by offering a primary material that appears formless, aimless, without closure or coherent narrative order. Such technique—for it is highly crafted and conscious—she attributes to a feminine quality of seeing and experiencing.

The long, uncut visual sequences of *Aurélia Steiner, dite Aurélia Melbourne* combine with the off-screen spoken track to create a new and heightened sense of the phantasmatic. The "words to say it" are, in Duras's representation, owned by the speaking subject whose story is told in her own voice, a voice accorded primacy because the visual can only intensify its meaning, not alter it. For the eighteen-year-old author addresses an absent "you," a genderless, unspecified other. This other—a loved object lost through death, disappearance or separation—confronts the filmmaker with the necessity of mourning. Immortalized in turn by the cinematic apparatus, the object is rescued from the finality of total loss, recovered from the oblivion of repression, only to live again for the benefit of others, and hence restored to the speaking, filming subject. As our spectator's gaze travels the familiar banks of the river, the road of water itself a metaphor of desire, the filmmaker takes us through the artifacts of human commerce—bridges, cathedrals, onlookers—in a ceaseless, inexorable flow of movement:

> Where are you? What are you doing? Where did you lose your way? Where did you lose your way while I cry out that I'm afraid? . . . I see your eyes. I see that the river's sky is blue, that same liquid blue color of your eyes. I see it is not true. That when I write to you no one is dead. And that you too are here on this desert continent.

The wish to see and to be seen, present in other Duras texts from *Le Ravissement de Lol V. Stein* to *L'Homme assis dans le couloir,* reasserts itself here in cinematic form. Here, too, the Durassian discourse of love and death, of pleasure inextricably combined with loss, absence, and even destruction, is intensified by the look of the other that engenders desire:

> It was later, yes, afterwards, that it happened. A very, very long time, nothing. And then, your eyes. Your eyes on me . At first the blue, liquid and empty, of your eyes. And then you saw me.

At the moment these words are intoned, a coal barge appears on the river, moving from left to right toward the camera, penetrating the visual sphere. This instance is the first moment in *Aurélia Steiner, dite Melbourne* that an object advances toward the viewer's gaze, marking the light reflecting off the water in a metonymy of desire of the other. Duras's visual and aural structures proceed thus in tandem throughout the film, undercutting the viewer's desire to identify the absent voice, as the river too is cut through by bridges linking its banks.

Such subtle interpenetration of image and sound overtake the spectator, leaving him in thrall—despite the avowed distancing strategies of the artist—to its hallucinatory visceral effects. In a chapter in *Les Quatre concepts fondamentaux de la psychanalyse*, translated as "Of the Gaze as Object petit a," Lacan describes the dialectic of the eye and the gaze in relation to the picture, arguing that there is a lack of coincidence between them that he calls a "lure":

> when, in love, I solicit a look, what is profoundly unsatisfying and always missing is that you never look at me from the place from which I see you. . . . At the scopic level, we are no longer at the level of demand, but of desire, of the desire of the Other. . . . Generally speaking, the relation between the gaze and what one wishes to see involves a lure. The subject is presented as other than he is, and what one shows him is not what he wishes to see. It is in this way that the eye may function as 'objet petit a,' that is to say, at the level of the lack. (*op. cit.*, 103–4)

Duras too speaks of a lack, from the place from which she writes and sees, as creator of words and images eventually to become signifiers for other subjects. In an interview, she states:

One says things through absence, through "manque d'être,
manque d'amour, manque de désir." . . . I love to film at the
very minimum: the emptiness of a beach gives me great pleasure. I can say, for example, that I have a brother who died
during the war at twenty-eight, such an abomination that I
wanted to die. Suddenly I understood that this young man
had been a great, great love for me, an immense love. . . . Yet
nothing can bear witness to incest, which is not representable. That is the paradox I show in my cinema, that impossibility. I show what is not representable, that is what
haunts and interests me.[6]

The unrepresentable is for her doubly absent, a search for true
speech transmitted from the unknown. Such subversion at the
level of the signifier, in which silence and passivity become the
strength of the feminine subject, defies translation, itself a form of
transference.

Duras states the origins, the trajectories, the endings of love
and desire of her primarily female speaking subjects, suspended in
the simultaneous creation and negation of language. "When I am
writing I am not dying," she remarks in her interview in *Cahiers
du Cinéma*, for which she was given carte blanche:

Before films there are books; before books, nothing. . . . I always want to be reading while shooting a film, but I cannot
because I must look while the camera is on. . . . For me
cinema is an adjunct of writing . . . yet I feel guilty for having
deserted the word in favor of the image. The place of writing
is magnificent, unique, terrifying . . . the written part of a film
is for me cinema. (*op. cit.*, 5–6)

Duras's films make demands on the spectator. They both in-
vite and repel our desire, both promise and refuse to gratify.
Reading them as a text—for pleasure, for obliteration, for reconnec-
tion with those extreme questions that constitute her life as a
writer—means submitting oneself to the contradictory perceptual
and subjective operation of which Lacan speaks. And, although
cinema, like psychoanalysis, is anything but absolutely neutral,
this paradoxical configuration of desire-demand-lack can be imagined as a countertransferential text, a term I use in a very approxi-
mate way, as Lacan uses the term "love" in relation to positive

transference. To surrender to the lure of the cinematic transference requires, in the case of Duras, a sense of psychic safety coupled with danger—both the risk of engulfment by the specular seduction and the desire to remain beyond the pull of narrative. To be sure, learning to look at a Duras film demands apprenticeship, as she informed us long ago in *Hiroshima mon amour* by exhorting the viewer to learn to look: at pain, at the outsider, the marginal, the woman, the repressed, the unrepresentable. "I am speaking of writing," she says in a documentary film of herself at work shooting *Agatha* in 1981: I also speak of writing even when I seem to be talking about filmmaking. I don't know how to talk about anything else. . . . I am not completely responsible for what I write . . . a word contains a thousand images" (*Apostrophes*).

If Marguerite Duras has acquired, along with Jacques Lacan, an emblematic value, associated with the rupture of expectations both narrative and psychological, it is in part because her cinema insists on narrating while at the same time deconstructing, in the manner of the avante-garde, the narrative impulses of the audience. Like those of Godard and Straub, both of whom she admires, her films have come increasingly to a disjuncture between sound and image, an emptying out of theatricality, of *mise-en-scène*, in favor of movement through space. With the gradual disappearance of characters and their replacement with voices-off (as evident in *Aurélia Steiner, dite Melbourne*), there is an intensification of the dialectic of sound and image, space and time, a *prise de pouvoir* of the text in tension with the resistance of the image. Although there are several Aurélia Steiners—named Melbourne, Vancouver, and Paris—they are, according to Duras, the same: ageless, eternal. "There is no difference," she writes, "between Aurélia's eyes and the sea, between her piercing gaze and the end of time" (90). Aurélia-Melbourne is eighteen, the age of Duras when she left her home in Saigon, the age of the protagonist of *Hiroshima mon amour* when she lost her first lover, the German soldier shot at the end of the Occupation, and three years older than the adolescent narrator of *L'Amant* whose lover is Chinese. Here as elsewhere, Duras's subject is the memory of forgetfulness; the fact of knowing that one has forgotten is, for Duras, memory.

> But who are you? Who? How could that have happened? How could it be that that happened? You, no longer here. . . . I don't know anymore. I'm aware only of that love I have for

you. Extreme. Terrifying. And that you are not here to release me from it. Never. I have never separated you from our love.

There are also references to the Holocaust, the "universe concentrationnaire," the ovens near Cracow, as the letter or letters urge the interlocutor to remember to listen, just as Duras the director addresses the spectator by insisting on the primacy of both image and sound, thwarting our desire to privilege the one over the other. We—Aurélia/Duras/the viewer—are drawn into the circulation of desire of the spoken and imaged texts as the off-screen voice apostrophizes:

How can we reach the end of our love? Listen. Beneath the vaults of the river to those waves breaking . . . listen again. Those illusory fragments I told you about have disappeared. We ought to draw ourselves nearer to the end, the end of our love. Don't be afraid anymore.

As cinematic spectators, we are both "voyeurs" and "auditeurs," excluded and forgotten by those phantasms with which we are projectively identified, seeking our absence in the very plenitude of visual and auditory fulfillment. If Lol V. Stein's pleasure depends upon her detachment from gratification, ours as spectators is intimately bound up with it. Between us and pleasure lies that zone that Lacan refers to as "correct distance," the privileged field wherein one can experience the object without fear either of the suffocation that arises through excessive closeness or the detachment that results from too great a separation. To experience pleasure, the viewer must establish in relation to the visual text a space of receptivity, which we alone create within ourselves. In the cinema of Marguerite Duras, there is the possibility for experiencing pleasure in this way: its primal material seems formless, aimless, without closure or conventional narrative order. This she attributes to a feminine quality of seeing and experiencing: "It is as a woman that I cause things to be seen in this way" (*Apostrophes*).

Duras's search is for traces of the past, for clues in the service of a reconstruction that takes place only gradually, like the analytic process, over and over, with infinitely repeated variations. In so doing, she transgresses the boundaries between imaginary and real, fiction and autobiography, repressed history and enacted story. In *Les Yeux verts*, Duras notes that what she seeks in her films is the primary state of the text, as one tries to remember a distant interval event not lived but heard told. Its meaning, she believes, comes later and has no need of her authorship, for the voice of the reading alone will impart that meaning without intervention on her part. For this to be accomplished, everything must be read, including what she calls the "empty place."

In his "Hommage fait à Marguerite Duras," Lacan suggests that if Duras's art makes her the ravisher, we as readers (and spectators) are the ravished.[7] Writing, speaking, and seeing from the phantasmal place of her own desire, Duras insists upon the obsessional and deceptively simple questions that continue to torment human beings, despite efforts to gain distance from them: why do we love, suffer, die? What do we want from the indescribably and eternally lost object—man, woman, child? How is anything possible without absolute love, absolute desire? By permitting the viewer a major role in her cinematic project, Duras discovers a language adequate to these questions, to speak the unspoken, hear the unheard.[8]

Notes

1. Marguerite Duras, "Les Yeux verts," *Cahiers du cinéma*, nos. 312–313 (June 1980): 23. Translations mine.

2. Marguerite Duras, *Aurélia Steiner, dite Melbourne* (1979), 16mm. Film courtesy of French-American Cultural Services and Educational Aid, New York City. All transcriptions and translations of the film text are mine.

3. Jacques Lacan, *The Four Fundamental Concepts of Psychoanalysis* (New York: Norton 1978). See also D.W. Winnicott, *Through Paediatrics to Psychoanalysis* (London; International Psychoanalytical Library, 1973); *The Maturational Processes and the Facilitating Environment* (London: International Psychoanalytical Library, 1963); and *Playing and Reality* (London: Tavistock, 1971).

4. Marguerite Duras, text of *Hiroshima mon amour*, directed by Alain Resnais (New York: Grove Press, 1961).

5. Interview with Marguerite Duras on *Apostrophes*, Bernard Pivot, interviewer/producer. Radio-télévision française, Station 2, translation mine.

6. Marguerite Duras, "Le Malheur merveilleux: Pourquoi mes films?" *Cahiers du Cinéma,* June 1980:79–86.

7. Jacques Lacan, "Hommage fait à Marguerite Duras, du *Ravissement de Lol V, Stein,* in Marguerite Duras, Collection Ça/Cinema (Paris: Editions Albatros, 1981).

8. For more detailed analysis, see my "Cinematic Countertransference: Duras and Lacan." PsychCritique 2:1 (1987): 17–23, and "Seeing Subjects: Women Directors and Cinematic Autobiography," in *Life/Lines: Theorizing Women's Autobiography,* eds. B. Brodzki and C. Schenck (Ithaca: Cornell University Press, 1988) 338–50.

Index